Updating Support Skills from Microsoft Windows NT 4.0 to Microsoft Windows 2000

Updating Support Skills from Microsoft Windows NT 4.0 to Microsoft Windows 2000

iUniverse.com, Inc.

San Jose   New York   Lincoln   Shanghai

Published by iUniverse.com, Inc.

For information address:
iUniverse.com, Inc.
5220 S 16th, Ste. 200
Lincoln, NE 68512
www.iuniverse.com

Cover Creation by Shay Jones

Graphic Production by Matt Bromley, Associate Consultant
Domhnall CGN Adams, Corporation Sole—http://www.dcgna.com
5721-10405 Jasper Avenue
Edmonton, Alberta, Canada T5J 3S2
(780) 416-2967—dcgna@yahoo.com

CD-ROM Duplication by Paragon Media, Seattle, Washington

ISBN: 0-595-14812-3

Printed in the United States of America

.

Acknowledgments

We are pleased to acknowledge the following professionals for their important contributions in the creation of this study guide.

Technical Writer—Caleb Thompson, MSC, MCT, MCSE, MCP+I, A+, Network+

Editors—Anita Crocus and Nina Gettler

Indexer—Loral Pritchett

Cover Creation, Text Conversion and Proofing—Shay Jones, AA, MCSE, MCP

Technical Reviewer—Travis McElfrcsh, MCT, MCSE+I, MCP+SP, Director, E-Commerce Technology Research and Training

Graphic Designer—Matt Bromley

V.P., Publishing and Courseware Development— Candace Sinclair

Course Prerequisites

The Updating Support Skills from Microsoft Windows NT 4.0 to Microsoft Windows 2000 study guide targets individuals who have the following skills in administering Microsoft Windows NT 4.0:

- Creating and administering user and group accounts

- Troubleshooting problems that prevent users from logging on to a network and managing network resources

- Setting up and administering permissions for files and folders

- Taking ownership of folders

- Troubleshooting when users are unable to gain access to disk resources

- Creating, administering and troubleshooting a printing environment

- Monitoring network resources

- Backing up and restoring files and folders

- Administering the Windows NT Server and Windows NT Workstation operating systems in real-world situations

- Installing and configuring Windows NT

- Creating and implementing system policies

- Creating and managing partitions, file systems, and fault-tolerant volumes

- Supporting running applications under Windows NT

- Identifying network components and describing their function on a Windows NT–based computer

- Installing and configuring network transport protocols.

- Installing and configuring network services on Windows NT Server

- Implementing remote access service (RAS)

- Installing client software

- Implementing and troubleshooting directory replication

- Recognizing problems related to the boot process

- Determining the appropriate action to take for common problems

- A thorough understanding of DHCP, WINS, and Internet Protocol (IP) subnetting and routing

- Experience supporting networks and end users

The Updating Support Skills from Microsoft Windows NT 4.0 to Microsoft Windows 2000 exam tests an individual's knowledge for providing Microsoft Windows NT 4.0 support for a Microsoft Windows 2000-based network upgrade.

In addition, we recommend that you have a working knowledge of the English language, so that you are able to understand the technical words and concepts this study guide presents.

To feel confident about using this study guide, you should have the following knowledge or ability:

- The desire and drive to become an MCSE certified technician through our instructions, terminology, activities, quizzes, and study guide content

- Basic computer skills, which include using a mouse, keyboard, and viewing a monitor

- Basic networking knowledge including the fundamentals of working with Internet browsers, e-mail functionality, and search engines

- IP, remote connectivity and security

Hardware and Software Requirements

To apply the knowledge presented in this study guide, you will need the following minimum hardware:

- For Windows 2000 Professional, we recommend 64 megabytes of RAM (32 megabytes as a minimum) and a 1-gigabyte (GB) hard disk space.

- For Windows 2000 Server, we recommend a Pentium II or better processor, 128 megabytes of RAM (64 megabytes minimum), and a 2-GB hard drive. If you want to install Remote Installation Server with Windows 2000 Server, you should have at least two additional gigabytes of hard disk space available.

- CD-ROM drive

- Mouse

- VGA monitor and graphics card

- Internet connectivity

To apply the knowledge presented in this study guide, you will need the following minimum software installed on your computer:

- Microsoft Windows 2000 Advanced Server

- Microsoft Internet Explorer or Netscape Communicator

Symbols Used in This Study Guide

To call your attention to various facts within our study guide content, we've included the following three symbols to help you prepare for the Updating Support Skills from Microsoft Windows NT 4.0 to Microsoft Windows 2000 exam.

 Tip: The Tip identifies important information that you might see referenced in the certification exam.

 Note: The Note enhances your understanding of the topic content.

 Warning: The Warning describes circumstances that could be harmful to you and your computer system or network.

How to Use This Study Guide

Although you will develop and implement your own personal style of studying and preparing for the MCSE exam, we've taken the strategy of presenting the exam information in an easy-to-follow, ten-lesson format. Each lesson conforms to Microsoft's model for exam content preparation.

At the beginning of each lesson, we summarize the information that will be covered. At the end of each lesson we round out your studying experience by providing the following four ways to test and challenge what you've learned.

Vocabulary—Helps you review all the important terms discussed in the lesson.

In Brief—Reinforces your knowledge by presenting you with a problem and a possible solution.

Activities—Further tests what you have learned in the lesson by presenting ten activities that often require you to do more reading or research to understand the activity. In addition, we have provided the answers to each activity.

Lesson Quiz—To round out the knowledge you will gain after completing each lesson in this study guide, we have included ten sample exam questions and answers. This allows you to test your knowledge, and it gives you the reasons why the "answers" were either correct or incorrect. This, in itself, enhances your power to pass the exam.

You can also refer to the Glossary at the back of the book to review terminology. Furthermore, you can view the Index to find more content for individual terms and concepts.

Introduction to MCSE Certification

The Microsoft Certified Systems Engineer (MCSE) credential is the highest-ranked certification for professionals who analyze business requirements for system architecture, design solutions, deployment, installation, and configuration of architecture components, as well as troubleshooting system problems.

When you receive your MCSE certification, it proves your competence by having earned a nationally-recognized credential as an information technology professional who works in a typically complex computing environment of medium to large organizations. It is recommended that a Windows 2000 MCSE candidate should have at least one year of experience implementing and administering a network operating system environment.

To help you bridge the gap between needing the knowledge and knowing the facts, this study guide presents Updating Support Skills from Microsoft Windows NT 4.0 to Microsoft Windows 2000 knowledge that will help you pass this exam.

The MCSE exams cover a vast range of vendor-independent hardware and software technologies, as well as basic Internet and Windows 2000 design knowledge, technical skills and best practice scenarios.

 Note: This study guide presents technical content that should enable you to pass the Updating Support Skills from Microsoft Windows NT 4.0 to Microsoft Windows 2000 certification exam on the first try.

Updating Support Skills from Microsoft Windows NT 4.0 to Microsoft Windows 2000 Study Guide Objectives

Successful completion of this study guide is realized when you can competently upgrade, install and configure Microsoft Windows 2000 from a Windows NT 4.0 environment. Furthermore, the objectives require skills and knowledge for optimizing a performance-based network that supports job-related tasks using the Windows 2000 operating system.

You must fully comprehend each of the following objectives and their related tasks to prepare for this certification exam:

- Install Windows 2000 and describe tools used for unattended installations

- Install, configure, and troubleshoot the DNS Server Service

- Explain the relationship between the Active Directory structure and a network's organization

- Install and configure Active Directory in a network

- Populate Active Directory and manage Active Directory objects

- Upgrade a Windows NT 4.0 network to Windows 2000

- Install and configure RIS

- Deploy RIS images to workstations

- Manage desktop environments by using Group Policy

- Manage software by using Group Policy

- Install and configure Terminal Services

- Configure and support Routing and Remote Access in Windows 2000

- Configure Smart Cards, security policies, Internet Protocol Security (IPSec), and the Encrypting File System (EFS)

- Support DHCP and WINS in Windows 2000

- Manage file resources in Windows 2000

- Create and manage dynamic volumes

- Implement disaster-protection and disaster-recovery techniques in Windows 2000

Figures

Figure 10.18 Backup Utility Welcome Page 553
Figure 10.19 What to Back Up 556
Figure 10.20 Backup Selection 557
Figure 10.21 Backup Destination 558
Figure 10.22 Backup Label 560
Figure 10.23 When to Back Up 560
Figure 10.24 User Account Information 561
Figure 10.25 Backup Schedule 562
Figure 10.26 Backup Property Page 563
Figure 10.27 Backup Job Information 564
Figure 10.28 Restore Options 565
Figure 10.29 How to Restore 566
Figure 10.30 Restore Property Page 567
Figure 10.31 System State Selection 569
Figure 10.32 NTDSUTIL.EXE 570

List of Tables

Table of Contents

Lesson 5   Upgrading a Windows NT 4.0
Network to Windows 2000 223

Introduction and Installation of Windows 2000

As more and more companies discover the benefits of networking, the need for secure and stable servers and workstations has increased. In addition, the need to keep operating systems "user-friendly" has not diminished. Seeing this trend, Microsoft has created Microsoft Windows 2000. Windows 2000 incorporates Plug-and-Play technology, support for over 6,500 hardware devices that Microsoft Windows NT 4.0 did not support, and several tools familiar to Microsoft Windows 98 users and administrators. These features run atop the Windows NT 4.0 kernel structure, preserving the stability Windows NT 4.0 is known for, and maintaining a level of security unmatched by Windows 95 and Windows 98.

After completing this lesson, you should have a better understanding of the following topics:

*   Windows 2000 Introduction

*   Microsoft Windows 2000 Family

*   Windows 2000 Installation

*   Windows 2000 Automated Installation

*   Remote Installation Service (RIS)

*   Disk Duplication

*   Windows 2000 Installation Troubleshooting

Windows 2000 Introduction

Windows 2000 is the newest Windows-based operating system from Microsoft and unites two of their most popular operating systems, Windows 98 and Windows NT 4.0.

Windows NT 4.0 is a stable, secure, and robust operating system, whereas Windows 98 is known for its ease of use. Both operating systems have their strengths and weaknesses. Windows NT 4.0, for example, does not fully support Microsoft's implementation of automatic hardware detection and configuration, Plug and Play (PnP). It also lacks support for some of the more common hardware devices on the market today, including the Universal Serial Bus (USB).

Although Windows NT 4.0 lacks hardware support, it is much more stable and secure than Windows 95 and Windows 98. These operating systems have sacrificed stability and network security for compatibility. With Windows 2000, Microsoft forgoes some backward-compatibility features, because Microsoft recognizes that a stable and secure system is more important in a network than one that runs outdated programs and supports older hardware.

 Note: Stability in an operating system is often achieved by limiting which programs run in that operating system. Windows NT 4.0 is stable in part because programs that try to directly access the hardware do not run in it.

Understanding New Features of Windows 2000

Although it is easiest to think of Windows 2000 as a combination of Windows NT 4.0 and Windows 98, it contains many new features which did not previously exist on any Microsoft platform. For example, Microsoft has concentrated on redesigning network organization by implementing a new directory service called Microsoft Active Directory. There are also considerable changes to server management, with management tools now centralized in the Microsoft Management Console (MMC).

Some of the new features build on previous elements of Windows NT 4.0. Network security is an important feature of Windows NT 4.0, and Windows 2000 adds several new security features to those of Windows NT 4.0.

Microsoft Active Directory

Active Directory provides a new way of organizing a network. Based on a hierarchical structure, Active Directory provides a flexible and expandable network architecture. This structure supports a variety of clients, including Windows 3.11, Windows 95/98, Windows NT 4.0, and even UNIX and Macintosh clients. In order to make migration (upgrading a network from an older network operating system to a new one) as easy as possible for system administrators, Active Directory has been designed to work in conjunction with the existing Windows NT 4.0 domain model. Nonetheless, there are many reasons to migrate to an Active Directory-based network.

Active Directory allows for a far more intuitive structuring of users, groups, and resources on the network. It permits the grouping of resources, rather than just the grouping of users. Using these groups, you can assign permissions and delegate administrative tasks based on resource allocation.

Active Directory requires the use of the Domain Name Service (DNS). As a result, Microsoft has made DNS integration much easier to implement and maintain than in Windows NT 4.0. DNS now supports dynamic updates because Active Directory updates DNS automatically, eliminating the need to update the DNS table manually. The integration of Active Directory and DNS also means that the incorporation of the Internet and Internet-based technologies is more intrinsic in Windows 2000-based networks.

Microsoft Management Console (MMC)

Another significant change in the Windows environment is the way the management of Windows 2000 has become more centralized. All of the main administrative tools are accessed through the MMC. Introduced with Internet Information Service (IIS) for Windows NT 4.0, the MMC provides a common interface through which many different tools can run in the form of snap-ins (or consoles). Tools that include User Manager, Disk Manager, Server Manager, and Event Viewer are no longer separate tools in Windows 2000. They are now snap-ins for the MMC.

Security Features

Security features have also been enhanced in Windows 2000. In addition to requiring a valid logon to access any resources on the network or any computer running Windows NT 4.0, Windows 2000 also supports file-level encryption, Internet Protocol Security (IPSec), and Smart Card support.

Microsoft Windows 2000 Family

Microsoft has released four different Windows 2000 products: Windows 2000 Professional, Server, Advanced Server, and Datacenter Server. Although each has a unique purpose in the structure of your network, they share many features. Similar to Windows NT 4.0, options differ among Windows 2000 products.

Understanding Windows 2000 Professional

Windows 2000 Professional has been designed as the operating system for workstations, portable computers, and stand-alone computers. It is intended to replace Windows 98 and Windows NT 4.0 Workstation. It is not designed to act as a file or application server. Although much of the user interface has not changed from Windows NT 4.0 or Windows 98, Windows 2000 Professional has a few enhancements that are designed to make the system easier to use.

Microsoft has hidden or removed some of the options available to users, which simplifies the interface by giving you fewer choices. For example, Windows 2000 features a customized Start Menu, which only displays recently used programs and files. In addition, shortcuts to the administrative tools do not appear on the Start Menu by default. The Logon and Shutdown dialog boxes have also been simplified.

Tip: You can customize the Start menu to show those features that are hidden by default.

Microsoft has also added a Graphical User Interface (GUI) program for task scheduling, appropriately named the Scheduled Task Wizard. You no longer need to use the "**AT**" command and its unfriendly command-line interface to schedule programs. Programs and scripts can be set to run on specific dates and at specific times using the Scheduled Task Wizard (Figure 1.1). The Wizard leads you through the process, allowing you to first choose the program or script, then how often you want it to run. You can access the Wizard through the Control Panel, Scheduled Tasks folder.

Figure 1.1 Scheduled Task Wizard

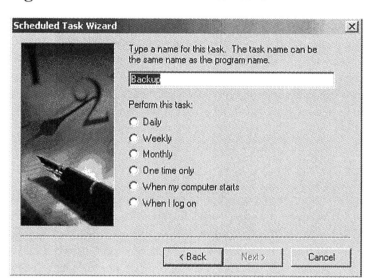

Portable Computer Enhancements

Windows 2000 Professional includes several new features that enhance the use of portable computers. For example, Windows 2000 supports the Advanced Configuration and Power Interface (ACPI) that allows "hot swapping" of hardware (the addition and removal of hardware without turning the computer off). ACPI also integrates the operating system and the computer's system Basic Input-Output System (BIOS) for advanced power management. If your computer does not support ACPI, Windows 2000 offers Advanced Power Management (APM), which supports power management but not hardware configuration.

Network folders can now be accessed when your computer is disconnected from the network with a new feature called Offline Folders. Using the Offline Folders option, you can copy the contents of a network folder onto your hard drive for use while you are disconnected from the network. Upon reconnecting to the network, the Synchronization Manager automatically compares the items in your offline folders to those on the network folder and updates the network folder with the changes you made. This ensures that you are always working on the most recent version of your documents, even when disconnected from the network.

Both laptop and desktop users can take advantage of a new shut down option called hibernate. When preparing to hibernate, Windows 2000 Professional copies the contents of the Random Access Memory (RAM) to the hard disk and then allows the computer to be shut off (or turned off automatically if APM is enabled). When the computer is turned on after hibernation, the system restores the configuration to exactly where it was prior to hibernation. As an extra safety precaution, Windows 2000 always locks the computer during hibernation. Only the person last using the computer or an administrator can unlock it. Hibernation requires an amount of hard drive space equal to the amount of RAM installed in the system (if you have 64 MB of RAM, hibernation requires 64 MB of free hard drive space).

Internet Enhancements

In accordance with Microsoft's efforts to make Windows 2000-based networks interface with the Internet, Windows 2000 Professional offers many Internet-based features. Microsoft has included built-in support for Virtual Private Networks (VPNs). Windows 2000 also includes the Internet Printing Protocol (IPP), which allows you to print to any printer on a Windows 2000 network that is connected to the Internet (assuming, of course, that you have the appropriate permissions). It also allows you to view the status of a printer using a Web browser, as well as download and install the latest printer drivers automatically. Windows 2000 ships with Microsoft Internet Explorer 5 and Microsoft Outlook Express 5 for connecting to the Internet and for sending and receiving e-mail.

Understanding Windows 2000 Server

Microsoft Windows 2000 Server, as the name implies, is designed as the operating system for your network servers. It includes all of the features and enhancements of Windows 2000 Professional (except hibernation), and also supports the numerous server services unavailable on Windows 2000 Professional. Most important among these services is the Active Directory service. As previously discussed, Active Directory is the new service that defines and supports the organization of your network. In Windows 2000, domain controllers are servers providing the Active Directory service.

Like Windows 2000 Professional, Windows 2000 Server makes use of the MMC to centralize management tools. Any services running on the server can be managed through the MMC, including DNS, Dynamic Host Configuration Protocol (DHCP), and Internet Information Services (IIS). Because the MMC is modular, which allows the addition of snap-ins at any time, other services that provide a snap-in can be managed in this centralized way. As an example, Microsoft Proxy Server 2.0, which was written for Windows NT 4.0, works with Windows 2000 Server (with an update patch), in part because it is designed to use the MMC.

Another major change in Windows 2000 Server over its Windows NT 4.0 predecessor is the addition of Remote Installation Services (RIS). RIS allows you to install Windows 2000 Professional on client computers across your network from a central server. RIS supports PnP hardware detection, which allows you to perform automatic installations on computers with different hardware.

Understanding Windows 2000 Advanced Server

Windows 2000 Advanced Server includes all of the features of Windows 2000 Server, but is much more scalable. Windows 2000 Advanced Server supports up to 8 GB of physical RAM on an Intel-based computer (32 GB on Alpha-based computers), and up to eight processors. Furthermore, Windows 2000 Advanced Server supports Windows clustering. The Windows Cluster service allows you to join a group of servers to act as a single server and allows strong fault tolerance (if one of the servers in a cluster fails, another assumes the roles of the failed computer) and load balancing (clustering distributes network demands to all of the servers in a cluster rather than to just one).

Windows 2000 Advanced Server is the Windows 2000 version of Windows NT 4.0 Enterprise Server.

 Tip: Windows Clustering allows several servers to act as one server, which provides load balancing and fault tolerance.

Understanding Windows 2000 Datacenter Server

The most powerful member of the Windows 2000 family is Windows 2000 Datacenter Server. It expands the features of Windows 2000 Advanced Server. Whereas Windows 2000 Advanced Server supports eight processors,

Windows 2000 Datacenter Server supports up to 32 processors. It also supports up to 64 GB of physical memory on Intel-based computers (32 GB on Alpha-based servers). This is accomplished through Microsoft's implementation of Physical Address Extensions (PAEs) created by Intel. PAEs allow an operating system to take advantage of 36-bit memory addressing, rather than the 32-bit addressing that has been the standard for years.

The ability to support such large amounts of RAM and processing power makes Windows 2000 Datacenter Server an appropriate choice for the most demanding computing needs. Large data warehouses, E-commerce servers, and computers used for scientific and engineering modeling will benefit from running Windows 2000 Datacenter Server.

Comparing Windows 2000 Products

Each member of the Windows 2000 Server family builds upon a less-powerful sibling. Matching the operating system to the demands of the server is an important task. Table 1.1 summarizes the features of each of the four Microsoft Windows 2000 Family members.

Table 1.1 Windows 2000 Key Features

Operating System	Description
Windows 2000 Professional	--Designed as the desktop operating system --Designed to replace Windows 95, Windows 98, and Windows NT 4.0
Windows 2000 Server	--Designed as the operating system for most servers in your network --Has all of the features of Windows 2000 Professional, plus support for server services (Active Directory, DHCP, DNS, and more)
Windows 2000 Advanced Server	--Designed for servers in a large enterprise network --Contains all of the features of Windows 2000 Server --Supports more RAM and CPUs
Windows 2000 Datacenter Server	--The most powerful Windows 2000 product --Supports more RAM and CPUs --Designed for the largest networks and data warehouses

Windows 2000 Installation

There are three ways to install Windows 2000: locally from a CD-ROM, over the network, or remotely over the network. The installation can also be automated, which simplifies the job of the network administrator.

Preparing for Installation

Before installing Windows 2000, you must spend time preparing. A poorly planned installation usually leads to a reinstallation. The old adage "measure twice, cut once" applies to installing operating systems as well. Think through the installation process thoroughly before beginning.

Tip: Microsoft likes administrators to plan ahead. You should expect questions on the exam about installation planning, including hardware requirements, the role of servers and workstations, and licensing.

You should be able to answer the following questions before you begin an installation:

- Does the hardware meet the minimum requirements of the version of Windows 2000 you are installing?

- Are the computer and devices in the computer listed on Microsoft's Hardware Compatibility List (HCL)?

- How do you want the hard drive partitioned?

- Which file system (NTFS, FAT, or FAT32) best suits your needs?

- Will this computer join a domain or workgroup?

If you are installing one of the Windows 2000 Server products, there are two additional questions you should ask:

- What role will this server play in the network?

- What licensing mode is most appropriate?

Hardware Requirements

As Microsoft products become more feature-rich, they need computers that can run these features. The hardware requirements for Windows 2000 are higher than those for Windows NT 4.0. Windows 2000 Professional (Table 1.2) and Windows 2000 Server (Table 1.3) have different hardware requirements, which reflect the enhanced options and capabilities of the latter. You should be familiar with both the hardware requirements and recommendations for each platform.

 Note: A server running on minimum hardware requirements usually will not serve a network of more than a few users with any acceptable level of performance.

Like Windows NT 4.0, Windows 2000 is designed to run on Intel-based computers and computers using the Alpha processor. With Windows 2000, Microsoft has abandoned support for the PowerPC processor.

Table 1.2 Windows 2000 Professional Hardware Requirements

Component	Required Hardware	Recommended Hardware
CPU	--Pentium 166 MHz *or* Compaq Alpha-based Processor	--Pentium II or higher Compaq Alpha-based Processor
Memory (RAM)	--32 MB (48 MB for Alphas)	--64 MB or more (96 MB for Alphas)
Hard Drive Space	--685 MB free space (351 MB for Alphas)	--1 GB or more free space
Other Drives	--12x CD-ROM --High-density 3.5-inch disk drive as drive A	--32x CD-ROM or faster --High-density 3.5-inch disk drive as drive A
Input / Output Devices	-Keyboard --Mouse	--Keyboard --Mouse

 Note: A CD-ROM is not required if Windows 2000 and all other applications are installed over the network. A floppy drive is not required if the computer supports booting from a CD-ROM or network card.

Table 1.3 Windows 2000 Server Hardware Requirements

Component	Required Hardware	Recommended Hardware
CPU	--Pentium 166 MHz *or* Compaq Alpha-based Processor	--Pentium II or higher *or* Compaq Alpha-based Processor
Memory (RAM)	--64 MB (96 MB for Alphas)	--128 MB or more
Hard Drive Space	--685 MB free space (367 for Alphas)	--1 GB or more free space
Other Drives	--12x CD-ROM --High-density 3.5-inch disk drive as drive A	--32x CD-ROM or faster --High-density 3.5-inch disk drive as drive A --Tape Backup
Input Devices	--Keyboard --Mouse --Network Card	--Keyboard --Mouse --Network Card

In addition to the minimum hardware requirements, it is also important to check the latest version of Microsoft's Hardware Compatibility List (HCL) for hardware compatibility. The HCL can be found on Microsoft's Web page at http://www.microsoft.com/hcl.

After hardware is tested for compatibility, it is included on the HCL. However, this list is not and can never be complete. Microsoft could not possibly test the hundreds of thousands of devices available in the personal computer industry. If a device in your computer is not on the HCL, it does not mean that Windows 2000 will not work with it. Many devices emulate other devices which may be included on the HCL.

For example, you may have an older DTC SCSI (Small Computer Systems Interface) controller card that does not appear on the HCL. However, in reading the documentation that came with the SCSI card, you notice that it emulates the Adaptec AHA-1520 SCSI card that is on the HCL, so you can be fairly certain your card will work with Windows 2000. If a particular device is not on the HCL and it does not emulate other devices, do not give up all hope: the device may still work. However, if it is crucial device (like a hard disk controller or network card), you should consider replacing it with one that is on the HCL before beginning the installation of Windows 2000.

Note: Microsoft does not support hardware problems for hardware not listed on the HCL. Realistically, most of the components you purchase today are included on the HCL or emulate a component that is on the list.

Disk Partitioning and Formatting

Before a hard drive can be used by the operating system, it must be partitioned. Partitions are logical (not physical) divisions of the hard drive. A partition acts like an independent drive with its own drive letter, even though it may be on the same physical hard disk as several other partitions. A hard disk may contain one or several partitions.

In Windows 2000, a hard disk may contain up to four partitions that may be any combination of primary partitions and extended partitions, as long as at least one primary partition is present. A primary partition is one from which the operating system can boot; the primary partition contains the Windows 2000 boot files. The primary partition is also marked as the active partition (meaning it is bootable). An extended partition is a logical division of the hard disk that can be further sectioned into logical drives. A logical drive, like a primary partition, acts as an independent drive with its own drive letter but it cannot be an active (bootable) partition.

Figure 1.2 shows a disk with a primary partition (drive C), one extended partition and two logical drives (drives D and E) within the extended partition.

Figure 1.2 Partitioned Hard Disk

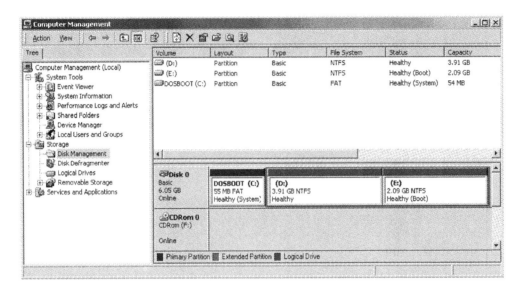

When installing Windows 2000, you copy the boot files to the active, primary partition (usually drive C). In Windows 2000 and Windows NT 4.0 terminology, this is called the system partition. The system files are copied to the **\WINNT** directory on the partition you specify during setup. This partition, called the boot partition, can be the same as the system partition, but does not have to be.

Tip: The boot partition is the partition that contains the Windows 2000 system files and can be on any partition. The system partition is the partition that contains the hardware-specific boot files; it must be the active primary partition. The boot partition and system partition can be the same partition.

Installation of Windows 2000 requires a minimum partition size of 685 MB for the boot partition. If you plan on installing many services on top of the Windows 2000 Server installation, you will need considerably more space.

When planning your installation partitioning scheme, perhaps the most important thing to remember is that once you create the boot and system partitions and load the operating system, it is difficult to change the size of these partitions. To change the size of the partitions, you must use a third-party utility like Partition Magic from PowerQuest, or back up your data, repartition, reload Windows 2000, then restore the data.

The other important drive space consideration before installation is choosing the file system. Like Windows NT 4.0, Windows 2000 supports the 16-bit File Allocation Table (FAT) file system and Windows NT File System (NTFS). NTFS has been updated to version 5 and called Windows 2000 File System. Windows 2000 also supports the 32-bit File Allocation Table (FAT32) file system.

In general, you should choose to use NTFS whenever possible. NTFS Version 5 provides file- and folder-level security, disk compression, disk quotas, and encryption. None of these security features are available on FAT and FAT32 volumes. The only scenario where one of the FAT file systems should be considered is when you are setting up a dual/multiple-boot computer. A multiple-boot computer is one where you have installed more than one operating system. For example, you may want to have both Windows 98 and Windows 2000 Professional installed on one computer. Windows 98 supports both FAT and FAT32, but does not support NTFS. In such a situation, you must make sure that the primary active partition is formatted as FAT or FAT32.

Tip: Setting up a dual-boot computer compromises system security and performance. Because of this, Microsoft strongly discourages a dual-boot configuration on servers.

Joining the Network

Before installing the operating system, it is important to determine what type of network the computer will join. If the computer is joining a workgroup, you only need to supply the workgroup name during setup. If the computer is joining a domain, you need the following:

- A domain name

- A computer account

- An available DNS server and domain controller

Active Directory uses the domain name that is entered during installation to define the network. A computer account must be created in the domain before or during installation. A domain administrator can create the account ahead of time, or you can create it during installation if you have administrative privileges for the domain. Like the installation of Windows NT 4.0, if you opt to create the computer account during installation, you are prompted to enter the username and password of an account with domain administrative privileges. Also like Windows NT 4.0, a domain controller must be available when attempting to join the domain. In addition, because Active Directory is dependent upon DNS, a DNS server must be accessible over the network.

Role of the Computer on the Network

The final planning consideration before installation is the role of the computer on the network. Not only does the role of the computer affect installation choices, it also influences the hardware choices. If you are installing a version of Windows 2000 Professional, you have no choice regarding the role of the computer. It will act as a workstation on the network, whether you have set up the network as a workgroup or domain. However, when installing one of the versions of Windows 2000 Server, you should consider the following questions:

- What kind of server do you need?

- What services will the server provide?

- How much network traffic will this server handle?

- What licensing mode do I want to use?

The first three questions are interrelated. The role of the server and the services it provides determine in part how much traffic is directed to the server. Although these questions make little difference during installation, they do affect your hardware choices. If you are installing a Web server that handles hundreds of thousands of requests daily, loading Windows 2000 on a computer with the minimum hardware requirements is not appropriate.

When you install a Windows network, you need a license to run an operating system on the server. You also need a license to run an operating system on each client. These licenses are included in the purchase of the software. In fact, you are not purchasing any software; you are purchasing the right to load and run the software. In addition to these licenses, you need a Client Access License (CAL) for each client that connects to your server.

 Note: You never actually purchase software from Microsoft. You purchase the CD-ROM and the right to load and run the software on a computer.

The CAL licensing modes are the same in Windows 2000 as they were in Windows NT 4.0 - you must choose between Per Seat and Per Server. Per Server allows a certain number of clients to connect to the server. Per Seat allows a client to access any number of servers. To clarify, let's look at a simple scenario.

Your network consists of 1 server and 100 client computers. Your company runs 24 hours a day, and at any given time you never have more than 50 employees accessing the network. In this case, Per Server licensing mode makes the most sense. You can purchase 50 CALs and have all 100 clients on your network. This is legally acceptable because you never have more than 50 computers accessing the server at any given time. The alternative (Per Seat) would require you to purchase a 100 CALs.

Now suppose your company grows and you add a new server. Naturally, you want the clients to be able to access both servers. You could buy 50 CALs for the new server, and continue with Per Server licensing. At this point, you have purchased 100 CALs. Had you chosen Per Seat, you would have also purchased 100 CALs.

If you add yet another server, and continue using Per Server Licensing, you need to purchase 50 more CALs. You have actually purchased more CALs than you have clients! Microsoft acknowledges that networks tend to grow, so they allow a one-time-only conversion of licenses from Per Server to Per Seat. You cannot convert licenses from Per Seat to Per Server.

When choosing the licensing mode, consider the number of servers in your network. If you have a small number, Per Server may make more sense. If you are uncertain about which licensing mode to choose, choose Per Server. If you find that Per Server was not an appropriate choice, you can do a one-time conversion of your CALs to Per Seat.

Note: If you are uncertain about what licensing mode to choose, choose Per Server. You can always convert (once) to per seat licensing if you later decide that is what you need.

Installing Windows 2000 Locally

A local installation of Windows 2000 occurs when you are working on the computer where you are installing Windows 2000. There are two ways to install Windows 2000 locally on a computer. You can install the operating system using the CD-ROM (and floppy disks, if necessary), or you can install from a network share (an installation folder that is accessible over the network).

The beginning of the installation procedure (the text mode) for Windows 2000 has not changed much from the Windows NT 4.0 installation, but there are some differences.

 Tip: You should have experience running through the installation procedure before taking the exam.

The following installation procedures address Windows 2000 Professional and member servers running Windows 2000 Server.

CD-ROM Installation

If your computer supports booting from a CD-ROM, you can begin installation by inserting the Windows 2000 compact disc into the CD-ROM drive and turning on the computer. When the CD-ROM begins to boot, it prompts you to "Press any key to boot from the CD." If you do not press a key within a few seconds, the computer attempts to boot from the hard drive.

Note: Unlike the Windows NT 4.0 CD boot process, you must actively inform the setup program in Windows 2000 that you want it to run.

If the computer does not support booting from the CD-ROM, you can boot the computer using the setup disks included with the CD-ROM. If you do not have these disks, they can be made using the **MAKEBOOT A:** command. Booting from either the CD-ROM or floppies launches the boot program **WINNT.EXE**, which loads a minimal version of Windows 2000 into memory. With this, the first stage of Setup has begun.

In the Windows NT 4.0 installation, Setup stops after loading the basic drivers and asks if you have other disk controllers to load. In Windows 2000 Setup, the program prompts you to press **F6** if you have third-party drivers for SCSI and Redundant Array of Independent Disks (RAID) controllers. Setup does not stop and wait for user input. If you do not press **F6**, Setup continues automatically using the drivers it has loaded.

The next several screens should look familiar to anyone who has loaded Windows NT 4.0. You must choose the boot partition on which the system files are stored. If you have not yet defined any partitions, you have the option to create, delete, and format partitions.

Note: Although you can create all of the partitions in the Setup program, it is best to create only the system and boot partition(s) now. You have more control over the creation of partitions using Disk Management from within Windows 2000.

Once you choose (or create) a partition for installation of Windows 2000, you have the option to format the partition with one of the file systems discussed above (FAT, FAT32, or NTFS). If the partition is already formatted, you have the option to leave the file system intact. You may also choose the directory in which to install the system files (called the system root). The default location has not changed; it is still the \WINNT folder on the boot partition. Setup then copies the appropriate files to the system root, and automatically restarts the computer.

After rebooting the computer, the Graphical User Interface (GUI) portion of Setup runs. Windows 2000 automatically sets up security features and, after displaying an informational screen, detects and configures any devices in your computer. This detection process is part of the PnP, and may take quite a while to complete. Hardware that is PnP compliant is automatically configured. Legacy devices (those that are not PnP-compliant) are examined for their hardware settings. When finished, Setup requests the following information:

- Regional settings (location, date and time, keyboard and language settings)

- Name and organization

- Licensing mode (if you are installing a version of Windows 2000 Server)

- Computer name

- Password for the administrator account

After entering this information, you get a prompt to choose the optional components you would like to install. There are many optional components from which to choose. Table 1.4 lists the component, provides a brief description, whether it is available in Windows 2000 Professional or Server installations, and whether it is a new feature of Windows 2000.

Table 1.4 Optional Windows 2000 Components

Component	Description	Server or Professional Installation	New Windows 2000 Feature
Internet Information Services (IIS) (loads by default)	FTP and Web servers, and tools necessary to administer them	Both	No
Microsoft Indexing Service	Indexes data stored on the computer or network and allows full-text searches	Both	Yes

Component	Description	Server or Professional Installation	New Windows 2000 Feature
Management and Monitoring Tools	Tools to improve network performance and monitoring	Both	No
Networking Services	DHCP, DNS, TCP/IP, print server, file and print services, and more	Both	Some
Other Network File and Print Services	Includes support for Macintosh and UNIX-based computers	Both	No
Message Queuing Services	Uses Active Directory to store messages and allows interoperability of messaging applications	Both	Yes
Remote Storage	Allows direct access to tape media as if it were an extension of an NTFS volume	Server	Yes
Terminal Services	Allows Microsoft clients (Windows 3.11, 95, 98, and Windows NT 4.0) to run a virtual Windows 2000 desktop and other applications remotely	Server	Yes
Certificate Services	Creates X.509 digital certificates, used for authentication on the network and over the Internet	Server	No
Cluster Service	Enables Microsoft clustering	Advanced Server and Datacenter	Yes
Microsoft Script Debugger (loads by default)	Debugging features for Microsoft ActiveX scripts	Both	Yes
Remote Installation Services (RIS)	Used for remote installation of Windows 2000 Professional	Server	Yes

After choosing the optional components you wish to install, Setup prompts you for the correct date and time. Active Directory uses the date and time for replication of its database. Therefore, it is very important that this information is correct, especially on domain controllers.

Tip: Active Directory uses a computer's date and time for replication of the Active Directory database. Make sure the computers on your network are synchronized, especially domain controllers.

The next stage of Setup installs and configures the network. Setup automatically detects your Network Interface Card (NIC). If it fails to detect a NIC, Setup simply continues on to the next step, skipping over this part of the installation. When you install a NIC later, you must also configure the network settings. If Setup found a NIC, you may then choose whether you want a typical network installation, which includes loading Client for Microsoft Networks, File and Printer Sharing, and the TCP/IP protocol or indicate whether you want to customize the installation. By default, Windows 2000 Setup looks for a DHCP server and uses it for the dynamic (automatic) assignment of the IP address.

Note: NetBEUI, Microsoft's own protocol, does not install by default. To use NetBEUI on your network, you must install it.

The Setup program asks you to enter the name of the domain or workgroup to which this computer will belong. If a computer account has not yet been created in the domain, you get a prompt for a username and password, as mentioned above.

During the final stage of installation, Setup copies the remaining files needed, applies the settings you have specified, saves the configuration settings, and removes the temporary files used to run the Setup program. The computer reboots, and you are presented with the Windows 2000 logon screen.

Installing Windows 2000 Over the Network

When faced with the task of installing Windows 2000, on many computers installation over the network saves considerable time.

When installing over a network, all of the aforementioned hardware requirements apply, but the additional following conditions must exist:

*   A distribution folder (a shared folder that contains the files necessary to install Windows 2000) must be created and made available over the network.

*   A boot floppy disk that loads the network protocol(s) and the drivers for the NIC must be made. This allows the client computer to connect to the distribution folder when booted from the floppy.

*   The local hard drive must have at least one formatted partition. The Setup program copies temporary files to this partition.

Once these requirements are met, you can boot the computer from the network boot floppy and connect to the distribution folder. Run **WINNT.EXE** to start the Setup program. **WINNT.EXE** creates a temporary folder (named **$WINNT4.~LS**) on the local hard drive and copies the installation files to this folder. Unlike the Windows NT 4.0 installation, the boot floppies are not created by default. The Setup program restarts the local computer and begins the installation of Windows 2000, as described for the CD-ROM installation.

WINNT.EXE Switches

Much like the installation of Windows NT 4.0, you can modify the Windows 2000 version of **WINNT.EXE** using switches. A switch is an addition to the command that specifies how you should execute the command. It is typically preceded by a forward slash (/). Table 1.5 lists the switches that you can use with **WINNT.EXE**.

Note: Unlike Windows NT 4.0, you cannot create boot floppies using **WINNT.EXE**. Create startup disks by running **MAKEBOOT.EXE** from the **\bootdisk** folder on the Windows 2000 compact disc.

Table 1.5 Optional WINNT.EXE Switches

Switch	Description
/a	Enables the accessibility options during Setup
/i:inf	If you are using a setup information file (see the section on automating installation), specifies the name of the file
/l	Creates a log file, **$WINNT.LOG**
/r:folder	Allows you to install a folder within the **\WINNT** directory during setup
/rx:folder	Allows you to copy a temporary folder during setup. This folder is deleted when Setup finishes
/s:source	Defines the location of source files; used in conjunction with /u
/t:temp_drive	Forces Setup to use a particular drive for the temporary setup files. By Default, setup uses the drive with the most free space
/UDF:ID [UDF_file]	Requires setup to use an UDF file and specifies an ID within that file
/unattend:answer_file	Performs an unattended installation and defines the name of the answer file. Requires the use of the /s switch

Windows 2000 Automated Installation

One of the goals of network administrators is to reduce the amount of time spent installing operating systems and software on client computers. A significant way to reduce the overall time spent installing systems is by automating the setup procedure. In Windows NT 4.0 and Windows 2000, this means creating an answer file (also known as the **UNATTEND.TXT** file), and often a Uniqueness Database File (UDF). The answer file is used to automatically answer the prompts you see during installation. A complete answer file allows the installation of the operating system without any user intervention after turning the computer on.

The UDF is a supplement to the answer file, supplying computer-specific information like the IP address and the computer name. Using both an answer file and an UDF allows an administrator to install Windows NT 4.0 on many computers, as long as they all have the same hard disk controllers and hardware. However, these installation scripts are difficult to create in Windows NT 4.0, and errors are common.

Using Setup Manager Wizard

With Windows 2000, Microsoft has vastly improved the process of creating answer files and UDFs by introducing the Setup Manager Wizard. The Setup Manager is part of the Resource Kit, which is included on the Windows 2000 CD-ROM. To install the Setup Manager, you first install the Resource Kit. The Setup Manager can then be found in the Tools Management Console.

When you run the Setup Manager, you have the option of creating a new answer file from scratch, creating a new one that duplicates the computer on which the Wizard is running, or editing a previously created answer file (Figure 1.3).

Figure 1.3 Windows 2000 Setup Manager Wizard

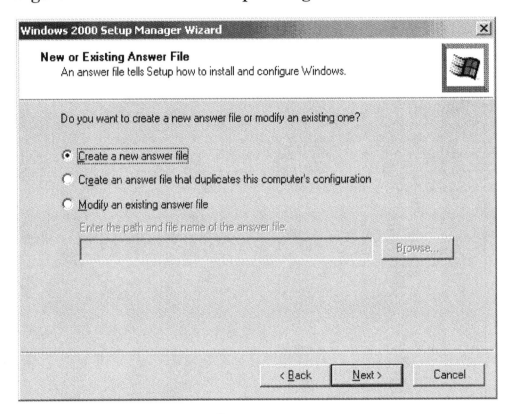

If you are creating a new answer file, you must specify the type of answer file you want to create. Setup Manager can create an **UNATTEND.TXT** file for Windows 2000 Professional and Windows 2000 Server installations. You can also use it to create a **REMBOOT.SIF** file for use with Remote Installation Services (RIS) and a **SYSPREP.INF** file for use with the System Preparation Tool (called "Sysprep Install") (Figure 1.4).

After choosing the file to create, Setup Manager Wizard asks you to select a level of user intervention during Setup. You may choose from the following:

Provide Defaults—Setup provides default answers, but requires the user to review them before proceeding.

Figure 1.4 Answer File Options

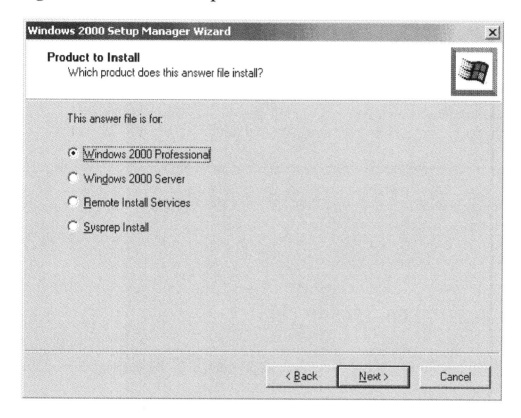

After choosing the file to create, Setup Manager Wizard asks you to select a level of user intervention during Setup. You may choose from the following:

Provide Defaults—Setup provides default answers, but requires the user to review them before proceeding.

Fully Automated—You supply all of the answers; the user has no input.

Hide Pages—For any screen that is completed by the answer file, the user cannot see the settings.

Read Only—The user can see the pages, but cannot change settings.

GUI Attended—Only the text mode of Setup is unattended (the GUI portion of installation requires user input).

The Setup Manager Wizard then displays several screens on which you enter the necessary information. Requested are the registration code, computer name (enter as many names as you like, import them from a text file, or have Setup Manager automatically create them), administrator password, display settings, and network settings.

 Tip: Spend time going through the Setup Manager Wizard. Automation of the installation process is a key feature of Windows 2000 with which you should be familiar.

Finally, you may remember a utility for Windows NT 4.0 named **SYSDIFF.EXE**. This program allows you to take a "snapshot" of a system before and after installing any applications. You can apply the difference to new installations, essentially automating the installation of applications. The use of **SYSDIFF.EXE** has not changed with Windows 2000.

Remote Installation Service (RIS)

RIS takes the procedure of performing network installations one step further. RIS allows you to install Windows 2000 Professional on client computers without physically being at the client computer. The advantages of RIS are as follows:

- Simplifies management (hardware-specific files are not needed)

- Helps in recovery of crashed client computers

- Reduces administrative time, therefore, the Total Cost of Ownership (TCO)

Preparing to Use RIS

You must install RIS software on an NTFS-formatted partition that is accessible over the network. This partition can be on any Windows 2000 Server (either a domain controller or a member server), but it cannot be the same partition that contains the Windows 2000 Server system files. The partition must be large enough to hold the RIS software and the Windows 2000 Professional installation images.

Tip:RIS uses DNS, DHCP, and Active Directory for remote installations. The services don't need to be on the RIS server, but must be accessible over the network.

Installing a RIS Server

There are two stages for installing RIS on a server. The first stage copies necessary files from the Windows 2000 CD. Copying files can take place during installation of the server or after the server has been installed through Add/Remove Programs in the Control Panel. To begin the installation, follow these steps:

1. From the Start Menu, choose Settings, and then select Control Panel.

2. From the Control Panel, double-click Add/Remove Programs to display the Add/Remove Programs window.

3. Choose the Add/Remove Windows Components option (Figure 1.5).

Figure 1.5 Add/Remove Programs

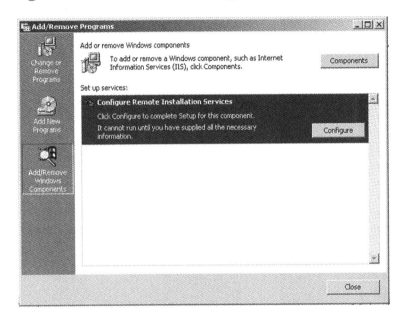

4. From the list of Windows components, choose the checkbox next to Remote Installation Services, then select Next (Figure 1.6).

5. Setup copies the necessary files to your hard disk.

6. Choose Finish.

7. Setup prompts you to reboot the server.

After rebooting the server, you must begin the second stage of installation. To continue the installation, follow these steps:

1. From the Start Menu, choose Programs, Administrative Tools, and then select Configure Your Server.

2. From the "Configure Your Server" window, choose Finish Setup.

    The Add/Remove Programs control panel opens, with Configure Remote Installation Services selected

Figure 1.6 RIS Installation

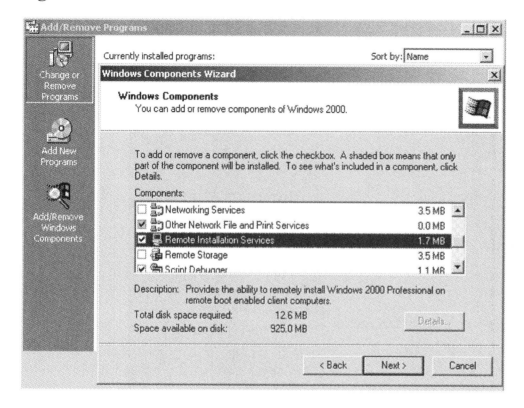

3. Choose Configure, and then select Next.

    The Remote Installation Services Setup Wizard displays

4. Type the directory name where you want to install RIS, and then choose Next.

 Note: The RIS installation directory cannot be on the system partition and must be for-matted with the NTFS file system.

5. From the Initial Settings window, choose a RIS option to either begin responding to client requests immediately or after you enable the service and then select Next.

6. Type the path to the installation files, and then choose Next.

    Typically, this will be the drive letter containing the Windows 2000 Professional CD-ROM, unless you have copied the Windows 2000 Professional files to another location

7. Type a name for the installation folder, and then choose Next

    As an option, you can type a "friendly" name for the installation folder and also include a text-based comment. These settings appear when you begin a remote installation and help identify the correct installation.

8. Choose Next to review the final settings and then select Finish.

Installing the RIS Client

The client computers, which receive the remote installation, must be able to access the network. Like a network installation, you can create a network installation boot disk and boot the client computer from this disk. RIS comes with a remote boot disk generator called **RBFG.EXE**. This program can be found in the **\REMOTEINSTALL\ADMIN** folder on your RIS server.

You can achieve a more efficient remote installation if the client computer supports booting from the NIC. The network card must have Pre-Boot Execution Environment (PXE) bootable Read Only Memory (boot ROM). In addition, the BIOS on the client computer must support booting from a NIC and must be configured to do so. If these conditions exist, you can simply turn on the computer and have the installation of Windows 2000 begin.

The most efficient method for performing a remote installation is to use Net PCs. A Net PC is a PC98-compliant computer that relies on the network for some of its functionality. PC98-compliant refers to a document published annual by Microsoft and Intel and distributed to hardware manufacturers. It represents computer standardization, which helps Microsoft implement new features like RIS.

Generally, Net PCs are not as upgradeable as other computers, and typically do not contain CD-ROM drives or floppy drives. The two major benefits to Net PCs are reduced cost and greater security (without a floppy drive, it is difficult for a user to copy information from the PC). The Net PC is designed to boot from its NIC and install an operating system over the network.

Note: Microsoft has put quite a bit of work into the integration of Net PCs with the Windows 2000 environment. RIS support and Terminal Services are two examples of their efforts.

Whether performing a remote installation using a Net PC or a standard computer, the RIS procedure follows six steps (Figure 1.7).

Figure 1.7 Six Steps for a RIS Remote Installation

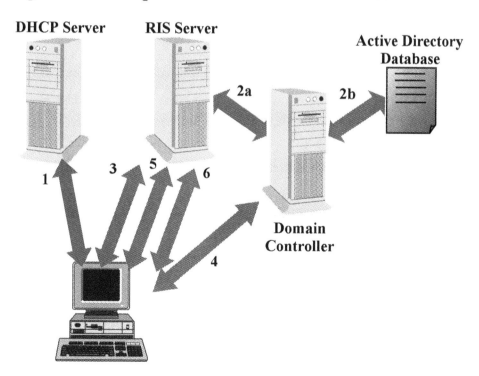

1. When the client computer is first turned on, it sends out two requests: a DHCP request to obtain an IP address, and a query to discover what RIS servers are available. With these requests, the client attaches a Globally Unique Identifier (GUID), which allows the client to be identified on the network. The DHCP Server grants an IP address to the client; the RIS server sends the client its own IP address and the name of the boot file the client should request. The user get a prompt to hit **F12** to confirm this RIS server as a host.

2. Once the client computer accepts the RIS server, the server searches the Active Directory server to see if an account for the client computer exists. RIS queries the Active Directory database for the client's GUID. If a computer account does not currently exist in the Active Directory, one is created during step 6.

3. The RIS server sends the Client Installation Wizard (CIW) to the client and prompts the user to log on to the network.

4. The user logs on to the network. Based on the user's logon credentials (which RIS checks against the Active Directory), RIS makes available to the user only those installation options and files for which the user has permission.

5. The user get a prompt to choose an operating system and installation option. If only one choice exists, no prompt appears. In either scenario, the user is warned that installation will reformat the hard disk and all data will be lost. The user must confirm before installation continues.

6. The operating system installation begins. The installation is performed as an unattended installation, so the end user is not required to enter any information.

Creating an Image Using the Remote Installation Preparation Wizard

You can use RIS to install Windows 2000 Professional on clients' computers. With the addition of the Remote Installation Preparation Wizard (**RIPREP.EXE**), you can also use RIS to install applications. RIS does not actually install the operating systems or applications but rather installs an image of them. To create an image, follow these steps:

1. Use Remote Installation Services to install the operating system on a client computer.

2. Install any additional applications manually.

3. Run **RIPREP.EXE**

4.   **RIPREP.EXE** guides you through the last two steps of preparing the image and copying the image to the RIS server.

When you complete this process, clients who access the RIS server can choose to install the image. When RIS finishes, each client has an identical installation of Windows 2000 Professional and the applications. This process is very similar to preparing a system for disk duplication.

Disk Duplication

Disk duplication is the process of setting up one computer exactly as you want it, taking a "snapshot" of the hard drive, and copying this image to as many other computers as you desire. It is, in essence, cloning. Windows 2000 does not offer disk duplication, but it does include a utility that makes duplication of Windows 2000 computers much easier. The tool is called the System Preparation Tool (**SYSPREP.EXE**), and is used in conjunction with a third-party duplicator. It is similar to **RIPREP.EXE**.

Using the System Preparation Tool

The problem with disk duplication and Windows NT 4.0 is one of Security Identifiers (SIDs). Every Windows NT 4.0-based computer has a SID, a unique number that identifies the computer on the network. When you duplicate a Windows NT 4.0 computer, you also duplicate the SID, and this creates problems. The problem becomes most significant when duplicating servers and domain controllers. The System Preparation Tool assists you in the duplication process by solving the SID problem.

 Note: Windows 2000 does not include disk-duplicating software.

To begin the disk duplication process, follow these steps:

1.   Install and configure Windows 2000 on a master computer.

2.   Install and configure any applications on the same computer.

3. Run **SYSPREP.EXE**.

4. Run the Setup Manager Wizard (optional).

5. Restart the computer and run the disk duplication program of your choice.

6. Save the disk image to a network share or CD-ROM.

7. Copy the image to new computers, using the disk duplication program.

The first two steps involve installing the operating system and any applications you want onto a computer. This computer should have a similar configuration to the computers on to which the image will be copied. They must have the same Hardware Abstraction Layers (HALs) and hard disk controllers.

The System Preparation Tool prepares the computer for duplication by deleting the SIDs and any other computer-specific or user-specific information. It also creates a minimal setup program that runs the first time the destination computer is restarted. You can run **SYSPREP.EXE** with the following switches (Table 1.6).

Table 1.6 SYSPREP.EXE Switches

Switch	Description
-quiet	Requires no user intervention.
-pnp	Requires the Setup program to detect PnP devices on the destination computer.
-reboot	Restarts the master computer instead of shutting down.
-nosidgen	Does not generate a new SID for the destination computer.

After running **SYSPREP.EXE**, the computer is ready for disk duplication. However, you may choose to run the Setup Manager Wizard to create a **SYSPREP.INF** file. Like an **UNATTEND.TXT** file, **SYSPREP.INF** supplies the answers needed for the minimal setup program that runs after duplication.

The final steps to disk duplication involve using a third-party disk duplication utility, like Ghost from Symantec. These programs make an image of the hard drive and save it as a file. They then have the ability to convert the image file back to a partition on any destination computer. The entire duplication process is significantly faster than installation of the operating system. If applications are installed, the time saved can easily justify the cost of the disk-duplicating software.

 Note: In addition to disk-duplicating software, there are hardware devices that duplicate entire hard drives. These devices can be even faster than their software counterparts and can simultaneously duplicate four or more drives.

Windows 2000 Installation Troubleshooting

If the computer on which you are installing Windows 2000 is functioning properly, and the hardware is on the HCL, the installation of Windows 2000 typically proceeds without a problem. However, there are times when problems arise. Troubleshooters are tools you can use to diagnose Windows 2000 problems.

Using Troubleshooters

One of the best resources for diagnosing and fixing problems related to

Windows 2000 is the "Troubleshooters" section of Windows 2000 Help. On a computer running Windows 2000 Professional, follow these steps:

1.   From the Start Menu, choose Help.

2.   From the Windows 2000 Help window, choose the Contents page.

3.   Choose Troubleshooting and Maintenance and then select Windows 2000 Troubleshooters.

To find the troubleshooters on a computer running Windows 2000 Server, follow these steps:

1. From the Start Menu, choose Help.

2. From the Windows 2000 Help window, choose the Contents page.

3. Choose Troubleshooting and Additional Resources, select Troubleshooting, and then select General Troubleshooting.

These sections provide step-by-step questions to help you diagnose and solve problems. The troubleshooters are also available on the Internet, at the following Microsoft Web sites:

http://windows.microsoft.com/windows2000/en/professional/help/
(for Windows 2000 Professional)

http://windows.microsoft.com/windows2000/en/server/help/
(for Windows 2000 Server)

Knowing that you can access the troubleshooters from the Internet is important when you are trying to diagnose an installation failure.

Diagnosing Installation Problems

Although the installation procedure is fairly robust, there are times when the installation does not progress as expected. Table 1.7 provides an overview of the more common text-mode installation problems and how to fix them.

Table 1.7 Common Text-Mode Installation Problems

Problem	Solution
Setup fails to read boot floppies	■ Make new floppy disks using the **MAKEBOOT A:** command ■ Boot from the CD-ROM, if possible
Computer fails to boot from CD-ROM	■ Make sure the BIOS supports this feature ■ Make sure the BIOS is configured to boot off of the CD-ROM before the hard drive (Since every BIOS setup is different, refer to your computer manuals or the manufacturer for more information)
Setup fails to detect the hard drive or CD-ROM	■ Make sure the hard disk or CD-ROM are detected by the BIOS ■ Verify the hard disk or CD-ROM are on the HCL
Setup fails when copying files from CD-ROM	■ Make sure the CD-ROM is on the HCL and is connected properly ■ Check the CD for physical damage (scratches or finger prints, for example) ■ Try another CD, if possible
Insufficient Disk Space	■ The partition to which you are installing Windows 2000 is too small ■ Re-run setup and repartition the drive to create a larger partition

Table 1.8 shows the most common GUI-mode installation problems.

Table 1.8 Common GUI-mode Setup Problems

Problem	Solution
Failure of Dependency Service to Start.	■ Check the NIC settings ■ Check that you have the proper protocol installed ■ Make sure the computer name is unique on your network
Inability to connect to a domain controller	■ Make sure you entered the correct domain name ■ Make sure the network cable is plugged in to the NIC ■ Make sure the DNS server and the domain controller are online ■ Check NIC settings ■ Make sure you using the proper protocol for the network
Computer locks up during Plug and Play detection	■ Do you have a hardware conflict? If you are comfortable working inside the computer, remove any extra expansion cards (leave only the video card, NIC, and drive controller cards) and re-run setup ■ Check cable connections to the drives and make sure the expansion cards are installed properly in the computer

The most elusive problems during setup, whether in the text-mode or GUI-mode, are intermittent failures and lock-ups. When a problem does not occur at a specific time during installation, it is much more difficult to track down the cause. The following are suggested remedies:

Disable the cache—Refer to your computer's manuals for more information on disabling the cache memory. If this solves the problem, re-enable the cache after installation. If the problems return, you may have bad cache memory.

Check or replace the RAM—A faulty RAM chip can cause intermittent problems. If you are comfortable working inside your computer, you can try replacing the RAM. Alternatively, run a third-party diagnostic tool to check the RAM for problems. Occasionally, you need to slow the computer's access to the RAM by adding a wait state in the system BIOS. Again, consult your computer's documentation on changing BIOS settings.

Check for viruses—A boot-sector virus can cause intermittent problems, and will remain on the drive even if you repartition and reformat the drive. Use a third-party virus scanning software to check the hard drive.

Vocabulary

Review the following terms in preparation for the certification exam.

Term	Description
ACPI	Advanced Configuration and Power Interface is a configuration standard for laptop computers.
Active Directory	The foundation of Microsoft's new network architecture.
active partition	The partition from which an operating system boots.
APM	Advanced Power Management is a union of the BIOS and operating system to manage power.
BIOS	Basic Input-Output System is the code the computer uses to boot.
CAL	Client access license is a license for a client to access a server.
CIW	Client Installation Wizard.
clustering	Grouping two or more servers together for combined processing.
CPU	Central Processing Unit.
DHCP	Dynamic Host Configuration Protocol.
DNS	Domain Name Service resolves IP addresses to hostnames, and hostnames to IP addresses.
domain	A logical grouping of computers in a network.
dual-boot, multiple-boot	Setting up a computer to boot from more than one operating system.

Term	Description
dynamic DNS	The ability of DNS to automatically update itself using the Active Directory database.
extended partition	A partition that can contain logical drive s.
FAT	A File Allocation Table is a 16-bit file system format.
FAT32	A File Allocation Table is a 32-bit file system format.
fault tolerance	The ability of a system to recover from failure.
file-level encryption	Requiring permission to open or read files.
GUI	Graphical User Interface.
GUID	A client uses a Globally Unique Identifier during a RIS installation to identify himself.
HAL	Hardware Abstraction Layer.
HCL	Hardware Compatibility List.
hibernate	A method of shutting down Windows 2000 that restores the system state upon waking.
hot swapping	Interchanging hardware components while the computer is running.
IIS	Internet Information Service.
IP address	A number that identifies a computer on a TCP/IP -based network.
IPP	Internet Printing Protocol allows printing across the Internet.
IPSec	Internet Protocol Security is an addition to the TCP/IP protocol.

Term	Description
legacy	Hardware that does not support PnP.
local installation	Installing software on the computer at which you are working.
logical drive	A logical division of the extended partition that has its own drive letter.
MMC	Microsoft Management Console is a tool that centralizes administrative tools.
network share	A folder that is accessible over the network.
NIC	Network Interface Card is the hardware inside a computer that accesses the network.
NTFS	Windows 2000 File System is a file system format.
offline folders	Network shares that are available even when not connected to the network.
PAE	Physical Address Extensions allows programs to access RAM beyond 4 GB.
partition	A logical division of a hard disk.
Per Seat	A licensing mode that assigns a CAL to a specific client machine.
Per Server	A licensing mode that assigns a series of CALs to a server.
PnP	Plug and Play is Microsoft's hardware detection and configuration procedure.
primary partition	The partition from which an operating system can boot (if it is also active).
primary partition	The partition from which an operating system can boot (if it is also active).

Term	Description
protocol	A set of rules that define a network language.
PXE	Pre-Boot Execution Environment; allows a computer to boot from the NIC.
RAID	Redundant Array of Independent Disks.
RAM	Random Access Memory is used to store active programs and the operating system.
RIS	Remote Installation Service is used to install Windows 2000 remotely.
ROM	An addition to a command that defines how the command should be executed.
SCSI	Small Computer Systems Interface.
SID	Security Identifier.
Smart Card	Read-only memory is used to permanently store code the computer uses.
snap-in	A credit card-sized device that securely stores security information.
switch	A module for the Microsoft Management Console (MMC).
system root	The folder or directory into which Windows 2000 is installed; usually **C:\WINNT.**
TCO	Total Cost of Ownership.
TCP/IP	Transmission Control Protocol/Internet Protocol is a network protocol and the protocol used for the Internet.
USB	Universal Serial Bus is an interface for connecting devices to a computer.

Term	Description
VPN	Virtual Private Network uses the Internet to transfer private information.
USB	Universal Serial Bus is an interface for connecting devices to a computer.
VPN	Virtual Private Network uses the Internet to transfer private information.

Lesson 1 Activities

1. Explain Microsoft clustering.

2. List the six steps involved in a remote installation.

3. Explain the difference between the system partition and the boot partition.

4. Explain how RIS could be helpful after a computer crashes.

5. Describe the Microsoft Management Console (MMC).

6. Schedule a task to run every time you log in.

7. List the minimum hardware requirements for both Windows 2000 Professional and Windows 2000 Server running on an Intel-based computer.

8. Explain the purpose of an answer file (**UNATTEND.TXT**).

9. List the **WINNT.EXE** switches and what they do.

10. Explain the difference between Per Server and Per Seat licensing modes, and when each is an appropriate choice.

Answers to Lesson 1 Activities

1. Clustering is the process of making two or more servers act as one server. This creates more processing power and fault tolerance than any one server can provide.

2. The RIS steps are: 1) client asks for and receives an IP address and the location (IP address) of a RIS server, 2) the RIS server checks the Active Directory database for client information, 3) RIS sends the CIW to the client, 4) the client logs on to the network, 5) the user chooses an installation option, and 6) the installation begins.

3. The system partition contains the boot files (the files needed to boot the computer) and is always an active and primary partition. The boot partition contains the system files (the **\WINNT** directory) and can be any partition (including the system partition).

4. If you use the same image for all client computers on your network and if you have used Remote Installation with **RIPREP.EXE**, you have a complete image of a "master" computer. If a computer crashes, you can replace the computer, boot from a network floppy, and run a remote installation. The destination computer will have an exact image of the master computer.

5. The MMC is a program that centralizes the administrative tools for Windows 2000. Tools come in the form of snap-ins, which are modules that run within the MMC. As developers create new tools for Windows 2000, they can make them compatible with the MMC. This provides administrators a familiar interface for all tools.

6. From the Start Menu, choose Settings, and then select Control Panel. Open the Scheduled Tasks Control Panel, and then open "Add Scheduled Task." Choose Next, select a program to run (Calculator, for example), and then select Next again. Select When I Log On, and choose Next. Enter your username and password, confirm the password, and select Next. Choose Finish.

7. Windows 2000 Professional: Pentium 166, 32MB RAM, 685MB free disk space, 12x CD-ROM, floppy drive, keyboard, mouse.

    Windows 2000 Server; Pentium 166, 64MB RAM, 685MB free disk space, 12x CD-ROM, network card, floppy drive, keyboard, mouse.

8. The answer file automatically provides the information the Setup program needs to install Windows 2000. A complete answer file assures that the end user does not need to know any of the information needed to install the operating system.

9. **WINNT.EXE** can be run with the following switches:

   /a = enables the Accessibility Options

   /i = specifies the name of an information file

   /l = creates a log file (**$WINNT.LOG**)

   /r = creates a subfolder into the **\WINNT** directory

   /rx = creates a temporary folder

   /s = specifies the location of source files

   /t = defines the drive to use for the temporary directory

   /unattend = performs an unattended installation and specifies the file to be used

   /UDF = defines the UDSF file to use in an unattended installation

10. A Per Server license allows one client to access that server. If you have few servers and more computers than users at any given time, Per Server is a good choice. A Per Seat license allows a client to access any server on the network. If you have many servers or if most of your computers are used at the same time, choose Per Seat.

Lesson 1 Quiz

These questions test your knowledge of features, vocabulary, procedures, and syntax.

1. What is the tool used to prepare a hard disk for cloning to other computers?
    A. **DUPLICATE.EXE**
    B. **PRIPREP.EXE**
    C. **SYSPREP.EXE**
    D. **DUPREP.EXE**

2. Internet Information Services is included in which Windows 2000 product?
    A. Windows 2000 Professional
    B. Windows 2000 Server
    C. Both A and B
    D. Neither A nor B

3. Which of the following is true about Active Directory?
    A. It only supports Windows 2000 clients
    B. It works with pre-existing Windows NT 4.0 domains
    C. It runs on all versions of Windows 2000
    D. It runs on Windows NT 4.0 domain controllers

4. When performing a network installation, the boot disk must:
    A. Be purchased from Microsoft
    B. Load the protocols used on the network
    C. Contain all of the Windows 2000 files
    D. Be reformatted after each installation

5. The partition from which a computer boots is the _____ and _____ partition.
    A. Active, extended
    B. Inactive, boot
    C. Active, boot
    D. Primary, active

6. The program to duplicate hard drives included with Windows 2000 is called:
    A. Duplicator Service
    B. **CLONE.EXE**
    C. **DUPREP.EXE**
    D. Windows 2000 has no disk duplicating program

7. What is the program used to create an answer file called?
    A. Setup Manager Wizard
    B. The MMC
    C. The CAL
    D. Answer File Wizard

8. During a Remote Installation, who authenticates the client?
    A. A domain controller
    B. The DCHP server
    C. The RIS server
    D. The client is not authenticated

9. A _____ computer is a computer that relies on the presence of a network in order to boot.
    A. stand-alone
    B. client-side
    C. NetPC
    D. NotPC

10. . What is the default protocol installed during Windows 2000 Setup?
    A. NetBEUI
    B. IPX/SPX
    C. TCP/IP
    D. IIS

Answers to Lesson 1 Quiz

1. Answer C is correct. **SYSPREP.EXE** prepares a hard disk for duplication by removing the SID and any other computer-specific files.

    Answer B is incorrect, because **RIPREP.EXE** is used for preparing for a remote installation using RIS.

    Answers A and D are incorrect; these filenames don't exist.

2. Answer C is correct. All versions of Windows 2000, including Professional and Server, include the option to load Internet Information Services (IIS).

    Therefore, answers A, B, and D are incorrect.

3. Answer B is correct. Active Directory is designed to work with pre-existing Windows NT 4.0 domains, so that the migration from Windows NT 4.0 to Windows 2000 is seamless.

    Answer A is incorrect because Active Directory, while it must run on a Windows 2000 server, supports many different clients.

    Answer C is incorrect; Active Directory must run on one of the three versions of Windows 2000 Server. Windows 2000 Professional cannot be used as an Active Directory server.

    Answer D is incorrect; although Active Directory supports Windows NT 4.0 clients, it must be run on a Windows 2000 server.

4. Answer B is correct. The boot disk must load the proper protocols in order for the client to access the network and the distribution folder.

    Answer A is incorrect. Microsoft does not sell network boot disks.

    Answer C is incorrect. A 1.44-MB boot floppy cannot contain the several hundred Megabytes of data needed to load Windows 2000.

    Answer D is incorrect.

5. Answer D is correct. The bootable partition is always the active partition, and is always a primary partition.

    Answer A is incorrect. You cannot boot from an extended partition, or from logical drives within that partition.

Answer B is incorrect. There is no such thing as an inactive partition.

Answer C is incorrect. The boot partition is the partition that contains the system files. It is the system partition that contains the boot files.

6. Answer D is correct. Microsoft has not incorporated any program into Windows 2000 that actually duplicates hard drives. You must purchase a third-party solution.

    Answers A, B, and C are incorrect. None of these exist.

7. Answer A is correct. Setup Manager allows you to create both the unattend.txt file and Uniqueness Database File (UDF).

    Answer B is incorrect; the MMC (Microsoft Management Console) is used to centralize management tools.

    Answer C is incorrect. CAL stands for Client Access License; it is not a program.

    Answer D is incorrect. There is no Answer File wizard.

8. Answer A is correct. A domain controller is always responsible for authenticating clients.

    Answer B is incorrect. The DHCP server is responsible for giving the client an IP address, but not for authentication.

    Answer C is incorrect. The RIS server supplies the client computer with information about the remote installation and provides the necessary files for installation.

    Answer D is incorrect. A client cannot participate on a Windows 2000 network without authentication.

9. Answer C is correct. A NetPC has a bootable NIC, and uses the network to obtain boot files.

    Answer A is incorrect. A stand-alone computer is one that is not attached to a network.

    Answers B and D are incorrect.

10. Answer C is correct. TCP/IP is the protocol of the Internet. It is now the default protocol loaded in Windows 2000.

    Answers A and B are incorrect. Although NetBEUI and IPX/SPX are network protocols, they are not loaded by default.

    Answer D is incorrect. IIS is not a protocol, but a network service.

Lesson 2

Implementing DNS, DHCP, and WINS

A key aspect of Microsoft Windows 2000 is Active Directory, Microsoft's new network directory service. Active Directory requires two other two network services to work. These services are the Domain Name System (DNS) and Dynamic Host Configuration Protocol (DHCP). Active Directory is dependent on these services to organize and maintain the network. There have been significant changes to both DNS and DHCP in Windows 2000 that have led to a change in the role of the Windows Internet Naming Service (WINS). Whereas WINS is a very important part of Windows NT 4.0 networks, its importance is de-emphasized in Windows 2000.

After completing this lesson, you should have a better understanding of the following topics:

*   Domain Name System (DNS)

*   DNS Installation

*   DNS Configuration

*   DNS Zone Configuration

*   DNS Testing

*   Dynamic Host Configuration Protocol (DHCP)

*   DNS Dynamic Update Protocol

*   Windows Internet Naming Service (WINS)

Domain Name System (DNS)

DNS is a record-keeping service responsible for maintaining a database file of information about the computers on your network. The information in this file includes the names and addresses of the computers and may contain information about the role of each computer on the network. The purpose of this database file, and of DNS in general, is to simplify network use. It also makes Web browsing and most other Internet-related activities possible.

When you access the Internet, you typically enter a server name into the address section of a Web browser (like www.lightpointlearning.net), and a Web page appears. Most users take for granted that they can access another computer over the Internet by entering its name. However, the Internet is based entirely on the Transmission Control Protocol/Internet Protocol (TCP/IP) network protocol that uses numbers, not names, to identify computers. DNS is the service responsible for converting these TCP/IP numbers (called IP addresses) into familiar names, and converting names to addresses.

Understanding IP Addressing

TCP/IP is a protocol suite. A protocol is like a language computers use to communicate with one another. A protocol suite is a collection of protocols and applications that are intricately related to one another. In the TCP/IP protocol suite, TCP is one protocol and IP is another. Other members of the TCP/IP protocol suite include DNS, DHCP, and WINS.

Like all other network protocols, TCP/IP has a method for identifying each object on a network. Every object or host (a computer or printer, for example), has a unique IP address. An IP address is a 32-bit number that is written as four octets separated by decimals, such as 192.168.25.1. The actual address is a series of 32 bits (binary digits or 0s and 1s). The IP address 192.168.25.1 looks like this to a computer:

11000010101010000001100100000001

These IP addresses are the only way that hosts can be located and accessed on the network. All transactions between computers are based on the IP addresses of the sending and receiving computers. When developing a TCP/IP-based network, you must make sure that a unique IP address is assigned to each host on the network.

Note: Each host on a TCP/IP network must have a unique IP address, or network conflicts will occur.

TCP/IP is the protocol of the Internet. Although the current version (IP Version 4, or IPv4) was completed in the 1970s, it is the single most widely used protocol today. It is a very robust protocol, and was designed to run on very large networks. Engineers saw the need for a protocol that was routable (it could carry information from one network segment to another) and very reliable. TCP/IP was designed specifically for networks like the Internet because it can be passed from one segment to another and can carry information reliably over less-than-perfect transmission lines.

It is so well designed that the newest version (IP Version 6, or IPv6) will not significantly change the way the protocol works, but only add more IP addresses. Currently, IPv4 uses 32-bit IP addresses, which allows for 2^{32} IP addresses (about 4.3 billion addresses). IPv6 will support 128-bit addressing, for a maximum of 2^{128}, or about $3.4x10^{38}$ IP addresses.

IP addresses are a bit cumbersome at 32 bits. If users had to remember the 32-bit IP address of every computer on their network to send or receive information, the network would not be very user-friendly. With the move toward 128-bit addresses, this situation is not going to improve. Imagine having to remember the address of your favorite Web page as the following IP address:

011011000110110011100101001101001101100011001001100110011001010110 11011000110110011100101001101001101100011001001100110011001 10010101

or even this

192.168.12.5.20.12.7.46.33.17.8.211.18.31.100.50

The following is an example of how the IPv6 address will appear in hexadecimal (how IPv6 addresses will likely be written):

4A3F:AE67:F418:DC55:3412:A9F2:0340:EA1D

DNS provides a way for the TCP/IP network to be more friendly. DNS converts IP addresses into names users are more likely to remember and also converts the names back into IP addresses as necessary. In many ways, it is like a phonebook. You can find someone's phone number by looking up their name, and reverse phonebooks allow you to look up a number to find a person. In the case of DNS, the phonebook (DNS) dials the phone, so users do not need to know the number.

Understanding the Domain Namespace

More specifically, a name server (a computer running the DNS) translates IP addresses into Fully Qualified Domain Names (FQDNs). A FQDN is the name of a computer (also called the host name), plus the full name of the domain in which the computer exists. The full domain name is defined by the domain namespace in which a computer is located.

The domain namespace is a hierarchical structure that organizes groups of computers on the Internet. The term domain defines a level within this hierarchical structure. There are three main levels in the domain name system: the root-level domain, top-level domains, and second-level domains (Figure 2.1).

Figure 2.1 Domain Namespace

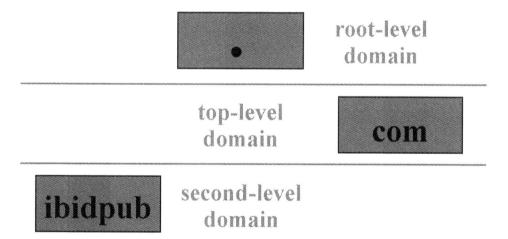

The root-level domain is at the top of the domain namespace hierarchy. It does not have a label, but is represented by a period (.). All domains on the Internet are members of the root domain. Below the root domain are a series of top-level domains. These domain names consist of two- or three-letter names that define the type of domain.

Examples of top-level domains including the following:

com = Commercial organizations

org = Non-profit organizations

edu = Educational institutions

gov = Non-military U.S.American Government organizations

net = Networks

mil = U.S. military

Some two-letter country abbreviations are as follows:

ca = Canada

de = Germany

Below the top-level domains are second-level domain names. These second-level domains contain hosts (host refers to any object on a TCP/IP network) and other domains, called subdomains. Second-level domains are typically company, agency, or university names. Let's look at an example.

Suppose you have a company named IBID Publishing, Inc., and you have an Internet domain name of ibidpub.com. The domain name officially ends with a (.) that represents the root domain. The period is often omitted, since all domains are members of the root domain. The .COM is the top-level domain for corporations. Your company chose the name ibidpub because it represents the company's name.

Within your company, you have a Web server named www. The FQDN for your Web server is www.ibidpub.com. It includes the host name (www), plus the full domain name (the root-, top-, and second-level domains).

 Note: The domain namespace is maintained by the non-profit organization InterNIC. To obtain a second-level domain name, you must register it with them at http://www.internic.net. When you register, they assign the IP address of your DNS server to the domain name.

Now, let's suppose that your company has several divisions. In an effort to organize the network structure, you gave each division a subdomain name, based on the division's role within your company. One of these subdivisions, Sales, wishes to have its own Web server. They have named the Web server webby. The FQDN for the computer may look something like this:

webby.sales.ibidpub.com

Notice that com and ibidpub have not changed because you added information below these levels on the hierarchy (Figure 2.2).

Figure 2.2 Domain Name Structure

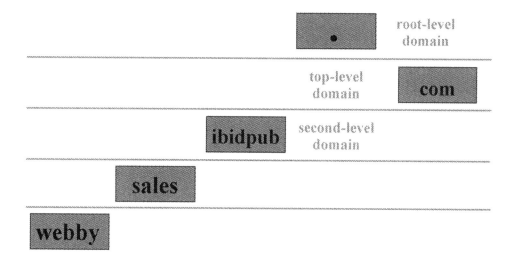

A name server is responsible for resolving the FQDN to the IP address assigned to the computer. If the computer named webby.sales.ibidpub.com has an IP address of 169.254.30.3, a name server is responsible for knowing this IP address and making the conversion to and from the name when required.

Understanding DNS Zones

A zone, or zone of authority, is the portion of the domain namespace for which a domain name server is responsible. This is an important concept in understanding of how DNS works. No DNS server can possibly know all of the 4.3 billion IP addresses and the FQDN that maps to each one. Before the advent of Windows 2000, mMost DNS servers hadhave to be updated manually. If, as an administrator, you would have to manually update a DNS server to know about all of the computers on the Internet, you have an impossible task on your hands.

Tip: Traditionally, a DNS server is manually configured and updated with every change in IP address or host name for computers within its zone of authority. Windows 2000 eliminates this inconvenience by supporting dynamic updates.

The concept of zones allows a DNS server to be responsible for a limited amount of informationonly so much. For information beyond the DNS's zone of authority, the DNS shifts the responsibility to a higher-level name server. This is called a forward lookup query.

A DNS server contains information in a lookup zone. A forward lookup zone maps FQDNs to IP addresses. A reverse lookup zone converts IP addresses to FQDNs.

Resolving DNS Names

When you ask for information from a DNS server (for example, when you browse the Iinternet using FQDNs), your computer (the client) sends a request to the DNS server for your zone that is configured as the default name server.

Note: The default name server is manually configured within the TCP/IP Properties sheet and can also be assigned dynamically using DHCP.

The request is called a recursive request. The client computer is saying, "give me an address, or give me an error, but don't give me partial information." The default (also called local) name server needs to resolve a host name to an IP address, so it first looks for the host name in its own database file. If it finds the host name and IP addresses are found, the local name server sends this information back to your client.

However, the request for an IP address is frequently beyond the zone of authority for the local name server, such as the information is not in the local DNS database. A local name server may only have information about computers on your local network. More often than not, the IP address you need is beyond your Local Area Network (LAN). If this is the case, your default DNS server must find the information for you (Figure 2.3).

Figure 2.3 Recursive Request to DNS Server

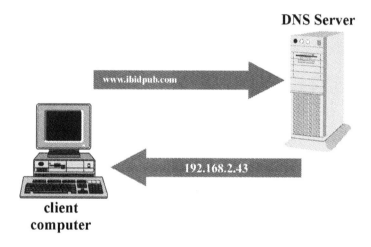

Let's go back to our scenario. You are working at a client computer in the **ibidpub.com** domain. Using a Web browser, you type in the Universal Resource Locator (URL) http://www.cityu.edu. The DNS server for your company (perhaps it is called dns_server.ibidpub.com) does not know the IP address for the computer called www in the domain **cityu.edu**, so it performs a query of its own to find the answer. Your local DNS server sends an iterative request to a root-level domain server. An iterative request simply asks for the best answer it can get, even if it contains only partial information. The iterative request process is as follows:

1. The root name server receives a request from your local name server to resolve www.cityu.edu.

2. The root name server does not know about a computer named www, or a domain named **.cityu**, but it does have information about the first-level domain named **.edu**. The root name server sends back the IP address of a top-level domain name server within the **.edu** domain (Figure 2.4).

Figure 2.4 Iterative Request Response from Root

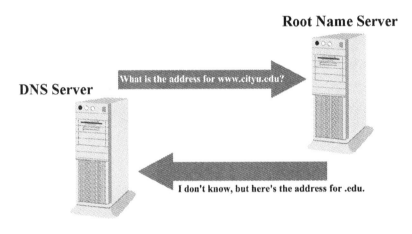

 Note:The client computer has sent a recursive request for an IP address. It does not want the IP address for any other computer. Therefore, your local name server does not send the IP address it just received from the root-level name server. Instead, the name server uses it to find a better address.

3. The local name server sends a request to the top-level domain name server for the **.edu** domain.

4. The top-level name server knows nothing of a computer named www, but it does know how to find the DNS server for **cityu.edu**. The top-level name server sends the IP address for a DNS server for cityu.edu back to your local DNS server (Figure 2.5).

Figure 2.5 Iterative Request Response from Top-Level

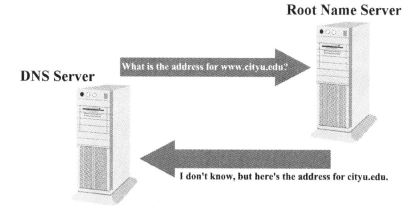

5. Your local DNS server sends a request to the **cityu.edu** DNS server.

6. The name server for **cityu.edu** knows about a computer called **www** (it is within the name server's zone), and sends the IP address for **www** back to your local name server.

7. At this point, your local DNS server has an IP address for the computer you requested and it sends the information back to your computer (Figure 2.6).

Figure 2.6 IP Address Resolution

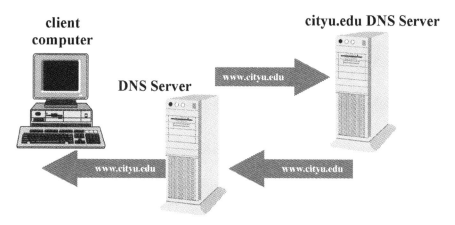

8. Your computer contacts www.cityu.edu using the IP address, and your Web browser displays the Web page (Figure 2.7).

Figure 2.7 Web Page Access

1. The following list reviews the 10 steps for resolving an IP address:

2. The client contacts the local DNS server with a recursive request.

3. The local DNS server contacts a root-level domain name server.

4. The root-level DNS returns an IP address for a first-level name server.

5. The local DNS sends a request to the first-level DNS.

6. The first-level DNS send back the IP address for a second-level DNS.

7. The local DNS sends a request to the second-level DNS.

8. The second-level DNS sends back the IP address of the computer.

9. The local DNS sends the IP address to the requesting client.

10. The requesting client sends a request for information directly to the target computer (in this case, it asks for a Wweb page from the computer **www**).

11. The target computer sends the requested information.

DNS Installation

It is not difficult to install and configure DNS. You install DNS, like other Windows 2000 network services, is installed using the Add/Remove Programs Control Panel. However, before beginning the installation, you must change two settings on the server.

Preparing to Install DNS

Before you can install the DNS service on a Windows 2000 server, you must first prepare the server for installation by assigning a static IP address and configuring the DNS settings.

Resolution of an FQDN to IP address depends on DNS. For clients to resolve names, they must always know where to find their primary name server which must therefore. Therefore, the name server must have a static (unchanging) IP address. If the IP address of the name server changes, clients cannot find the name server and therefore cannot resolve IP addresses for any other computers.

Tip:The DNS server needs to have a static IP address. Otherwise, computers can not find the DNS server or the IP address for any other computer.

For the server to perform forward lookup queries, DNS needs to have answers to the following questions:

*   Where am I within the domain namespace?

*   What are my member domains?

*   What is my zone of authority?

Looking back at our scenario, the DNS server called dns_server.ibidpub.com is a second-level name server and a member of the **ibidpub** domain, which is a member of the first-level **com** domain. It may contain several subdomains, including one named **sales**. A name server for the domain **sales.ibidpub.com**, called **dns_server.sales.ibidpub.com**, is a name server within the subdomain **sales** in the second-level domain **ibidpub**, which is in the first-level domain **com**. The zone of authority for either of these name servers may include all of the hosts within the domain as well as the DNS servers for domains above and below this domain.

Changing the IP Settings

The IP address settings can be changed manually as followsby following these steps:

1. From the desktop, right-click My Network Places, and then choose Properties.

2. Right-click Local Area Connection, and then choose Properties.

3. From within the Local Area Connection window, choose Internet Protocol (TCP/IP), and then select Properties (Figure 2.8).

Tip: You can also display the properties for the Internet Protocol (TCP/IP) by double-clicking on the selection.

Figure 2.8 TCP/IP Properties

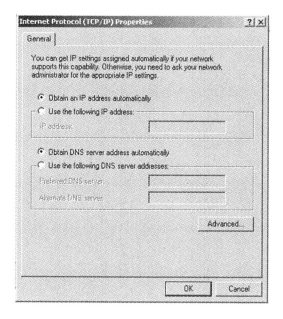

4. From within the Internet Protocol (TCP/IP) Properties window, choose Use the following IP addresses, and then enter an IP address, subnet mask, and (optionally) default gateway.

5. Choose OK, and then select OK again. A reboot is not required to make these changes effective.

Entering the Domain Name

To change the domain name, follow these steps:

1. From the desktop, right-click My Computer, and then choose Properties.

2. From within System Properties, choose the Network Identification pproperty page. (Figure 2.9)

Figure 2.9 System Properties Network Identification Page

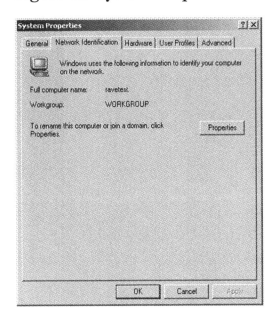

3.   Choose Properties.

4.   From ,the Identification Changes window, choose More.

5.   Type the full domain name for this computer, and then choose OK. Do not include the computer name (Figure 2.10).

Tip: Do not enter the FQDN for the Primary DNS suffix of this computer information. When you choose OK, you see the computer's FQDN listed under the Full Computer Name heading.

Figure 2.10 DNS Suffix Designation

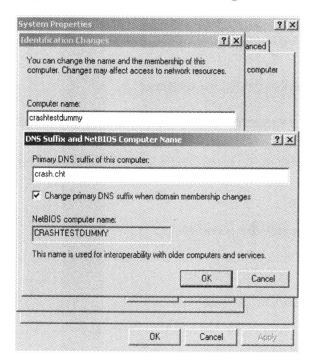

6. Choose OK, and then select OK again.

7. Choose OK to close System Properties, and then select Yes to reboot the server.

Installing DNS

After preparing the server, you can begin installation of DNS. You can install DNS can be installed during or after installation of the operating system. During the installation of Windows 2000 Server, when you are prompted to select Windows 2000 components, you can select the DNS service, which is in the details listing of Network Services. If you have already have installed Windows 2000 Server installed, you install the DNS service by following these steps:

1. From the Start Menu, choose Settings, and then select Control Panel.

2. Double-click Add/Remove Programs.

3. Choose Add/Remove Windows Components.

4. From Windows Components, choose Networking Services, and then select Details.

 Tip: You can also view the Details by double-clicking the component.

5. In the Subcomponents list, choose the box next to Domain Name System (DNS), and then choose OK (Figure 2.11).

6. Choose Next to begin the installation process.

7. When Windows 2000 is finished installing the software, choose Finish.

8. Close the Add/Remove Programs Control Panel. Notice that, unlike Windows NT 4.0, you do not need to reboot the servera reboot of the server is not needed.

Behind the scenes, the installation process performs the following tasks:

•   Installs the DNS service

•   Starts the DNS service without a reboot

•   Installs the DNS snap-in for the Microsoft Management Console (MMC), and adds a shortcut to this console in the Administrative Tools menu

Figure 2.11 DNS Selection

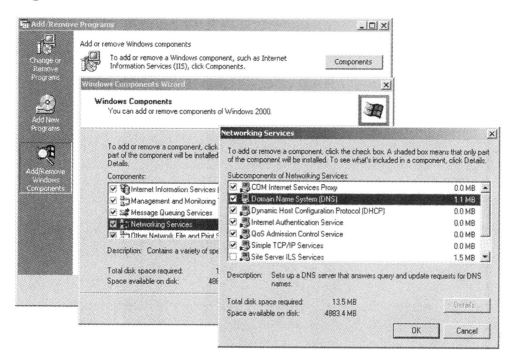

- Creates the folder, **\WINNT\System32\Dns**\WINNT\System32\Dns, which contains the database files DNS uses and a cache file that contains the addresses of all of the root servers on the Internet

- Adds the following entry to the Registry:
  HKEY_LOCAL_MACHINE\System\CurrentControlSet\Services\DnsHKEY_LOCAL_MACHINE\System\CurrentControlSet\Services\Dns

Note:The DNS installation also creates a boot file in the DNS folder. This is not a required part of DNS, but is included to ease migration offor a DNS server running Berkeley Internet Name Domain (BIND). The Bboot file from the older server can be copied to the Windows 2000 Bboot file.

DNS Configuration

Once DNS is installed, it must be configured. Configuration of DNS is done through the DNS snap-in for the MMC. The MMC provides a common interface for administrative tools (called snap-ins or consoles). Every snap-in has a similar interface, so that learning to use one tool helps in learning others.

Configuring DNS

The following explanation of DNS configuration uses the previously- created company, ibidpub.com. The root domain is ibidpub.com, and these steps pertain to installtioninstalling and configurationconfiguring of the first DNS server for the root domain. The FQDN for this server is dns_server.ibid-pub.com.

1. From the Start Menu, choose Programs, Administrative Tools, and then select DNS.

2. In the left pane of the DNS console, choose the plus sign (+) next to the name of your server to expand the container.

 Tip: You can also expand a container by double-clicking the name of the container.

3. Right-click the server, and choose Configure the server.

4. Choose Next to begin the Configure DNS Server Wizard.

5. Choose This is the first server on this network, and then select Next.

6. Choose Yes, create a forward lookup zone, and then select Next.

7. Since "this is the first DNS server in the domain," choose Standard primary, and then select Next (Figure 2.12).

Figure 2.12 DNS Server Wizard

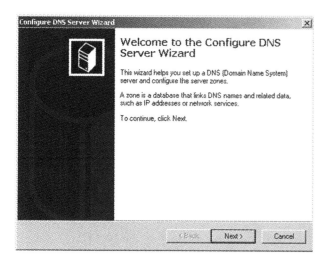

8. Type a name for the zone, and then choose Next. In our example, you would type **ibidpub.com** (Figure 2.13).

Figure 2.13 DNS Zone Naming

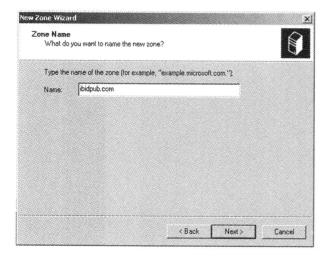

Note:Notice that you cannot create an Active Directory-integrated zone unless Active Directory is installed. An Active Directory-integrated zone is stored in the Active Directory database.

9.   Accept the default filename, or type a different filename and then choose Next.

10. Choose Yes, create a reverse lookup zone, and then select Next.

11. Choose Standard primary, and then select Next.

12. Choose Network ID, type the first three groups of 8 numbers (octets) of the IP ADDRESS, and then select Next (Figure 2.14).

Figure 2.14 Reverse Lookup Zone Naming

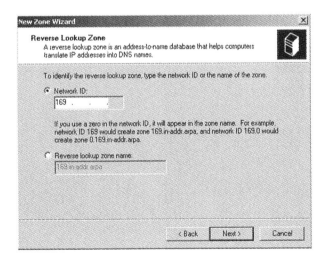

13. Accept the default filename, or create a new one, and then choose Next.

14. Review the DNS settings, and then choose Finish.

Tip: The default filename is the zone name appended with .DNS, and is stored in the **\WINNT\System32\dns**\WINNT\System32\dns folder.

DNS Zone Configuration

There are three types of zones supported by Windows 2000: standard primary, standard secondary, and Active Directory-integrated. The standard primary database is the master copy of the zone information. Changes and updates are made to this file. The standard secondary zone contains a copy of the master file.

Secondary DNS servers are installed for two reasons: 1) fault tolerance, in case the primary server fails, and 2) load-balancing. If the number of DNS requests overburdens the DNS server, setting up a secondary DNS server will handle half of the requests. As mentioned above, the third type of zone, an Active Directory-integrated zone, stores the DNS database within the Active Directory database. This allows it to be copied to all domain controllers during replication. Replication is the process of copying the Active Directory database among domain controllers.

Tip:Windows NT 4.0 supports primary and secondary DNS zones. In Windows 2000, these zones are called standard zones, because Windows 2000 also supports Active Directory-integrated zones.

Configuring Zone Transfers

In addition to choosing the type of zone to configure, you can also configure how often the zones are copied from the master DNS server to any secondary DNS servers (called zone transfers). The zone transfer process occurs when a master DNS server copies zone information to secondary DNS servers. A master DNS server is the source of zone information and can be either a primary or secondary DNS server (Figure 2.15).

Figure 2.15 Two Master DNS Servers and Two Secondary Servers

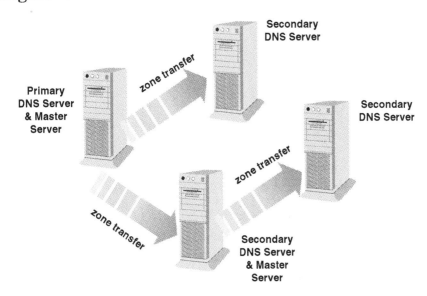

Zone transfers happen after one of the following events:

- The master server sends notification to the secondary server(s) that a change to the DSN database has occurred

- The secondary server sends a query to the primary server asking for any changes. This request happens if the refresh interval on the secondary server has elapsed

There are two methods for transfer of the zone information. Both Windows NT 4.0 and Windows 2000 support a Full Zone Transfer (AXFR). This transfer method replaces the entire zone database.

When a secondary DSN server queries the master server, it compares its own database serial number to that on the master. If the master has a newer file, the secondary requests the entire contents of the newer file. Although this ensures that the secondary server has all of the changes, it can generate significant network traffic. Windows 2000 also supports Incremental Zone Transfers (IXFR). If there are changes to the master database file, the changes are stored in a cache file until the secondary servers have received the changes. The secondary server requests only the changes.

Using Active Directory-Integrated Zones

As mentioned, Windows 2000 supports a new form of DNS zone, the Active Directory-integrated zone. The zone database files are stored in the Active Directory rather than the **\WINNT\System32\Dns**\WINNT\System32\Dns folder. Whenever the Active Directory replicates, DNS information also replicates. Active Directory-integrated zones can only be created on Active Directory networks, and only on DNS servers that use the dynamic update protocol.

Active Directory-integrated zones support Sservice (SRV) Rresource records, which identify computers in the DNS database file based on their role in the network. This allows a client computer to query the DNS server for the IP addresses of all domain controllers, without knowing any domain controller's FQDN. These records are also supported in standard DNS zones, but they are not automatically created as they are when using an Active Directory-integrated zone.

Testing DNS

Before fully integrating a DNS server into your network, it is a good idea to make sure it is working properly. You can test the DNS service in two ways. First, the DNS console has a built-in monitoring tool that allows you to perform simple and recursive queries. Second, as in Windows NT 4.0, you can also use the command **NSLOOKUP.EXE** from a command prompt.

Using the DNS Console to Test DNS

1. From the Start Menu, choose Programs, Administrative Tools, and then select DNS.

2. In the left pane of the DNS console, right-click the server you wish to test, and then choose Properties.

3. From within the Properties, choose the Monitoring property page (Figure 2.16).

Figure 2.16 Monitoring Property Page

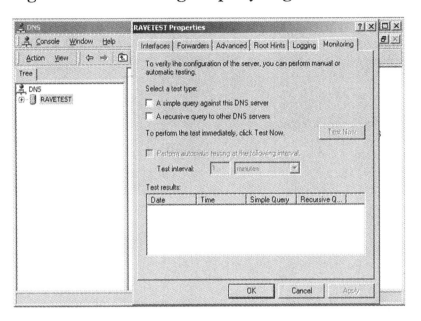

A simple query tests the DNS server on which the test is run. A recursive query tests other DNS servers within the domain.

Tip: You can configure the DNS server to perform these tests automatically and on a regular interval from the Monitoring property page.

4.   Choose the test(s) you wish to perform, and then select Now.

5.   Choose OK.

Using NSLOOKUP

The command-line utility **NSLOOKUP.EXE** (Name Server Lookup) is included with TCP/IP, and is installed when you install TCP/IP is installed. The Windows 2000 version of **NSLOOKUP** runs in interactive and non-interactive modes. To perform only one query of a name server, running the command in non-interactive mode is appropriate. However, if you want to make several queries of a name server, run the command in interactive mode.

To run the command interactively, type **NSLOOKUP.EXE** at a command prompt. The program contacts the default name server and allows you to enter a command for the server. For a list of commands available, type **?** at the prompt. To exit the **NSLOOKUP.EXE** interactive mode, type **EXIT**.

Running the command in non-interactive mode functions like the **NSLOOKUP** command in Windows NT 4.0. At a command prompt, type the following:

* **NSLOOKUP [-OPTION(S)] [COMPUTER-TO-FIND|-SERVER]**

* **OPTION** is one or more nslookup options (use **?** to list commands)

* **COMPUTER-TO-FIND** is the name of the computer or an IP address you want DNS to resolve

* **SERVER** specifies which DNS server to use for the lookup

Dynamic Host Configuration Protocol (DHCP)

DHCP is a service that assigns IP addresses to client computers when the computers become active on a network. In addition to assigning an IP address, you can configure DHCP can be configured to issue other TCP/IP-related settings, such as the default gateway and DNS server addresses to clients. The use of DHCP greatly simplifies network administration in TCP/IP-based networks. Without DHCP, you must manually assign an IP address to each host on the network, and keep track of which IP addresses have been used. Manual configuration can lead to accidentally assigning duplicate IP addresses in the network. A duplicate IP address causes conflicts on the network and prevents hosts with identical IP addresses from participating in network activity.

The inclusion of DHCP in Windows NT 4.0 was a welcome change for network administrators. However, the Windows NT 4.0 version of DHCP did not have any enhancements for use with DNS. With an increase in the importance of the Internet and DNS, Microsoft has increased the functionality of DHCP to work with DNS.

Understanding New Features of DHCP

The new Windows 2000 version of DHCP contains many new enhancements not found in previous Microsoft versions of DHCP. These features include the following:

- DHCP server authorization

- Superscopes and multicast scopes

- Option classes

- Client-side assignments

- Monitoring and reporting

- DNS–DHCP integration

DHCP Server Authorization

In Windows NT 4.0-based networks, any user could implement a DHCP server on the network. You did not have to have Domain administrative rights to add a DHCP server. This situation had the potential to cause serious IP conflicts. In Windows 2000, a DHCP server must be authorized in Active Directory before it can begin assigning IP addresses to clients.

When a DHCP server boots, it queries the Active Directory for a list of authorized servers. If the DHCP server is not on that list, the DHCP server generates an error in the system log and stops the DHCP service. After that, it periodically queries the Active Directory to see if it has been authorized.

Superscopes and Multicast Scopes

A scope is a range of IP addresses from which the DHCP server can issue an address to a requesting client. Windows 2000 DHCP supports two scope options beyond the standard IP address scope.

A superscope combines IP addresses from more than one range of IP addresses (or logical subnets). In other words, if you have clients all on the same physical network, belonging to two logical subnets, you can build a superscope to manage both groups from one DHCP server. Superscopes are also useful when expanding a subnet beyond the originally-planned size, or if you are replacing an existing address range with a new one.

Configuring a multicast scope allows DHCP to assign a multicast IP address to selected clients. Multicast IP addresses are used by applications that send information simultaneously to many computers (like streaming audio and video-conferencing). Implementing a multicast scope can reduce overall network traffic by directing the information to many clients rather than having an application direct the information to one client at a time.

Option Classes

Another new feature of the Windows 2000 DHCP service is the implementation of option classes. In previous versions of DHCP, all clients received the same configuration from a DHCP server. In Windows 2000, you can configure the DHCP server to issue different TCP/IP settings to different clients, based on the client computer's vendor-specific information (like the brand of computer), and user-defined classes.

For example, you may want some users to have Internet access through a proxy, but others to have no Internet access. By defining user classes, you can assign particular computers- appropriate IP information.

Client-Side Assignments

In Windows NT 4.0-based networks, if a DHCP server is unavailable when a DHCP client requests an address, the client reports an error and is unable to participate on the network. Windows 2000 supports a new system that allows a client computer to assign itself an IP address if a DHCP server is unavailable. This system is called Automatic Private IP Addressing (APIPA). The IP address that a client issues himselfitself is always in the form of 169.254.x.y, where x and y representare values between 0 and 254. The subnet mask is set to 255.255.0.0. With APIPA, you can run a Windows 2000-based network with automatic assignment of IP addresses, whenyet no DHCP server is installed. When the client computer assigns itself an address, it sends out a broadcast to make sure no other computers on the network are using the same IP address. The client computer uses this address until a DHCP server provides it updated IP information.

 Note: The range of IP addresses from 169.254.0.1 through 169.254.255.254 is reserved; any IP address within this range cannot be used on the Internet.

The APIPA feature is enabled by default and can only be disabled through editing the registry. Instructions on disabling APIPA can be found in the Windows 2000 Help file.

Monitoring and Reporting

You may view statistics regarding the DHCP server within the DHCP console (the MMC console used for configuring DHCP). These statistics include the following:

*   The start and up times for the server

*   The number of addresses available

*   The number of leases being granted per second

*   The total number of scopes and addresses on the server

To obtain this information, follow these steps:

1.   From the Start Menu, choose Programs, Administrative Tools,, and then select DHCP.

2.   From the left pane of the DHCP console, right-click the server, and then choose Display Statistics.

3.   The data is presented as a table in a separate window. Choose Close when you are finished reviewing the information.

 Note: You can leave the statistics window open and monitor changes in the DHCP statistics by choosing Refresh.

Installing and Configuring DHCP

Like the DNS service in Windows 2000 server, you can install DHCP can be installed by opening the Add/Remove Windows Components section of the Add/Remove Programs Control Panel. To install DHCP, follow these steps:

1. From the Start Menu, choose Settings, and then select Control Panel.

2. Double-click Add/Remove Programs.

3. Choose Add/Remove Windows Components.

4. From Windows Components, choose Networking Services, and then select Details.

5. In the Subcomponents list, choose the box next to Dynamic Host Configuration Protocol (DHCP), and then select OK.

6. Choose Next to begin the installation process.

7. When Windows 2000 is finished installing the software, choose Finish.

8. Close the Add/Remove Programs Control Panel.

Installation of the DHCP service does not require a reboot of the server.

Creating and Configuring a DHCP Scope

To configure a scope in DHCP, follow these steps:

1. From the Start menu, choose Programs, Administrative Tools, and then select DHCP.

2. From the left pane of the DHCP console, right-click the server, and then choose New Scope (Figure 2.17).

Figure 2.17 New DHCP Site Creation

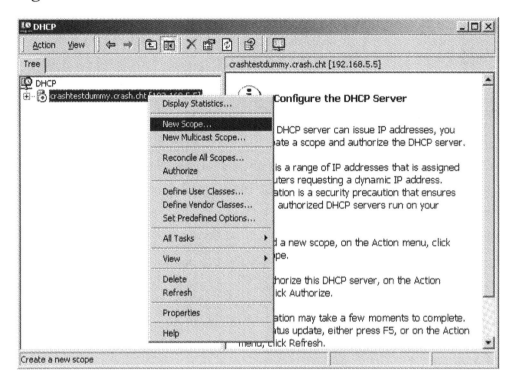

3.   Choose Next to begin the New Scope Wizard.

4.   Type a name and description for the scope, and then choose Next.

5.   Type the Start and End IP addresses for the range that the scope includes, type a subnet mask (or a length, in bits), and then choose Next (Figure 2.18).

6.   To exclude any IP addresses from the range you created, type the Start and End IP addresses of the excluded range, choose Add, and then choose Next.

7.   Type the lease duration and then choose Next.

Note: The default lease duration is 8 days.

To configure additional DHCP settings, choose Yes, I want to configure these options now, and then choose Next. If you do not wish to configure, choose No, I will configure these options later, and then select Next.

Figure 2.18 Scope Range Configuration

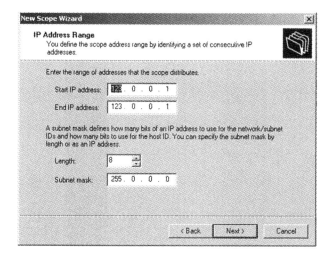

9. Type the IP address for the default gateway (router) DHCP clients will use, choose Add, and then select Next.

10. Type the name of the parent domain for the clients, type the IP address for the DNS servers the clients will use, choose Add, and then select Next (Figure 2.19).

Note: If you do not know the IP address for a DNS server, you can enter the server name and choose Resolve. The DNS service resolves the IP address for you, and automatically puts it in the IP address box.

Figure 2.19 DNS Settings in the DHCP Scope

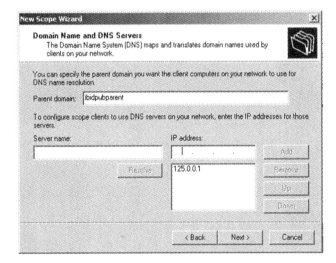

11. Type the name or IP address of any WINS servers on the network. If you type the name, choose Resolve to have DNS determine the IP address for you. Choose Add, and then select Next.

12. To activate the scope immediately, choose Yes, I want to activate the scope now, and then choose Next. Otherwise, choose No, I will activate this scope later, and then select Next.

13. Choose Finish to close the wizard.

Creating a Superscope

To configure a superscope, follow these steps:

1. From the Start menu, choose Programs, Administrative Tools,, and then select DHCP.

2. From the left pane of the DHCP console, right-click the server, and then choose New Superscope.

3. Choose Next.

4. Type a name for the superscope, and then choose Next.

5. Choose one or more scopes from the list, and then choose Next.

Tip: You can choose more than one scope at a time by pressing and holding down the Control key while selecting scopes.

6. Choose Finish.

Creating a Multicast Scope

To create a multicast scope, follow these steps:

1. From the Start menu, Programs, choose Administrative Tools,, and then select DHCP.

2. From the left pane of the DHCP console, right-click the server, and then choose New Multicast Scope.

3. Choose Next.

4. Type a name and description for the multicast scope, and then choose Next.

5. Type the Start and End IP addresses for the multicast scope, the Time To Live (TTL), and then choose Next.

Note: A multicast IP address must be between 224.0.0.0 and 239.255.255.255.

6. To exclude any addresses from the range you defined, type the Start and End IP addresses for the excluded range.

7. Choose Add, and then select Next.

8. Type the Lease Duration, and then choose Next.

 Tip: The default lease duration for multicast scopes is 30 days.

9. Choose whether you want to activate the scope now or later, and then select Next.

10. Choose Finish.

DNS Dynamic Update Protocol

DNS is designed as a static service that requires an administrator to manually update the DNS database file when a change occurs in the IP address or host name of a computer. The administrator has to handle aAny additions or removals to the network are handled manually. However, with the Windows 2000 DNS and DHCP services, you can implement dynamic updates to the DNS database file using the DNS dynamic update protocol. The DNS dynamic update protocol allows client computers to automatically update the DNS database file without requiring you to implement the changes.

Configuring Dynamic Update Protocol

Dynamic updates work in conjunction with the DHCP service so that when a client receives an IP address from DHCP, both the client and the DHCP server can update the DNS database. In

Windows NT 4.0, if an administrator uses the DHCP service to assign IP addresses, computers are not easily accessible using FQDNs, since a client's IP address can potentially change with every boot. This requires a reliance on the WINS service (discussed later in this lesson), a service that generates significant network traffic, is incompatible with non-Windows clients, and is not supported over the Internet.

To configure DNS for dynamic updates, follow these steps:

1. From the Start menu, choose Programs, Administrative Tools,, and then select DNS.

2. From the left pane of the DNS console, expand the server, expand Forward Lookup Zones, right-click the zone you wish to configure, and then choose Properties (Figure 2.20).

Figure 2.20 Zone Properties

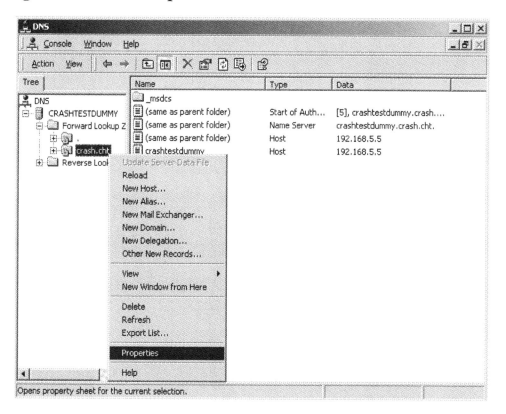

3. Choose Yes from Allow dynamic updates? and then select OK (Figure 2.21).

4. Close the DNS console.

Figure 2.21 Dynamic DNS Update Activation

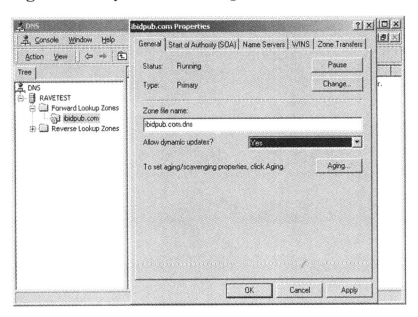

The DHCP service must also be configured to enable the dynamic update protocol. You can configure DHCP through the DHCP console by following these steps:

1. From the Start Menu, choose Programs, Administrative Tools,, and then select DHCP.

2. From the left pane of the DHCP console, right-click the server, and then choose Properties.

3. From Properties, choose the DNS property page (Figure 2.22).

Figure 2.22 Dynamic Update Options

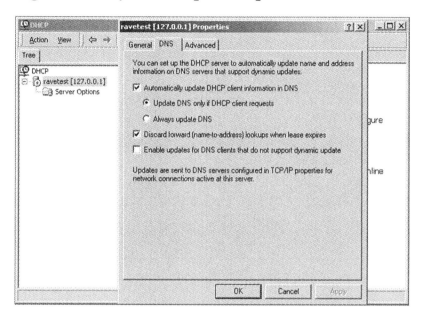

4. Choose Automatically update DHCP client information in DNS. You can select any of the following options, (Table 2.1). After making your selections, select OK.

Table 2.1 Dynamic DNS Update Options

Option	Description
Update DNS only if DHCP client requests	Updates the DNS database only if the client computer requests the update. This requires a client computer that supports dynamic updates.
Always update DNS	Updates the DNS database regardless of what the client computer does.
Discard forward (name-to-address) lookups when lease expires	Removes client records from the DNS database when an IP address lease expires.
Enable updates for DNS clients that do not support dynamic update	Handles all aspects of the dynamic update for clients that do not support dynamic updates.

5.   Close the DHCP console.

Windows Internet Naming Service (WINS)

WINS is a Microsoft-specific service that resolves IP addresses to NetBIOS names. NetBIOS is a network protocol that was originally designed to run in unison with NetBEUI. However, as the importance of TCP/IP has increased, fewer networks use the NetBEUI protocol. NetBIOS has been redesigned to work within the TCP/IP protocol suite.

The NetBIOS name is often referred to as the WINS name, or the computer name. In Windows NT 4.0, the WINS name and the host name are the same by default, but can be manually configured to be different.

Despite the fact that WINS names are only used by Microsoft computers and some network applications, the use of NetBIOS names is extensive in many networks. One of the advantages of WINS over DNS is that WINS has a dynamic database. When a client's IP address changes, the WINS server updates its records without user intervention. However, with the new implementation of Dynamic DNS, the importance of this feature in WINS has diminished.

Understanding New WINS Features

Despite the lessening importance of WINS in the Windows 2000 network, Microsoft has added to the functionality of the WINS service. Much of this effort is undoubtedly for backward compatibility, allowing you to implement Windows 2000 servers into a pre-existing network that relies on WINS. Many of the changes to WINS are administrative. WINS is now configured through the MMC, so it has enhanced administrative tools. For example, you can search and filter the results for specific records within the WINS database file, delete dynamic and static records, perform options on more than one record at a time, and export the database as a comma-delimited text file. The two most significant server-side changes to WINS are the introduction of persistent connections and manual tombstoning.

Persistent Connections

In Windows NT 4.0, when a WINS server replicates the database to other WINS servers (replication partners), it has to first establish the connection, then transfer the data, and then terminate the session. With Windows 2000, a WINS server can maintain a persistent connection with one or more other WINS servers. This connection reduces transfer time during replication and generates less network traffic.

Manual Tombstoning

In previous versions of WINS, if a record is marked for deletion, it can be overwritten by an unmarked record during replication. In Windows 2000, you can mark a record for deletion and ensure that this tombstone mark is replicated to the other WINS servers.

Vocabulary

Review the following terms in preparation for the certification exam.

Term	Description
Active Directory-integrated zone	A DNS zone that is stored in the Active Directory database and is copied during Active Directory replication .
APIPA	Automatic Private IP Addressing is the ability of a client computer to assign its own IP address in the absence of a DHCP server.
AXFR	Full zone transfer occurs when the primary DNS server transfers the database file in its entirety to secondary servers.
BIND	Berkeley Internet Name Domain
bit	A binary digit, a bit is represented by a 0 or 1.
broadcast	Method of sending information to all computers on a TCP/IP network.
DHCP	Dynamic Host Configuration Protocol is a service for automatically assigning IP addresses and settings.
directory	A listing of the objects in a network and their associated properties.
directory service	A service that maintains a network directory. Active Directory is a directory service .
DNS	Domain Name System is a service that resolves IP addresses to host names or host names to IP addresses.
domain name server	A server running the DNS service.

Term	Description
domain namespace	The hierarchical structure of domain names from the root domain down through first-level and second-level domains and subdomains.
Dynamic Update Protocol	A protocol that allows clients and the DHCP server to update the DNS database as changes occur on the network.
forward lookup query	The process a DNS server uses when trying to resolve a host name or IP address beyond its zone of authority.
forward lookup zone	The portion of the DNS database file used for resolving host names to IP addresses.
FQDN	Fully Qualified Domain Name is the host name appended with the full domain name in the form of host name.domain2.domain1.
host	Any object (computer, printer, etc.) on a TCP/IP network.
host name	The name of a host on a TCP/IP network; DNS resolves host names to IP addresses.
IP address	The 32-bit number used to identify hosts on a TCP/IP network in the form of aaa.bbb.ccc.ddd.
IPv4	IP version 4 is the current version of the IP protocol that supports 32-bit addressing.
IPv6	IP version 6 is the proposed new version of the IP protocol that will support 128-bit addressing.
iterative request	A complete or partial request for information. DNS servers send lookup queries as iterative requests.
IXFR	Incremental zone transfer is when the primary DNS server sends only the changes to secondary servers.

Term	Description
LAN	A Local Area Network is a small network of computers within a single building or office.
lookup zone	The scope of information a DNS server has within its database file.
manual tombstoning	Marking a record for deletion in WINS.
master DNS server	The DNS server that contains a master copy of the database file. It can be a primary or secondary DNS server.
multicast	A method of simultaneously sending information to several computers over a TCP/IP network.
multicast scope	A range of IP addresses defined in the DHCP service reserved for multicasts.
NBT	NetBIOS over TCP/IP allows the use of NetBIOS names on a TCP/IP-based network.
NetBEUI	A protocol designed by Microsoft, originally designed for small single-segment networks.
NetBIOS	Network Basic Input-Output System is a protocol that uses names to identify computers on a network. It was originally designed as part of NetBEUI.
NetBIOS name	A name assigned to a computer on a NetBIOS-based network to identify it. Also called a WINS name.
NSLOOKUP.EXE	A command-line program used for testing DNS.
option classes	Settings within DHCP that allow you to assign IP addresses based on user-definable parameters.
persistent connections	A setting in Windows 2000 WINS that allows WINS servers to replicate data without establishing a connection every time.

Term	Description
primary DNS server	The DNS server that has the master database file. Changes to the DNS file occur on the primary DNS server.
protocol	The set of rules computers use to communicate over a network.
protocol suite	A collection of protocols designed to work in unison. TCP/IP is an example of a protocol suite.
recursive request	A request for complete information. A client sends a recursive request to a DNS server for the IP address of another computer.
replication	The process of copying database information from one server to another, which is used by DNS, Active Directory, and WINS.
reverse lookup zone	The portion of a DNS database file that resolves IP addresses to host names.
root-level domain	The domain under which all computers on the Internet belong that is represented as (.).
scope	In DHCP, a range of IP addresses that the DHCP server can issue to requesting clients.
secondary DNS server	A DNS server that receives a copy of the master DNS database file through replication. Changes to the DNS file cannot be made on a secondary server.
second-level domain	In the namespace, one level below first-level domains. Typically a company name, university name, or other unique and identifiable name.
segment	One section of a TCP/IP network separated from other segments by a router.
SRV records	Service Resource records

Term	Description
static IP address	An IP address that does not change and is manually entered when configuring TCP/IP on a host.
subdomain	In the domain namespace, one or more levels below the second-level domain, usually used for organizational purposes within a corporation or other large network.
superscope	A DHCP scope that contains several smaller scopes.
TCP/IP	Transmission Control Protocol / Internet Protocol is the protocol of the Internet and many smaller networks.
top-level domain	In the domain namespace, the first level below the root level; typically a two- or three-letter domain name (for example, com, edu, gov, ca).
TTL	Time To Live
URL	Universal Resource Locator is the address used to connect to hosts and resources over the Internet using a Web browser.
WAN	A Wide Area Network is one or more LANs connected over a distance of miles.
WINS	Windows Internet Naming Service is a service that keeps track of NetBIOS names on a network.
zone transfers	The process of sending the DNS database file from the master DNS server to secondary servers.
zone, zone of authority	The group of computers for which a DNS server has domain name information.

In Brief

If you want to...	Then do this...
Resolve host names to IP addresses.	Use DNS to perform a forward lookup query.
Resolve IP addresses to host names.	Use DNS to perform a reverse lookup query.
Have every client on your network receive an IP address when they boot up.	Install and configure the DHCP service.
Keep the DNS file in Active Directory.	Install DNS, DHCP, and Active Directory on your network. Then create Active Directory-integrated zones on the DNS server.
Test the DNS service from a command prompt.	Use **NSLOOKUP.EXE**.
Test the DNS service from within Windows 2000.	Use the DNS console. Open the monitoring page within the server Properties window.
Assign every client the same DNS server, WINS server, and default gateway without having to configure each computer.	Configure the DHCP server to send this information with every response to a DHCP request.
Make all Compaq computers on your network logically separate from all other computers by placing them on their own IP segment	Use DHCP to configure and implement a vendor-specific option class. Assign all Compaq computers a different range of IP addresses and a different subnet mask.
Alleviate network traffic to your DNS server.	1) Install and configure a secondary DNS server; or, 2) Create one or more subdomains, each with its own DNS server.
Resolve NetBIOS names on your network to IP addresses.	Install a WINS server.

Lesson 2 Activities

Complete the following activities to better prepare you for the certification exam.

1. Install the DNS service on a computer. Create a fictitious name for your domain, and make this computer the primary name server. If you have the resources, configure a secondary DNS server as well.

2. On a Windows 2000 server running DNS, open the **\WINNT\System32\Dns** folder. Open the file named **CACHE.DNS** with Notepad. What information is in this file? Why is it there?

3. From a command prompt, use the **IPCONFIG** command. What information is listed about your computer? Now try the **IPCONFIG /ALL** command.

4. Set up a Windows 2000 computer to use automatically configured TCP/IP settings. Reboot and check the IP address and subnet mask. What is the default gateway?

5. Install the DHCP service on a Windows 2000 server. Configure DHCP to assign a default gateway and the IP address of a DNS server. Reboot the client used in Activity #2. What is the IP address of the client now? Does it have a default gateway and preferred DNS server?

6. On the DHCP server, determine what three vendor-specific option classes are installed by default when DHCP is installed. In the Microsoft Windows 2000 option class, what are the three options that are pre-defined?

7. From a computer with Internet access, use **NSLOOKUP.EXE** to resolve a host name to an IP address. Try resolving www.lightpointlearning.net. What happens?

8. Use the ping command to "ping" a host name on a server. For example, at a command prompt, type **PING** www.lightpointlearning.net. What happens? What happens if you ping this server more than once?

9. Change the domain name for the DHCP server, and reboot when requested to do so. Then open the DHCP console. What is listed?

10. Install the WINS service on a Windows 2000 server and explore the WINS configuration options.

Answers to Lesson 2 Activities

1. DNS is installed in the Add/Remove Windows Components section of the Add/Remove Software Control Panel. Options can be configured using the DNS console, located under Administrative Tools in the Start Menu.

2. The **CACHE.DNS**CACHE.DNS file contains the IP addresses for the root-level domain name servers. Without these, your local DNS server would not be able to perform forward lookup queries.

3. The **IPCONFIG** command lists the domain name, the DNS servers' IP addresses, the client's IP address and subnet mask, and the default gateway. Typing **IPCONFIG /ALL** displays all of the TCP/IP configuration settings, including the host name, node type, description, physical address (also known as the MAC address), whether DHCP is enabled (and if so, what the lease settings are), and more.

4. Use the **IPCONFIG** command to find this information. The IP address will be 169.254.x.y, where x and y are values between 1 and 255. The subnet mask will be set to 255.255.0.0, and there will be no default gateway will be configured.

5. The client should have an IP address within the range you defined in the DHCP scope. It should also have the default gateway you defined in the advanced settings for the scope.

6. Open the DHCP console, right-click the server, and choose set predefined options. The three vendor-specific option classes are: 1) Microsoft Options, 2) Microsoft Windows 2000 Options, and 3) Microsoft Windows 98 Options. Within the Windows 2000 options, the three options are: 1) disable NetBIOS Option, 2) release DHCP Lease on Shutdown, and 3) default router metric base.

7. You should receive an IP address for every host name. If you try resolving www.lightpointlearning.net, you receive multiple IP addresses. Microsoft is distributing the load on their Web server by actually having several Web servers mapped to the host name **www**.

8. If you ping a host name, the ping command first asks DNS to resolve the host name to an IP address. Ping reports the IP address, then attempts a connection. In the case of www.lightpointlearning.net, if you repeat the command, you may notice that the IP address has changed. Again, there is more than one computer with the FQDN www.lightpointlearning.net.

9. After changing the domain for the DHCP server, the DHCP console lists the old server's FQDN only. In order to manage the DHCP server under the new domain name, you need to right-click DHCP, choose Add Server, and enter the name of the server.

10. WINS installs in the Add/Remove Windows Components section of the Add/Remove Software Control Panel. Options can be configured using the WINS console, which is under Administrative Tools in the Start Menu.

Lesson 2 Quiz

These questions test your knowledge of features, vocabulary, procedures, and syntax.

1. How long is a standard (IPv4) IP address?

    A. 72 bits

    B. 32 bits

    C. 36 bits

    D. 128 bits

2. Which of the following can DHCP assign automatically?

    A. NetBIOS name

    B. DNS zone transfer (IXFR)

    C. DNS server address

    D. Replication address

3. What is the function of WINS?

    A. Resolve NetBIOS names to host names

    B. Resolve NetBIOS names to IP addresses

    C. Resolve IP addresses to street addresses

    D. Resolve IP addresses to host names

4. Which of the following is used to configure DNS for automatic updates?

    A. DNS to DHCP Update (DDU)

    B. **DCPROMO.EXE**

    C. DNS Updater

    D. DNS Dynamic Update Protocol

5. Which of the following allows a Windows 2000 client to assign itself an IP address?

    A. Automatic Private IP Addressing (APIPA)

    B. Auto-Assign Boot Process (AABP)

    C. Independent IP Addressing (IIPA)

    D. Internet Reservation IP Assignment (IRIPA)

6. Which of the following describes a FQDN:

    A. Defines the number of host names within a domain

    B. The domain name of the DNS server

    C. The host name and the entire domain name of any computer

    D. Configures when installing WINS

7. Which of the following is utilized when a client computer asks for an IP address resolution?

    A. An iterative request

    B. A recursive request

    C. A ping packet

    D. A DHCP query

8. To test IP-to-host name resolution, which of the following would you use?

    A. The DHCP console

    B. **NSLOOKUP.EXE**

    C. WINS

    D. Both A and B

9. When you use Windows NT 4.0 and Windows 2000 together in a network, which protocol is used for zone transfers ?

    A. AXFR

    B. IXFR

    C. DHCP

    D. WINS

10. Which of the following is the default IP address utilized by Windows 2000 client in the absence of a DHCP server?

    A. 192.168.52.4

    B. 254.196.3.10

    C. 169.192.4.52

    D. 169.254.5.63

Answers to Lesson 2 Quiz

1. Answer B is correct. The current version of the IP protocol (version 4, or IPv4), uses 32-bit addresses.

    Answers A, C, and D are incorrect. Answer D is close; IPv6, the replacement of IPv4, will support 128-bit addresses.

2. Answer C is correct. In addition to an IP address, a DHCP server can issue several other TCP/IP settings, including DNS server addresses, the default gateway, the domain name, and WINS server addresses.

    Answer A is incorrect. NetBIOS names cannot be chosen from a pool, but are configured during the initial installation of the operating system.

    Answer B is incorrect. A client does not need to know anything about DNS zone transfers.

    Answer D is incorrect. There is no replication address setting.

3. Answer B is correct. WINS resolves NetBIOS names to IP addresses.

    Answer D is incorrect. DNS resolves IP addresses to host names

    Answers A and C are incorrect.

4. Answer D is correct. The DNS database can be automatically updated using the DNS Dynamic Update Protocol, and configuring both DNS and DHCP to use it.

    Answers A, B, and C are incorrect.

5. Answer A is correct. If a Windows 2000 client cannot locate a DHCP server during the boot process, it assigns itself a temporary IP address until a DHCP server becomes available. This process is called APIPA.

    Answers B, C, and D are incorrect. They are all fictitious terms.

6. Answer C is correct. An FQDN includes both the host name and the full list of domains to which the computer belongs.

    Answer D is incorrect. WINS uses NetBIOS names, not FQDNs.

    Answers A and B are incorrect.

7. Answer B is correct. When a client computer asks DNS to resolve an address, the client needs to know the IP address for the target computer, not the address of some computer along the way. A request for the full address (or an error if the address cannot be resolved) is a recursive request.

    Answer A is incorrect. When a DNS server looks for an address beyond its zone of authority, it requests information from other DNS servers in an iterative request, accepting partial answers that help find the final IP address.

    Answers C and D are incorrect.

8. Answer B is correct. IP-to-host name resolution is done by the DNS service. You test DNS by using either the DNS console or **NSLOOKUP.EXE**.

    Answers A and D are incorrect. DHCP assigns IP addresses and other TCP/IP information; it has nothing to do with host name resolution.

    Answer C is incorrect. WINS resolves NetBIOS names to IP addresses, and is a service, not a testing utility.

9. Answer A is correct. Although Windows 2000 supports full (AXFR) and partial (IXFR) zone transfers, Windows NT 4.0 only supports full transfers.

    Answer B is incorrect. Only Windows 2000 supports partial zone transfers

    Answers C and D are incorrect. Neither one is related to DNS zone transfers.

10. Answer D is correct. When a client cannot find a DHCP server to fulfill its request for an IP address, it assigns itself one from the pool of addresses in the range of 169.254.0.1 through 169.254.255.254.

    Answers A, B, and C are incorrect. These addresses to not fall within the scope of addresses that have been reserved for APIPA.

Active Directory Installation and Configuration

Microsoft Active Directory is the directory service of Microsoft Windows 2000. A directory service stores, maintains, and supplies directory information to the network. Directory information can include details about resources on the network such as shared folders, printers, users, and groups. Active Directory provides a centralized system of organizing, classifying and managing this information. Understanding the components of Active Directory and the installation of Active Directory is fundamental to building a Windows 2000 network.

After completing this lesson, you should have a better understanding of the following topics:

*   Active Directory Overview

*   Active Directory Installation Requirements

*   Active Directory Logical Structure

*   Active Directory Physical Structure

*   Active Directory Installation

Active Directory Overveiw

Active Directory is the directory service upon which Windows 2000 networks are constructed. Active Directory makes resources available to users on a network. Because Active Directory provides for a centralized view of the network, users do not need to know the physical location of a resource in order to access it. A user in Seattle can locate a database file stored on a server in Tokyo as easily as one stored on a server down the hall. To the user, all resources appear to be part of one system, not individual, isolated units. The physical structure of the network—how the computers are wired together, where the servers are located, etc.—should be of no concern to a user. Active Directory makes the physical structure of the network transparent.

In addition to making network resources easier to find, Active Directory also centralizes administration and allows delegation of administrative tasks to users or groups. Unlike Microsoft Windows NT 4.0, you can assign administrative rights to groups of objects, as well as groups of users. Active Directory is also sectionalized; as an organization grows and changes, so does the Active Directory. Active Directory has been designed to support millions of objects and thousands of servers on a network, but works equally well with a single server and a few hundred objects.

Using Active Directory-Supported Technologies

One of the major strengths of Active Directory is its interoperability with other directory services and a variety of networking applications. To this end, Active Directory supports many existing networking standards and protocols (Table 3.1). Active Directory also provides support for Application Programming Interfaces (APIs) that make possible communication to other directory services, including those running on other platforms like UNIX or Novell.

Table 3.1 Active Directory-Supported Technologies

Protocol Standard	Definition
Transmission Control Protocol / Internet Protocol (TCP/IP)	The protocol of the internet that transmits information over a network using IP addresses.
Dynamic Host Configuration Protocol (DHCP)	Assigns IP addresses to computers automatically.
Domain Name Service (DNS)	Stores information about IP addresses and ho st names.
DNS Dynamic update protocol	Allows DNS to be updated by the DHCP server and DHCP clients.
Simple Network Time Protocol (SNTP)	Provides a way to synchronize clocks over the Internet .
Lightweight Directory Access Protocol (LDAP), Version 3	Accesses a directory service on a server for client compu ters.
LDAP C	A C language program interface for LDAP .
LDAP Data Interchange Format (LDIF)	Provides directory synchronization.
Kerberos (Version 5)	An authentication / network security implementation.
X.509 v3 certificates	An authentication / network security implementation.

Understanding Active Directory Naming Conventions

Users and applications find resources in the Active Directory by searching for the name of the resource or the name of some property of that resource. Active Directory uses four different naming conventions, allowing users and applications to use the format most appropriate for them. The names must be unique within the Active Directory forest (the entire Active Directory repository). The four naming conventions are as follows:

Distinguished name—In Active Directory, every object has a distinguished name. The distinguished name not only identifies the object, but the entire domain path in which the object is located.

It is similar to a Fully Qualified Domain Name (FQDN) in that a distinguished name lists the object name plus the domain information. The distinguished name for a user named Sally Jones in the lightpointlearning.net domain is as follows:

DC=net,DC=lightpointlearning,CN=Users,CN=Sally Jones

DC is a domain component and CN is a common name. The hierarchical structure ensures that the distinguished name is unique.

Relative distinguished name—The relative distinguished name is the part of the distinguished name that relates only to the object. As a distinguished name is like an FQDN, the relative distinguished name is analogous to the host name. In the provided example, the relative distinguished name for the container object is Users, and the relative name for the user object within that container is Sally Jones. Active Directory does not allow two objects within the same container to have the same relative distinguished name.

User principal name—The user principal name is the user's logon name and the DNS domain name in which the user account is located. The user principal name is often the user's e-mail address, and it can be used to log on to the network. If the user Sally Jones has a logon name of JonesS, her user principal name may be joness@lightpointlearning.net.

Globally Unique Identifier—Every object in Windows 2000 receives a Globally Unique Identifier (GUID) when it is created in the Active Directory. The GUID is a 128-bit number that is guaranteed to be unique. Like the Security ID (SID) assigned to a user, group, or computer in Windows NT 4.0, the GUID stays with an object, even if it is moved or renamed. In Windows 2000, GUIDs are assigned to every object in the Active Directory, not just users, groups, and computers. This allows applications to access components in the Active Directory even if the components have been moved or renamed.

Examining Active Directory and the Domain Name Service (DNS)

DNS provides name resolution (translation of host names to IP addresses) and controls the DNS namespace. A namespace is a logical area within which a name can be resolved to an address. Active Directory uses the DNS naming scheme to name Active Directory domains. Although Active Directory and DNS use the same domain names, they manage different namespaces, and each performs a different type of name resolution.

Active Directory relies upon DNS to find a computer on the network. Once the computer is found, Active Directory handles name resolution for objects on that computer. You cannot install and run

Active Directory on a server without the DNS service present on the network. The DNS service does not need to be running on the same server as Active Directory, but it must be available. DNS does not require the presence of Active Directory, but Active Directory requires DNS. More specifically, Active Directory requires a DNS service that supports Service Location (SRV) resource records, which provide information on the role of servers in the domain.

 Tip: A DNS record for a host (computer) is in a different namespace from the Active Directory record for that same computer's domain account.

The DNS database is a list of computers in the network and their IP addresses.

The DNS server also contains SRV records. Active Directory uses the SRV information to help clients find services running on servers. For example, when a user logs on to the network, the client computer queries the DNS server for the IP address of a domain controller. The DNS server knows which computers on the network are domain controllers by using the SRV records. It sends the IP address for a domain controller back to the client computer, and the user logs on.

 Note: If DNS is not available when you install Active Directory, the Active Directory installation asks if you would like to install DNS at the same time. If you chose not to, Active Directory will not run until DNS is properly installed.

Active Directory Installation Requirements

An understanding of the installation of Active Directory is crucial in implementing a successful Windows 2000 network. Active Directory is the core of Windows 2000 and is what differentiates Windows 2000 from Windows NT 4.0. Like any other installation, careful planning and network design are important. This section discusses what you need to install Active Directory, and what decisions should be made before beginning the installation process.

Defining Active Directory Installation Requirements

Active Directory must be installed on a server running Windows 2000 Server, Windows 2000 Advanced Server, or Windows 2000 Datacenter Server. The computer must meet the minimum hardware requirements to run Windows 2000, and the hardware should be listed on the Microsoft Hardware Compatibility List (HCL).

 Note: Although the hardware requirements for Windows 2000 Server do not change with Active Directory installed, a minimum of 128-MB of Random Access Memory (RAM) is recommended, even for a small LAN.

The server assigned as the domain controller (the computer running Active Directory) must have adequate disk space on an NTFS-formatted partition. A minimum of 1-GB free space is recommended. In addition, the server must have the TCP/IP protocol installed and be configured to use DNS. Although Active Directory does not rely entirely on the system time and date for replication, it is important to make sure these are set correctly prior to installation.

The network on which the domain controller will be installed must use TCP/IP (it can use other protocols in addition to TCP/IP) and must have at least one DNS server that supports SRV records. It is also recommended, but not required, that the DNS server supports the DNS dynamic update protocol.

 Note: If a DNS server is unavailable on the network when you begin the Active Directory installation, Active Directory offers to install the DNS service on the Active Directory server.

If you are creating a domain controller in a pre-existing Windows 2000 domain, you must have the necessary administrative rights to the network before beginning installation.

Planning Active Directory Installation

Before installing the first domain controller, you must have a concept of the overall network plan. The first domain controller you install becomes the domain controller for the root domain. It is from the root domain that other domains (child domains) are created. Although you can create child domains and separate domains in the same forest, you cannot create a domain above the root. Planning and mapping out the logical structure of your organization's network is a fundamental step. Your map should include the domains and trees within the forest, as well as the domain names you will use. If your company has an Internet presence, you must also make sure that the root domain name is registered for use on the Internet. When planning a network structure, make sure you plan for growth in your organization.

 Note: Registration of Internet domain names is handled by the nonprofit organization InterNIC, found on the Internet at www.internic.net.

Choosing Active Directory Installation Options

When you begin the Active Directory installation, you must choose what part of the network the computer will control. You have six choices for the role of the domain controller. Your choices depend on your first selection. Initially, you can choose to set up either of the following:

• A domain controller for a new domain

• A domain controller for an existing domain

If you choose to install a domain controller for an existing domain, you are asked to select the domain, and the Active Directory installation proceeds. If you choose to set up a controller for a new domain, you may then choose to create either of the following:

• A new domain tree

• A new child domain

If you choose to create a new child domain, you are asked to supply the name of the parent domain. If you choose to create the root domain for a new domain tree, you have the following two more options:

• Create a new forest

• Join an existing forest

Active Directory Logical Structure

Active Directory networks are based on a hierarchical structure. The basic unit of structure in Active Directory is the domain. A domain is a logical grouping of objects that share a common directory database. In any given domain, there is only one Active Directory database, and this database contains information about all of the objects within the domain.

Within a domain, you may have smaller Organizational Units (OUs). OUs are similar to groups in Windows NT 4.0. They are used to gather objects with similar attributes for the purpose of simplifying management. Unlike global and local groups in Windows NT 4.0, OUs can be used to group all objects, not just users. OUs are called container objects because they contain other objects and other OUs.

A collection of domains that share the same DNS namespace is called a tree. The DNS namespace is the logical region in which a DNS server can resolve host names to IP addresses. In a tree, all domains that branch from the root (the first domain that was created) are called child domains. For example, in a domain named lightpointlearning.net, the namespace is lightpointlearning.net. If there is a child domain named sales.lightpointlearning.net, both domains share a similar namespace: lightpointlearning.net. These two domains form a tree.

Tip: The highest-level domain (the root) must be the first domain created in your network. Once you create the first domain, you cannot create a domain above it in the hierarchy; only child domains and other trees can be created.

In addition to creating a child domain under an existing domain, you can also create an independent domain that does not share the same namespace as the root. Although the two domains (or two domain trees, as the case may be) do not share a common namespace, they are both part of your organization. The term forest describes the situation when two or more trees exist that do not share a common namespace. They share information only if you implement trusts.

Structuring Active Directory Domains

The overall unit of organization in the Active Directory is the domain. A domain is a logical collection of objects (computers, printers, users, and more) that share a common directory database. Domains are not confined or defined by any physical boundaries. Each domain has one or more domain controllers—computers that store the Active Directory and make it available to other computers.

The Active Directory structure is divided into domains for security and administrative purposes. A company's network may be composed of several domains. The administrator for any given domain has administrative rights for only that domain (unless specifically granted rights to other domains). This allows for delegation of control and administrative responsibility. Every domain also has its own security policies.

In Windows NT 4.0, every domain has only one Primary Domain Controller (PDC) and ideally has one or more Backup Domain Controllers (BDCs). In the Windows NT 4.0 domain structure, the PDC has the master (read-and-write) copy of the domain information. The BDCs receive a read-only copy of the directory information during the process of replication. In Windows 2000 domains, all domain controllers are peers (they are equal). This is known as a multi-master replication model. Changes can be made to the Active Directory database on any one of the controllers, and the changes are replicated to the other domain controllers.

 Note: A domain controller is responsible for the Active Directory in one domain, and one domain only.

In order to ease migration (upgrading) of a Windows NT 4.0 network to a Windows 2000 network, Active Directory servers support two modes of operation: mixed-mode and native-mode. In mixed-mode (the default), your network supports both Windows 2000 domain controllers (using Active Directory) and Windows NT 4.0 domain controllers. The PDC of your Windows NT 4.0 domain is the first domain controller to be upgraded to a Windows 2000 server running Active Directory. In mixed-mode, this server has most of the features of Active Directory, but also acts as a PDC to the BDCs still running on the network. Once all of the remaining BDCs have been upgraded to Windows 2000, you can convert the domain to native-mode.

 Note: Only the PDC and BDCs need to be upgraded to Windows 2000 before converting your domain to native-mode. Member servers and workstations do not need to be upgraded to run in a native-mode Active Directory network.

A few features of Active Directory, including group nesting and security-type universal groups, are not available until a network is running in native-mode.

Converting an Active Directory Domain From Mixed-Mode to Native-Mode

When you begin migrating your Windows NT 4.0 network to Windows 2000, all domain controllers run in mixed-mode. To convert your Active Directory-based network to native-mode, follow these steps:

1. From the Start Menu, choose Programs, Administrative Tools and then select Active Directory Domains and Trusts.

2. In the left pane of the Active Directory Domains and Trusts console, right-click the icon that represents the server and then choose Properties (Figure 3.1).

Figure 3.1 Server Properties

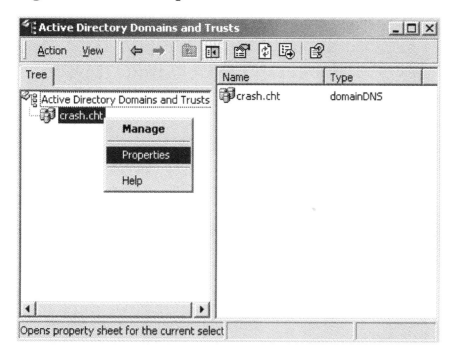

3. On the Server Properties page, choose the General Properties page, and then select Change Mode (Figure 3.2).

Figure 3.2 Change Mode Option

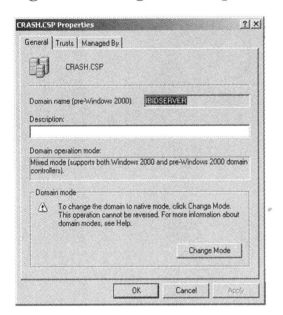

4.   Choose Yes to confirm the warning.

5.   Close the Server Properties window. Your domain is now running in native-mode.

 Warning: Converting a domain from mixed-mode to native-mode is a one-time, one-way option. You cannot change from native-mode back to mixed-mode.

Implementing Organizational Units (OUs)

Within a domain, objects are organized in Organizational Units (OUs). An OU is a container object containing other objects and OUs. In Windows NT 4.0, you combine domain users into global groups for the purpose of organizing and implementing security policies. You may also create local groups, into which you place global groups and users. In Windows 2000, this grouping concept—for the sake of organization and security—is no longer limited to users. All objects within the Active Directory can be placed into OUs, better reflecting the structure of your organization.

For example, your company may have two locations, one in New York and the other in Seattle. You have chosen a single domain model for your company. You would like the administrator in New York to be able to manage objects in her region while you administer the objects in Seattle. You can create two organizational units, one for New York and the other for Seattle and assign appropriate permissions to these OUs.

When you assign permissions to an OU in Active Directory, you have a large degree of flexibility. You can assign full administrative control to an OU and all of the objects within the OU or you can limit the amount of control. This allows you to maintain levels of administrative ability. Perhaps the administrator in New York has an assistant who handles user accounts and forgotten passwords. You can assign this assistant permission to change user accounts and passwords within the New York OU, but not change settings for any other objects within that OU.

The structure and use of OUs in one domain do not effect the structure and use of OUs in another domain. In addition, the administrative rights you assign to an OU in one domain do not effect the OUs in other domains.

 Note: Many companies find that when planning an upgrade from Windows NT 4.0 to Windows 2000, their multiple domain models are no longer needed. Even with millions of objects, Active Directory allows a high degree of organization within a single domain through the use of OUs.

Creating an Organizational Unit

To create an OU, follow these steps:

1. From the Start menu, choose Programs, Administrative Tools and then select Active Directory Users and Computers. The Active Directory Users and Computers window displays.

2. From the left pane, right-click icon that represents the server, choose New and then select Organizational Unit (Figure 3.3).

Figure 3.3 New Organizational Unit Selection

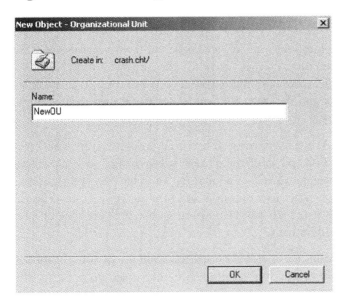

3. In the Create New Object (Organizational Unit) window, enter a name for the OU in the Name box and choose OK.

Designing Structural Trees and Forests

As a domain is a logical collection of computers that share the same directory database, a tree is a collection of domains that share a continuous namespace. For example, you create a domain called cityu.edu. This is your root domain that was the first one created for your company's network. Any subdomains (child domains) to this domain will be part of the cityu.edu domain tree, and they will be named *something*.cityu.edu. All domains within this tree share the common namespace cityu.edu.

You may also create a domain that is not a child to your original root domain. Suppose that your company (City University, cityu.edu) joins another company (LightPoint Learning, lightpointlearning.net). You may decide to keep lightpointlearning.net in its own domain for administrative reasons or to maintain a separate presence on the Internet. Both domains are part of your organization, but do not share a common namespace. These domains make up a forest. A forest is a collection of multiple domains that do not share a contiguous namespace (Figure 3.4).

Figure 3.4 Trees and Forest

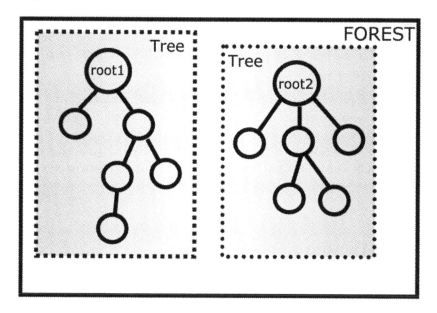

Although the two companies (City University and LightPoint Learning) do not share a common namespace, they are two trees in the same forest. Within every forest, at least one global catalog server exists that contains the global catalog, a listing of resources available throughout the forest.

Building Trust Relationships

A trust relationship is a logical connection between two domains that allows the domains to share resources and administrative tasks. Windows 2000 supports two types of trusts: one-way, non-transitive trusts and two-way, transitive trusts.

 Note: You can only implement one-way, non-transitive trusts in Windows NT 4.0 networks.

Examining One-Way, Non-transitive Trusts

In a one-way trust, one domain can trust another domain to receive useful information from it without requiring the second domain to trust the first. You can represent the trust as a line connecting the two domains. The line has an arrow at one end which points to the trusted domain. A non-transitive trust means that the trust relationship only includes the two domains.

As an example, suppose there are three domains in a forest: ibidpub.com, cityu.edu, and lightpointlearning.net. If you set up a one-way trust so that ibidpub.com trusts cityu.edu, cityu.edu does not trust ibidpub.com. Resources in the cityu.edu domain are available to the ibidpub.com domain, but objects in the ibidpub.com domain are not available to cityu.edu. If lightpointlearning.net trusts ibidpub.com, it does not automatically trust cityu.edu. In other words, it doesn't inherit the trust between ibidpub.com and cityu.edu (Figure 3.5).

Figure 3.5 One-Way Non-Transitive Trusts

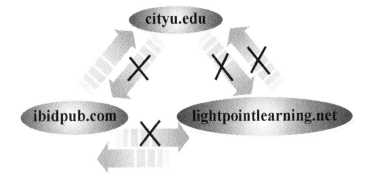

Exploring Two-Way, Transitive Trusts

If a two-way trust is created between domains, both domains trust each other. If you draw the trust as a line, a two-way trust is a line with an arrow at both ends. Each domain has access to objects in the other. If ibidpub.com trusts cityu.edu, cityu.edu also trusts ibidpub.com.

In a transitive trust, the trusts of one domain are passed on to domains that trust it. For example, if lightpointlearning.net trusts ibidpub.com and ibidpub.com trusts cityu.edu, then lightpointlearning.net trusts cityu.edu (Figure 3.6).

Note: Two-way, transitive trusts are the default between Windows 2000 domains.

Figure 3.6 Two-Way Transitive Trusts

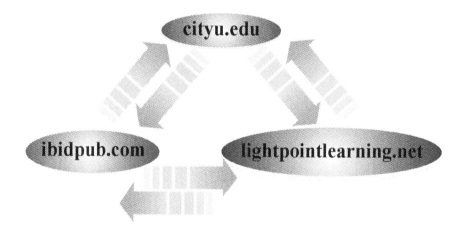

Describing Operations Masters

Certain domain controllers play a special role in a domain. The operations these domain controllers perform must only be carried out at one place in the domain or forest at any time. A domain controller that handles any of these operations is called an operation master. In every Active Directory forest, the following five operation master roles must be filled:

Schema master—The schema master controls all updates and changes to the schema (the entire database and all objects within the forest).

Domain naming master—This domain controller handles the addition and removal of domains in the forest.

Relative Identifier (RID) master—The RID master allocates identifiers that are unique within each domain.

PDC emulator—You need this controller when the network includes computers that are not running Windows 2000. It acts like the PDC for a Windows NT 4.0 network and receives preferential replication of password changes. If a user logon at an Active Directory domain controller fails, the domain controller sends the request to the PDC emulator to see if a password change has occurred that has not yet been replicated to all domain controllers.

Infrastructure master—The infrastructure master tracks changes to domain group membership.

 Note: Each domain has one RID master, one PDC emulator and one infrastructure master. A forest can have only one schema master and one domain-naming master.

Active Directory Physical Structure

It is important to separate the logical organization of an Active Directory network from the physical structure. Although Active Directory makes it possible for users to access resources regardless of their physical location, you must consider the physical structure of the network when planning an Active Directory installation. The physical structure of the network and Active Directory determine when and where network traffic occurs.

Within Active Directory, you can define sites. Just as a domain represents a logical grouping of objects on a network, a site represents a physical grouping of objects. A site is a physical collection of one or more IP subnets that are connected by a high-speed link. A subnet is one portion of a TCP/IP network. In this case, a high-speed link is any link that supports transmission rates of at least 10 Mbps (standard Ethernet or faster). You define a site in order to direct network traffic and reduce replication (copying of the Active Directory database) over slow links.

Because sites are physical constructs and domains are logical constructs, the two are mutually exclusive. A site can contain several domains or portions of several domains. A single domain may have several sites.

Understanding Active Directory Replication

Replication is the process of transferring the Active Directory information among all of the domain controllers within a domain. Connection objects handle transfer among servers. A connection object is an object within the Active Directory on one domain controller that points to another domain controller. Domain controllers that are linked by connection objects are called replication partners.

For every pair of replication partners, there are two connection objects, one on each server. Controller A has a connection object that allows it to receive information from Controller B. Controller B has a connection object that allows it to receive information from Controller A. Connection objects may be created manually by an administrator. They are also created automatically by the Knowledge Consistency Checker (KCC) which is a built-in process on all domain controllers. It is responsible for maintaining the Active Directory replication. The KCC checks the replication process at regular intervals to make sure replication occurs properly.

 Note: Replication data transfers among domain controllers using the Remote Procedure Call (RPC) over IP protocol. When a data transfer among domains occurs, it can be transmitted using RPC over IP or using the Simple Mail Transfer Protocol (SMTP).

Within any domain, there may be several sites. Replication must occur among all domain controllers within a domain, regardless of their physical location. Although connection objects establish replication between any two-domain controllers, there are differences in the replication procedure depending on site configuration.

Replicating Within a Site

Within a site, replication occurs on a change notification basis. When you make a change on a domain controller, it waits a specified amount of time and then sends notice to the other domain controllers to inform them of the change. If no changes have occurred over a longer specified period of time, a domain controller begins the replication process to make sure no changes were missed.

Tip: The default time for change notification is 5 minutes. The default time for replication if no changes have been logged is 6 hours.

Between domain controllers within the same site, replication data is not compressed. Rather than use domain controller resources to compress and decompress the data, Windows 2000 sends the data uncompressed. This causes a temporary decrease in network bandwidth. But remember, a site is a collection of computers connected by a high-speed link (10 Mbps or faster).

Certain changes to the Active Directory require immediate replication when possible. The following security-related changes are replicated on an Urgent Replication basis:

- Changes to the account lockout policy

- Changes to the domain password policy

- Changes to the password on a computer account

- Replication of a locked-out account

- Changes to the Local Security Authority (LSA)

Replicating Between Sites

Replication between sites must take into consideration the slower (or more unreliable) connections between domain controllers. Between sites, replication does not occur on a change notification basis but on a user-configurable schedule. The two values that can be configured for replication are as follows:

Schedule—The times at which replication may occur.

Interval—How often the domain controllers check for changes during the specified schedule time.

Replication traffic between sites is compressed to conserve bandwidth. Typically, the data is compressed 10 to 15%; this adds processing overhead to the domain controllers, but minimizes the network traffic generated.

Tip: Urgent replication is only available between domain controllers in the same site. It does not occur between sites.

Creating and Updating Site Locations

In order to create a site, you must be a member of the Enterprise Admins group or have the name and password for an account in that group. Site creation and configuration requires a series of steps.

Creating a Site

To create a new site, follow these steps:

1. From the Start Menu, choose Programs, Administrative Tools and then select Active Directory Sites and Services. The Active Directory Sites and Services window displays.

2. Within the left pane, right-click the Sites folder and then choose New Site (Figure 3.7).

Figure 3.7 New Site Selection

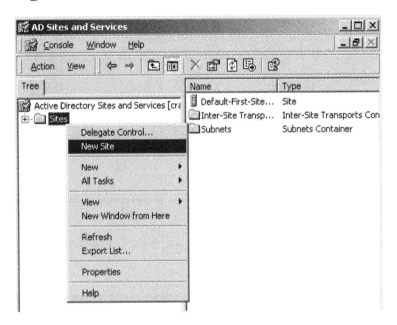

3. From within Create New Object – Site, type in a name for the site and choose a site link from the list (there will only be one if you have not created others; Figure 3.8).

4. Choose OK.

Figure 3.8 Available Site Link Selection

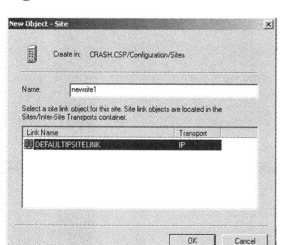

A window displays reminding you to complete a series of other steps that include the following:

*   Configuring site links

*   Adding subnets

*   Adding or moving domain controllers to this site

Configuring Site Links and Bridges

Site links map the connections between sites and dictate when and how replication occurs. Site links not only delineate the site boundaries, but also provide the cost of replication between any two sites. Costs are arbitrary numbers that you enter (between 1 and 32,767), based on the type of physical link between sites. The numbers you choose should accurately reflect the differences between site connections. If the link between Seattle and New York is four times faster than the link between New York and Lebanon, the site link cost should be four times higher between New York and Lebanon.

A site link bridge combines one or more site links that use the same protocol. For example, if the site link between Seattle and New York and the link between New York and Lebanon both use RPC over IP, you could create a site link bridge that included all three sites. The cost associated with this bridge is cumulative. If the cost of Seattle to New York is 16, and the cost between New York and Lebanon is 64, the site link bridge has a cost of 80. By default, all site links for the same protocol belong to the same site link bridge. You need not create one. You can disable this transitive feature of bridges, which allows you to manually configure all site link bridges.

To create a site link, follow these steps:

1. From the Start Menu, choose Programs, Administrative Tools and the select Active Directory Sites and Services. The Active Directory Sites and Services window displays.

2. In the left pane, choose the plus (+) sign to expand the Sites folder and then expand Inter-Site Transports.

Tip: You can expand a container in the left pane by either clicking the associated plus (+) sign or double-clicking the container.

3. Depending on the protocol you are using, right-click either IP or SMTP and then choose New Site Link (Figure 3.9).

Figure 3.9 New Site Link Selection

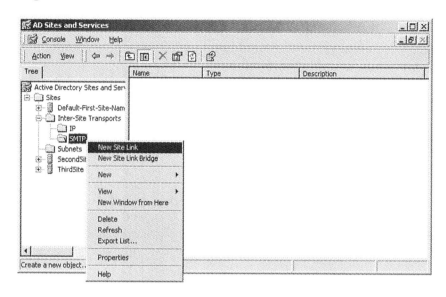

 Note: When you right-click IP or SMTP, you also have the choice to create a new site link bridge.

4. From New Object—Site Link, enter a name for the site link in the Name: box.

5. In the Sites not in this site link box, choose two or more sites to include in the site link and then select Add (Figure 3.10).

Figure 3.10 Site Link Inclusion

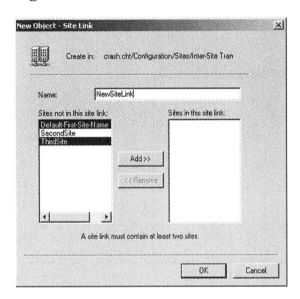

6.   Choose OK.

Once you have created the site link, you can associate a cost, replication interval and schedule for it.

Tip: On a new site link, the default setting for the cost is set to 100; the default setting for the replication interval is three hours; the default setting for the schedule is set to allow all hours.

To configure the site link you have just created, follow these steps:

1. From the Start Menu, choose Programs, Administrative Tools and select Active Directory Sites and Services. The Active Directory Sites and Services window displays.

2. In the left pane, expand the Sites folder, expand Inter-Site Transports and then choose IP (or SMTP if that is the protocol you used).

3. On the right pane, right-click the site you created and choose Properties (Figure 3.11).

Figure 3.11 Site Properties Window

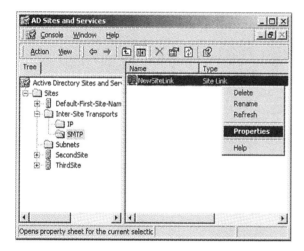

4. From Properties, choose the General Property page.

5. Enter the cost and replication interval in the appropriate boxes and then choose Change Schedule (Figure 3.12).

Figure 3.12 Cost and Replication Interval Values

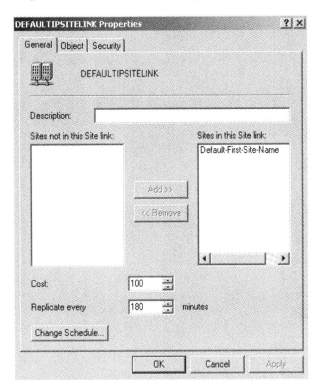

6   From Schedule, adjust the schedule by selecting one of the following options:

- Selecting the hours during which replication will be available and then choosing Replication Available, or

- Selecting the hours during which replication will not occur and then choosing Replication Not Available (Figure 3.13)

7.   Choose OK in each open window to save your configuration changes.

Figure 3.13 Replication Schedule Adjustment

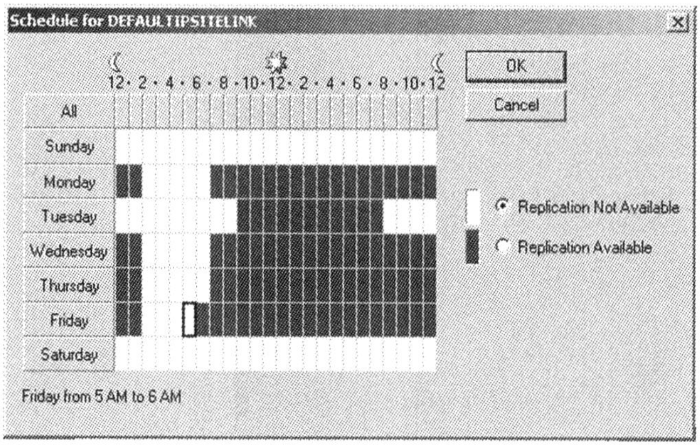

Creating Active Directory Subnets

When you create a site, you are defining a subnet within the TCP/IP network. After creating the site, you must define the subnet using an IP address and subnet mask. To create a subnet, follow these steps:

1. From the Start Menu, choose Programs, Administrative Tools and then select Active Directory Sites and Services. The Active Directory Sites and Services window displays.

2. In the left pane, expand the Sites folder, then right-click Subnets and then choose New Subnet (Figure 3.14).

3. In the Address: box, enter the IP address for the computer and in the Mask: box enter the subnet mask for the computer (Figure 3.15).

4. Choose the site that will be associated with this subnet, and then select OK.

Figure 3.14 New Subnet Selection

 Note: When you enter the IP address and subnet mask, the name of the subnet is automatically created. Creating the subnet name involves ANDing the binary numbers of the IP address and the subnet mask.

Figure 3.15 IP Address and Subnet Mask

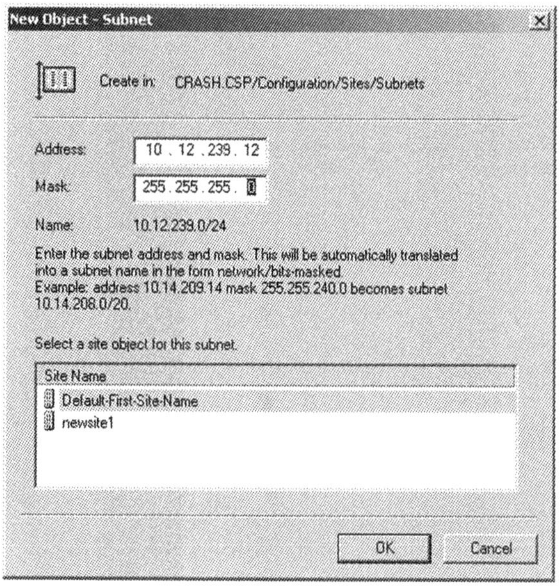

Moving Server Objects

If you create sites before creating additional domain controllers, the domain controllers are automatically assigned to the appropriate site during installation of Active Directory. Active Directory uses the IP address and subnet mask of the domain controller to create a server object in the corresponding site. If, however, you have installed domain controllers before creating sites, the domain controllers will need to be moved to the appropriate sites. To move a domain controller, follow these steps:

1. From the Start Menu, choose Programs, Administrative Tools and then select Active Directory Sites and Services. The Active Directory Sites and Services window displays.

2. In the left pane, expand the Sites folder, expand the site that contains the domain controller you wish to move and then expand the Servers folder (Figure 3.16).

Figure 3.16 Server Object Relocation

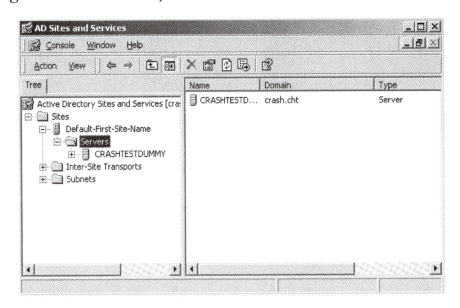

 Note: By default, domain controllers are placed in the site named Default-First-Site-Name.

3. Right-click the server object and then choose move.

4. From the Move Server window, choose the destination site and then click OK.

Creating a Connection Object

Connection objects define the connections between domain controllers for replication. Normally, connection objects are created automatically by the KCC. To configure a connection object manually, follow these steps:

1. From the Start Menu, choose Programs, Administrative Tools and then select Active Directory Sites and Services. The Active Directory Sites and Services window displays.

2. In the left pane, expand the Sites folder, expand the site that contains the server, expand Servers and then expand the icon that represents the server that will receive replication information.

3. Choose NTDS Settings, then right-click NTDS settings and then choose New Active Directory Connection (Figure 3.17).

Figure 3.17 New Active Directory Connection

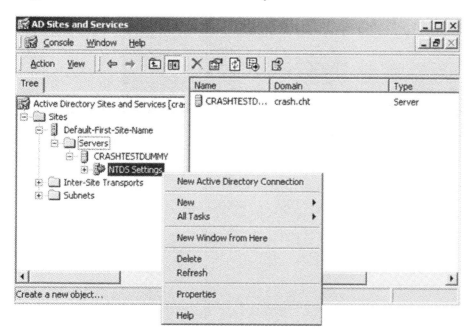

4. From the Find Domain Controllers window, choose a server that will supply the replication information, choose OK and then select OK again (Figure 3.18).

Figure 3.18 Domain Controller Selection

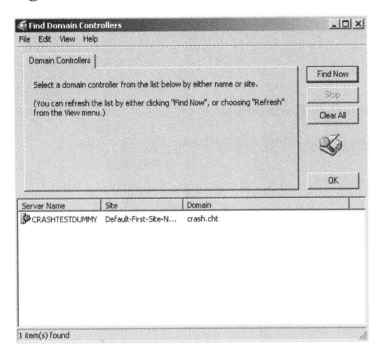

Creating a Global Catalog Server

Every forest has at least one global catalog server. Unlike a domain controller, which only contains information about objects in its domain, the global catalog server contains information about resources throughout the forest. If a client is looking for all of the users named Sally in the forest, the global catalog server can process this query. Without a global catalog server, the client would have to separately query every domain within the forest.

Every forest must have at least one global catalog. In native-mode, the global catalog is used to complete the logon authentication process. Therefore, it is advisable for larger networks to set up several domain controllers as global catalog servers to expedite the logon process and provide fault tolerance. If the global catalog server fails, users cannot log on to the network, but they can log on to the local computer.

Tip: Members of the Domain Admins group can log on to the network even if the global catalog server is unavailable.

Because the global catalog servers are designed to handle requests to locate resources throughout the forest, placing global catalog servers in each site speeds up requests and minimizes cross-domain network traffic. To create an additional catalog server, follow these steps:

1. From the Start Menu, choose Programs, Administrative Tools and then select Active Directory Sites and Services. The Active Directory Sites and Services window displays.

2. From the left pane, expand the Sites folder and then expand the site container that contains the server you want to create (let's call it the target server).

3. Under this site, expand the Servers folder and then expand the icon that represents the target server (Figure 3.19).

Figure 3.19 Global Catalog Server Selection

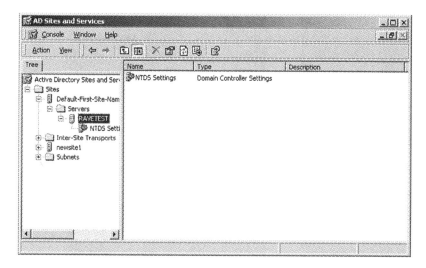

4. Choose the NTDS Settings icon, then right-click NTDS Settings and then select Properties (Figure 3.20).

Figure 3.20 Server Properties Page

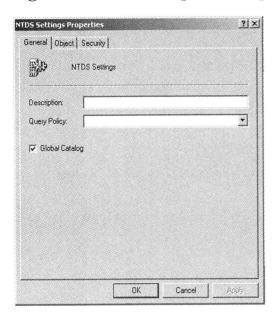

5. From the NTDS Settings Properties page, choose the General property page, and then select Global Catalog.

6. Choose OK.

Active Directory Installation

In Windows 2000, any server can be promoted from a member server (a server that plays no role in managing Active Directory) to a domain controller using **DCPROMO.EXE**. Unlike Windows NT 4.0, the role of domain controller in Windows 2000 is not determined during the initial installation of the operating system.

Using the Domain Controller Utility (DCPROMO)

To start installation of Active Directory, run the domain controller promotion utility (**DCPROMO.EXE**) on a Windows 2000 server. **DCPROMO.EXE** runs the Active Directory Installation wizard, which guides you through the installation of Active Directory.

You can also use the program **DCPROMO.EXE** to demote a domain controller to a member server. This is a new feature of Windows 2000. In Windows NT 4.0, once you install a domain controller, it remains a domain controller until Windows NT 4.0 server is reinstalled. In Windows NT 4.0, domain controllers cannot be demoted, and member servers cannot be promoted. The ability to promote and demote servers in Windows 2000 simplifies the installation process because you use the same installation process for all servers.

When **DCPROMO.EXE** installs Active Directory on a server, it installs three Active Directory consoles for the Microsoft Management Console (MMC). These consoles are as follows:

Active Directory Users and Computers—Use this console to administer and publish information in the Active Directory. In this console, you create, modify and delete objects.

Active Directory Domains and Trusts—Use this console to administer domain trusts and to change the domain mode from mixed-mode to native-mode.

Active Directory Sites and Services—Use this console to manage replication among domain controllers.

Establishing a Root Domain

When you install the first Active Directory server on a network, you are creating a new forest. At the same time, you are creating the root domain. All subsequent domains will either be child domains of this first one, or new domains within the same forest. To create a new root domain for a forest, follow these steps:

1. From the Start Menu, choose Run.

2. In the Open box, type **DCPROMO**, and then choose OK.

3. When the Active Directory Installation Wizard displays, choose Next.

4. Choose Domain controller for a new domain and then choose Next.

5. Choose Create a new domain tree and then select Next.

6. Choose Create a new forest of domain trees and then select Next.

7. Enter the full DNS name for the new domain and then choose Next (Figure 3.21).

Figure 3.21 New DNS Domain Name Entry

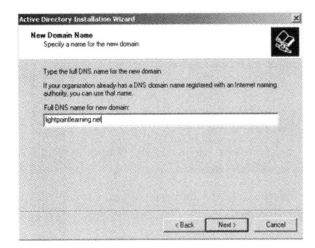

8. Enter the Domain NetBIOS name, and then choose Next.

 Note: Pre-Windows 2000 computers use the NetBIOS name to identify the new domain.

9. Choose the directories in which to store the Active Directory database and log files and then select Next.

Tip: The default directory for both the Active Directory log files and the Active Directory database is **\WINNT\NTDS**.

10. Choose a directory for the public files within Active Directory and then select Next.

Tip: The public directory for Active Directory must be on a volume formatted with NTFS Version 5. The default is **\WINNT\SYSVOL**.

11. If you have not yet installed DNS, the wizard will ask if you want to install and configure DNS as part of the Active Directory installation. Choose Yes or No, as appropriate, and then select Next.

12. Choose whether you want to allow pre-Windows 2000 servers (such as Remote Access Service (RAS) servers) to read Active Directory information, and then select Next.

Warning: Enabling support for pre-Windows 2000 servers gives the Everyone user group permission to read any attribute of every user object in the Active Directory! You should only enable it if absolutely necessary.

13. Enter a password, confirm it and then choose Next.

Note: The password you create when installing Active Directory is used to start a domain controller in Directory Services Restore Mode, a special boot option used for recovering faulty domain controllers.

14. Read the summary information to ensure it is correct and then choose Next.

15. The Active Directory Installation begins. When prompted, choose Finish and then select Restart Now.

After you complete the Active Directory Installation wizard, **DCPROMO.EXE** installs the Active Directory software, converts the server to a domain controller and adds the three Active Directory consoles to the Administrative Tools menu.

Adding a Domain Controller

A domain can be managed using only one domain controller. However, it is wise to create at least one other domain controller for fault tolerance and load balancing. If you have only one domain controller and it fails, users cannot log on to your network. The cost of a "down" network usually far exceeds the cost of a second domain controller. Multiple domain controllers are needed in larger networks to disperse the network demands. Active Directory not only controls user logons, but also handles all requests to locate resources on the network. Too few domain controllers in a network result in an overall drop in network performance.

To add a domain controller to an existing domain, follow these steps:

1. From the Start Menu, choose Run.

2. In the Open box, type **DCPROMO** and then choose OK.

3. When the Active Directory Installation Wizard displays, choose Next.

4. Choose Additional domain controller for an existing domain and then select Next.

5. In the Network Credentials window, enter the username, password, and domain name for the domain you wish to join.

 Note: The user name you provide must be for a user with administrative rights to the domain.

---

6. Enter the DNS name of the domain this controller will join and then choose Next.

7. Choose the directories in which to store the Active Directory database and log files and then select Next.

8. Choose a directory for the public files within Active Directory and then select Next.

9. Read the summary information to ensure it is correct and then choose Next.

10. The Active Directory Installation begins. When prompted, choose Finish and then select Restart Now.

After you complete the Active Directory Installation wizard, **DCPROMO.EXE** converts the server to a domain controller, replicates the Active Directory from an existing domain controller and adds the three Active Directory consoles to the Administrative Tools menu.

Creating a Child Domain

A child domain is a domain created after the root domain. It shares the same DNS namespace as the root domain. Child domains are usually created for organizational and administrative purposes. Like the root domain, you create the domain when you install the first domain controller for the domain. Begin the installation process by running **DCPROMO.EXE**. Follow these steps to complete the installation:

1. From the Start Menu, choose Run.

2. In the Open box, type **DCPROMO** and then choose OK.

3. When the Active Directory Installation Wizard displays, choose Next.

4. Choose Domain controller for a new domain and then select Next.

5. Choose Create a new child domain in an existing tree and then select Next.

6. Enter the username, password, and domain name for the root domain.

 Note: The user account specified must be a member of the Enterprise Admins group. You must have Enterprise Administrative rights to add a new domain to an existing tree.

7. Specify the DNS name for the existing parent domain and for the new domain and then choose Next.

8. Enter the domain NetBIOS name and then choose Next.

9. Choose the directories in which to store the Active Directory database and log files and then select Next.

10. Choose a directory for the public files within Active Directory and then select Next.

11. Choose whether you want to allow pre-Windows 2000 servers (such as RAS servers) to read Active Directory information and then select Next.

12. Read the summary information to ensure it is correct and then choose Next.

13. The Active Directory Installation begins. When prompted, choose Finish and then select Restart Now.

After you complete the Active Directory Installation wizard, **DCPROMO.EXE** installs the Active Directory software, converts the server to a domain controller and adds the three Active Directory consoles to the Administrative Tools menu.

Creating a Directory Tree

After a root domain has been established, you may choose to create a new tree within the forest. If you create a domain that is not a child to another domain it becomes a separate tree in the same forest. If your organization is composed of several semi-independent entities, you may choose to have each entity in its own domain. To create a new domain in a forest, follow these steps:

1. From the Start Menu, choose Run.

2. In the Open box, type **DCPROMO** and then choose OK.

3. When the Active Directory Installation Wizard displays, choose Next.

4. Choose Domain controller for a new domain and then select Next.

5. Choose Create a new domain tree and then select Next.

6. Choose Place this new domain tree in an existing forest and then select Next.

7. Enter the username and password for an account with Enterprise Administrative rights and domain name for the root domain and then choose Next.

8. Specify the DNS name for the new tree and then choose Next.

9. Enter the Domain NetBIOS name and then choose Next.

10. Choose the directories in which to store the Active Directory database and log files and then select Next.

11. Choose a directory for the public files within Active Directory and then select Next.

12. Choose whether you want to allow non-Windows 2000 servers (such as RAS servers) to read Active Directory information and then select Next.

13. Read the summary information to ensure it is correct and then choose Next.

14. The Active Directory Installation begins. When prompted, choose Finish and then select Restart Now.

After you finish entering the information in the Active Directory Installation Wizard, Active Directory is installed, the server converts to a domain controller and the Active Directory consoles are added to the Administrative Tools menu.

Vocabulary

Review the following terms in preparation for the certification exam.

Term	Description
API	Application Programming Interface
BDC	The Backup Domain Controller is the computer in a Windows NT 4.0 network that receives a read-only copy of the directory database.
child domain	A domain that shares a common namespace with the domain above it in the hierarchy.
CN	The Common Name is one component of the distinguished name in the Active Directory naming convention.
connection object	An Active Directory object that points a domain controller to its replication partners.
console	A module that is designed to work in the MMC to provide a central location for management.
container object	An Active Directory object that contains other objects.
continuous namespace	The hierarchical structure of a domain tree where each layer of the tree shares a common DNS domain name.
DC	The Domain Component is one part of the distinguished name in the Active Directory naming convention.
DCPROMO.EXE	The domain controller promotion utility is used to promote member servers to domain controllers and demote controllers to member servers.
directory database	A database file that contains directory information.
directory service	A service that provides network information to users and applications.

Term	Description
distinguished name	An Active Directory name that lists an object's relative distinguished name and the containers in which the object is found.
DNS	The Domain Name Service translates IP addresses to host names.
domain	A logical grouping of computers that share a common directory database.
domain naming master	An operations master that controls the addition and removal of domains in the forest.
forest	Two or more domains that do not share a common namespace.
FQDN	The Fully Qualified Domain Name is composed of a host name and the full domain name (www.cityu.edu).
global catalog server	An Active Directory domain controller that contains information on objects in the entire forest, not just one domain.
GUID	The Globally Unique Identifier is a 128-bit number assigned to every object in the Active Directory and is guaranteed to be unique.
HCL	The Hardware Compatibility List published by Microsoft that lists hardware tested to work with Windows 2000.
infrastructure master	An operations master that controls changes in group membership within a domain.
interval	The setting that determines how often domain controllers look for changes in the Active Directory.
IP address	A 32-bit number that identifies a computer on an TCP/IP network.

Term	Description
KCC	The Knowledge Consistency Checker is a service that automatically creates connection objects and ensures replication occurs properly.
LAN	Local Area Network
LDAP	Lightweight Directory Access Protocol
LDIF	LDAP Data Interchange Format
migration	The process of changing a computer or network from an old er operating system to a newer one.
mixed-mode	When Windows 2000 domain controllers support both Active Directory and older Windows NT 4.0 directory service s.
MMC	The Microsoft Management Console provides a centralized, common interface for management tools (consoles or snap -ins).
multi-master replication	All replication partners are peers—they all contain read -write copies of the directory database.
name resolution	The process of converting a network address to a name or a name to an address.
namespace	The logical region in which a name can be resolved to an address.
native-mode	When all Windows 2000 domain controllers only support Active Directory, and no longer function as do main controllers for a Windows NT 4.0 network.
non-transitive trust	A trust relationship that exists between two domains and cannot be inherited by other domains.
NTFS	New Technology File System
one-way trust	A trust relationship where one domain trusts another without the second domain trusting the first.

Term	Description
operation master	A domain controller that performs a special role in the domain or forest that can only be performed by one domain controller.
OU	Organizational Units are used to group objects within the Active Directory for management and administrative purposes.
PDC	In Windows NT 4.0, the Primary Domain Controller is the only domain controller with a read-and-write copy of the directory information.
PDC emulator	An operations master that acts as a Windows NT 4.0 PDC for non-Windows 2000 computers in a domain.
peers	Two or more computers that have equal importance or act in the same role.
RAM	Random Access Memory is the memory a computer uses to run the operating system and programs.
RAS server	Remote Access Server
relative distinguished name	The portion of the distinguished name that applies specifically to the object and not to its containers.
replication	Copying of the Active Directory database between domain controllers.
replication partners	Two computers that are configured to transmit the directory database with each other.
RID	The Relative Identifier is a number assigned to objects in a domain. Every RID is unique within the domain.
RID master	An operations master responsible for allocating RIDs to domain controllers so that the domain controllers can assign the RIDs to objects.
RPC	Remote Procedure Call

Term	Description
schedule	The time period during which replication can occur between sites.
schema	The entire scope of an Active Directory forest. The schema defines all objects within an Active Directory.
schema master	An operations master that controls all changes to the schema .
SID	Security ID
site	A physical grouping of computers where all computers a re members of the same TCP/IP subnet connected by a high-speed link.
site link	Defines the connection between sites and dictates when and how replication will occur.
site link bridge	A collection of two or more site links .
SMTP	Simple Mail Transfer Protocol
SNTP	Simple Network Time Protocol
SRV	Server location resource records are stored in the DNS database and define the role of a server on the network.
subdomain	A domain below another in the namespace (see child domain).
TCP/IP	Transmission Control Protocol / Internet Protocol is the network protocol used by DNS, Active Directory, and the Internet.
transitive trust	A trust relationship where the trusts between two domains are inherited by their subdomains .
tree	Two or more domains that share a common DNS namespace.
two-way trust	A trust relationship where both domains trust each other.
user principal name	A user's login name and domain name (joe@domain.com).

In Brief

If you want to...	Then do this...
Create an OU	Use the Active Directory Users and Computers console.
Upgrade a member server to a domain controller	Run the **DCPROMO.EXE** command.
Change your domain from mixed-mode to native-mode	Use Active Directory Domains and Trusts.
Use Windows NT 4.0 RAS servers in your Windows 2000 domain	Enable Support for Windows NT 4.0 RAS Servers during the Active Directory Installation Wizard.
Change a domain controller to a member server	Run the **DCPROMO.EXE** command.
Add a server to a site after the site has been created	Use the Active Directory Site and Services console.
Make a server join in a site automatically once the site has been created	Assign the server an appropriate IP address and subnet mask before creating the site. When the site is created, the server is automatically placed within the site.

Lesson 3 Activities

Complete the following activities to better prepare you for the certification exam.

1. Plan an Active Directory network for the following fictitious company. The company consists of two previously independent companies that have their own domain name. Each domain has three child domains. Your company has three locations: Nada (Fiji), Anchorage, and Seattle. Both domains have resources in all three locations. When drawing up the plan, take into consideration the physical connections among these sites.

2. Install Active Directory on a Windows 2000 server as the root domain of your fictitious company in Activity 1. Allow the Active Directory Wizard to install the DNS service, if needed.

3. Load Active Directory on a second computer. This computer should be the domain controller for a child domain under the one created in Activity 2. It should also be placed in a different IP subnet from the root domain.

4. Create two sites. Assign each site to one of the IP subnets created in Activities 2 and 3. Put the root domain controller in one site and put the second domain controller in the other.

5. Make the second domain controller a global catalog server.

6. Change the mode of the entire forest from mixed-mode to native-mode.

7. Configure replication to occur between the sites only during the hours of 10:00 p.m. and 6:00 a.m. on weekdays, and all day on weekends. During these times, domain controllers should check for Active Directory database changes once every hour.

8. Determine what connection objects have been created on the root domain controller.

9. Disable the default bridging of site links on the root domain controller. This process is not mentioned in the text, but think about logical places to find this setting.

10. Uninstall Active Directory from the second computer.

Answers to Lesson 3 Activities

1. Your company will have two trees, one for each domain name. You will create three sites, one representing each of the three geographic regions. Within each site, there will be computers that belong to either domain. It is a good idea to put at least one domain controller for each domain in each site. Costs for site links will probably be higher between Fiji and Anchorage than between Seattle and Anchorage. You may also wish to have a global catalog server at each site.

2. First, make sure the computer is the member of the domain (right-click My Computer, choose Properties, Network Identification, Network ID) and has a static IP address. Then run **DCPROMO.EXE** and follow the prompts in the wizard to make this computer the first controller in the domain and the first computer in the forest.

3. Make sure the computer is a member of the domain you created in Activity 2 and has a static IP address that is in a different subnet than the root domain. Run **DCPROMO.EXE** and follow the wizard. Make this computer the domain controller for a new domain in an existing tree.

4. From either domain controller, open the Active Directory Sites and Services console. Right-click Sites and choose New Site. Create both sites this way. Assign subnets to each site (in the same console) and move the domain controllers to the appropriate sites.

5. Open the Active Directory Sites and Services console, expand the server name, right-click NTDS Settings and choose Properties.

6. The change from mixed-mode to native-mode must be made on all domain controllers. From each domain controller, open Active Directory Domains and trusts. The Server Properties window has an option to change modes.

7. Open Active Directory Sites and Services. Replication scheduling is found in the properties window for the sites you created earlier. Use the graphical depiction of the week to select the hours when replication can occur. Enter the time (in minutes) for the interval.

8. On either domain controller, open Active Directory Sites and Service console. Expand the Sites folder, expand the server name corresponding to the root domain controller and select the NTDS Settings. The connection objects are listed on the right pane.

9. By default, site bridge links are automatically created. Although the method for disabling this feature is not mentioned in the text, the steps are very similar to creating a site link. Start by opening the Active Directory Sites and Services console. Expand the Sites folder, then expand Inter-site Transports. Right-click IP (or SMTP if appropriate) and choose Properties. Notice the check box labeled Bridge all site links. Clear it and choose OK.

10. Active Directory is uninstalled using **DCPROMO.EXE**. Follow the steps in the wizard.

Lesson 3 Quiz

These questions test your knowledge of features, vocabulary, procedures, and syntax.

1. What do you call two computers that exchange directories?
    A. Trusts
    B. Active Directory partners
    C. Connection objects
    D. Replication partners

2. Which of the following support two-way trusts?
    A. Windows 2000 servers
    B. Windows NT 4.0 servers
    C. Both A and B
    D. Neither A nor B

3. What defines the hours during which replication may occur between sites?
    A. Interval
    B. Schedule
    C. Replication duration interval (RDI)
    D. Copy rate

4. What does Active Directory require?
    A. SRV records
    B. DNS
    C. TCP/IP
    D. All of the above

5. What do you call the number assigned to site links to represent their relative speeds?
    A. Link rate
    B. Expense
    C. Cost
    D. Bridge

6. Which of the following domain controllers contains information about the entire forest?

    A. Global catalog server

    B. Forest-wide domain controller (FWDC)

    C. Root

    D. Replication master

7. What is the process that automates replication and creates connection objects?

    A. TCP/IP

    B. KCC

    C. DNS

    D. DHCP

8. **DCPROMO.EXE** is used to do what?

    A. Promote Windows 2000 Professional to Windows 2000 Server

    B. Promote Windows 2000 Server to a Domain Controller

    C. Promote Windows 2000 Server to Windows 2000 Advanced Server

    D. Promote Windows NT 4.0 Server to Windows 2000 Server

9. Which is the default directory for Active Directory log files?

    A. **\WINNT\SYSTEM32**

    B. **\WINNT\ADLOG**

    C. **\WINNT\NTDS**

    D. **C:\ADLOG**

10. You can convert the domain mode from _____ to _____.

    A. Active Directory, Windows NT 4.0

    B. Server, replication

    C. Mixed-mode, native-mode

    D. Native-mode, mixed-mode

Answers to Lesson 3 Quiz

1. Answer D is correct. Replication partners send each other the changes to the Active Directory, so that both are continually updated.

   Answer A is incorrect. Trusts define connection between domains

   Answer B is incorrect. This is a non-existent term.

   Answer C is incorrect. Connection objects are objects within the Active Directory that point to replication partners.

2. Answer A is correct. Two-way trusts are only supported by Windows 2000 servers.

   Answers B, C, and D are incorrect.

3. Answer B is correct. The schedule defines the times during which replication may occur.

   Answer A is incorrect. The interval defines how often replication partners will ask for changes during the scheduled time.

   Answers C and D are incorrect. Neither of these exists.

4. Answer D is correct. Active Directory requires the TCP/IP protocol, DNS, and SRV records within the DNS service to function.

   Answers A, B, and C are incorrect.

5. Answer C is correct. You assign a cost to each site link to represent its relative speed compared to other site links on the network.

   Answer D is incorrect. A bridge is a collection of two or more site links.

   Answers A and B are incorrect. These are fictitious names.

6. Answer A is correct. The global catalog server contains information about objects throughout the forest. This allows a user to query the entire forest to find resources.

   Answer C is incorrect. The root is the first domain controller in a tree and may also be the global catalog server, but not necessarily.

   Answers B and D are incorrect.

7. Answer B is correct. The Knowledge Consistency Checker (KCC) creates connection objects and ensures that replication occurs when it is supposed to.

    Answer A is incorrect. TCP/IP is a network protocol.

    Answer C is incorrect. DNS is the service that provides IP-to-host name resolution.

    Answer D is incorrect. DHCP is the service that automatically assigns IP addresses to clients.

8. Answer B is correct. DCPROMO.EXE is used to promote a Windows 2000 server to a domain controller or to demote a domain controller to a member server.

    Answers A and C are incorrect. DCPROMO cannot be used to upgrade one edition of Windows 2000 to another. You must purchase the other edition.

    Answer D is incorrect. You can only upgrade Windows NT 4.0 Server to Windows 2000 Server using the Windows 2000 Server CD-ROM.

9. Answer C is correct. The default location for the Active Directory database and log files is **\WINNT\NTDS**.

    Answers A, B, and D are incorrect.

10. Answer C is correct. You can perform a one-time only conversion of the network from mixed-mode to native-mode.

    Answer D is incorrect. You cannot perform the conversion from native-mode to mixed-mode; the conversion is a one-way option.

    Answers A and B are incorrect.

Lesson 4

Active Directory Management

Management of the Microsoft Windows 2000 domain is based on management of the Microsoft Active Directory. Active Directory is the directory service that centralizes administrative control of the objects within domains and forests. The Active Directory is based on a hierarchical structure, allowing you to organize network resources in a way that makes sense for both users and administrators. Using Active Directory, you have the ability to group users and objects and delegate control of these groups to managers and administrators throughout your company.

After completing this lesson, you should have a better understanding of the following topics:

*   Active Directory Objects

*   Active Directory Groups

*   Active Directory Security

Active Directory Objects

All resources within a domain are represented in the Active Directory as objects. Objects include user accounts, computer accounts, printers, and shared folders. You create objects in the Active Directory to represent the actual resources in the network and to provide organization. Objects used specifically to organize other objects are called Organizational Units (OUs). You create OUs to provide a structure to the domain that is not bound by the physical structure of the network. For example, two laser printers can be placed in the same OU even if they are in different countries. OUs are created to manage the resources and to control network access to the objects within the OU. Creating an OU also allows you to delegate administrative control to resources. In this section, you will learn how to create and manage three Active Directory objects: OUs, user accounts, and computer accounts.

Using Organizational Units (OUs)

An OU is a container object within which you place other Active Directory objects. A container object is an object in the Active Directory structure that contains other objects, including user and computer accounts, groups, and other OUs. A container object is much like a folder in the file system. For example, you have a folder in Windows 2000 named My Documents that contains files you have created. You may wish to create subfolders within the My Documents folder to further organize your files. Unlike folders in the file system, OUs are not limited to one type of object (files); an OU can contain any Active Directory object.

Organizing the network benefits both administrators and users of the network. For administrators, you create OUs to represent the administrative structure of the network. For example, if you have a group of administrators who are responsible for managing all of the printers throughout the domain, you can create an OU that contains the printers and assign administrative control of this OU to the group. You may have another administrator who is responsible for user accounts. You can create an OU for user accounts and assign administrative control to this OU.

For users, OUs can make objects appear together in the network even if they are physically disparate. Often a user looks for a resource (like a database file), but may not know where the resource is located. In Microsoft Windows NT 4.0, the user needs to know the server on which the file is stored in order to access the file. With Active Directory in Windows 2000, the user can search the Active Directory for the file based on its name or other identifiable attributes. The user can also browse the Active Directory and find resources within the OUs you have created.

Creating an OU

To create an OU, follow these steps:

1. From the Start Menu, choose Programs, Administrative Tools and then select Active Directory Users and Computers.

2. In the left pane of the Active Directory Users and Computers console, right-click on the container in which you want to create an OU, choose New and then select Organizational Unit (Figure 4.1).

Figure 4.1 OU Creation

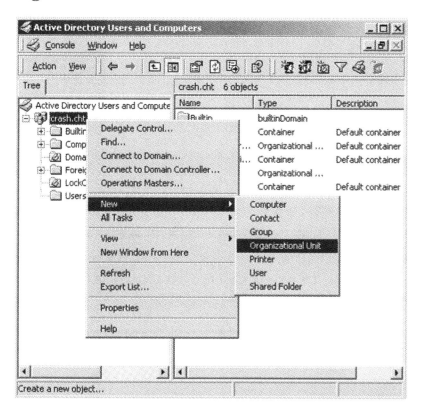

Tip: To navigate down through the containers in Active Directory, click on the plus sign (+) next to a container to expand it. You may also expand a container by double-clicking the container name.

3.   In the New Object—Organizational Unit window, enter a name for the OU and then choose OK.

4.   The OU appears in the Active Directory tree, under the container in which it was created.

Managing User Accounts

A user account is an account used to authenticate a user during logon to the domain. Like user accounts in Windows NT 4.0, Active Directory user accounts are used to grant and deny permissions to network resources. Unlike Windows NT 4.0 user accounts, Windows 2000 user accounts can be created on any domain controller. Because Active Directory uses multiple-master replication, accounts can be created on any domain controller.

User accounts can be created within any container in Active Directory, including at the domain level. Generally, you will create user accounts within OUs you have implemented. If you create a user account at the domain level, you limit your ability to delegate control over this account and to increase the overall complexity of the domain structure.

Tip: Before creating user accounts, it is good practice to create appropriate OUs for users and then place the user accounts in these OUs.

Creating an Active Directory User Account

You create user accounts within the Active Directory Users and Computers console. To create a user account, follow these steps:

1. From the Start Menu, choose Programs, Administrative Tools and then select Active Directory Users and Computers.

2. Right-click the OU in which you want to create the user account, choose New and then select User.

3. In the New Object—User window, enter the first name, middle initial and last name of the new user.

 Note: The information in the Full name: box is automatically created as you enter the first and last names and middle initial. You can also manually enter a full name or edit this information.

4. Enter a user logon name and then choose Next (Figure 4.2).

Figure 4.2 Logon Name Assignment

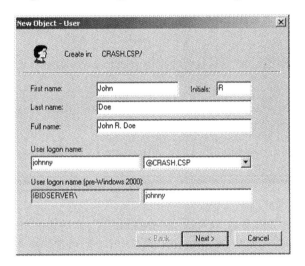

5. Enter a password, confirm the password, choose the password options according to your network plan and then select Next. You may choose to:

•   Require the user to change the password at next logon

•   Disallow the user from changing his or her password

•   Prevent the password from expiring

•   Disable the account

•   Review the summary information and then choose Finish.

Modifying an Active Directory User Account

Once a user account has been created in the Active Directory, you may wish to modify it to reflect changes in the role of the user within your company. More often, you may need to modify a user account when a user forgets his or her password. To modify an Active Directory user account, follow these steps:

1. From the Start Menu, choose Programs, Administrative Tools and then select Active Directory Users and Computers.

2. In the left pane of the Active Directory Users and Computers console, choose the container in which the user account is located. You may have to expand higher-level containers to find the container in which the user account resides (Figure 4.3).

Figure 4.3 User Account Modification

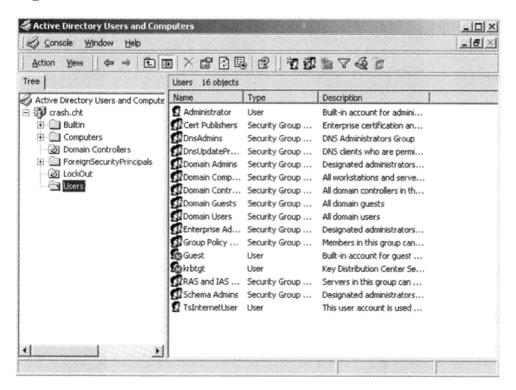

3. In the right pane, right-click the user account and choose Properties.

Note: You can also access user account properties by double-clicking the user account object.

4. From the user Properties window, you can modify user settings, including:

*   Group membership

*   Remote access rights

*   User profile

*   Logon hours

*   Terminal services access

You can also add the following detailed user information:

*   Telephone number(s)

*   E-mail address

*   Web page address

*   Mailing address

*   Title

*   Department

*   Managing supervisor

5. After making changes, choose OK.

Creating a Local User Account

Active Directory user accounts are used throughout the network to authenticate users and determine permissions. You may want to create a local user account (one that is not stored in the Active Directory) on a server or workstation. The following steps will guide you through creating a local user account.

 Note: You cannot create local user accounts on domain controllers. All accounts created on a domain controller are stored in the Active Directory and are replicated to all other domain controllers.

1. From the Start Menu, choose Programs, Administrative Tools and then select Computer Management.

Tip: You can also open the Computer Management console by right-clicking My Computer and selecting Manage.

2. In the left pane of the Computer Management console, click the plus sign (+) next to Local Users and Groups to expand the container.

3. Right-click Users and choose New User (Figure 4.4).

Figure 4.4 Local User Account Creation

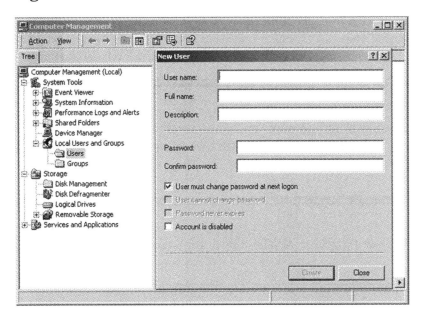

4.   In the New User window, enter a username, password and confirm the password. Optionally, you may enter the user's full name and a description. These fields help identify more clearly the user associated with a username.

5.   Choose the password options according to your network plan and then select Next (Figure 4.5). Similar to the options when creating a domain user account, you may choose to:

•   Require the user to change the password at next logon

•   Disallow the user from changing his or her password

•   Prevent the password from expiring

•   Disable the account

Figure 4.5 Local User Account Password Options

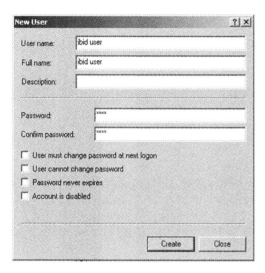

6. Choose Create. If necessary, create other accounts in the same fashion. When finished, select Close.

7. In the left pane, choose Users and verify that the account(s) you created are listed in the right pane.

Modifying a Local User Account

Modifying a local user account is similar to modifying an Active Directory user account, but offers fewer choices. To modify a local user account, follow these steps:

1. From the desktop, right-click My Computer and then choose Manage.

2. In the left pane of the Computer Management console, expand the Local Users and Groups container and choose the Users folder.

3. In the right pane, right-click the user account you wish to modify and choose Properties (Figure 4.6).

Figure 4.6 Local User Account Properties

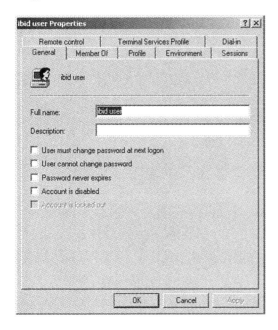

4.   In the User Properties window, you may specify the local groups to which this user account belongs, the user profile information, and remote access (dial-in) permissions. When you are finished with modifications, choose OK.

Exploring Computer Accounts

A computer account, like a user account, authenticates and grants permission to computers on an Active Directory network. Like computers in Windows NT 4.0, computers running Windows NT 4.0 and Windows 2000 must have a computer account in the domain in order to join the domain.

Creating a Computer Account in Active Directory

A computer account can be created in any Active Directory container, including the domain-level container. However, if you create a computer account at the domain level, you reduce your delegation options and may increase the complexity of your network. Like user accounts, it is best to implement OUs and organize computer accounts within these OUs.

To create a computer account, perform the following tasks:

1. From the Start Menu, choose Programs, Administrative Tools and then select Active Directory Users and Computers.

2. In the left pane of the Active Directory Users and Computers console, expand the Active Directory tree to show the OU in which you will create the new computer account.

3. Right-click the OU, choose New and then select Computer.

4. In the New Object—Computer window, enter the computer name (Figure 4.7).

Figure 4.7 New Computer Account Name Assignment

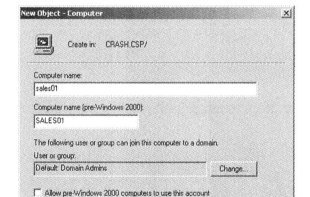

5. You can assign permission to add this computer to the domain to an individual user or group of users by following these steps:

    a. Choose Change.

    b. In the Select User or Group window, choose the user or group and then select OK.

Note: The default permission allows members of the Domain Admins group to add computers to the domain.

6. If the computer account you are adding will belong to a pre-Windows 2000 computer, choose Allow pre-Windows 2000 computers to use this account and then select Next.

7. If this computer account will be assigned to a managed computer (one that will be installed using Remote Installation Services (RIS)), choose This is a managed computer, enter the computer's Globally Unique Identifier (GUID) and then select Next.

 Note: The GUID is used by RIS to add the computer to the domain during a remote installation of Windows 2000. If you specify a GUID, you will be asked which RIS server will support the client during installation.

8. Review the summary information and then choose Finish.

Managing Active Directory Objects

One of the most useful features of Active Directory is its ability to transcend the physical structure of a network and allow you to organize objects in logical groupings. Active Directory is flexible and changeable. If an object needs to be moved from one OU to another, it can be moved without the need to delete the old object and create a new one. In addition, Active Directory provides a search utility to find objects within the Active Directory.

Moving Active Directory Objects

You will need to move objects in the Active Directory when administrative or organizational needs call for a change. For example, you may wish to move an administrator's user account to a different OU to reflect the administrator's change in responsibilities.

When you move an object, the following rules apply:

- Permissions granted directly to the object remain with the object

- Permissions assigned to the old OU do not move with the object

- Objects inherit the permissions of the new OU

To move an object in Active Directory, start by opening the Active Directory Users and Computers console:

1. From the Start Menu, choose Programs, Administrative Tools and then select Active Directory Users and Computers.

2. In the left pane, choose the OU that contains the object you wish to move. This may require expanding several containers (Figure 4.8).

Figure 4.8 Object Relocation

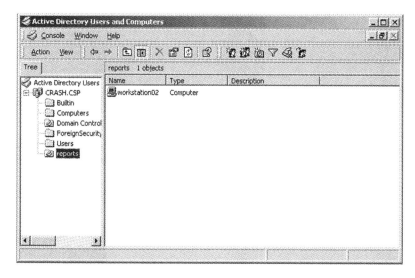

3. In the right pane, right-click the object you wish to move and choose Move.

4. In the Move window, choose the destination OU for the object and then select OK. Again, this may require expanding several containers (Figure 4.9).

Figure 4.9 Destination OU Selection

5. In the left pane, choose the target OU, and verify that the object has been moved (it appears in the right pane).

Tip: You can simultaneously move multiple objects to the same destination. When selecting the object to move, hold down the control key and select multiple objects. All selected objects will be moved to the same destination OU.

Locating Active Directory Objects

Finding objects within the Active Directory can be difficult, especially in larger networks. However, Active Directory includes a Find feature that allows you to search the directory for objects based on the type of object and any number of attributes of the object.

 Note: The Find feature is available to users with administrative access to the Active Directory. Other users can search the Active Directory by selecting the Start Menu, choosing Search and then selecting the type of search they wish to perform.

To locate an object from within Active Directory, use the Find command as follows:

1. From the Start Menu, choose Programs, Administrative Tools and then select Active Directory Users and Computers.

2. In the Active Directory Users and Computers console, choose the domain in which you wish to search, select Action and then select Find.

3. In the Find menu, choose the type of object you wish to find.

4. In the In menu, choose an option to either search the domain or the entire directory.

5. Specify the criteria you wish to locate and then choose Find Now (Figure 4.10).

Figure 4.10 Active Directory Find Utility

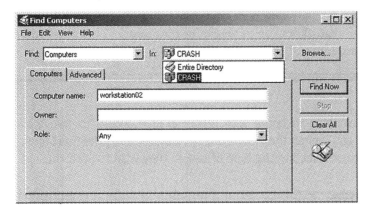

Notice that as you choose the object type, your choice for searchable attributes changes. Your basic choices include the following:

Users, Contacts, and Groups—Name and description

Computers—Computer name, owner, and role

Printers—Name, location, and model

Shared Folders—Name and keywords

Organizational Units—Name

Custom Search—A wide variety of choices

The custom search allows you to find an object based on less-often-used criteria. These choices are also available by selecting the Advanced page for each object type. For example, an advanced search on user accounts allows you to find a user based on over 50 attributes, including the user's phone number, division, department, title, or office location.

Note: You can search all of the information you enter when creating and modifying user accounts.

When the search is complete, the results display at the bottom of the window. Depending on the type of objects searched, you can perform various administrative tasks from this location. For example, after a search for user accounts, you can right-click any of the accounts listed to perform the following:

- Rename the account

- Delete the account

- Add the account to a group

- Disable the account

- Reset the password

- Move the account to a new OU

- Open the home page (Web page) for the user

- Send e-mail to the user

- Create a shortcut to the user object

- Access the Properties page for the user account

Active Directory Groups

You can organize users within the Active Directory using groups. Like Windows NT 4.0, you place user accounts into groups to simplify management. You assign security permissions to the group object rather than to each individual, greatly reducing administrative overhead.

Defining Active Directory Group Types

In Windows NT 4.0, group management is relatively simple. There are two group types: global and local. Users are placed in global groups, global groups are placed in local groups, and local groups are assigned security permissions. This model is known as the A-G-L-P model (**a**ccounts are placed in **g**lobal groups, which are placed in **l**ocal groups, which are assigned **p**ermissions).

In Windows 2000 Active Directory, the naming and function of groups has changed significantly. Active Directory supports two group types: security groups and distribution groups. Within either of these groups, you may create one of three group scopes: domain local, global, or universal.

 Note: Some of the group scopes and their options are only available in a native-mode domain. For example, you cannot create universal group scopes in mixed-mode domains.

Although both group types may be used on your Active Directory network, your network requirements dictate the type of group you create. Both group types serve a unique purpose within the domain:

Security Groups—These groups grant or deny permission to network resources. User accounts and computer accounts may be added to a security group. Security groups can also be used for e-mail distribution.

Distribution Groups—These groups are used specifically for sending e-mail messages to groups of users. E-mail-enabled applications, like Microsoft Exchange Server, use distribution groups. You cannot assign security permissions to distribution groups.

At first glance, it appears as though distribution groups are unnecessary, since security groups can be used for the assignment of permissions and for e-mail distribution. However, security groups decrease server performance during the logon process. If you want to generate an e-mail distribution group that does not need permissions associated with it, create a distribution group.

Note: When a user logs on to the network, Windows 2000 generates an access token for that user. All security groups to which the user belongs are added to this token, creating a demand on the server and generating more network traffic. Distribution groups are not added to the token.

Defining Active Directory Group Scopes

Both security and distribution groups have a scope attribute. The scope determines membership in the group and where in the network the group is used. There are three group scopes:

Domain local groups—Use domain local groups to grant permissions to resources within the local domain only. Members of a domain local group can come from any domain in the forest.

Global groups—Global groups are assigned permissions to resources anywhere in the forest, but members can only come from the domain in which the global group is created.

Universal groups—Universal groups can contain members from any domain in the forest and may be assigned permissions to any resource in the forest.

Membership in these group scopes depends upon the domain mode. By default, an Active Directory domain runs in mixed mode, which supports Active Directory-based and Windows NT 4.0-based domain controllers. If your network consists of only Active Directory domain controllers, it is wise to switch the network to native mode. Native mode permits additional group memberships not available in mixed mode. Table 4.1 defines the membership and permission rules for each of the three scope types in mixed-mode and native-mode domains.

Table 4.1 Group Scope Membership Rules

Group Scope	Available Members (mixed mode)	Available Members (native mode)	Membership	Granted Permissions
Domain local	User accounts and global groups from any domain.	Any user account, global group, or universal group in the forest or other domain local groups from the same domain.	Domain local groups in the same domain.	Resources in the same domain.
Global	User accounts from the same domain.	User accounts and global groups from the same domain.	Any universal or domain local group in the forestor global groups in the same domain.	Resources in any domain in the forest.
Universal	Not available.	Any user account, global group, or universal group in the forest.	Any domain local or universal group in the forest.	Resources in any domain in the forest.

Selecting and Managing Active Directory Groups

Choosing which group to use is an important consideration in your overall network structure. Universal groups can be granted permission to any resource in the forest and may contain user accounts from any domain in the forest. In short, this means you can use universal groups for all your security needs. However, you should not always use universal groups, especially on larger networks with more than one global catalog server.

All three-group scopes are listed in the global catalog (the catalog of all objects in the forest). Members of universal groups are also listed in the global catalog, whereas members of domain local and global groups are not. Each change to a universal group's membership replicates to all global catalog servers, whereas membership in the other two groups does not affect the global catalog. Therefore, changes to universal groups cause more network traffic.

Note: On a small network with only one global catalog server, exclusive use of universal groups may be acceptable. However, it is not a good habit to develop, especially as your network grows.

A second drawback of universal groups is an increase in access token sizes. When a user logs on to a domain, the access token contains only those global and domain local groups that apply to the local domain. However, it also must contain every universal group in which the user is a member, even if the universal group is not used in the local domain.

Tip: A good way to use universal groups is to limit universal group membership to domain local groups and global groups, not individual user accounts. When you need to change user membership, make the change in the global or domain local group so no replication traffic is generated.

Planning a Group Strategy

Much like group management in Windows NT 4.0, there is a recommended method for placing user accounts in groups and assigning permissions to groups. In general, the A-G-L-P rule holds true with Windows 2000. In this case, user accounts should be placed in global groups. Global groups can only contain user accounts from the same domain. The global groups are then placed in domain local groups, and the domain local groups are assigned permissions to resources. In a multiple-domain network, place the global groups in a universal group and then place the universal group in domain local groups, conforming to the A-G-U-L-P model.

For example, suppose your company has two locations, one in Seattle and one in Prague. Each location is represented by its own domain tree within your company's forest. You want sales managers in both regions to have the same access to monthly sales records throughout the forest. The most effective solution is as follows:

1. Create a global group in each domain named Seattle_Sales and Prague_Sales.

2. Add the appropriate user accounts in each domain to that domain's global group.

3. Create a universal group named Sales_Univ and add the two global groups to Sales_Univ.

4. Create domain local groups wherever access to sales resources is needed and assign the appropriate permissions.

5. Add the Sales_univ group to the domain local groups (Figure 4.11).

Figure 4.11 A-G-U-L-P Example

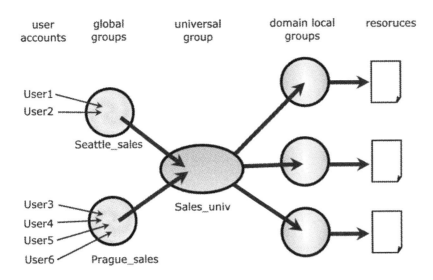

If you need to grant or deny access to the sales records for a user, change the user account membership in the global group only. By removing a user from the global group, you prohibit access to the sales records and you do not generate any replication traffic between global catalog servers.

Creating Active Directory Groups

You create Active Directory groups from within the Active Directory Users and Computers console. To create a new group, perform the following steps:

1. From the Start Menu, choose Programs, Administrative Tools and then select Active Directory Users and Computers.

2. In the left pane of the Active Directory Users and Computers console, expand containers and OUs as necessary to find the OU that will contain the new group.

3. Right-click the OU in which the group will be created, choose New and then select Group (Figure 4.12).

Figure 4.12 New Group Creation

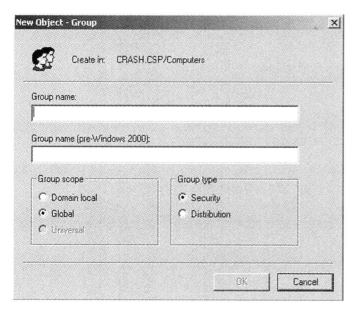

In the New Object—Group window, enter a name for the new group, choose the group scope, select the group type and then select OK. Notice that the group scope Universal is unavailable if this is a mixed-mode domain (Figure 4.13).

Figure 4.13 New Group Definition

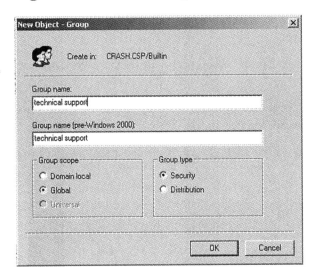

Adding Members to an Active Directory Group

Once you create a group, you must add members. Group membership depends in part on the type and scope of the group, but can include user accounts, other groups, and computer accounts.

 Note: Computer accounts can be granted permissions to resources.

To add a member to a group, follow these steps:

1. From the Start menu, choose Programs, Administrative Tools and then select Active Directory Users and Computers.

2. In the left pane of the Active Directory Users and Computers console, expand the containers and OUs necessary to find the group in which members will be added and then choose the container that holds the group.

3.   In the right pane, right-click the group and choose Properties.

4.   From the Group Properties window, choose the Members property page and then select Add (Figure 4.14).

Figure 4.14 Members Property Page

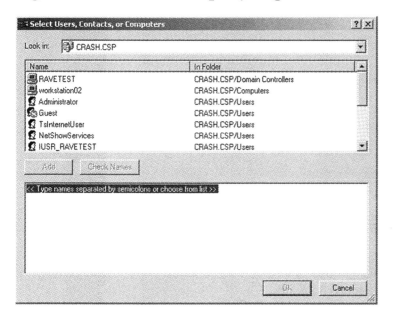

Tip: You can also double-click on an object in the right pane to open the Properties page.

5.   Choose a domain from which to obtain user and group accounts, select the accounts you wish to add and then select Add. Once you have added the accounts, click OK (Figure 4.15).

Figure 4.15 Group Accounts

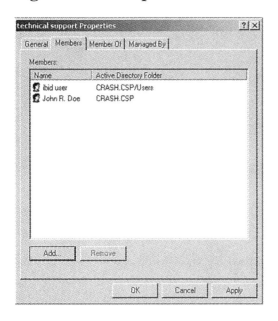

 Note: You can choose multiple user and group accounts by pressing and holding the Control key while selecting accounts.

6.   Verify that the appropriate accounts are listed in the Members: display and then choose OK.

This procedure is the most efficient way to add multiple users to one group. There are times, however, when you will want to add one user to multiple groups. If this is the case, follow these steps:

1.   From the Start menu, choose Programs, Administrative Tools and then select Active Directory Users and Computers.

2.   In the Active Directory Users and Computers console, expand the containers and OUs necessary to find the container that holds the user account and then choose that container.

3. In the right pane, right-click the user and choose Properties.

4. From the User Properties window, choose the Member Of property page and then select Add (Figure 4.16).

Figure 4.16 Member Of Property Page

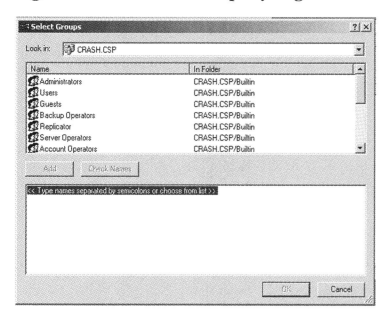

5. Choose the group or groups in which the user will be a member, select Add and then click OK.

6. Verify the group membership listing is correct and then choose OK.

Modifying Active Directory Groups

In Windows NT 4.0, you can add and remove members of local and global groups on the Primary Domain Controller (PDC), but you cannot modify the group (except to delete it). Unlike Windows NT 4.0 groups, Active Directory groups can be changed after they have been created. You can change both the type and scope of an Active Directory group.

Tip: To change group types and modes, the domain must be running in native mode.

To change the group type or scope, follow these steps:

1. From the Start menu, choose Programs, Administrative Tools and then select Active Directory Users and Computers.

2. In the Active Directory Users and Computers console, expand the containers and OUs necessary to find the group and then choose the container that holds the group.

3. In the right pane, right-click the group and choose Properties.

4. From the Properties window, choose the General properties page, select the new group type or scope and then choose OK.

The following rules apply to changing the group scope:

*   A global scope can only be changed to a universal scope

*   A global group cannot be changed if it is a member of another global group

*   A domain local group can only be changed to a universal group

*   The domain local group cannot be changed if it contains other domain local groups

Note: Group scopes can only be changed from scopes with more restrictive membership rules to scopes with less restrictive rules.

Deleting Active Directory Groups

You may decide to delete a group in the Active Directory. When a group is created, it is assigned a Security ID (SID), which is a unique number used to identify the group. When you delete a group, the SID is also deleted and cannot be recreated. In other words, if you delete a group and then create a new one with the same name, the new group does not inherit the membership or permissions of the deleted group. To delete a group, follow these steps:

1. From the Start menu, choose Programs, Administrative Tools and then select Active Directory Users and Computers.

2. In the left pane of the Active Directory Users and Computers console, expand the containers and OUs necessary to find the group and then choose the container that holds the group.

3. In the right pane, right-click the group and choose Delete.

4. Choose Yes to confirm the deletion.

Active Directory Security

Every object in the Active Directory has its own security descriptor called the Discretionary Access Control List (DACL). When you assign permissions to an object, they are stored in the DACL. This allows you to specifically control access privileges to every object throughout the forest. However, assigning permissions to every object would be an administrative nightmare.

Like using groups to simplify management of user accounts, you can simplify management of objects by using OUs. You can create an OU and place objects with identical permission requirements in that OU. This method requires you to grant access permissions once—to the OU—and not to each object within the OU.

Using Active Directory Permissions

To make an Active Directory object available to users on the network, an administrator or the object owner assigns access permissions. The object type determines the permissions you can assign to the object. For example, you can assign the Manage Documents permission for a printer object, but not for a computer object. The following are the five standard permissions available for most objects:

Read—Allows a user with read permission to view the object and objects contained within this object. The user can also view object attributes, the object owner, and the Active Directory permission assigned to the object.

Write—Allows a user to change object attributes, but not object permissions. Write must be combined with the Read permission for the user to make changes.

Create All Child Objects—Allows a user to create objects within the OU.

Delete All Child Objects—Allows a user to delete any type of object contained in the OU.

Full Control—Allows a user to change permissions, take ownership, and perform all of the functions of the other standard permissions.

In addition to these standard permissions, Windows 2000 offers special permissions that allow you to assign permissions on a more detailed level. For example, when you grant the standard Read permission, you are actually granting the List Contents, Read All Properties, and Read Permissions special permissions. Special permissions allow you to fine-tune the access a user or group has to an object. You may wish to grant permission to view the OU and its contents, but not view the permissions assigned to it.

With the use of global, domain local, and universal security groups, it is likely that a user account will be assigned multiple permissions to the same object. For example, a user may be a member of two different global groups. Each of these global groups is in a different domain local group, and each of those local groups has been granted different permissions to the same object. The user, then, has two different permissions for the same object. When multiple permissions are granted to a user account, the effective permission is the combination of all granted permissions (Figure 4.17).

 Note: The principle of effective permissions has not changed from Windows NT 4.0. The effective permission is still the combination of all assigned permissions.

When you are determining effective permissions in Windows NT 4.0, the access permission "No Access" overrules all other permissions. If a user belongs to a group with Full Control access to a shared folder and also belongs to a group with No Access permission to the same folder, the user is denied access to the folder.

Figure 4.17 Effective Permissions

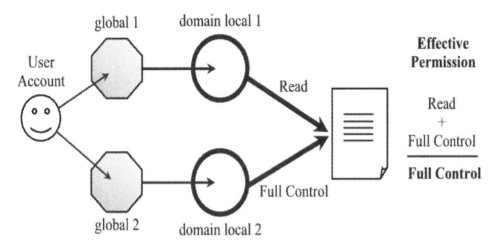

The No Access permission is not included in Windows 2000. Instead, you can deny specific permissions. For each permission you grant to a user, you may also deny that same permission to another user. A denied permission takes precedence over a granted permission, much like No Access takes precedence over all other permissions in Windows NT 4.0.

 Warning: Be careful denying access. Make sure that at least one user account is granted Full Control to an object or you may have an Active Directory object that is inaccessible to everyone, even an administrator.

Granting Active Directory Permissions

When you grant permission for an object, you are editing that object's DACL. To add or change a permission, follow these steps:

1. From the Start Menu, choose Programs, Administrative Tools and then select Active Directory Users and Computers.

2. In the Active Directory Users and Computers console, choose View and then select Advanced Features (Figure 4.18).

 Tip: By default, you cannot view the security settings of Active Directory objects, even if you are logged on as an administrator. You must enable Advanced Features to view and change permissions.

Figure 4.18 Active Directory Advanced Features

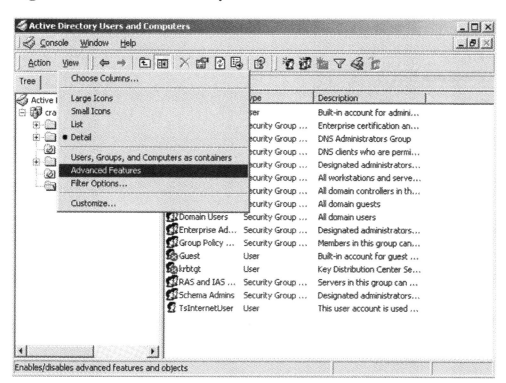

3. In the left pane, expand containers as necessary to find the object on which you are changing permissions.

4. Right-click the object and choose Properties.

5. From the Object Properties window, choose the Security property page (Figure 4.19).

 Note: If the object is an OU or a container, it appears in the left pane. Otherwise, it appears in the right pane.

Figure 4.19 Securities Property Page

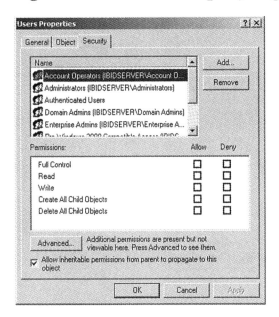

6. If you are adding a new user or group account, choose Add, select the user or group account(s) you are adding, select Add and then choose OK (Figure 4.20).

Figure 4.20 Permissions

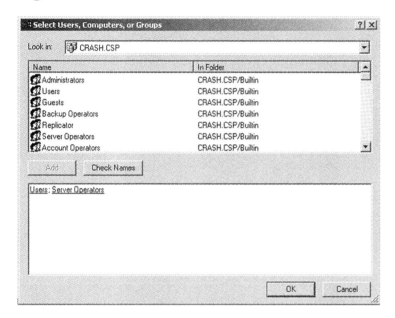

7. To grant permissions to an account, choose the account name and then select the permissions you wish to grant in the Allow list.

8. To deny permissions, choose the user or group account and then select the permissions you wish to deny in the Deny list (Figure 4.21).

Figure 4.21 Standard Permissions

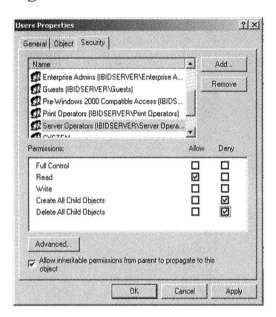

To view or assign special permissions, follow these steps:

1. Below the list of standard permissions, choose Advanced.

2. In the Access Control Settings window, choose the Permissions property page and then select View/Edit.

3. In the Permission Entry page, choose the Properties page and then select the special permissions you wish to allow or deny (Figure 4.22).

4. Choose OK in each open window to save your configuration changes and return to the Active Directory Users and Computers console.

Figure 4.22 Special Permissions

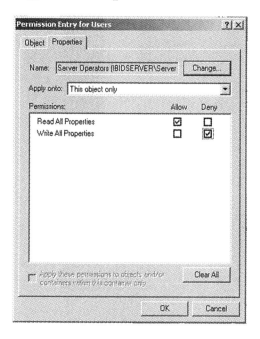

Using Permission Inheritance

To simplify administration, Windows 2000 allows you to assign permissions to an OU and have those permissions automatically assigned to all child objects (objects within the OU). For example, if you have assigned an administrator Full Control for an OU that contains User Accounts, the administrator has full control for all user accounts within that OU. You may then prevent inheritance of permissions on individual child objects as necessary. To apply permission inheritance, begin by opening the Active Directory Users and Computers console:

1. From the Start Menu, choose Programs, Administrative Tools and then select Active Directory Users and Computers.

2. In the Active Directory Users and Computers console, choose View and verify that Advanced Features is checked.

3. Right-click the object or OU on which you are changing inheritance and then choose Properties.

4. From the Object Properties window, choose the Security property page and then select Advanced.

5. Choose the entry you wish to view or change and select View/Edit.

6. In the Apply onto: menu, choose the appropriate option. For example, to have the permission propagate to all child objects, select "This object and all child objects" (Figure 4.23).

Figure 4.23 Permission Inheritance

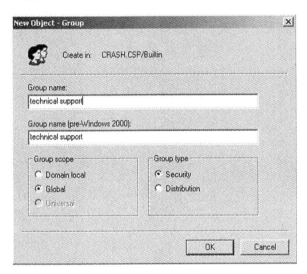

7. Choose OK in each open window to save your configuration changes and return to the Active Directory Users and Computers console.

To prevent a child object from inheriting the permissions of the parent object, follow these steps:

1. From the Start Menu, choose Programs, Administrative Tools and then select Active Directory Users and Computers.

2. In the Active Directory Users and Computers console, choose View and verify that Advanced Features is checked.

3. Right-click the object on which you are preventing inheritance and then choose Properties.

4. From the object properties window, choose the Security property page.

Note: Inherited permissions appear in the list of permissions as gray boxes with check marks. Permissions directly granted to an object appear as white boxes with check marks.

5. Choose the box next to Allow inheritable permissions from parent to propagate to this object to uncheck it (Figure 4.24).

Figure 4.24 Disallowing Inherited Permissions

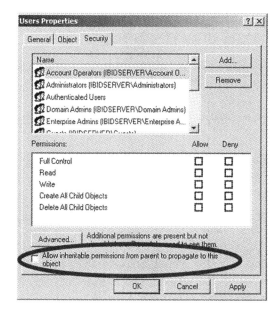

6. From the security window, choose an option (Table 4.2)

Table 4.2 Inherited Permission Options

Option	Description
Copy the inherited permissions.	Preserves permissions inherited from the parent.
Remove the inherited permissions.	Keeps only those permissions that have been assigned directly to the object.

7. Choose Copy or Remove, as appropriate, and then select OK.

Changing Object Ownership

When you create an object in the Active Directory, you become the owner of the object. Each object in the Active Directory has an owner, and this owner controls access to the object.

 Note: If a user creates an object, the user is the owner. If an administrator creates an object, the Administrators group is the owner.

Ownership of an object changes only when another user takes ownership. By default, only users with Full Control to an object can take ownership. However, an owner (or user with Full Control) can assign the Modify Owner permission to another user. This user, in turn, can take ownership of the object.

 Note: For security reasons, you can take ownership of an object, but cannot assign ownership to another user. If, as the owner of an object, you make detrimental changes to the object, you cannot hide the fact that you were the owner.

To take ownership of an object, follow these steps:

1. From the Start Menu, choose Programs, Administrative Tools and then select Active Directory Users and Computers.

2. In the Active Directory Users and Computers console, choose View and verify that Advanced Features is checked.

3. Right-click the object on which you want to take ownership and then choose Properties.

4. From the object Properties window, choose the Security property page and then select Advanced.

5. From the Access Control Settings window, choose the Owner property page, select your user account from the Change owner to: list and then Select OK in each open window to save your configuration changes.

 Tip: If you are a member of the Administrators group, you may also select that group from the list. This makes the administrators group the owner.

Delegating Administrative Control in Active Directory

The task of managing and administering Active Directory can be more work than one person can handle. The hierarchical structure of Active Directory allows you to delegate administrative control over certain portions of the directory, decreasing your workload and administrative responsibility. Delegation of administrative tasks also allows you to structure the Active Directory to better reflect your company's organizational structure.

You can customize and assign administrative roles within the Active Directory in two ways: use the Delegation of Control Wizard and customize the Microsoft Management Console (MMC).

Using the Delegation of Control Wizard

The Delegation of Control Wizard allows you to grant permission to a user or group for an OU. Using the wizard, you can delegate control over a OU, allowing a user to create and modify objects within that OU. To run the Delegation of Control Wizard, start by opening the Active Directory Users and Computers console:

1. From the Start Menu, choose Programs, Administrative Tools and then select Active Directory Users and Computers.

2. In the left pane, expand OUs and containers as necessary to find the OU on which you wish to delegate control.

3. Right-click the OU and choose Delegate Control (Figure 4.25).

Figure 4.25 Control Delegation

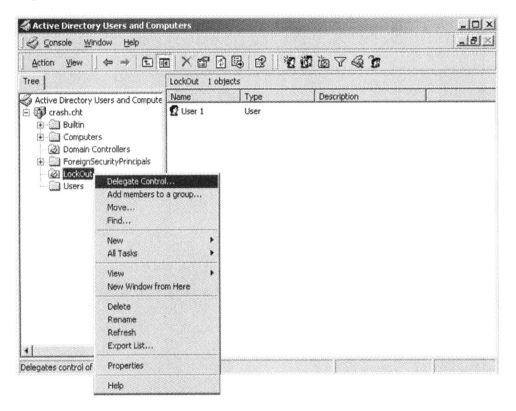

4. Choose Next to start the wizard and then select Add to select users and groups.

5. From the Select Users, Computers, or Groups window, choose the users and groups to whom you are delegating control, select Add, and then choose OK.

6. Confirm the names displayed and then choose Next.

7. In the Tasks to Delegate page, you have the choice to assign common tasks or create a custom task. To assign common tasks, choose the tasks you wish to delegate from the list and then select Next (Figure 4.26). To create a custom task, select "Create a custom task to delegate" and then select Next.

Figure 4.26 Task Delegation Selection

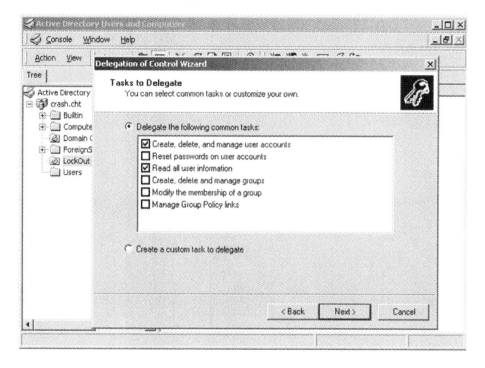

7. If you chose to delegate common tasks, review the summary information and then choose Finish to complete the wizard. If you chose to create a custom task, select "Only the following

objects in the folder," select the objects to which control will be delegated and then select Next (Figure 4.27).

8. Choose the level of permission you want to delegate to those objects you selected on the previous wizard page and then select Next.

9. Review the summary information and then choose Finish.

Figure 4.27 Custom Task Creation

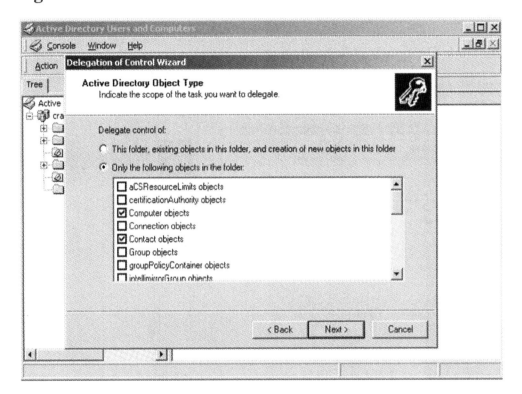

Customizing the Administrative Tools

A powerful feature of Windows 2000 for delegation of administration is the ability to customize the MMC. Used in conjunction with the Delegation of Control wizard, the customization of the

MMC allows you to limit not only what an administrator can manage, but what tools that administrator can use.

The MMC provides a centralized location for many administrative tools. Administrative tools mentioned in this lesson include the Active Directory Users and Computers and the Computer Management consoles. Both of these tools have similar interfaces because they are snap-ins, tools that run within the MMC shell.

After delegating control of certain OUs within the Active Directory, you can send a customized MMC that only contains the needed snap-ins to the administrator. The customized console can be sent through e-mail, stored in a shared folder on the network, or posted to a Web page.

 Note: Customized MMC consoles are saved as files with the .MSC extension.

To create a customized MMC console, start by opening the MMC:

1. From the Start Menu, choose Run, type **MMC** in the Open: box and then select OK. The MMC opens with an empty console named Console1 (Figure 4.28).

Figure 4.28 Empty MMC Console

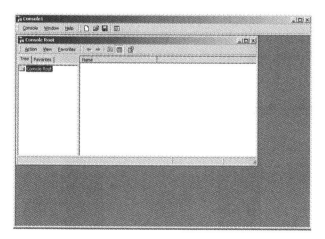

2. From within the MMC, choose Console and then select Add/Remove Snap-in.

3. From the Add/Remove Snap-in window, choose the Standalone property page and then select Add.

4. From the Add Standalone Snap-in window, choose the snap-in you wish to add and then select Add. Notice that the snap-ins you add are listed in the Add/Remove Snap-in window. Continue to add the desired snap-ins and then choose Close (Figure 4.29).

Figure 4.29 New Console Snap-ins

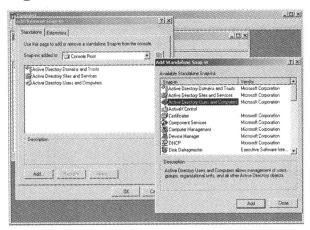

 Note: Some snap-ins you add require additional information. For example, if you add the Computer Management snap-in, you must specify what computer this console will manage.

5. Verify the list of snap-ins you have added and then choose OK.

    The left pane of the console displays the snap-ins you added (Figure 4.30). Leave this window open.

Figure 4.30 New Console Display

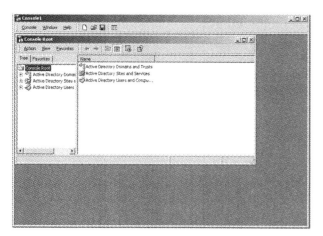

Before saving the console, you must set the mode. There are two modes: author mode and user mode. A user has full control of a console running in author mode, including the ability to add and remove snap-ins. Author mode is the default, but is often not the appropriate choice if you are sending the console to another user.

User mode prohibits the user from adding or removing snap-ins to the console and optionally prohibits the user from customizing and saving changes to the console. Within user mode, you may choose one of the three following types of access:

Full Access—This user mode allows users to use all portions of the console tree and open new windows within the MMC.

Limited Access, Multiple Windows—This user mode allows users to open new windows within the MMC, but restricts user access to a portion of the console.

Limited Access, Single Window—The user is restricted to using only portions of the console and cannot open new windows.

To set the mode of the console, return to the new console you have been creating and then follow these steps:

1. Choose Console and then select Options.

2. Rename the console, choose a console mode, select which, if any, of the three additional restrictions you want to apply and then select OK (Figure 4.31).

Figure 4.31 Console Mode

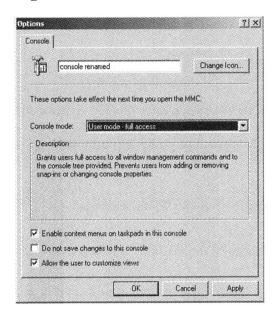

3. From the Console window (now titled with the name you assigned), choose Console and then select Save.

4. Name the console (the name should end in .MSC), choose a folder in which to save the console and then select Save.

You can now distribute the console to the appropriate users. The user only needs to open this file, and the MMC opens with this console.

Vocabulary

Review the following terms in preparation for the certification exam.

Term	Description
access token	The information created when a user logs on to a network that contains the user's assigned permissions and group memberships.
A-G-L-P	The group model used in Windows NT 4.0, in which user accounts are placed in global group s, which are placed in local groups and are assigned permissions.
A-G-U-L-P	A group model in which user accounts are placed in global groups, which are (optionally) placed in universal group s, which are placed in domain local groups and are assigned permissions.
author mode	A console mode that allows the user to add and remove snap-ins from the MMC.
child object	An Active Directory object that is contained within another Active Directory object.
container object	An Active Directory object that contains other objects.
DACL	The Discretionary Access Control List for any object contains the list of permissions assigned to that object.
distribution group	A group type used exclusively for e-mail distribution.
domain local group	A group scope that may contain users from any domain and may be assigned permissions to resources in the same domain.
effective permission	The combination of all permissions assigned to user and the groups to which that user belongs.

Term	Description
global catalog	Information on objects in the entire forest, stored in—and replicated between—the global catalog servers.
global group	A group scope that may contain users only from the same domain, and may be assigned permission to resources in any domain.
Group scope	Defines how the group type will be used. The group scope may be domain local, global, or universal.
group type	Defines the purpose of the group. The group type is either security or distribution.
GUID	The Globally Unique Identifier is used by RIS to join the computer to a domain during an unattended remote installation of Windows 2000.
inheritance	The ability of a child object to be automatically assigned the same permissions as its container object.
mixed mode	A domain mode that supports both Windows 2000 and Windows NT 4.0 domain controllers.
MMC	The Microsoft Management Console provides a centralized location for administrative tools called snap-ins.
multiple-master replication	The copying of Active Directory information among domain controllers, in which the Active Directory can be updated on any domain controller.
native mode	A domain mode that supports only Windows 2000 domain controllers.
object	An item in the Active Directory.
organizational unit (OU)	An Active Directory object that contains objects that share similar characteristics.

Term	Description
owner	The user that creates an object or any user that has Full Control to the object and takes ownership.
PDC	The Primary Domain Controller in Windows NT 4.0 networks.
RIS	Remote Installation Services allows Windows 2000 Professional software to be installed across the network.
security group	A group type that is used for assigning permissions and may be used for e-mail distribution.
SID	The Security ID is a unique code assigned to each group and user account to identify that account on the network.
snap-in	An administrative tool designed to run in the MMC.
universal group	A group scope that can contain users from any domain and may be assigned permissions to resources in any domain.
user mode	A console mode that allows a user to use a customized console in the MMC, but not add or remove snap-ins.

In Brief

If you want to...	Then do this...
Group together objects that have the same security needs	Create an OU, assign permissions to the OU, and allow the child objects to inherit the permissions of the OU.
Place users from one domain into a group and assign the group permission to resources in a different domain	Use either a global or universal group.
Allow a user to manage one group of user accounts, but not have administrative rights to other user accounts	Place those user accounts that will be managed in their own OU and delegate control of that OU to the administrator.
Create a user account on a Windows 2000 member server	Use the Computer Management console. A member server does not contain the Active Directory, so you can only create a local user account.
Change a group type or scope	Open the properties page for the group and change the type or scope. If you are changing the scope, make sure the domain is running in native mode.
Search the Active Directory for all users who have "H" for a middle initial	Using Active Directory Users and Computers, use the Find utility to perform an advanced search on user attributes and search for all middle names that start with the letter H.
Combine users that receives the same e-mail newsletter once a week	Create a distribution group type.

Lesson 4 Activities

Complete the following activities to better prepare you for the certification exam.

1. Create two OUs in your domain named TestOU and SalesOU.

2. Create a user account within the TestOU named user1. Assign a password to the account and, for security, disable the account. You will not be logging on to the domain with this account.

3. Move the user1 user account to the SalesOU.

4. For the user1 user account, perform the following:

    *   Enter a mailing address

    *   Make the user the vice president of the Sales department

    *   Allow the user to access the server remotely, but require the server to call the user back to a preset number

5. Search for all users who are in the sales department. Verify that user1 appears in the list.

6. Within the SalesOU, make a Security group with a domain local scope named DL-Test.

7. Make user1 a member of DL-Test.

8. Change DL-Test to have a universal scope and then rename it to Uni-Test.

9. Using the Delegation of Control wizard, allow user1 to have the ability to add, remove, and manage user accounts in the SalesOU.

10. Create a custom console for user1 that includes the Active Directory Users and Computers, Disk Defragmenter, and Computer Management snap-ins. The Computer Management console should be for the local computer. Name the console User1 and set it to run in User mode, Full Access.

Answers to Lesson 4 Activities

1. Use Active Directory Users and Computers to create the OUs. You may create them anywhere in the Active Directory structure, but it may be wise to put them within the same container so that you can easily find them.

2. Again, use Active Directory Users and Computers. When creating the user account, you need to create a fictitious name for the user. In the second screen of the New Object—User, enter a password and choose Account is Disabled.

3. From within Active Directory Users and Computers, right-click the user account and choose Move.

4. Right-click the user account and choose Properties. From the User properties window, the mailing address is entered on the Address property page. Enter the user's title and department on the Organization property page and then set the remote access information on the Dial-in property page.

5. Right-click the server, and choose Find. In the Users, Contacts, and Groups page, select an advanced search. In the Field menu, select User and then select Department. Enter a Value of Sales, and then choose Find Now. Answer Yes to add the search criteria.

6. Right-click the SalesOU, choose New and then select Group. Make sure you select Domain Local for the scope and Security for the type.

7. Right-click the DL-Test group and choose Properties. Select the Members property page, click Add and add user1.

8. Right-click the DL-Test group and choose Properties. Select the universal group scope and then select OK. Right-click the DL-Test group again and this time choose Rename. Rename the group.

9. Right-click the SalesOU and choose Delegate Control. In the wizard, add user1 and then select Create, delete, and manage user accounts under the common tasks list.

10. From the Start Menu, choose Run and run MMC. In the blank MMC console, select Console and then select Add/Remove Snap-in. Add the necessary snap-ins. In the MMC, choose Console again and select Options. Name the console here and select User mode-full access.

Lesson 4 Quiz

These questions test your knowledge of features, vocabulary, procedures, and syntax.

1. A printer object is in the lasers1 OU. The Admin domain local group has Full Control to the Lasers1 OU. The printer is moved to the Lasers2 OU. The Admins group has been granted Manage Documents to the Lasers2 OU. What permissions does the Admin group have to the printer?

   A. Full Control

   B. Manage Documents

   C. Full Control and Manage Documents

   D. No Access

2. Caleb is a member of two groups: users and temp. The users group has been granted Read and Write permission to the Employee Public OU. The temp group has been granted the Read permission and denied the Write permission to the same OU. The Caleb user account has been granted Read, Write, and Create All Child Objects permission to the OU. What is Caleb's effective permission?

   A. Read, Write, and Create All Child Objects

   B. Read and Write

   C. Read and Create All Child Objects

   D. Read Only

3. If an object is moved from one OU to another, which of the following is true?

   A. Permissions granted to the object are lost

   B. Permissions granted to the original OU are moved with the object

   C. Permissions granted to the object are moved with the object

   D. Permissions granted to the original OU are removed from the OU

4. Members of which group type(s) are included in the global catalog?

   A. Universal only

   B. Global and domain local

   C. Global and universal

   D. Global only

5. Which group type can contain only user accounts and groups from the same domain as the group?
    A. Universal groups
    B. Global groups
    C. Domain local groups
    D. OU groups

6. Which of the following can be members of a domain local group running in native mode? (Select all that apply)
    A. Global groups
    B. Users from other domains in the forest
    C. Universal groups
    D. Other local groups from the same domain

7. Which mode allows a user to remove a snap-in to a customized MMC console?
    A. Author Mode
    B. User Mode, Full Control
    C. User Mode, Full Access
    D. Native Mode

8. Who can take ownership of an object?
    A. Members of Domain Admins only
    B. Members of Domain Users
    C. Any user with Full Control permission to the object
    D. Only the owner of the object

9. To which resources can a global group be granted permissions? (Select all that apply)
    A. Resources in the same domain
    B. Resources in other domains in the forest
    C. Only resources with associated local groups
    D. Only resources with associated universal groups

10. Which domain mode supports universal groups?
    A. Author Mode
    B. User Mode
    C. Mixed Mode
    D. Native Mode

Answers to Lesson 4 Quiz

1. Answer B is correct. When an object is moved from one OU to another, it inherits the permissions of the new OU.

    Answers A and C are incorrect. None of the permissions assigned to the old OU apply once the object is moved.

    Answer D is incorrect. No Access is not a valid permission in Windows 2000.

2. Answer C is correct. The effective permission is the combination of all other permissions. In this case, the combination is Read + Write + Create + Denied Write (Write has been denied, and a denied permission supercedes a granted permission).

    Answers A, B, and D are incorrect.

3. Answer C is correct. When an object is moved from one OU to another three rules apply: permissions assigned directly to the object remain with the object, permissions assigned to the original OU do not move with the object, and permissions assigned to the new OU are inherited.

    Answers A, B, and D are incorrect.

4. Answer A is correct. Members of universal groups are included in the global catalog.

    Answers B, C, and D are incorrect. Global and domain local groups are included in the global catalog, but the members are these groups are not.

5. Answer B is correct. Global groups may only contain user accounts from the same domain. A global group may also contain other global groups from the same domain if the domain is running in native mode.

    Answers A and C are incorrect.

    Answer D is incorrect. OU group is not a valid group type.

6. Answers A, B, C, and D are correct. In native mode, domain local groups may contain users from the same domain, users from any other domain in the forest, global groups and universal groups from any domain, and domain local groups from the same domain.

7. Answer A is correct. Author mode is the only console mode that allows snap-ins to be added or removed.

Answers B and C are incorrect. User mode allows a user to use the console and (sometimes) open new windows within the console, but does not allow the removal of consoles.

Answer D is incorrect. Native mode is a domain mode, not a console mode. 8. Answer C is correct. Any user with Full Control to an object may take ownership of that object.

Answers A, B, and D are incorrect.

9. Answer B is correct. A global group can be granted permission to resources located anywhere in the forest.

   Answer A is incorrect.

   Answers C and D are incorrect. Although it is a good idea to place global groups in either local groups or universal groups and then assign the local or universal group permissions, global groups can be assigned permissions.

10. Answer D is correct. Universal groups can only be created in native-mode domains.

    Answer C is incorrect.

    Answers A and B are incorrect. Author Mode and User Mode are console modes, not domain modes.

Lesson 5

Upgrading a Windows NT 4.0 Network to Windows 2000

Microsoft Windows 2000 supports many new networking technologies previously not available in Windows-based networks. Included in these new networking enhancements are improved security and administration features, enhanced Domain Name System (DNS) and Dynamic Host Configuration Protocol (DHCP) services and the implementation of Active Directory. Because each of these features greatly simplifies administration and use of the network, it is beneficial to network administrators to migrate (upgrade) their network to a Windows 2000-based network. Changing an entire network from Microsoft Windows NT 4.0 to

Windows 2000 involves four steps: planning the upgrade, upgrading the domain controllers, upgrading the member servers and then upgrading the client computers. Only the first two steps are absolutely necessary to begin using most of the features of Active Directory.

After completing this lesson, you should have a better understanding of the following topics:

* Network Upgrade Planning

* Root Domain Administration

* Domain Controller Upgrades

* Member Server Upgrades

* Client Upgrades

Network Upgrade Planning

When you decide to migrate your Windows NT 4.0 network to Windows 2000, you should have a clear idea of how you want the network to be structured, what roles current servers will perform in the new network and in what stages the migration will occur. In other words, migrating an entire network takes careful planning. Before beginning any operating system upgrades, you must do the following:

- Design an Active Directory network model that matches your current Windows NT 4.0 domain model

- Identify network requirements and test the domain controllers for Windows 2000 compatibility

- Develop a naming strategy for the network

- Implement a disaster recovery plan

Once you have performed these tasks, you can begin the upgrade process, starting with the domain controllers.

Choosing an Upgrade Model

When upgrading a Windows NT 4.0 network, take into consideration the current domain model used in the network. Because Windows NT 4.0 does not use Active Directory, domains and domain models are entirely different in Windows NT 4.0 from those in Windows 2000. Before discussing upgrade options, a review of Windows NT 4.0 domain models is necessary.

A domain is a logical collection of computers and network resources. In Windows NT 4.0, each domain has one Primary Domain Controller (PDC). The PDC contains the read-and-write copy of the directory database that lists all user accounts, computer accounts, and access permissions for the entire domain. Each domain may have one or more Backup Domain Controllers (BDCs). BDCs contain a read-only copy of the directory database and provide load balancing and fault tolerance if the PDC fails. When a user logs on to the domain, any one of the domain controllers can authenticate the user.

For organizational reasons, Windows NT 4.0 networks often contain more than one domain. If two or more domains need to share information (user accounts, for example), trusts are implemented among the domains to allow them to pass information. In Windows NT 4.0, trusts are always one-way, non-transitive trusts, meaning that any given trust only works in one direction, and no trusts are implied. Trusts are represented by arrows to indicate their unidirectional nature. When one domain

(Domain A) trusts another domain (Domain B), Domain A can access the user and groups accounts stored in Domain B (Figure 5.1).

Figure 5.1 One-Way Trust

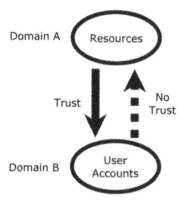

You can assign permission to resources in Domain A to user accounts in Domain B, but the inverse is not true. Resources in Domain B (the trusted domain) are not available to user accounts in Domain A. To have Domain B trust Domain A, you must implement a second one-way trust.

In Windows NT 4.0 terms, a domain that is trusted by another domain is known as the master domain. A domain that trusts another domain is called a resource domain. The combination of domains and trusts results in four possible Windows NT 4.0 domain models. These models are as follows:

Single Domain Model—The single domain model is the simplest. In this model, there is only one domain that contains all user and group accounts, as well as all resources. No trusts are needed, since there are no other domains to trust (Figure 5.2).

Figure 5.2 Single Domain Model

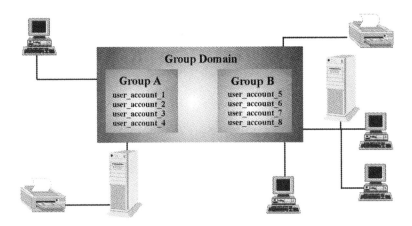

Single Master Domain Model—In the single master domain model, one domain (the master domain) contains all of the user and group accounts for the entire organization. Other domains contain the network resources. These resource domains trust the master domain, which allows them to assign permissions on local resources to users and groups from the master domain. This model allows for centralized administration of user accounts and localized control of resources (Figure 5.3).

Figure 5.3 Single Master Domain Model

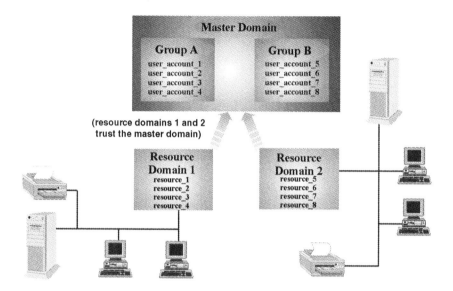

Multiple Master Domain Model—In a multiple master domain model, two or more domains contain the user and group accounts. Like a single master domain model, other domains contain resources and trust the master domains in order to obtain the user and group accounts. Typically, a multiple master domain model is used when a corporation is too large for a single master domain model or when geographical or political reasons dictate separate control of user and group accounts (Figure 5.4).

Figure 5.4 Multiple Master Domain Model

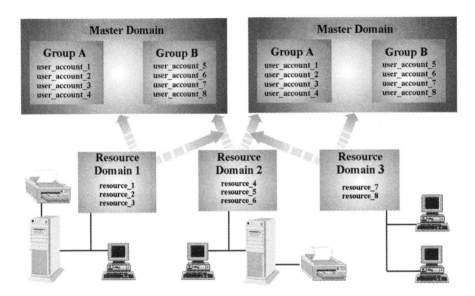

Complete Trust Domain Model—In the complete trust model, each domain contains user and group accounts and resources. Each domain serves as both a master domain and a resource domain because each domain trusts all other domains. This creates potentially dozens of trusts and a lack of any centralized control of the network. This type of domain model is used in corporations that require total autonomy over user accounts and resources. It is also found in poorly-planned networks (Figure 5.5).

 Note: The total number of trusts that need to be created in a complete trust model is determined by multiplying the number of domains (n) by the number of domains less one: n * (n-1) = trusts

Example: a network with 5 domains requires 20 trusts.

Figure 5.5 Complete Trust Domain Model

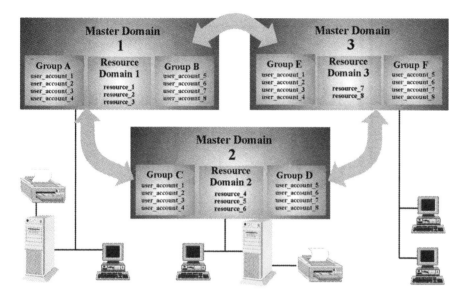

Windows 2000 Active Directory networks do not use the Windows NT 4.0 models. Domains are most often built on a hierarchical structure using DNS domains and as such, trusts are not needed between domains.

When creating an Active Directory network, you first create a root domain. This root domain is the foundation of your company's network. Domains created after this are either child domains (domains that share a common DNS domain name with the root) or are separate domains within the same forest (Figure 5.6). A series of domains that share a common namespace (portion of the DNS name) is called a tree. Domains or domain trees that have a namespace different from the root domain are said to be separate trees in the same forest. Trusts are not needed between domains in the same tree but are needed between trees in the same forest. Trusts implemented in Windows 2000 are two-way, transitive trusts.

Figure 5.6 Active Directory Forest

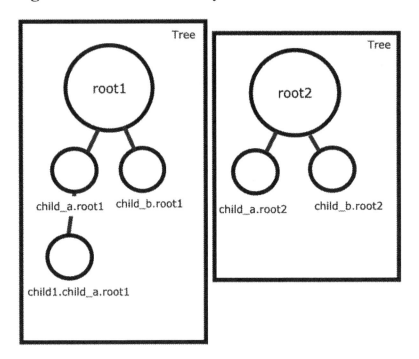

When migrating a Windows NT 4.0 network model to a Windows 2000 Active Directory network, consider the following rules:

Single domain model—create a single Active Directory domain (the root). No other model planning is needed (Figure 5.7).

Figure 5.7 Single Domain Migration

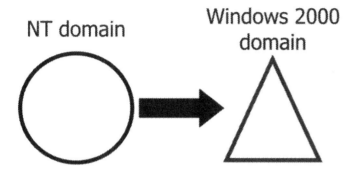

Single master domain model—make the Windows NT 4.0 master domain the Active Directory root domain. Make each of the resource domains child domains to the root (Figure 5.8).

Figure 5.8 Single Master Domain Migration

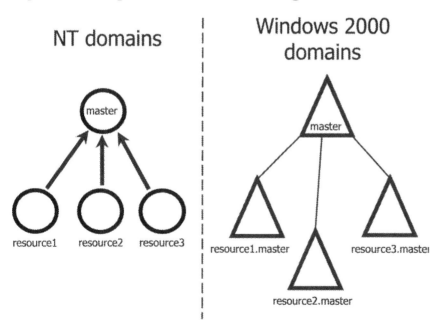

Multiple master domain model—create a new root domain. This domain will not contain any user or group accounts (it is an empty place-holder). Make each of the Windows NT 4.0 master domains a child domain to the root and make each of the resource domains a child domain to one of the former master domains (Figure 5.9).

Figure 5.9 Multiple Master Domain Migration

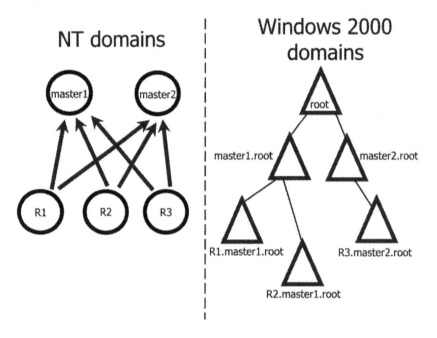

Complete trust model—create an empty root domain and make every Windows NT 4.0 domain a child to this domain. Since each domain is a child within the same tree, you eliminate the need to con-figure and maintain trusts between any of the domains (Figure 5.10). Alternatively, you can make each domain a separate tree in the same forest. This requires the use of trusts.

Figure 5.10 Complete Trust Domain Migration

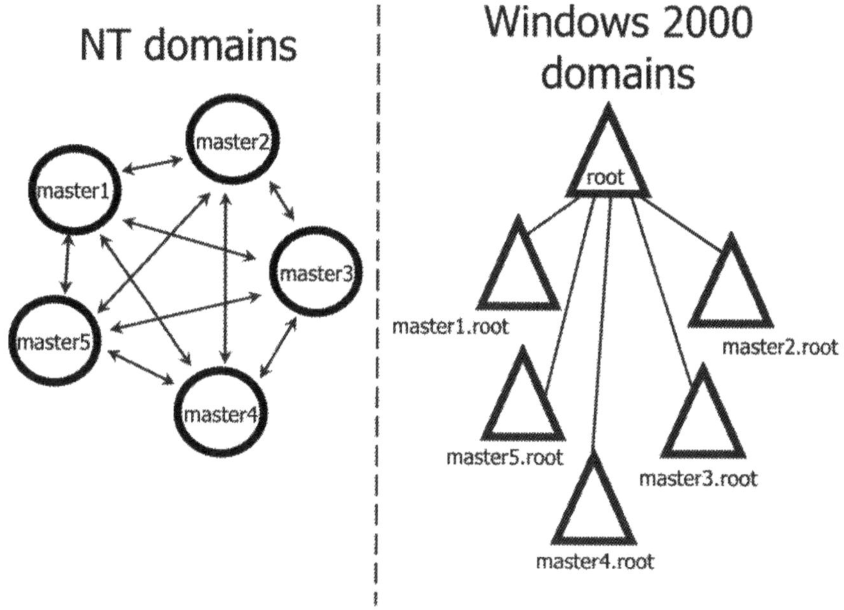

Identifying Network Requirements

Before you begin the upgrade process, make sure that the network has the needed services available and that the domain controllers are going to be capable of running Windows 2000.

A network running Active Directory must have the DNS and DHCP services. These services do not need to be running on a domain controller, but both services need to be available to the Active Directory domain controllers. In addition, the DNS service must support dynamic updates and service (SRV) resource records. Dynamic updates allow the DHCP service and clients to automatically update the DNS database as changes occur. SRV records allow computers to identify the role of other computers listed in the DNS database.

Note: The DNS dynamic update protocol is defined in the Request For Comments (RFC) 2136. SRV resource records are defined in RFC 2052. RFCs can be found at the following Web address: http://www.rfc-editor.org.

In addition to these two network requirements, you must make sure that the domain controllers are capable of running Windows 2000. Make sure that the minimum hardware requirements for Windows 2000 Server are met. Also consult the Microsoft Hardware Compatibility List (HCL). The HCL lists the hardware that has been tested and verified to work with Windows 2000. If your hardware is not on this list, it may not work with Windows 2000 unless it emulates (acts like) a piece of hardware on the list. It may be best to replace server components not listed on the HCL rather than take chances.

 Note: The latest version of the HCL can be found at the following Web address: http://www.microsoft.com/hcl.

Another useful tool for determining whether a computer is compatible with Windows 2000 is the Check Upgrade utility. To run the check, insert the Windows 2000 CD. From the Start menu, choose Run, enter the following command and then select OK.

D:\i386\winnt32.exe /CheckUpgradeOnly

Alternately, you may run a batch file. In the I386 folder on the Windows 2000 CD, double-click the file **CHKUPGRD.BAT**. This batch file runs the command presented above. Entering the command or executing the batch file runs the Windows 2000 Setup program in a special diagnostics mode that checks the computer for hardware and software incompatibilities with Windows 2000 and generates a report (Figure 5.11).

Figure 5.11 Check Upgrade Utility

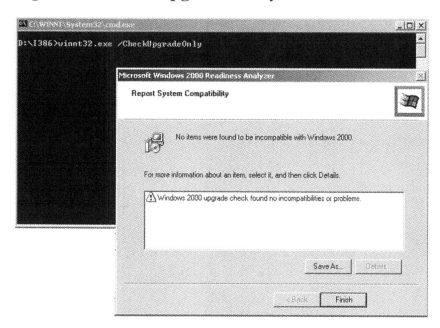

Implementing a Naming Strategy

Windows 2000 uses DNS domain names to name the Active Directory domains. The DNS namespace is a hierarchical structure in which each child domain name is added to the domain name of the parent domain (Figure 5.12). This is the structure of the Internet and is used by Active Directory as well.

Figure 5.12 DNS Namespace

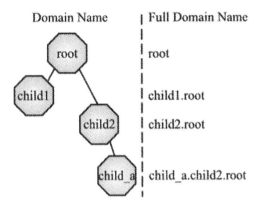

Each child must have a unique name within its parent domain. By requiring a unique name within the parent domain, the full domain also remains unique. Two domains in different parents can be given the same name because their full domain name will be different (Figure 5.13).

Figure 5.13 Two Domains With the Same Name

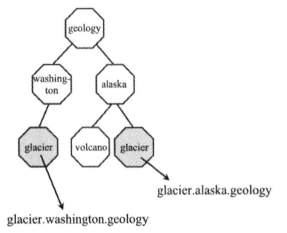

Because every Active Directory domain has a corresponding DNS domain name, your domain names should use standard DNS characters or Unicode characters. Furthermore, to make the network user-friendly, you should strive for short but meaningful domain names. In DNS, the maximum length for each domain name is 63 characters. The total domain namespace cannot exceed 255 characters.

Note: Unicode characters are non-ASCII characters used to support multiple languages. Unicode characters can be used only if all DNS servers on your network support Unicode.

Designing a Site Structure

Active Directory provides your network with a logical structure that is not bound to the physical configuration of the network. In general, the physical construction of the network should not dictate the logical structure in any way. However, domain controllers within a domain replicate (copy) the directory database amongst each other.

This replication uses a significant portion of the network bandwidth and is best carried out over fast network connections. When it is necessary to replicate information over slow links, it is best to configure the times when the replication will occur. This is accomplished by configuring sites. A site is a collection of computers that are all connected by a relatively fast connection (10 Mb or faster). Replication within a site occurs automatically. You can control replication between sites by creating site links.

Sites and domains are independent of one another. A domain may span multiple sites, and one site may contain several domains (Figure 5.14). For each domain in any given site, you should have at least one domain controller. This domain controller provides Active Directory services to local clients. Without a domain controller in the same site, a client logging on to the domain needs to contact a domain controller in another site, generating network traffic across a slow link.

Figure 5.14 Multiple Sites and Domains

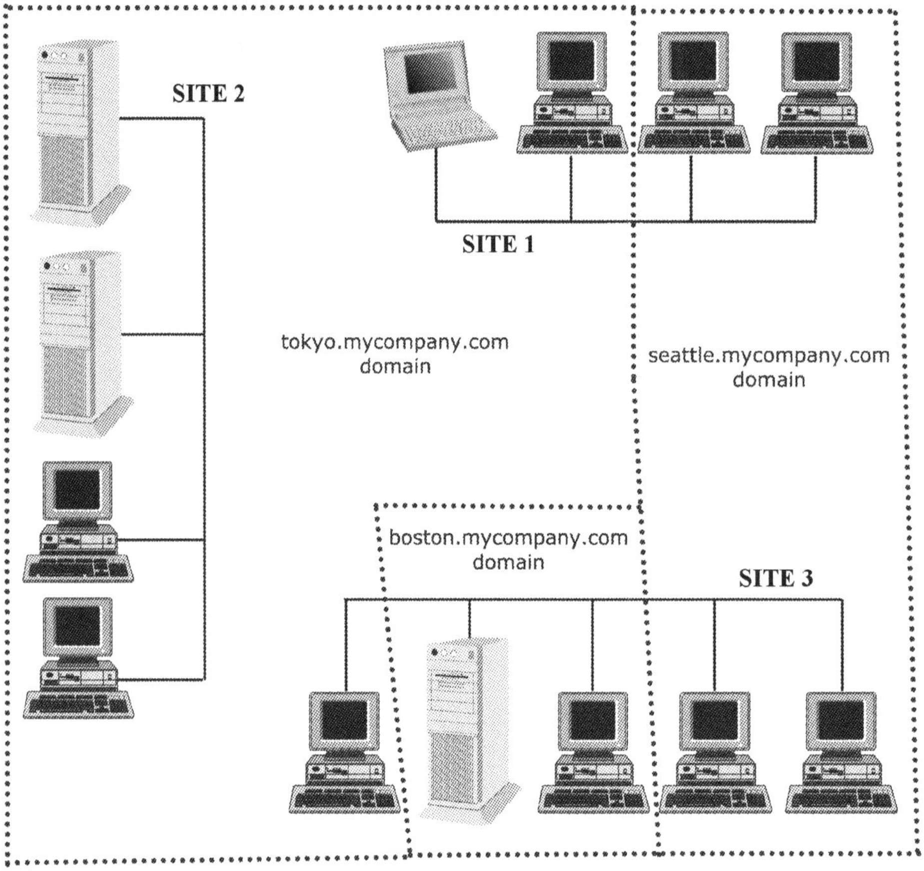

Planning where to place sites is dictated mainly by the physical nature of your network. Wherever a group of computers is connected to the remainder of the network by a slow link, that group of computers should be placed in their own site. Sites and site links are created after Active Directory has been installed. Once the sites have been created, domain controllers can be "moved" to sites. You do not physically move the domain controllers, but rather assign a new site location within the Active Directory.

If you create the sites early in the migration process after installing only a few Windows 2000 domain controllers, Windows 2000 domain controllers will be automatically placed in their appropriate sites as they are created. This reduces the administrative tasks you must perform.

Preparing for Problems

The final planning stage before migrating your network involves preparing for failure. Although the upgrade process is straightforward and relatively smooth, you should create a rollback strategy in case the upgrade fails. A good rollback strategy is one that permits you to return the network to its pre-upgrade state quickly, so that production is not stopped for long.

To migrate your network, the first server you upgrade to Windows 2000 is the PDC. In Windows NT 4.0, the PDC is the only computer in the domain that contains a read-and-write copy of the Windows NT 4.0 directory database. In other words, to perform the migration, you must first upgrade the most important server on your Windows NT 4.0 network. Although it seems risky to upgrade your most important server first, there is an easy rollback method that involves one of the BDCs on your network.

In Windows NT 4.0, the BDCs contain a read-only version the directory information. A BDC can be promoted to a PDC when the PDC is unavailable on the network. Because you can promote a BDC to a PDC if necessary, you can use one of the BDCs as a backup of the PDC. To implement the roll-back strategy, follow these steps:

1. Perform a full backup of your PDC.

Tip: Before you perform any software upgrades (especially to the operating system), make a complete backup of the computer that is being upgraded. If your rollback strategy fails, you can always restore from a tape backup.

---

2. Synchronize a BDC with the PDC so that it has the latest changes to the directory database. Although you can use any BDC, it is a good idea to choose one that does not perform other network duties, such as act as a file or print server, since this server will be taken offline during the upgrade of the PDC.

3.   Remove the BDC from the network.

4.   Begin the upgrade of the PDC to Windows 2000.

If the upgrade of the PDC fails, bring the BDC back online, and promote it to a PDC. This restores your network to its state prior to the failed upgrade (except the network will have one less BDC), and users will have suffered little interruption in productivity. You may then opt to restore the PDC using the tape backup and attempt another upgrade.

Root Domain Administration

After planning, the next stage in migrating a Windows NT 4.0 network to Windows 2000 is creating the root domain for the new Active Directory structure. The root domain is always the first Active Directory domain created, and it forms the foundation for all other domains in your forest. All child domains share the root domain name, so naming and planning the root are important steps in the process. When establishing the root domain, you will do one of two things:

•   Upgrade an existing Windows NT 4.0 domain to a Windows 2000 root domain

•   Create a new root domain

The choice depends on your current Windows NT 4.0 domain model. If you have a single domain or single master domain model, upgrade the single domain or master domain to the root domain. If your company has a multiple master or complete trust domain model, create a new root domain.

Upgrading an Existing Domain to the Root Domain

When your company uses a single Windows NT 4.0 domain model, the existing Windows NT 4.0 domain becomes the root domain. When migrating a single master Windows NT 4.0 domain model, the master domain becomes the root domain, and the resource domains become child domains to the root.

As you upgrade a domain controller from Windows NT 4.0 to Windows 2000 and Active Directory, the upgrading process preserves most of the directory database objects. These objects are:

User Accounts—The existing user accounts are placed in the Active Directory Users container.

Computer Accounts—Existing Windows NT 4.0 computer accounts are placed in the Active Directory Computers container.

Global Groups—Global groups created in Windows NT 4.0 are copied to the Active Directory Users container.

Local Groups—Local groups created on the Windows NT 4.0 domain controller are placed in the Active Directory Users container.

Built-in Groups—All groups built in to Windows NT 4.0 are moved to the Active Directory Built-in container.

In addition to the directory database objects, the migration from Windows NT 4.0 to Windows 2000 also preserves permissions assigned to files (on NTFS volumes) and printers and maintains group memberships.

Creating a New Root Domain

If your existing Windows NT 4.0 network is based on the multiple master or complete trust domain model, you need to create a new Active Directory root domain. In either of these models, more than one Windows NT 4.0 domain contains user and group accounts. You cannot combine the user and group accounts from several Windows NT 4.0 domains into one Active Directory domain. However, you can create a root domain that contains none of the user or group accounts, then migrate each of your master domains to child domains under the root. This method allows you to maintain the prevailing structure of your Windows NT 4.0 domain while benefiting from the many features of Active Directory. The drawback to creating an "empty" root domain is the need for at least two domain controllers in the root that are not heavily used as domain controllers.

 Warning: The root domain, even if empty, should have at least two domain controllers. If you have only one domain controller in the root and it fails, you face restoring from backup or reconstructing the entire Active Directory structure, not just the root domain.

When you create the new root domain, you install Windows 2000 Server on a computer that is not currently a Windows NT 4.0 domain controller. You then promote the member server to a domain controller for a new root domain in the forest. Once created, you upgrade the PDC from each of the master domains, making it a domain controller for a new child domain of the root (Figure 5.15).

Figure 5.15 Multiple Master Domain Migration

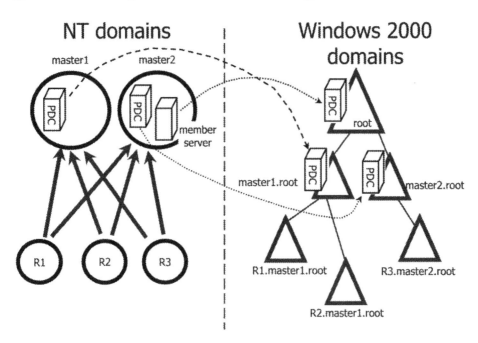

Using Organizational Units (OUs)

In Windows NT 4.0, domains are created to provide organizational structure. Although the added organization is often needed, the addition of domains and trusts to a network complicates administration. In Windows 2000 and Active Directory, rather than creating new domains, you create Organizational Units (OUs) to provide structure. These OUs may contain user and group accounts, computer accounts, and any network resources. OUs may be created to reflect your company's organizational structure (geographic, political, or departmental) or may reflect the administrative structure of the company (Figure 5.16).

Figure 5.16 Organizational Unit Uses

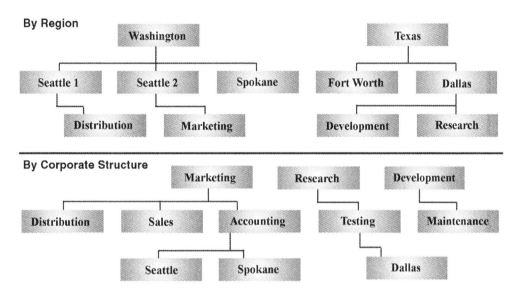

Domain Controller Upgrades

When migrating your Windows NT 4.0 network to Windows 2000, the first computers to be upgraded to the new operating system are the domain controllers. You first upgrade the PDC and then migrate the BDCs. Member servers and client computers can be updated at any time after the PDC has been upgraded.

In Windows 2000, no distinction between domain controllers exists. All domain controllers contain a read-and-write copy of the Active Directory database. In Windows NT 4.0, only the PDC has a read-and-write copy; the BDCs hold a read-only copy. Because all domain controllers in Windows 2000 are peers, when you upgrade your Windows NT 4.0 domain controllers to Active Directory domain controllers, you need not concern yourself with the previous role of the computer. As long as the computer is a Windows NT 4.0 domain controller, it becomes a Windows 2000 domain controller. However, the Windows 2000 setup does not allow you to upgrade a BDC until the PDC has been upgraded.

Identifying Upgrade Options

This discussion of migrating the network to Windows 2000 focuses entirely on upgrading Windows NT 4.0. However, you may still be running an older version of Windows NT on your network. In addition, you may also want to convert a current Windows NT 4.0 member server (one that is not serving as a domain controller) to a Windows 2000 domain controller. The upgrade options available to you are listed in Table 5.1.

Table 5.1 Windows 2000 Server Upgrade Options

If you have...	You can upgrade to...	And then you can...
Windows NT 4.0 PDC or BDC	Windows 2000 domain controller	
Windows NT 3.51 or 4.0 member server	Windows 2000 member server	Promote the member server to a domain controller
Windows NT 3.1 or 3.5 server	Windows NT 3.51 or 4.0 member server	Upgrade to Windows 2000 member server and then promote to a domain controller

 Note: The upgrade paths listed in Table 5.1 do not take hardware requirements into consideration. A server running Windows NT 3.1 is likely to need a hardware update before upgrading to Windows NT 4.0 and Windows 2000.

Preparing for Conversion

Before beginning the domain controller conversion from Windows NT 4.0 to Windows 2000, make sure the computer meets or exceeds the minimum hardware requirements for Windows 2000 Server. Table 5.2 lists the required and recommended minimum hardware requirements. Note that a server running Active Directory or any other network services (like DNS and DHCP) uses more hard disk space and memory.

Table 5.2 Minimum and Recommended Hardware Requirements

Component	Required Hardware	Recommended Hardware
CPU	--Pentium 166 MHz *or* Compaq Alpha-based Processor	--Pentium II or higher *or* Compaq Alpha-based Processor
Memory (RAM)	--64 MB (96 MB for Alphas)	--128 MB or more
Hard drive space	--1 GB for the operating system and Active Directory	--2 GB or more free space
Other drives	--12x CD-ROM --High-density 3.5-inch disk drive as drive A	--32x CD-ROM or faster --High-density 3.5-inch disk drive as drive A --Tape backup
Input devices	--Keyboard --Mouse --Network card	--Keyboard --Mouse --Network card

In addition to ensuring suitable hardware for the installation, you should perform the following four steps before starting an installation:

1. Back up all data on the server.

2. Remove virus protection software and any third-party network services.

3. Disconnect the serial cable to your Uninterruptible Power Supply (UPS), if applicable. During installation, Windows 2000 looks for devices on the serial ports. Problems may arise if the UPS is connected to the serial port during this detection process.

4. Set your computers' Basic Input-Output System (BIOS) to reserve Interrupt Requests (IRQs) for any non-Plug and Play (PnP) devices. If you do not reserve the IRQs needed for the non-PnP cards, Windows 2000 may assign the IRQs to other devices. Check with your computer manufacturer for information on making changes to the system BIOS.

Performing the Upgrade

The upgrade to Windows 2000 begins by running the Windows 2000 Setup from the Windows 2000 Server CD or from a network share. The network share can be any shared folder on the network that contains the Windows 2000 installation files. If you insert the CD, it automatically runs an introduction screen, from which you may choose "Install Windows 2000." Alternatively, you may run **WINNT32.EXE** from the \i386 directory on the CD or network share.

Upgrading a PDC

On the PDC, follow these steps to perform the upgrade:

1. Run **WINNT32.EXE** from the CD-ROM or network share.

2. Choose Upgrade to Windows 2000 (Recommended) and then select Next.

3. Read and accept the license agreement by selecting "I accept this agreement" and then choose Next.

4. The Windows 2000 Compatibility utility begins. Review the report and then choose Next if there are no incompatibilities.

 Note: You may see a message that the Directory Replicator service is incompatible with Windows 2000. The File Replication System in Windows 2000 replaces this service, and you may safely ignore this message.

5. The setup program copies necessary files to begin the upgrade, and then reboots the server.

6. The remainder of the upgrade to Windows 2000 continues without user intervention.

7. After installation is complete, the server reboots and automatically logs on using the administrator account and then starts the Active Directory Installation Wizard (**DCPROMO.EXE**). Choose Next to begin the wizard.

8. Since you are upgrading a PDC and this defines a new Windows 2000 domain, choose Create a new domain tree and then select Next.

9. Choose whether you are creating a new forest (if this is the first PDC you are upgrading) or if you are creating a new domain in an existing forest and then select Next.

 Note: Your choice whether to create a new forest or to join an existing forest depends on the type of Windows NT 4.0 domain model you are upgrading.

---

10. If you already have a DNS server that supports dynamic updates and SRV records running on the network, choose the option "Yes, I will configure the DNS client." Otherwise, select the option "No, just install and configure DNS on this computer" and then choose Next. The remaining steps assume you are installing DNS on this server.

11. Enter the DNS name for the new domain you are creating and then choose Next.

12. Choose the locations for the Active Directory files (or accept the defaults) and then select Next.

13. Choose a location for the Active Directory shared system volume and then select Next.

14. Decide whether non-Windows 2000 servers can have access to the Active Directory. Since you are likely to have non-Windows 2000 servers running at this stage of the network migration process, you may wish to choose Permissions compatible with pre-Windows 2000 servers. Make a selection and then select Next.

15. Enter and confirm a password for the administrator account and then choose Next.

16. Review the summary information and then choose Next.

17. Active Directory installation finishes and user, group, and computer accounts are imported into the Active Directory database. Choose Finish and then select Restart Now.

18. After rebooting, the domain controller runs as a Windows 2000 Active Directory domain controller and emulates a Windows NT 4.0 PDC (the domain runs in mixed mode).

Upgrading a BDC

You begin the upgrade of a BDC in the same manner as a PDC by running **WINNT32.EXE** from a CD or network share.

 Warning: Make sure the system clock on the BDC is synchronized with the clock on the Windows 2000 domain controller before beginning the installation process. If the clocks are significantly different, the Active Directory portion of installation fails.

The upgrade process for a Windows NT 4.0 BDC is the same as that for a PDC, with one minor difference during the Active Directory setup. As in the PDC setup, the Active Directory Installation Wizard begins automatically. When selecting Active Directory installation options, choose to make this computer an additional domain controller in an existing domain. When you upgraded the PDC, you created a new domain; you are now making the BDC a member of that domain.

 Note: The Windows 2000 Setup Wizard does not allow you to upgrade a BDC until the PDC has been upgraded. During the initial setup, the wizard confirms that the PDC is running Windows 2000.

Switching Domain Modes

Once you have upgraded all domain controllers in a domain to Windows 2000, you should convert the domain from mixed mode to native mode. Native mode allows you to take advantage of all of the

Active Directory features, whereas mixed mode has limitations. To switch the domain to native mode, follow these steps:

1. From the Start Menu, choose Programs, Administrative Tools and then select Active Directory Domains and Trusts.

2. In the left pane of the Active Directory Domains and Trusts console, right-click the icon that represents the domain controller and then choose Properties (Figure 5.17).

Figure 5.17 Server Properties

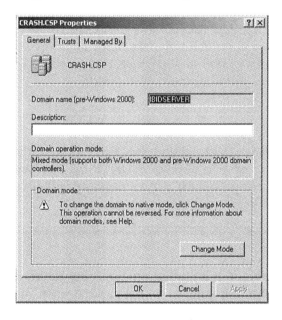

3. From the Server Properties page, choose the General Property page and then select Change Mode.

4. Choose Yes to confirm the warning.

5. Close the properties window.

6. Repeat this procedure for ALL domain controllers running in the domain. The domain is not running in native mode until all domain controllers have been changed.

Member Server Upgrades

You can upgrade Windows NT 4.0 member servers any time after you have upgraded the PDC. In fact, you do not need to upgrade the member servers at all to run your network with Active Directory. However, for users to take full advantage of the search capabilities of Active Directory, you should upgrade all servers to Windows 2000.

Upgrading a Member Server

As with all upgrades from Windows NT 4.0 to Windows 2000, run **WINNT32.EXE** from the Windows 2000 Server CD or from a network share containing the Windows 2000 installation files. Local user and group accounts are preserved during the upgrade. They are copied from the Windows NT 4.0 registry to the Windows 2000 registry, but they are not transferred to the Active Directory. As a member server, the computer did not provide directory services in Windows NT 4.0 and will not provide these services in Windows 2000 (unless it is promoted to a domain controller).

Authorizing a DHCP Member Server

If the member server is a DHCP server on the network, you must authorize the DHCP server in the Active Directory before beginning the upgrade. One of the new features of DHCP for Windows 2000 is the prevention of rogue DHCP servers on the network. All DHCP servers must be authorized by Active Directory before they can begin to issue IP addresses to requesting clients.

 Note: You only need to authorize a DHCP server if it is running on a member server. If DHCP is installed on a domain controller, it is automatically authorized when you first run the DHCP console and add the server.

To authorize a DHCP server, perform the following steps on any Windows 2000 computer running DHCP:

1. From the Start Menu, choose Programs, Administrative Tools and then select DHCP.

2. In the left pane of the DHCP console, choose DHCP.

3. From menu bar, choose Action and then select Manage Authorized Servers (Figure 5.18).

Figure 5.18 DHCP Server Authorization

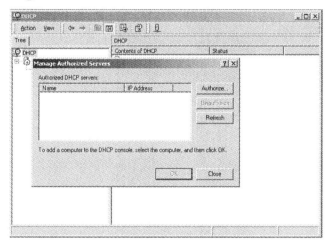

4. In the Manage Authorized Servers window, choose Authorize.

5. Enter the IP address or name of the DHCP server you wish to authorize, choose OK and then confirm the name or IP address by clicking Yes (Figure 5.19).

Figure 5.19 DHCP Server IP Address or Name

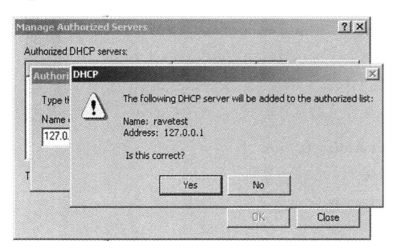

6.   The name or IP address for the DHCP is included in the list of Authorized DHCP servers. Choose Close.

Promoting a Member Server

Once you have upgraded a member server to Windows 2000, it is fully included in the Active Directory, but does not participate in managing or replicating the Active Directory database. In Windows NT 4.0, if you want to make a member server a domain controller, you must reinstall Windows NT 4.0. However, in Windows 2000 you can promote a member server to a domain controller. The promotion process is part of the installation of Active Directory, which is accomplished through the Active Directory Installation Wizard (**DCPROMO.EXE**).

 Note: When you promote a member server, the local user and group accounts are blended into the Active Directory database.

Client Upgrades

Once your network is running Windows 2000 and Active Directory, client computers can begin to use some of the functionality of Active Directory. In order to take full advantage of the features of Active Directory, you should upgrade your clients to Windows 2000 Professional. The upgrade of client computers can occur at any time after the domain controllers have been upgraded.

Identifying Upgrade Options

Upgrade options exist for computers running Windows NT Workstation 3.51 and 4.0, Windows 95, and Windows 98. Indirectly, you can also upgrade computers running Windows NT 3.1 and 3.5. Table 5.3 lists the upgrade options that are available.

Table 5.3 Windows 2000 Client Upgrade Options

If you have...	You can upgrade to...	And then you can...
Windows NT Workstation 3.51 or 4.0	Windows 2000 Professional	
Windows 95 or 98	Windows 2000 Professional	
Windows 3.1 or 3.11	Windows 95 or 98	Upgrade to Windows 2000 Professional
Windows NT 3.1 or 3.5	Windows NT Workstation 3.51 or 4.0	Upgrade to Windows 2000 Professional

For any of these upgrade paths to be effective, the computer must have the necessary hardware to run Windows 2000 Professional. The hardware should be listed on Microsoft's HCL. In addition, Windows 2000 Professional places higher demands on the computer hardware. Table 5.4 lists the required and recommended minimum hardware for Windows 2000 Professional. It is likely that computers running Windows NT 3.1 and 3.5 and Windows 3.1 have older hardware that may not be sufficient to run Windows 2000 Professional.

Table 5.4 Windows 2000 Professional Hardware Requirements

Component	Required Hardware	Recommended Hardware
CPU	--Pentium 166 MHz *or* Compaq Alpha-based Processor	--Pentium II or higher Compaq Alpha-based Processor
Memory (RAM)	--32 MB (48 MB for Alphas)	--64 MB or more (96 MB for Alphas)
Hard drive space	--685 MB free space (351 MB for Alphas)	--1 GB or more free space
Other drives	--12x CD-ROM --High-density 3.5-inch disk drive as drive A	--32x CD-ROM or faster --High-density 3.5-inch disk drive as drive A
Input / output devices	--Keyboard --Mouse	--Keyboard --Mouse

Preparing to Upgrade the Client

Before beginning an upgrade to Windows 2000 Professional, you should prepare the computer by following these steps:

1. Generate a compatibility report by running the Windows 2000 Compatibility Tool (as discussed above, run **WINNT32.EXE /CHECKUPGRADEONLY**).

2. Back up any important data stored on the client computer. Ideally, your network is configured such that the user's data and profile are stored on a server, and the client computer contains no data that needs to be backed up.

3. Some software requires an upgrade pack to work properly under Windows 2000. If software running on the client computer needs an upgrade pack, contact the software manufacturer to obtain this pack before beginning installation.

4. If you are upgrading a Windows 95 or Windows 98 computer, create a computer account for the computer in the domain.

Note: Computers which run Windows 95 and 98 do not need computer accounts to participate in Windows NT 4.0 or Windows 2000 domains, but computers which run Windows NT 4.0 and Windows 2000 do. When you upgrade a Windows 95 or 98 computer to Windows 2000, you must create a computer account in the domain for it.

Upgrading Windows Clients

If the client computer passes the compatibility test and has been backed up as necessary, you are ready to begin the upgrade process. The process differs for computers running Windows 95 and 98 and those running Windows NT 3.51 and Windows NT 4.0.

Upgrading Windows 95 and 98

To upgrade a client computer running Windows 95 or 98 to Windows 2000, perform the following tasks:

1. Run **WINNT32.EXE** from the Windows 2000 Professional CD or from a network share.

Note: If the client computer's CD-ROM supports Autoplay, the Windows 2000 Professional CD-ROM automatically starts and asks if you want to upgrade to Windows 2000. Choose Yes.

2. In the Windows 2000 Setup Wizard, choose Upgrade to Windows 2000 (recommended) and then select Next.

3. Read and accept the license agreement by selecting "I accept this agreement" then choose Next.

4. Read the summary information and then choose Next.

5. If you have upgrade packs for software running on the computer, choose "Yes, I have upgrade packs," then select Add and choose the location of the upgrade packs. Otherwise, select the option "No, I don't have any upgrade packs," and then choose Next.

6. You are prompted to change the file system to NTFS. If the computer will not be running with a dual-boot configuration (two operating systems loaded on the same computer), choose "Yes, upgrade my drive" and then select Next. To keep the file system as it is, select the option "No, do not upgrade my drive" and then select Next.

7. The Windows 2000 Compatibility utility begins. If you ran this before beginning the installation and corrected incompatibilities, you should not encounter any errors now. Choose Next after the upgrade report has been generated.

8. Choose Next again to begin copying files.

9. The computer automatically restarts after the file copy is finished.

10. The remainder of the upgrade proceeds without user intervention. After the final reboot, you must enter a password for the new administrator account and for any accounts used to log on to the client computer. Enter a password, confirm it and then choose OK. You can only enter one password for all accounts listed, so it is recommended that you change the passwords immediately after logging on to the Windows 2000 computer.

 Note: Computers running Windows 95 and 98 do not have user accounts. When you upgrade to Windows 2000, the local administrator account is created.

Upgrading Windows NT 3.51 and 4.0

To upgrade a computer currently running Windows NT 3.51 or 4.0, follow these steps:

1. From the Windows 2000 Professional CD or from a network share, run **WINNT32.EXE**.

2. Choose Upgrade to Windows 2000 (recommended) and then select Next.

3. Choose "I accept this agreement" and then choose Next.

4. If Windows NT 4.0 is running on a volume formatted with the FAT file system, you are prompted to change this volume to the NTFS file system. Choose your option and then choose Next. If Windows NT 4.0 is running on NTFS, you will not see this screen.

5. The Windows 2000 Compatibility utility begins. If there are no problems after the upgrade report has been generated, choose Next. As when upgrading the domain controllers, you may see a message about the Directory Replicator service. This message may be ignored.

6. The computer automatically restarts after the file copy is finished, and the remainder of the upgrade proceeds without user intervention.

Creating an Active Directory Client

You may be unable to upgrade some computers running Windows 95 and 98 because of insufficient hardware on those computers. These computers can still participate in an Active Directory network and support many Active Directory features if you install the Directory Services Client. The Directory Services Client allows Windows 95 and 98 computers to do the following:

- Use the Distributed File System (DFS)

- Search Active Directory

- Change passwords on domain controllers

The Directory Services Client requires Internet Explorer 4.01 or later with the Active Desktop component enabled. This is the default in Windows 98, but is not in Windows 95.

Installing the Directory Service Client

To install the Directory Services Client, follow these steps:

1. Insert the Windows 2000 Server CD in the CD-ROM drive.

2. From the Start Menu, choose Run, enter the following command in the Open box and then select OK:

    D:\CLIENTS\WIN9X\DSCLIENT.EXE (where D is your CD-ROM drive letter)

3. Choose Next to begin the Directory Services Client Wizard.

4. Choose Next again to begin copying files to the client computer.

5. When the copy process is complete, choose Finish and then select Yes to reboot the client computer. Installation is complete.

Vocabulary

Review the following terms in preparation for the certification exam.

Term	Description
bandwidth	The rate at which data can be carried across a network connection.
BDC	The Backup Domain Controller stores a read-only copy of the directory database in Windows NT 4.0.
BIOS	The Basic Input-Output System on a computer is the read-only programming used by the computer to access its hardware.
child domain	A domain under the root domain that uses part of the root domain's name as its own.
complete trust domain model	A Windows NT 4.0 domain model in which all domains are master domains and resources domains, and all domains trust one another.
CPU	Central Processing Unit
DFS	Distributed File System
DHCP	Dynamic Host Configuration Protocol assigns network addresses to client computers.
directory database	Contains user and group accounts and permissions to resources in the network.
Directory Services Client	Allows a Windows 95 or Windows 98 computer to participate on an Active Directory domain without upgrading the operating system to Windows 2000.
DNS	The Domain Name System translates computer names to network addresses and is a fundamental part of Active Directory and the Internet.

Term	Description
domain	A logical grouping of network resources.
dual-boot	Loading two operating systems on one computer, so that it may boot to either one based on user input.
dynamic update	A new feature of both DNS and DHCP that allows DHCP to update the DNS database as changes occur on the network.
FAT	The File Allocation Table is a file system supported by DOS, Windows, Windows 95 and 98, Windows NT 4.0, and Windows 2000.
forest	A collection of domains that do not share a common DNS namespace.
HCL	The Hardware Compatibility List is published by Microsoft and lists computer hardware that has been verified to work with Windows 2000.
IRQ	Interrupt Request is used by any device inside the computer to request information from the processor.
master domain	In Windows NT 4.0, a master domain is one that contains user and groups accounts and is trusted by other domains.
member server	A server that does not provide any directory service s to the network.
mixed mode	In Windows 2000, a domain mode that supports both Active Directory domain controllers and Windows NT 4.0 domain controllers.
multiple master domain model	A Windows NT 4.0 domain model in which more than one domain contains user and group accounts.
namespace	The hierarchical structure of the DNS naming system, in which a child domain's name contains the parent domain's name.

Term	Description
native mode	In Windows 2000, the domain mode that only supports Active Directory domain controllers.
network share	A folder that has been shared so that it is accessible over the network.
non-transitive trusts	A trust that exists only between two domains and is not inherited by other domains.
NTFS	The New Technology File System is a file system supported only by Windows NT 4.0 and Windows 2000.
OU	An Organizational Unit is used within the Active Directory to organize resources.
parent	A domain that contains a child domain, the parent is closer to the root than are its child domains.
PDC	The Primary Domain Controller is the only domain controller to contain the read-and-write copy of the directory database in Windows NT 4.0.
PnP	Plug and Play is Microsoft's hardware detection and configuration procedure.
RAM	Random Access Memory
replication	The process of copying the directory database from one domain controller to another.
resource domain	A domain that does not contain user and groups accounts and trusts a master domain.
RFC	A Request For Comments is a formal proposal defining a new technology or an update to an existing technology.
rollback strategy	A strategy that allows you to return a network to its previous state if problems arise during upgrades.

Term	Description
root domain	The first domain created in Active Directory.
single domain model	In Windows NT 4.0, a domain model that consists of only one domain.
single master domain model	In Windows NT 4.0, a domain model that consists of one master domain and numerous resource domains.
site	A collection of network resources joined by a fast connection (10 Mb or faster).
site links	A logical connection between sites that you create to govern replication between the sites.
SRV	The Service Resource record in DNS allows computers to search for servers in the DNS database based on the server's role in the network.
synchronize	To force replication between a BDC and PDC so that the BDC has the latest updates to the directory database.
tree	A series of domains, all sharing a common DNS namespace.
trust	A logical connection between two Windows NT 4.0 domains that allows the sharing of user and group information.
Unicode	Computer characters used to support languages other than English.
upgrade pack	A software update supplied by the software manufacturer that makes the application compatible with Windows 2000.
UPS	An Uninterruptible Power Supply is a battery that provides temporary power to your computer if the main power is lost.

In Brief

If you want to...	Then do this...
Make a Windows NT 4.0 member server a Windows 2000 domain controller	Upgrade the server to Windows 2000 by running **WINNT32.EXE** on the Windows 2000 Server CD and then promote it to a domain controller by running **DCPROMO.EXE**.
Allow a Windows 95 or Windows 98 client to take full advantage of an Active Directory-based network	Either upgrade the operating system to Windows 2000 Professional by running **WINNT32.EXE** or install the Directory Services Client by running **SCLIENT.EXE** on the Windows 2000 Professional CD.
Allow a Windows 3.11 client to take full advantage of an Active Directory-based network	Upgrade the client to Windows 95 or Windows 98. Then upgrade again to Windows 2000 or install the Directory Services Client.
Migrate a Windows NT 4.0 single domain model to Windows 2000	Make the single domain the root of a new tree in a new forest.
Migrate a Windows NT 4.0 single master domain model to Windows 2000	Make the master domain the root of a new tree in a new forest. Make all resource domains child domains under the root.
Migrate a Windows NT 4.0 multiple master domain model to Windows 2000	Create a new root domain. Make each of the master domains a child under this root, and make each resource domain a child under one of the master domains.
Migrate a Windows NT 4.0 complete trust domain model to Windows 2000	Create a new root domain and then make each domain a child under the root.
Migrate a complete trust model to Windows 2000, but allow each domain to have a unique and independent domain name	Make each domain the root of a new tree and create all trees in the same forest.

Lesson 5 Activities

Complete the following activities to better prepare you for the certification exam.

1. On a test (non-production) computer, format the hard drive and load Windows 95 or Windows 98. A basic installation will be fine. Then upgrade the computer to Windows 2000 Professional. MAKE SURE THIS IS A TEST COMPUTER THAT CONTAINS NO DATA. Also make sure the computer meets the minimum hardware requirements for Windows 2000 Server.

2. On the same computer, reformat the hard drive and load Windows NT Workstation 4.0. Format the partition that contains the operating system (the boot partition) with the NTFS file system. Perform an upgrade to Windows 2000.

3. Once again, reformat the hard drive and load Windows NT Server 4.0 as a Primary Domain Controller (PDC).

4. On the PDC, create at least two local groups, three global groups, and three user accounts. Give each an easily identifiable name (like Local1, Global2, or TestUser1). Place the user accounts into the global groups and make the global groups members of the local groups. How you distribute users and global groups is up to you, but make sure to record the memberships of the local and global groups for future reference. One option is to enter a description for each group that describes the members of the group.

5. Create two shared folders on an NTFS volume the PDC. Name them Test1 and Test2. Assign share permissions on the folders to the local groups you created in the previous activity. Again, record what permissions you assigned to each group for each share.

6. Upgrade the PDC to a Windows 2000 domain controller. Let the Active Directory Installation Wizard install and configure DNS.

7. Verify that all user and group accounts were migrated to the Active Directory correctly. Verify that permissions on the two shared folders were also retained.

8. The Windows NT 4.0 domain model for a hypothetical company contains three master domains named Sales, Marketing, and Research. Each user and group account is contained in one of these domains, based on the role of the user or group. The company has sales offices in Seattle, Tokyo, and Rome, marketing branches in Seattle and Rome, and research teams in Seattle and Tokyo. Currently, there is a separate resource domain for each city, and each resource domain trusts one or more of the master domains as necessary to obtain the user and group accounts. Determine

the type of domain model that is being used and then design a Windows 2000 network model to upgrade this existing Windows NT 4.0 domain model.

9. Determine the number of sites you should create for your domain model in Activity

8. Assume that groups in the same city have high-speed connections, and that all links between cities are slower than 10 Mbps.

10. Determine the minimum number of domain controllers your model needs. Each domain should have at least two. Take your site configuration into account as well.

Answers to Lesson 5 Activities

1. Consult other sources for formatting the hard drive and installing Windows 95 or Windows 98. Once Windows is installed, insert the Windows 2000 Professional CD and run **WINNT32.EXE**.

2. Again, consult a reliable source for information on reformatting a hard drive and installing Windows NT Workstation 4.0. During the installation of Windows NT 4.0, you are asked to format the drive. Choose NTFS. Once Windows NT 4.0 is installed, insert the Windows 2000 CD and run **WINNT32.EXE**.

3. Again, consult a reliable source for information on reformatting a hard drive and installing Windows NT Server 4.0. During the installation of Windows NT 4.0, you are asked what role the server will perform. Choose to make the server a Primary Domain Controller.

4. To create the user and group accounts, from the Start Menu, choose Programs, Administrative Tools and then select User Manager for Domains.

5. From the Start Menu, choose Programs and then select Windows NT Explorer. In the left pane of Windows NT Explorer, select the drive on which you are creating the shared folders. Choose File, select New and then choose Folder. While the name of the folder is highlighted, type in the name (Test1). Repeat this for Test2. In the right pane, right-click one of the new folders and select Sharing. Choose Shared As and then select Permissions. Choose the Everyone group, select Remove, and then choose Add. From the list of user and group accounts, choose the appropriate accounts to add, select Add and then choose OK. Assign the proper permissions to the accounts by selecting one account and then changing the selection in the Type of Access menu. Choose OK twice. Repeat these steps for the other folder.

6. Insert the Windows 2000 Server CD and run **WINNT32.EXE**. Since this is a PDC, the upgrade to Windows 2000 also includes the installation of Active Directory. During the installation of Active Directory, the wizard prompts you to install DNS. If you do not let Active Directory install DNS, Active Directory will not function properly after the final reboot.

7. To find the user and group accounts after the upgrade to Windows 2000 and Active Directory, from the Start Menu, choose Programs, Administrative Tools and then select Active Directory Users and Computers. In the left pane, expand the icon that represents the server and then select the container named "Users." The user and group accounts should all be listed in the right pane. Using the Windows Explorer, find the folders you created. Right-click on one, choose Sharing and then select Permissions.

8. Currently, this is a Windows NT 4.0 multiple master domain model. Although there are several possibilities to upgrade this, one solution is to create a new root domain (let's call it "root" for simplicity's sake). Make each of the master domains a child under the root: sales.root, research.root, and marketing.root. Under each of these domains, create a child domain for the city that needs accounts from the master. Under sales.root, create seattle.sales.root, tokyo.sales.root, and rome.sales.root. Under research.root, create the child domains seattle.research.root and tokyo.research.root and under the marketing.root domain, create the rome.marketing.root and seattle.marketing.root child domains. In total, there are 11 domains.

9. You should create three sites. Each site represents one of the cities and contains members of several domains.

10. The minimum number of domain controllers is two per domain, but you should also have a domain controller for each site in which a domain is represented. In our solution, there are 11 domains (therefore, 22 domain controllers needed). Since the sites match the location of the resource domains, each of the resource domains has domain controllers in the proper sites, so you do not need to add any more. However, you should make sure each of the master domains has a domain controller in the appropriate sites. The Research domain needs only two domain controllers (one in Tokyo and one in Seattle), so you don't need any more than the minimum. The same holds true for the Marketing domain (one domain controller in both Rome and Seattle). The Sales domain needs a domain controller in all three sites, so you need to add one more. Finally, the root domain should have a domain controller in each site. Because you already have two domain controllers for the root, you need to add only one more. This results in a total minimum of 24 domain controllers.

Lesson 5 Quiz

These questions test your knowledge of features, vocabulary, procedures, and syntax.

1. Which Windows NT 4.0 domain model has all user and group accounts located in one domain and resources distributed throughout several other domains?

    A. Single domain model

    B. Single master domain model

    C. Multiple master domain model

    D. Complete trust domain model

2. The connection between two Windows NT 4.0 domains that allows them to share account information is a

    A. trust

    B. site

    C. site link

    D. namespace

3. What is the maximum length for an entire DNS domain name?

    A. 63 characters

    B. 128 characters

    C. 255 characters

    D. There is no limit

4. Which Windows NT 4.0 domain model usually results in the most trusts?

    A. Single domain model

    B. Single master domain model

    C. Multiple master domain model

    D. Complete trust domain model

5. Which Windows NT 4.0 domain model uses the fewest trusts?

    A. Single domain model

    B. Single master domain model

    C. Multiple master domain model

    D. Complete trust domain model

6. Which of the following would be the best resource for technical information on network technology?
   A. Technical Information Sheet (TIS)
   B. Request From Client (RFC)
   C. Request For Comment (RFC)
   D. Resource of Technical Information (RTI)

7. Which of the following is the command to run the Check Upgrade Utility?
   A. WINNT.EXE /CHECKUPGRADEONLY
   B. WINNT32.EXE /CHECKUPGRADEONLY
   C. CHCKUPGD.EXE /WINNT32
   D. WINNT32.EXE /CHECKUPGRADE

8. Which of the following is a valid full domain name for a child domain immediately below a root domain named lightpointlearning.com?
   A. lightpointlearning.sales.com
   B. sales.seattle.lightpointlearning.com
   C. lightpointlearning.com.sales
   D. sales.lightpointlearning.com

9. Which of the following can be used as a Windows 2000 domain controller? (Choose all that apply)
   A. A Windows 2000 member server by running DCPROMO.EXE
   B. A Windows NT 4.0 member server on a Pentium 133 MHz with 64 MB RAM, by upgrading to Windows 2000 and then promoting to a domain controller
   C. A Windows NT 4.0 PDC running on a Pentium-II 350 MHz with 64 MB RAM by running DCPROMO.EXE from the Windows 2000 CD
   D. A Windows NT 4.0 PDC running on a Pentium-II 300 MHz with 128 MB by running WINNT32.EXE from the Windows 2000 CD

10. From which of the following client operating systems can a user log on to an Active Directory domain? (Choose all that apply)
    A. Windows NT Workstation 4.0
    B. Windows 98
    C. Windows 3.11
    D. Windows 2000 Professional

Answers to Lesson 5 Quiz

1. Answer B is correct. User and group accounts are stored in the master domain. If all accounts are in one domain, it must be a single master domain model.

    Answers A, C, and D are incorrect.

2. Answer A is correct. Trusts are implemented in Windows NT 4.0 domain models so that resource domains can utilize user and group accounts from master domains.

    Answers B and C are incorrect. Sites define physically separate portions of Windows 2000 networks, and site links define the connection between these sites.

    Answer D is incorrect. The DNS namespace defines the structure of DNS names.

3. Answer C is correct. The total length of a DNS name cannot exceed 255 characters.

    Answer A is incorrect. The maximum length of any one segment of a DNS name is 63 characters.

    Answers B and D are incorrect.

4. Answer D is correct. If there are more than two domains in a Windows NT 4.0 network, the complete trust model results in the highest number of trusts that need to be implemented.

    Answers A, B, and C are incorrect.

5. Answer A is correct. The single domain model always has the fewest number of trusts (0). Since there is only one domain, there are never any trusts.

    Answers B, C, and D are incorrect.

6. Answer C is correct. The best resource for technical information on most network technologies is to read the original Request For Comments (RFC).

    Answers A, B, and D are incorrect. They are all fictitious names.

7. Answer B is correct. To check a computer for Windows 2000 compatibility, run the Windows 2000 upgrade (which is always **WINNT32.EXE**) with the **/CHECKUPGRADEONLY** switch.

    Answer A is incorrect. Although the switch is correct, you must run **WINNT32.EXE**, not **WINNT.EXE**.

    Answers C and D are incorrect.

8. Answer D is correct. The full domain name for a child is the name of the domain, with the domain name of the parent appended.

   Answer B is incorrect. This is a valid domain name for a child in the lightpointlearning.com tree, but the child is two levels below the root, not immediately below. The parent of sales.seattle.lightpointlearning.com is seattle.lightpointlearning.com, not the root, lightpointlearning.com

   Answers A and C are incorrect. The naming order is incorrect.

9. Answers A and D are correct. To create a Windows 2000 domain controller, you can promote a current Windows 2000 member server (by running the Active Directory Installation Wizard, **DCPROMO.EXE**), or you can upgrade a current Windows NT 4.0 PDC to Windows 2000 by running **WINNT32.EXE** from the Windows 2000 CD. The installation of Active Directory (and the creation of a domain controller) is automatic if you are upgrading a Windows NT 4.0 domain controller.

   Answer B is incorrect. Although the steps listed work to make a Windows NT 4.0 member server a domain controller, this server does not meet the minimum hardware requirements for a Windows 2000 server.

   Answer C is incorrect. Although this PDC can be upgraded to Windows 2000 and it meets the minimum hardware requirements, running **DCPROMO.EXE** on a Windows NT 4.0 computer will not upgrade it.

10. Answers A, B, C, and D are correct. Any one of these operating systems can be used to log on to an Active Directory-based network.

Lesson 6

System Management

In Microsoft Windows 2000, most management tools are designed to run as snap-ins, modules that run within the Microsoft Management Console (MMC). The MMC provides a common interface so that you can quickly and easily learn and use each tool because all tools have similar features. You can also customize the MMC. You can create a console for the MMC that contains those tools you most often use. By opening this console, you have immediate access to the tools you need.

After exploring the MMC and its use, you will learn more about how Windows 2000 handles hardware support. You will learn the use of several MMC snap-ins to manage the hardware devices in your server and how to troubleshoot hardware-related problems.

You will also learn how to manage local user and group accounts. The lesson ends with a discussion of Group Policy. Group Policy allows you to manage a user's desktop environment, control the use of software and implement security policies. Group Policy can significantly raise the administrator's control over a network and lower the number of potential problems users face.

After completing this lesson, you should have a better understanding of the following topics:

*   The Microsoft Management Console (MMC)

*   Hardware Management

*   Group Policy

*   Software Management using Group Policy

272

Microsoft Management Console (MMC)

The MMC is a Windows 2000 interface that does not provide any system management capabilities, but provides a common interface in which management tools can run. When you run the MMC, you are actually opening a console. One or more tools are implemented in a console. These tools, which may include utilities for managing the Active Directory, user and group accounts, hardware devices, services, and applications, are called snap-ins. A snap-in is a tool that runs within a console, and a console is a window within the MMC shell.

Utilizing a Centralized System

By providing a common interface for all of the management tools in Windows 2000, the MMC centralizes control of the computer and of the entire network. Rather than run every system management tool as its own unique program, the MMC allows multiple tools to run together.

An example of this is the Computer Management console. To open the Computer Management console from the desktop, right-click My Computer and then choose Manage. Alternatively, you may open the Computer Management console from the Start Menu. From the Start Menu, choose Programs, Administrative Tools and then select Computer Management (Figure 6.1).

The Computer Management console contains several snap-ins that manage the computer. Included in this one console are snap-ins for several tools you should be familiar with from Windows NT 4.0: Event Viewer, System Information, and Services (formerly a control panel). Some of the tools are very similar to utilities in Windows NT 4.0, but have been renamed and updated, including Local Users and Groups (formerly named User Manager), Shared Folders (formerly part of Server Manager), Disk Management (formerly Disk Administrator), and Performance Logs and Alerts (formerly Performance Monitor). Some of the tools are completely new to Windows 2000. These tools include Disk Defragmenter, Indexing Service, Device Manager, and Removable Storage.

Figure 6.1 Computer Management Console

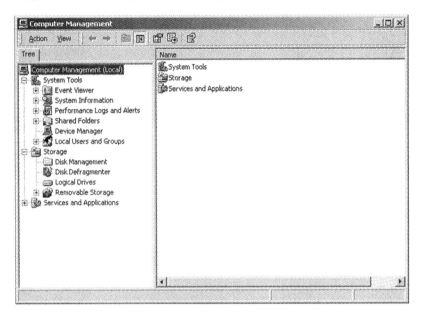

Working with Snap-Ins

Each snap-in in the MMC is designed to perform a different task, so there are many differences between the tools. However, all snap-ins must conform to the MMC, and so they all share some common features. The power of the MMC lies in this commonality. Once you learn to use the general features of one snap-in, you can begin to use a new snap-in much more easily.

The general form of a console includes two panes. The left pane is called the Tree pane, and contains a list of snap-ins included in the console (Figure 6.2).

Figure 6.2 Computer Management Console Tree Pane

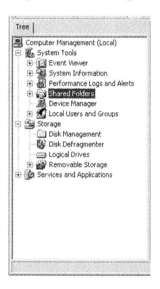

The Tree pane displays folders as well as snap-ins. Folders are MMC objects that contain other snap-ins. Folders have a small plus sign (+) symbol next to them. Clicking the plus sign (+) or double-clicking the folder name expands the folder, which reveals its contents. Some snap-ins may also be expanded, which reveals items within the snap-in. It is this branching, hierarchical structure that gives the name Tree to this left-hand pane (Figure 6.3).

Figure 6.3 Expanded Tree Pane

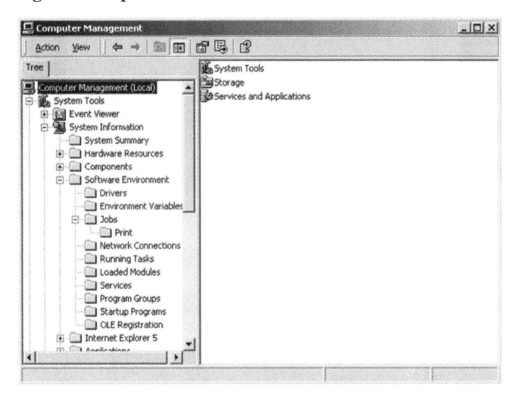

The right-hand side of the console contains the Details pane. If you choose a folder in the Tree pane, the Details pane displays the contents of the folder. If you select an object in the Tree pane, the Details pane displays the snap-in-specific information and features. The Details pane can display a variety of information, including Web pages, graphics (charts, tables, and pictures), and columns.

For example, in the Tree pane of the Computer Management console, expand System Tools, expand Event Viewer and then choose System. The Details pane displays the System Log for the Event Viewer with the information listed in columns (Figure 6.4).

Figure 6.4 System Event Log

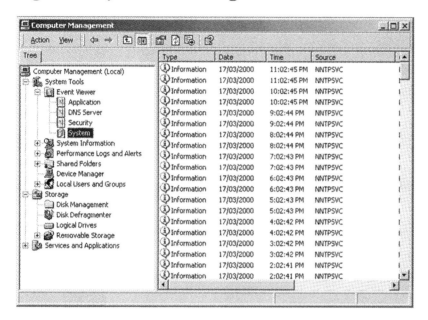

The columns in the Details pane can be rearranged and resized, and the data can be ordered by column type. As another example, in the Tree pane expand Storage and then choose Disk Management. The Details pane displays graphical information very similar to the Windows NT 4.0 Disk Administrator (Figure 6.5).

In this instance, the Details pane splits horizontally. The upper portion of the Details pane contains data listed in columns, and the lower portion contains a graphical representation of the physical and logical drives in the computer.

Figure 6.5 Disk Management Console

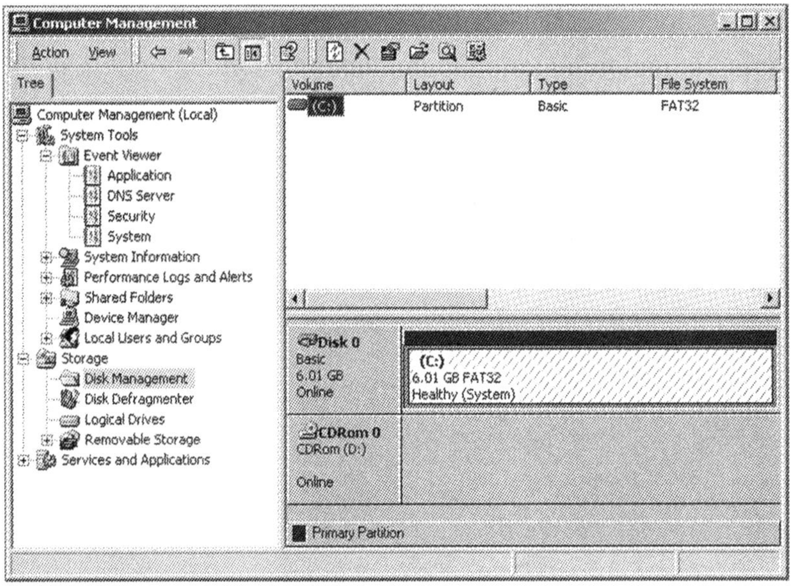

Creating Customized Tools

A powerful feature of the MMC is its ability to be customized. As you have seen, an MMC console may contain several snap-ins. The Computer Management console, for example, contains 13 snap-ins.

You can create a customized MMC console that contains the snap-ins you use most often. In addition, you can create customized consoles for other administrators. This allows you to delegate control of certain network aspects to other users and provide those users with only the tools they need. After creating a customized console, you can send it to the administrator through e-mail, store it in a shared folder on the network or post it onto a Web page.

Note: Customized MMC consoles are saved as files with the .MSC extension.

Hardware Management

In order for Windows 2000 or any other operating system to function properly, it needs to know how to communicate with the hardware (the physical devices inside and attached to the computer). Every device in a computer has an Input/Output (I/O) address. Like a street address for a house, the I/O address of a device provides a way for other devices and the operating system to communicate with it.

 Note: Every device in a computer MUST have a unique I/O address.

Many devices in a computer also have an Interrupt Request (IRQ). An IRQ allows a device to interrupt the Central Processing Unit (CPU) and request some of the CPU's time.

 Note: Ideally, every device in a computer has its own IRQ. Realistically, the limited number of IRQs means that two or more devices may share the same IRQ.

Today's computers have two types of devices, legacy and Plug and Play (PnP). A legacy device requires that you assign an address and IRQ before installing the device in the computer. Usually you assign these values by setting jumpers or dip switches (pins and switches) mounted on the device. A PnP device is one that can automatically receive its address and IRQ. Some PnP cards (those that use the Peripheral Component Interface (PCI) bus) receive this information every time the computer is turned on. Others (like those that use the Industry Standard Architecture (ISA) bus) receive the information from the operating system. To use ISA PnP cards, you must be running a PnP-compatible operating system.

Note: PCI cards receive their address and IRQ settings when the computer is turned on. By the time the operating system loads, these cards have their address and IRQ set and can be used by non-PnP operating systems like Windows NT 4.0.

Understanding the New Hardware Support in Windows 2000

Windows 2000 is a PnP operating system. Like Windows 95 and Windows 98, Windows 2000 automatically assigns I/O addresses and IRQs to PnP devices. Furthermore, Windows 2000 automatically detects new devices added to the system and loads drivers (software that allows programs to communicate with the device) for the device. This simplifies the addition and removal of hardware from a computer.

Windows NT 4.0 is not a PnP operating system by default, although PnP features can be enabled. Windows 95 and Windows 98 are PnP operating systems. Although Windows NT 4.0 is a stable operating system (far more stable than Windows 95 or Windows 98), it lacks support for much of the new hardware on the market. Windows 2000 aims to bridge this gap by providing PnP support while maintaining stability.

In addition to supporting PnP devices, Windows 2000 supports several newer technologies. These technologies, including the Universal Serial Bus (USB), Advanced Configuration and Power Interface (ACPI), multiple display support, and Infrared Data Association (IrDA), are also supported in Windows 98, but are not supported under Windows NT 4.0.

Supporting the Universal Serial Bus (USB)

USB provides a way to externally attach devices to a computer without requiring a separate controller for each device or a unique IRQ. There is a limited number of IRQs and an increasing number of devices which need these IRQs. The USB was designed to curb this problem.

Generally, when an external device (like a scanner or printer) is attached to a computer, it is connected through one of three ports: the parallel port, the serial port, or a Small Computer Systems Interface (SCSI) port. Serial ports, which were originally designed to support modems, transfer data very slowly.

There are typically two serial ports on a computer designated as COM1 and COM2. Parallel ports, which were originally designed to attach a printer to a computer, are faster than serial ports. Most computers have one parallel port (named LPT1), although many have a second port (LPT2). SCSI ports, which almost always must be added to a computer, are the fastest of these three ports. Each serial and parallel port uses its own IRQ and I/O address. In general, any given serial or parallel port can have only one device attached to it. This means that an IRQ is used for only one device.

SCSI controller cards also need their own I/O address and IRQ, but a SCSI controller can support six or more devices. In addition, an SCSI card supports both external devices and internal devices such as hard drives, CD-ROMs, and tape drives. Although this helps alleviate the IRQ problem, SCSI technology is much more expensive than other technologies.

 Note: There are several versions of SCSI. The original SCSI (SCSI-1) supports 6 devices in addition to the controller card. SCSI-3 supports 16 devices.

Like all other devices, a USB controller requires a unique I/O address and uses one IRQ. However, the USB can support up to 127 devices. USB ports are now standard on new computers and USB devices are common. In addition to PC manufacturers, Apple Macintosh computers also support USB. This universal acceptance and integration of the USB has resulted in low-priced USB devices.

 Tip: Windows 98 and Windows 2000 support the USB. Later versions of Windows 95 also support USB devices. Windows NT 4.0 does not support USB. According to Microsoft, they will not implement USB support for Windows NT 4.0 through a service pack or update.

Using Advanced Configuration and Power Interface (ACPI)

ACPI specification defines an interface to the computer hardware that allows an operating system to control the power management for the computer.

Windows 2000 uses ACPI to enable the power management features hibernate and standby and also uses ACPI with PnP to direct power to or from devices.

In Windows 2000, standby and hibernate are two shutdown options that are not available in Windows NT 4.0. In standby mode, Windows 2000 reduces power consumption on the computer so that only a minimum amount of power is used to keep information in the Random Access Memory (RAM).

On a portable computer, the screen, hard disk, and power to peripheral devices are turned off. In hibernate mode, Windows 2000 copies all of the information stored in RAM to a file on the hard disk and then turns the computer off. When the computer is turned on again, the data is placed back into the RAM so that the computer is restored to its exact state before hibernation. Hibernation is like standby mode, except the computer uses no power during hibernation, whereas standby requires a small amount.

A full implementation of ACPI and PnP allows a user to add a device to a computer without restarting the computer. An ACPI operating system manages power for the computer and its peripherals. This allows you to install hardware without rebooting because as hardware is installed, Windows 2000 automatically detects the new hardware, supplies necessary power and loads the necessary drivers.

 Warning: Only certain external devices should be installed with the computer running. When installing a new device, always follow the installation instructions that come with the device. Most internal devices and SCSI devices require the computer to be fully turned off before installation. Failure to do so may result in a damaged card, computer, and user.

Using Multiple Displays

Like Windows 98, Windows 2000 supports multiple video adapter cards and monitors. You can install more than one video card and display different information through each card. You can choose the primary display monitor, the relative position of each monitor to the others and extend the Windows desktop so that you can drag items from one screen to another or expand a window to display multiple screens.

Note: Multiple display support only works with Peripheral Component Interface (PCI) and Accelerated Graphics Port (AGP) video cards.

Working with Infrared Data Association (IrDA) Devices

Another new hardware technology supported by Windows 2000 is infrared data transmission. Infrared transceivers (devices that transmit and receive infrared signals) allow the transmission of information between a computer and a peripheral or between two computers without a physical connection. IrDA is an industry organization that establishes standards for infrared communication.

Currently, there are four IrDA standards: serial IrDA (IrDA-SIR), fast IrDA (IrDA-FIR), IrLPT printer support, and IrTran-P support. Windows 2000 supports all four of these technologies. IrDA-SIR supports data transmissions up to a maximum of 115,**000 bps (bits per second). IrDA-FIR supports communication at speeds up to 4 Mbps (Megabits per second). When you install an infrared port in Windows 2000, it appears as a local port. You can associate a printer (with an infrared port of its own) with this port, and Windows 2000 uses the IrLPT protocol to send the information to the printer. The IrTran-P protocol allows a Windows 2000 computer to receive digital images from a digital camera or other digital imaging devices.

 Tip: In Windows 2000, IrTran-P is a passive protocol. It listens for incoming data using the IrTran-P protocol but never initiates an IrTran-P connection.

Using the MMC to Manage Hardware

As with most other tools in Windows 2000, many of the tools used to manage hardware devices in Windows 2000 are snap-ins for the MMC and are found in the Computer Management console. Some tools, however, are found in the System Control Panel.

Working with Device Manager

The Device Manager provides a listing of all devices that Windows 2000 recognizes in the computer. The Windows 2000 implementation of Device Manager is similar to the Device Manager found in Windows 95 and 98, but is a snap-in for the MMC (Figure 6.6).

Figure 6.6 Device Manager Snap-In

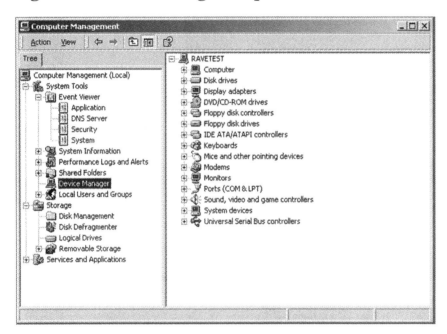

To open the Device Manager, follow these steps:

1. From the desktop, right-click My Computer and choose Manage.

2. In the Tree pane of the Computer Management console, expand System Tools and then choose Device Manager.

Alternately, open the System Properties window by following these steps:

1. From the Start Menu, choose Settings and then select Control Panel.

2. Double-click the System icon.

Tip: You can also access the System Properties window if you right-click My Computer and choose Properties.

3. From the System Properties window, choose the Hardware Properties page and then select Device Manager (Figure 6.7).

Figure 6.7 Hardware Property Page

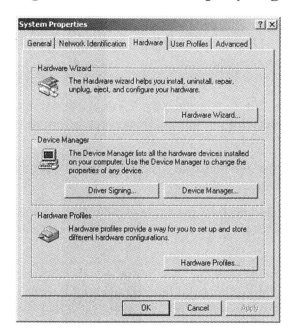

4.   The Device Manager opens in its own MMC console (Figure 6.8).

Figure 6.8 Device Manager Console

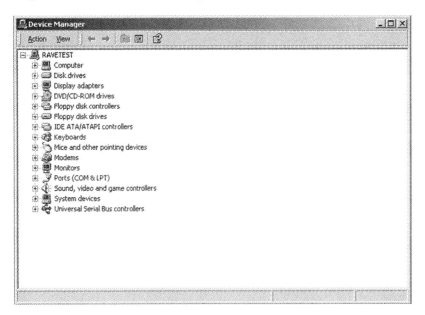

The Device Manager lists all devices inside or attached to the computer. By default, the devices are listed by type. To change the View type, from the Menu Bar choose View and then select the view type desired. You may choose to:

•   Display devices by type. In this view, each device type is represented by a branch. If you expand a branch, the Device Manager shows the installed devices of that type.

•   Display devices by connection. In other words, devices are listed based on how they are connected to the computer. This is convenient if, for example, you want to have all PCI devices listed together.

•   Display resources rather than devices. There are two choices that allow you to view the resources (memory address, IRQ, Direct Memory Access (DMA) setting, and Input/Output (I/O) setting). Like your choices for devices, you may view resources by type or by connection.

For anyone who has tried to hunt down an IRQ conflict in Windows NT 4.0, the ability to list devices and their IRQs so simply is a welcome change. Although Windows NT 4.0 had the System Diagnostics tool, the Device Manager provides much more information. The Device Manager does more than simply list devices and their resources. It shows devices that are not functioning properly with a bright yellow icon of an exclamation point and devices that have been disabled with an icon of a red X (Figure 6.9).

Figure 6.9 Disabled Device and Malfunctioning Device

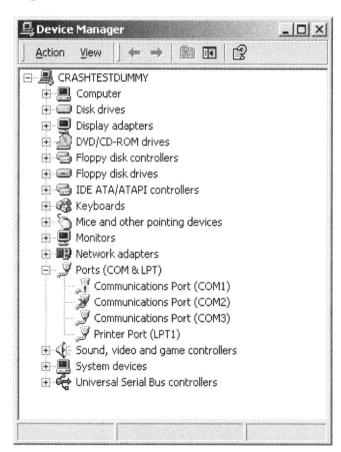

Using the Device Manager, you can also perform the following tasks on devices:

• Access detailed information about a device

• Enable and disable individual devices

• Change the drivers used for a device

• Manipulate the resource settings for a device

To access detailed information on any device, double-click the name of the device in the Device Manager. A properties window for the device displays. Most devices have at least three property sheets: General, Driver, and Resources (Figure 6.10). Many devices have a fourth property sheet that is specific to that type of device. For example, serial (COM) and printer (LPT) ports have a Port Settings page, and a USB controller has an Advanced page.

Figure 6.10 Device Property Window

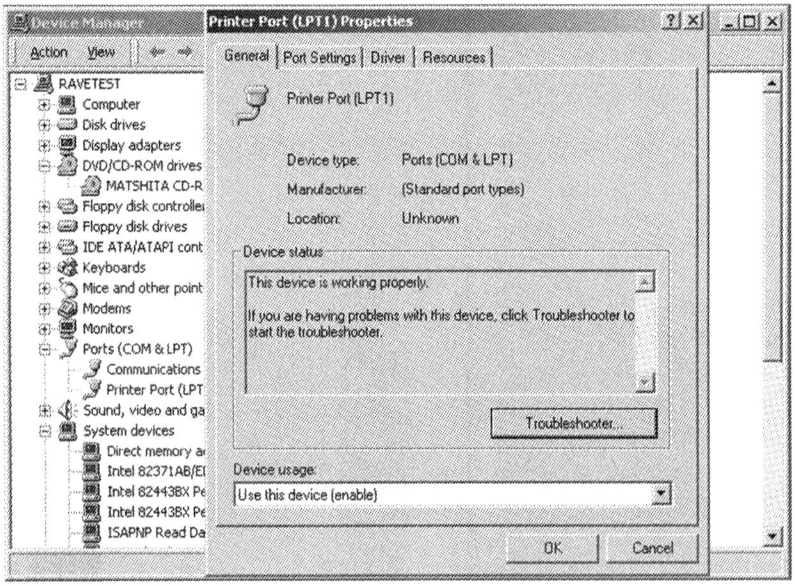

From the General property page, you can view the status of the device and can enable or disable the device. On the Driver property page, you can view the version, date, and provider of the driver used for the device. Clicking the Details button allows you to view which files are used for the driver and where they are located. From this page, you can also uninstall and update drivers. From the Resources property page, you can view the resources used by this device and view any resource conflicts involving the device. For some devices, you can also manually configure resource settings.

Managing Hardware with the Add/Remove Hardware Wizard

To simplify the process of adding new hardware, Windows 2000 has an Add/Remove Hardware Wizard. This wizard works in conjunction with PnP to automatically detect new hardware and assign resources to the device. If the device is not detected, the wizard also allows you to manually add and configure the device. The wizard can also be used to remove a device from the list of installed devices before physically removing the device.

To begin the Add/Remove Hardware Wizard, follow these steps:

1. From the Start Menu, choose settings and then select Control Panel.

2. Double-click Add/Remove Hardware and then choose Next to start the wizard (Figure 6.11).

Figure 6.11 Add/Remove Hardware Wizard

3. Choose whether you want to add (or troubleshoot) a device or remove the device. The remainder of the steps lead you through adding a new device. Select Add/Troubleshoot a device and then select Next.

4. The wizard begins an automatic detection of PnP devices. If it detects a new PnP device, Windows 2000 installs the necessary drivers and then presents a list of devices detected. Choose Next and then select Finish.

5. If the detection process fails to find any new PnP devices, it presents a list of known devices installed in the system. Heading this list is Add a new device (Figure 6.12).

Figure 6.12 Non-PnP Device Addition

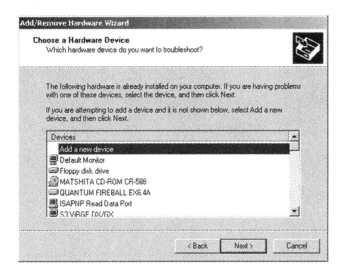

6. Choose Add a new device and then select Next.

7. Choose whether you want Windows 2000 to search for non-PnP devices or if you want to manually add a device. Allowing Windows 2000 to detect a device may result in a more accurate configuration, but Windows 2000 does not always detect non-PnP devices, and the process takes some time.

8. Choose whether you select to have Windows 2000 detect devices or whether you wish to manually add a device and then select Next.

If you chose automatic detection, Windows 2000 searches for devices based on device type. When it is finished, a list of detected new hardware displays (Figure 6.13). Choose the device(s) you wish to add (if not already selected) and then select Next. The drivers load, and the installation is completed. If you chose to manually add a device, you are presented with a list of device types. Select the device type and then select Next.

Figure 6.13 Automatic New Hardware Detection

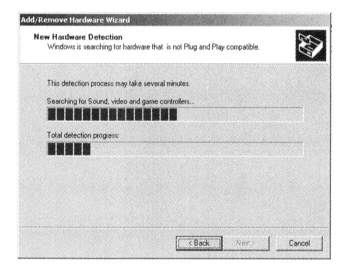

 Note: If the automatic detection of non-PnP devices fails, you have the option to manually add the device.

9. Depending on the device type you selected, you are usually presented with a list of manufacturers and models (Figure 6.14). In the left pane, choose the manufacturer of the device, select the model of the device in the right pane and then select Next.

10. If Windows 2000 cannot detect the settings for the device, a message displays. Choose OK.

11. Choose Interrupt Request, select Change Setting, enter a value for the IRQ and then select OK.

12. Choose Input/Output Range, select Change Setting, enter a value for the I/O range and then select OK.

Figure 6.14 Device Manufacturers and Models

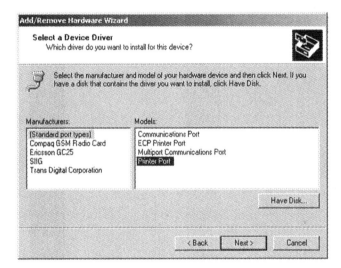

13. Confirm the settings you have entered and then select OK.

14. Choose Next and Windows 2000 copies the necessary drivers for the device.

15. Choose Finish to complete the installation process. If necessary, you are asked to restart the computer. Select Yes to reboot.

Note: Make sure the settings for IRQ and I/O address you enter match the settings on the device. If you are uncertain, check with the manufacturer of the device. Incorrect settings result in device conflicts and can cause a system malfunction.

Using Driver Signing

In order to ensure compatibility between a device and the operating system, Windows 2000 implements a new feature called driver signing. Driver signing helps prevent users from loading drivers that are not certified to work with Windows 2000 and prevent driver conflicts. All files on the Windows 2000 CD are digitally signed (marked by Microsoft as authentic). As an administrator, you can adjust the driver signing settings to customize driver restrictions.

To view and change driver signing options, perform the following steps:

1. From the desktop, right-click My Computer and then choose Properties.

2. In the System Properties window, choose the Hardware property page and then select Driver Signing (Figure 6.15).

Figure 6.15 Accessing Driver Signing Options

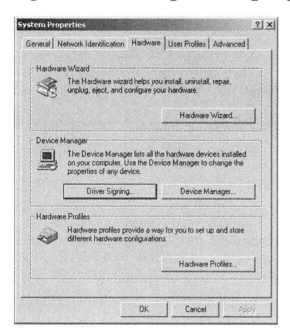

3.   You may choose the following options from the Driver Signing Options page:

•   Ignore the driver signing (which installs files whether they are signed or not)

•   Warn if the driver files you are using are not signed

•   Block the use of unsigned files

As administrator, you may also choose whether these settings should be applied to all users. Make your selections and then choose OK (Figure 6.16).

Figure 6.16 Driver Signing Options

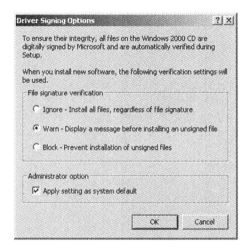

Tip: The default setting for driver signing warns if unsigned drivers are being used and applies the settings to all users who log on to the computer.

Creating Hardware Profiles

Hardware profiles define different computer hardware configurations. Hardware profiles are most commonly used with portable computers, which are likely to have two or more configurations (attached to a docking station and mobile, for example).

A portable computer may be attached to a docking station, a device that provides a connection to peripheral devices like an external monitor, a network card, additional drives, a keyboard, or mouse. At other times, you may use the portable computer at another location in an undocked configuration. The devices listed in the Device Manager will be different, depending on where the computer is used. In order to prevent device errors and conflicts, you can configure appropriate hardware profiles for each hardware configuration. You can choose the default profile and can configure Windows 2000 to prompt you to select a profile when the system boots.

To create a new hardware profile, open the System Properties sheet as follows:

1. From the desktop, right-click My Computer and choose Properties.

2. In the System Properties window, choose the Hardware properties page and then select Hardware Profiles (Figure 6.17).

Figure 6.17 Hardware Profiles Window

3. The default hardware profile (Profile 1) displays. To create a new profile, choose Profile 1 (Current) and then select Copy.

4. Assign a name for the new profile and then choose OK.

5. The new profile appears in the list of profiles (Figure 6.18).

Figure 6.18 New Hardware Profile

6. Choose the profile you want to have as the default and then select the up-arrow until the profile moves to the top of the list (Figure 6.19).

Figure 6.19 Default Profile Assignment

7. Choose OK to close the Hardware Profiles window and then select OK again to close the System Properties window.

To modify settings for a profile, you must reboot the computer. When you reboot, you are presented with a list of profiles from which to choose (Figure 6.20).

Figure 6.20 Hardware Profile Boot Menu

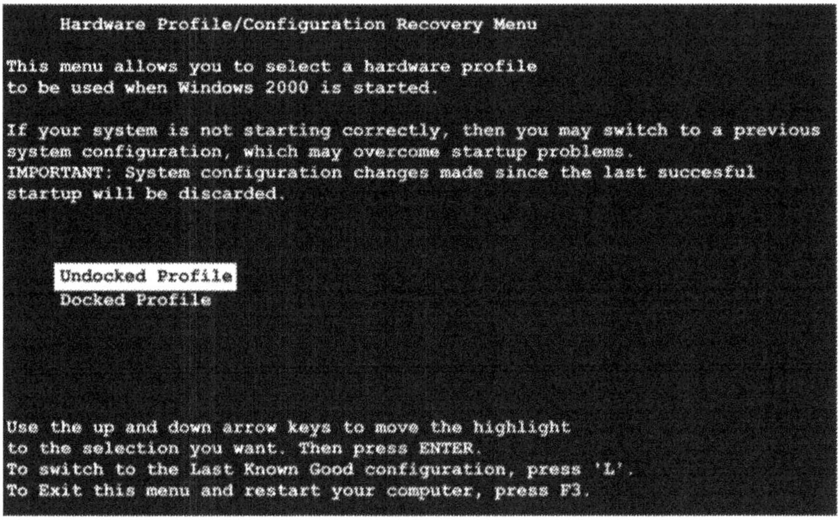

```
        Hardware Profile/Configuration Recovery Menu

This menu allows you to select a hardware profile
to be used when Windows 2000 is started.

If your system is not starting correctly, then you may switch to a previous
system configuration, which may overcome startup problems.
IMPORTANT: System configuration changes made since the last succesful
startup will be discarded.


        Undocked Profile
        Docked Profile




Use the up and down arrow keys to move the highlight
to the selection you want. Then press ENTER.
To switch to the Last Known Good configuration, press 'L'.
To Exit this menu and restart your computer, press F3.
```

If you do not make a selection within 30 seconds, the default profile is used. Using the arrow keys, choose the profile you wish to modify and then press the **ENTER** key. Once the computer has completely booted, log on to Windows 2000 using an account with administrative permissions.

To change the settings for a hardware profile, start by opening the Hardware Profiles window and proceed according to the following steps:

1. From the desktop, right-click My Computer and choose Properties.

2. Choose the Hardware properties page and then select Hardware Profiles.

3. Verify that the profile you wish to alter is the selected profile. If so, choose OK to close this window.

4. In the Hardware properties page, choose Device Manager.

5. In the Device Manager console make changes as necessary for this profile. For example, if you are configuring a profile for an undocked portable computer, you may wish to disable an external CD-ROM or keyboard.

Tip: If you are prompted to reboot the computer after making a change, choose No. This allows you to make several changes without rebooting after each change. Once you have made all changes, make sure you reboot the computer.

6. After making the changes, close the device manager, and close the System Properties window

7. You should reboot the computer to implement and test the changes. From the Start Menu, choose Shut Down, select Restart, and then select OK.

8. During the boot process, use the arrow keys to choose the desired profile, and then press **ENTER**.

Troubleshooting Hardware Problems

Although PnP technology generally reduces problems with conflicting hardware resources, you may find that a device is not functioning properly. The first step in diagnosing a suspected hardware problem is to open the Device Manager. To do so, right-click My Computer (on the desktop) and then choose Properties. In the System Properties window, select the Hardware properties page and then select Device Manager. Devices that are not functioning properly usually appear with a yellow exclamation point next to them (Figure 6.21).

Figure 6.21 Malfunctioning Device

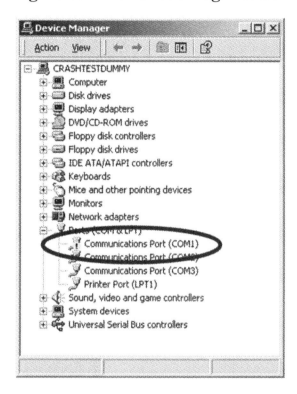

If the Device Manager shows a device that is improperly configured, you have two options to correct the problem. Both involve accessing the detailed information for the device. To do so, double-click the device name in the Device Manager (Figure 6.22).

Tip: Occasionally, a device has an incorrect resource configuration but the Device Manager does not show a problem. If you know which device is not working, check the resource settings, even if there is no yellow exclamation point.

Figure 6.22 Device Properties Window

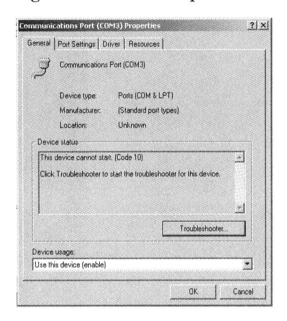

From the General property page of the Device Properties window, you can view the device status. Windows 2000 reports the suspected problem and how to correct it. A link to the Troubleshooter appears immediately below the Device Status information. Troubleshooter is part of the Windows 2000 Help file and is designed to step you through solving hardware-related problems. To start, choose Troubleshooter. Windows 2000 Help opens with the hardware troubleshooting guide (Figure 6.23). Follow the directions presented in the Help file.

Figure 6.23 Hardware Troubleshooting

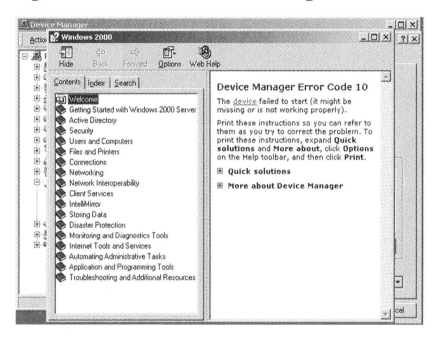

If you do not wish to run the Troubleshooter or if it does not resolve the conflict, you can try to manually configure the settings for the device. Do this from the Resource Properties page. If there is a button labeled Set Configuration Manually, choose it to view the current settings used by the device. Select one of the settings listed. The Conflicting Device List shows if this setting is causing a conflict with another device (Figure 6.24).

Figure 6.24 Conflicting Device

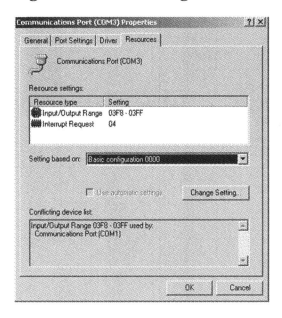

You may then choose Change Setting to change the setting to one that is not causing a conflict.

Tip: You cannot just change the resource setting in Windows 2000 and expect the device to work after rebooting. The settings on the device itself must also be changed. Refer to the device documentation to learn which settings are valid for the device and how to change them.

Group Policy

In Windows 2000, administration of user and computer accounts can be simplified by limiting what a user can do. In Windows NT 4.0, this can be accomplished by implementing account policies using the System Policy Editor. System policies restrict the desktop environment and force the system configuration settings on users.

In Windows 2000, you use Group Policy to define similar configurations for individual users and groups of users. Group Policy settings are part of the Active Directory as Group Policy Objects (GPOs). GPOs are associated with certain Active Directory containers, including sites, domains, and Organizational Units (OUs).

If you want to define a Group Policy that affects all users in a domain, associate the GPO with the domain object in Active Directory. If you want to implement a Group Policy for a choose group of users, place the users in their own OU and associate the GPO with that OU.

Although both are designed to do similar things, there are many differences between Windows NT 4.0 System Policy and Windows 2000 Group Policy (Table 6.1). Of note to administrators who have tried unsuccessfully to undo System Policy in Windows NT 4.0, Windows 2000 Group Policy changes can be easily removed.

In Windows NT 4.0, policy changes make permanent changes to the registry. To undo these changes, you have to create a new policy that exactly counteracts all other policy settings or manually edit the registry.

In Windows 2000, this is no longer necessary. Windows 2000 Group Policy is not only used to restrict the desktop environment. Group Policy settings can be configured to aid in the automation of software installations and upgrades. With a few changes in Group Policy settings, you can have users install an upgrade to an application without having to train them how to do it.

Table 6.1 Comparing System Policy to Group Policy

Feature	Windows NT 4.0	Windows 2000
Applies to	The entire domain only	Sites, domains, or OUs
Group Membership	May be further controlled by user membership in security groups	May be further controlled by user membership in security groups
Security	Not secure	Secure
Persistence	Makes permanent changes to registry	Changes do not persist in the registry
Use	Used to lockdown desktop (restrict use only)	Used to restrict use and to enhance use
Software Installation	Not used	Can be used to allow or require users to load new applications and updates to applications

Overall, Group Policy helps reduce the Total Cost of Ownership (TCO). TCO is the cost involved in building and maintaining a computer network. One of the major costs for corporations results from lost productivity at the desktop. If users have the ability to change their computer configurations, load third-party applications, or delete system files, there is a higher chance that their workstation will become unusable. The results are lost productivity for both the user and the system administrator who must correct the problems and a higher TCO for the company. By carefully constructing Group Policy settings, you can restrict the amount of user control over a workstation, which reduces the likelihood of problems.

Applying Group Policy

Group Policy settings are stored in two places, the Group Policy Template (GPT) and the Group Policy Container (GPC). The GPT is a folder hierarchy within the SYSVOL folder on all domain controllers and contains information on most of the Group Policy settings. The GPC, an Active Directory container, contains the information needed for replication of the Group Policy, including the version of the Group Policy, whether it is enabled or disabled and a list of extensions used in the GPO.

Like other objects in the Active Directory, each GPO is assigned a Globally Unique Identifier (GUID). The GUID is a 128-bit name used to identify the object within the Active Directory. Windows 2000 uses GUIDs so that objects can be renamed and moved within the Active Directory but can still be accessed because the GUID never changes.

 Tip: The GPT folder name corresponds to the GUID assigned to the GPO. GPTs are created in the following folder:

`WINNT\SYSVOL\SYSVOL\DOMAIN_NAME\POLICIES\{GUID_NAME}`

where **DOMAIN_NAME** is the name of the domain, and **GUID_NAME** is the 128-bit GUID assigned to the GPO.

Group Policy settings are applied to user accounts whenever the user logs on to the domain. GPOs associated with computer accounts are applied whenever the computer boots. The process of evaluating and loading GPOs requires some processing time and generates network traffic. Furthermore, many GPOs assigned to an account can become difficult to manage. For these reasons, you should consider the following guidelines when applying Group Policy:

- Limit the use of Block Inheritance and No Override (discussed later in the lesson). These options introduce another level of complexity to remembering what the effective policies are.

- Limit the number of GPOs associated with an account. The time it takes for a computer to start up and for a user to log on depends in part on the number of GPOs that must be evaluated.

- Disable portions of the GPO that are not being used. You can disable either the Computer Configuration or User Configuration portion of a GPO. If a GPO is specifically assigned to an OU which contains only user accounts, disable the Computer Configuration portion.

- Group similar settings in the same GPO. This helps you find policy settings more readily.

Creating a Group Policy Object (GPO)

When you create a GPO, you assign the GPO to an Active Directory object at the same time. The process of creating a new GPO to an OU or domain is done through the Active Directory Users and Computers MMC. To create a new GPO, follow these steps:

1. From the Start Menu, choose Programs, Administrative Tools and then select Active Directory Users and Computers.

2. In the Tree pane of the Active Directory Users and Computers console, choose the container for which you want to create a Group Policy (the target container). You may have to expand other containers to find the target container (Figure 6.25).

Figure 6.25 Target Container Selection

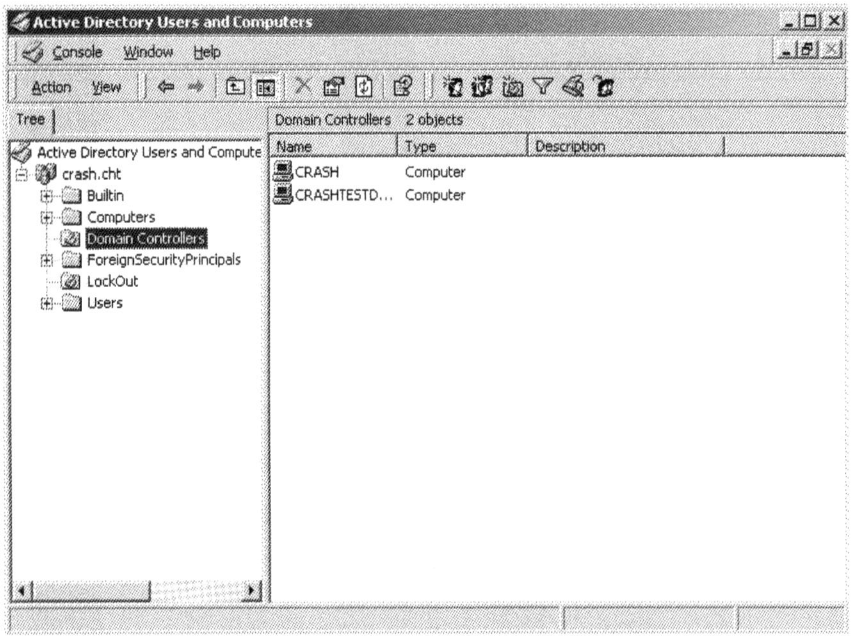

3. Right-click the target container and choose Properties.

Note: The target container must be an OU or a domain. You cannot assign Group Policy to other containers.

4. In the Container Properties page, choose the Group Policy property page (Figure 6.26). If a Group Policy property page is not available, you did not select a domain or OU for your target container.

Figure 6.26 Group Policy Property Page

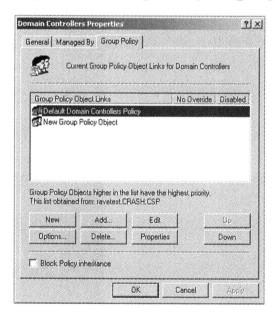

5. Choose New, type a name for the GPO, and then press **ENTER**.

If you have previously created a GPO and wish to associate it with an OU, access the Group Policy property page for the OU, as just described. Instead of clicking New in step 5, choose Add and follow these steps:

1. In the Add a Group Policy Object Link window, choose the location of the GPO. If you are uncertain where the GPO is located, select the All property page, where all of the GPOs in the Active Directory are listed.

2. Choose the GPO you wish to associate with this OU and select OK.

Associating a GPO with a Site

Creating and associating GPOs to sites (rather than domains and OUs) is done through the Active Directory Sites and Services console. To open the console, follow these steps:

1. From the Start Menu choose Programs, Administrative Tools and then select Active Directory Sites and Services.

2. In the Tree pane, right-click the site for which you are creating a new GPO and choose Properties.

3. In the Site Properties window, choose the Group Policy property page, select New and name the new GPO.

Configuring Group Policy

Once you have created a new GPO, you can alter the settings to suit your needs. Group Policy settings are made in the Group Policy snap-in for the MMC. This snap-in can be opened from within Active Directory Users and Computers or can be placed in its own MMC console.

Opening the Group Policy Snap-in

To open the Group Policy snap-in, first open the Group Policy property page for an OU to which the GPO is associated. To do so, follow these steps:

1. From the Start Menu, choose Programs, Administrative Tools and then select Active Directory Users and Computers.

2. In the Tree pane of the Active Directory Users and Computers console, choose the container associated with the GPO.

3.   Right-click the container and choose Properties.

4.   In the Container Properties page, choose the Group Policy property page.

5.   Choose the GPO you wish to configure and then select Edit.

Tip: To edit the GPO, you can also right-click the GPO name and choose Edit or double-click the GPO name.

6.   The Group Policy MMC snap-in displays (Figure 6.27).

Figure 6.27 Group Policy Snap-in

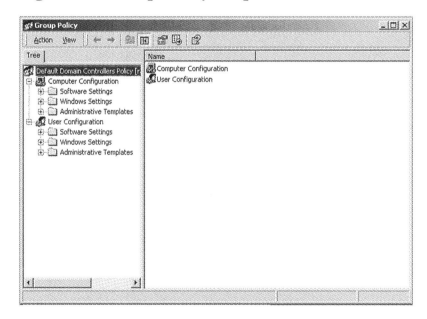

The Group Policy snap-in Tree pane has two main extensions (branches), Computer Configuration and User Configuration. Under each of these extensions are three folders. They are Software Settings, Windows Settings, and Administrative Templates. Although these three folders are found under both Computer Configuration and User Configuration, their contents differ depending on the extension to which they belong. For example, you can implement policies for the event log under the Computer Configuration extension, but you cannot do so under the User Configuration, since the event log is computer-specific, not user-specific.

Changing Administrative Template Settings

Each of the three folders contains policies that can be altered, and most have a unique and object-specific configuration. However, the objects contained within the Administrative Templates folder all share a common and simple interface. To change the settings for an object contained within the Administrative Templates folders, follow these steps:

1. From the Start Menu, choose Programs, Administrative Tools, and then select Active Directory Users and Computers.

2. In the Tree Pane, expand containers as necessary, right-click the Active Directory container that is associated with the Group Policy you will edit and then choose Properties.

3. In the Container properties window, choose the Group Policy property page and then double-click the name of the Group Policy you will edit.

4. In the Group Policy snap-in, expand either Computer Configuration or User Configuration, expand Administrative Templates, and then choose the subfolder that contains the settings you wish to alter (Figure 6.28). You may have to expand several levels of folders.

Figure 6.28 Administrative Template Choice

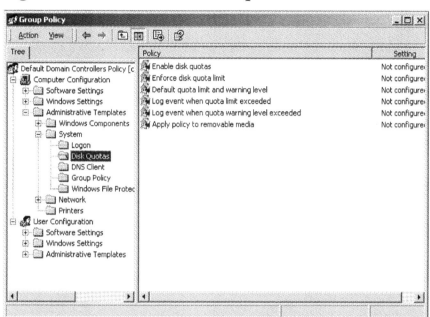

5. In the Details pane, double-click the name of the policy you will change.

Every Administrative Template shares a common interface (Figure 6.29). The Policy property page has three options: Not Configured, Enabled, and Disabled. The first option indicates this option has not been configured for the OU and will not override settings from higher-level containers. If the policy is enabled, settings are applied. If disabled, the settings are not applied to user (or computer) accounts in this OU.

Figure 6.29 Administrative Template

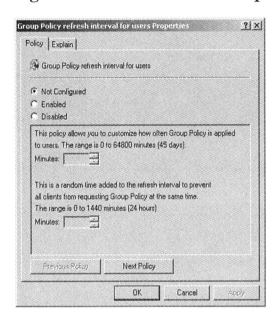

Each Administrative Template also has an Explain property page, which provides more detail about the policy. It contains Previous Policy and Next Policy buttons that allow you to scroll through policies within a folder without closing the Administrative Template each time (Figure 6.30).

Modifying Scripts

In a network environment, scripts are used to run batch files and applications when the script is executed. In Windows NT 4.0, you can create logon scripts that run when a user logs on to the network. The logon script is associated with a user account. Windows 2000 significantly expands the scripting possibilities. In Windows 2000, you can create logon and logoff scripts for a user account and can also create computer account scripts that run during the startup and shutdown process.

Figure 6.30 Administrative Template Explanation Page

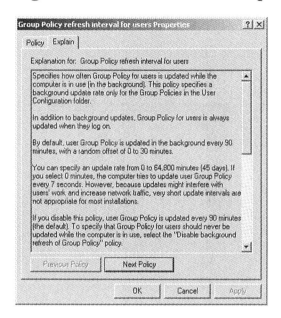

To view and modify Group Policy settings for scripts, start by opening the Group Policy console as follows:

1. From the Start Menu, choose Programs, Administrative Tools and then select Active Directory Users and Computers.

2. In the Tree Pane, right-click the container with the associated GPO and choose Properties.

3. In the Container property sheet, choose the Group Policy property page, select the GPO you wish to alter and then select Edit. The Group Policy Console displays.

4. In the Tree pane, expand Computer Configuration or User Configuration, expand Windows Settings and then choose Scripts.

Note: Startup and Shutdown scripts are found under Computer Configuration. Logon and Logoff scripts are located under User Configuration.

5. In the right-most pane, double-click the script you wish to alter.

6. The Script Property page displays. To add a script, choose Add. If a script already exists, you may select the script and select Edit or Remove (Figure 6.31).

Figure 6.31 Script Property Page

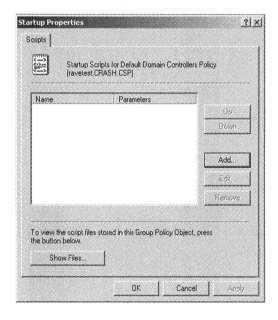

Tip: In the Script property page, you can also dictate the order in which scripts run by selecting a script and choosing Up or Down. Scripts at the top of the list execute before lower-listed scripts.

Understanding Security Settings

In addition to limiting what a user can do, Group Policy is used to enforce security settings for both user and computer accounts. Security settings that can be modified using GPOs include the following:

Account Policies—These settings allow you to set password restrictions, account lockout policies, and Kerberos (encryption) settings.

Note: Account policy settings, including password settings, account lockouts, and Kerberos settings can only be implemented at the domain level. If you apply these settings to an OU or site, they are ignored.

Local Policies—These settings can only be used on the local computer and include auditing policies.

Event Log—These settings allow you to set the configuration of the event log, formerly part of the Event Viewer in Windows NT 4.0.

Restricted Group—These settings allow you to manage membership in the built-in groups.

System Services—These settings allow you to configure settings for the system services. In Windows NT 4.0, similar settings are found in the Services Control Panel.

Registry—These settings control access to the system registry.

File System—These settings allow you to control access to folders and files.

Public Key Policies—These settings allow you to set the use of file-level encryption, certificate authorities, and other encryption settings.

IP Security Settings on Active Directory—These settings allow you to configure Internet Protocol Security (IPSec).

Configuring Folder Redirection

In Windows 2000, you can redirect a folder so that when users open the folder, they are actually accessing a network share. This allows you to standardize some folders (like the Start menu, which is actually a folder) and store the contents of folders (like My Documents) on a server, where the data can be backed up.

The five folders that can be redirected are as follows:

* Application Data

* Desktop

* My Documents

* My Pictures

* Start menu

To redirect a folder using GPOs, begin by opening the appropriate GPO in the Group Policy console. To do so, follow these steps:

1. From the Start Menu, choose Programs, Administrative Tools and then select Active Directory Users and Computers.

2. In the Tree pane of the Active Directory Users and Computers console, choose the container that is associated with the GPO.

3. Right-click the container and choose Properties.

4. In the Container Properties page, choose the Group Policy property page.

5. Choose the GPO you wish to configure and then select Edit.

6. In the Tree pane of the Group Policy console, expand User Configuration, expand Windows Settings and then expand Folder Redirection.

7. In the Tree pane, right-click the folder you want to redirect and choose Properties.

8. In the Target property page, choose either Basic or Advanced (Figure 6.32).

Figure 6.32 Folder Redirection

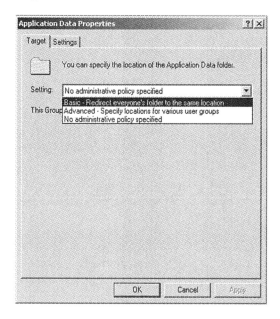

 Note: The Basic setting allows you to choose one network share for all user accounts. The Advanced option allows you to select a different network share for different security groups.

9. If you choose basic, enter the Universal Naming Convention (UNC) name for the network share. If you chose Advanced, select Add to add a security group and UNC.

Managing Group Policy Permissions

By default, Group Policy settings affect all user and computer accounts within the container to which the Group Policy has been associated. You can alter the permissions associated with a GPO to make users exempt from the GPO and to delegate control of the GPO to other administrators.

Tip: A user account must be assigned the Read and Apply Group Policy permissions for the GPO or the GPO has no effect on the user account.

There are times when a GPO may influence a broader range of user accounts than you would like. You have the option of creating additional OUs, placing accounts in these OUs and then creating new GPOs for the OUs. Alternatively, you may filter the scope of a GPO by creating security groups. A security group is a group of user accounts to which you may assign security settings. You can make some user accounts members of a security group and then deny the Apply Group Policy and clear the Read settings for that group. The GPO will not affect members of the group.

For example, suppose you have created an OU that contains both full-time employees and interns. You want to restrict computer usage for the interns but do not wish to impose the same restrictions on the full-time employees. You can create two security groups (maybe call them fulltime and interns) and place the appropriate accounts in each group. You would then assign the Apply Group Policy and Read permissions to the intern group and clear these settings for the fulltime group (Figure 6.33).

Figure 6.33 Group Policy Filtering

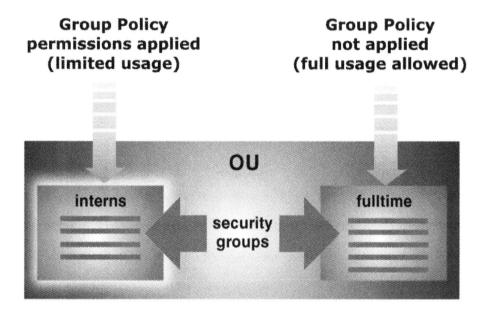

To delegate control of a GPO to other users, create a security group, placing appropriate user accounts in the group and assign the Read and Write permissions (or Full Control permission) to the group.

 Note: A group only needs the Read and Write permissions in order to fully manage a GPO. Full Control is not necessary and offers more control than you may wish to delegate.

To modify the permissions on a GPO, follow these steps:

1. From the Start Menu, choose Programs, Administrative Tools and then select Active Directory Users and Computers.

2. In the Tree pane of the Active Directory Users and Computers console, right-click the container that is associated with the GPO and then choose Properties.

3. In the Container Properties page, choose the Group Policy property page.

4. Choose the Group Policy you wish to alter and then select Properties.

5. Choose the Security property page and make changes to the permissions as necessary. When finished, select OK.

Note: The process of applying permissions to GPOs is identical to applying permissions to other Active Directory objects.

Managing Group Policy Inheritance

When a GPO is associated with a container (a site, domain, or OU), the child objects of that container are also associated with the GPO. In addition, you can associate multiple GPOs to a container. Windows 2000 determines which Group Policy to assign to a user or computer by analyzing each of the GPOs in a particular order. By default, Group Policy is inherited and cumulative.

Note: One Active Directory container may be associated with multiple GPOs, and one GPO may be associated with multiple containers.

When assigning Group Policy settings to a computer or user, Windows 2000 evaluates Group Policy settings starting with the Active Directory container farthest from the computer or user object. For example, suppose you have associated two Group Policy objects to the domain and one each to an OU within that domain and to an OU within that OU. You have also assigned a Group Policy object to the site in which the computer is located (Figure 6.34).

Figure 6.34 Basic Active Directory Structure with Group Policy

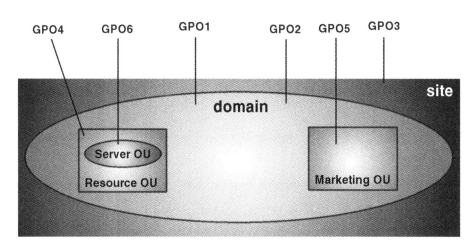

When a user logs on to the computer, Group Policy permissions are evaluated beginning with those associated with the site. Domain GPOs are then evaluated, followed by the higher level OU and then by the lower-level OU (which is closest to the user object in the Active Directory structure). In Figure 6.34, the order of GPOs evaluated for a user account in the Marketing OU is GPO3 (associated with the site), GPO1 (domain), GPO2 (domain) and then GPO5 (Marketing OU). A computer account in the Servers OU would have GPO3, GPO1, GPO2, GPO4 (Resources OU), and GPO6 (Servers OU) applied, in that order.

 Note: By default, Group Policy settings are cumulative. However, if two or more settings are in conflict, the more recently evaluated setting overrides the earlier-evaluated setting.

Group Policy settings can be enforced or blocked as necessary. For example, if you assign a GPO to a site, and you want to ensure that all user and computer accounts use this policy, regardless of other GPOs associated at lower levels, you can enforce the policy. Likewise, you may wish to make an OU exempt from the policies associated with higher level containers. You can block inheritance for this OU.

To enforce a policy from above, follow these steps:

1. From the Start Menu, choose Programs, Administrative Tools and then select Active Directory Users and Computers.

2. In the Tree pane, expand containers as necessary to find the container associated with the GPO.

3. Right-click the container and choose Properties.

4. In the container properties window, choose the Group Policy property page.

5. Choose the GPO you wish to enforce and then select Options.

6. Choose No Override and then select OK (Figure 6.35). A check mark appears in the No Override column next to the GPO name.

Figure 6.35 GPO Enforcement

To prevent an OU from inheriting the settings of a parent container, access the Group Policy property page for that OU, as described in the previous steps. On the Group Policy property page, choose Block Policy Inheritance (Figure 6.36).

Figure 6.36 Preventing GPO Inheritance

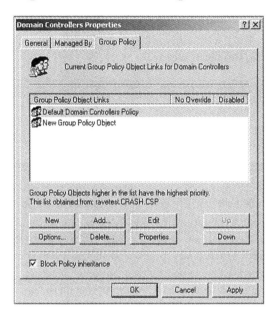

Software Management Using Group Policy

So far, you have seen how to use Group Policy to restrict what a user can do and to enforce settings and scripts for user and computer accounts. However, Group Policy can also be used to automate installation and upgrades to applications. Microsoft has created two new technologies, Windows Installer and Software Installation and Maintenance. Windows Installer enhances the way in which applications are installed, updated, and removed from a system. The Software Installation and Maintenance technology uses a combination of the features of Group Policy and Windows Installer technology, allowing you to deploy and manage applications with a minimal amount of administration.

Identifying Software Management Technologies

The new Windows Installer uses a Windows Installer package to install programs. Replacing the **SETUP.EXE** file used in older versions of applications, the package file initiates the installation and provides a custom installation, recovery from deleted files, and clean removal.

Tip: Windows Installer package file names end with the .MSI extension.

With a custom installation, not all features may be installed during the setup procedure, but appear to be available from within the application. The options are only installed when a user wants them. For example, a word processing program may have extensive foreign language support. Rather than loading these dictionaries and support files for every user (which takes time and disk space and may slow the application), they are available on an as-needed basis. A user attempting to access the Spanish dictionary, for example, is asked to wait a moment while the component is installed. Once installed, the component is available to the user each time.

Windows Installer supports recovery if one or more critical files needed to run the application are deleted or become corrupt. For various reasons, files may become unusable. With traditional installations, if any critical application file becomes corrupt, the entire application must be reinstalled. With Windows Installer, an application detects the absence or corruption of a file and acquires a new copy of the file from the original installation source.

A third benefit to Windows Installer is the ability to completely remove an application from a computer. Although many applications support uninstallation, Windows Installer ensures that the application does not leave orphaned files or deletes files used by other applications.

Windows Installer can perform these functions on a computer, even if the user currently logged on does not have permission to install applications. The installation process uses elevated privileges that supercede those of the user.

The Software Installation and Maintenance technology combines the features of the Windows Installer with Group Policy and Active Directory.

Using this technology, you can create GPOs that have the following ability:

*   Force an application to be installed when a user logs on

*   Make an application available to a user for installation

*   Implement upgrades and patches to software

*   Uninstall applications

This centralized approach to software management greatly reduces the time an administrator spends at client computers. Simply installing a patch for an existing application on each client computer may take several days. Creating a GPO to do the installation may take 15 minutes. When the user logs on, the patch automatically applies without further intervention.

 Note: The features of the Windows Installer and Software Maintenance technology require Group Policy. This technology only works on client computers running Windows 2000.

Deploying Software

Deploying software remotely using the Windows Installer and GPOs greatly reduces the time an administrator spends at client computers and reduces the TCO of the network. When you deploy applications, you may choose to assign or publish an application. Assigning an application ensures that the application is always available for a user or on a specific computer. Publishing an application makes it available for installation, but the user must actively begin the installation process.

Assigning Applications

You can assign applications to computer accounts or user accounts. Assigning an application to a computer account ensures that the application is available to any user who logs on to the computer and activates the program. Assigning an application to a user account ensures that the user is able to use the program, independent of which computer the user is logged on to.

Tip: When you assign an application to a computer, it automatically installs on the computer. When you assign an application to a user account, the application becomes available for installation but does not install unless the user activates the program.

When you assign a program, shortcuts to the program may be placed in the Start Menu and the desktop. When a user attempts to run the program, the program automatically installs and then executes.

To assign an application to a user or computer account, you must first have the Windows Installer package file with the extension .MSI.

1.   Place the .MSI file and all installation files in a shared folder.

2.   From the Start Menu, choose Programs, Administrative Tools and then select Active Directory Users and Computers.

3.   In the Tree Pane, expand containers as necessary, right-click the Active Directory container that is associated with the Group Policy you will edit, and then choose Properties.

4.   In the Container properties window, choose the Group Policy property page and then double-click the name of the Group Policy you will edit.

5.   In the Group Policy snap-in, expand either Computer Configuration or User Configuration, expand Software Settings, right-click Software Installation, choose New and then select Package (Figure 6.37).

Figure 6.37 New Software Package Selection

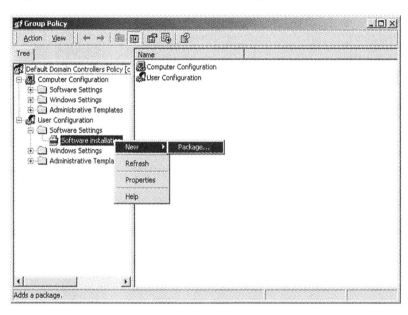

6. In the File Open window, choose the .MSI file from the network share you have created. Make sure you either enter the UNC for the network path and filename or browse the network share using My Network Places. Do not use the local address (for example, c:\installers\office.msi).

7. Choose Assigned and then select OK. After a moment, select Software Installation in the Tree pane, and the software package displays in the Details pane.

Publishing Applications

Publishing an application places the application in the Add/Remove Software control panel. The application does not automatically install, nor is a shortcut to the application placed on the desktop or Start Menu. A user will not know that the program can be installed without opening the Add/Remove control panel.

To publish an application, follow the steps above for assigning an application. In Step 7, choose Published instead of Assigned and then select OK.

Publishing Non-Windows Installer Applications

To assign an application, it must have an .MSI file and must be a Windows Installer application. However, you can publish applications that are not Windows Installer compatible by creating a .ZAP file. A .ZAP file is a text file that contains the information necessary to publish the application and can be created using any text editor.

Using a .ZAP file results in the following limitations to the installation:

* The application cannot be assigned to user or computer accounts; it can only be published

* The application will not automatically repair itself

* The application will probably require some user intervention

* The user must have permission to install the application

A .ZAP file has two sections, an Application section and an Extension section, identified by the headings [Application] and [Ext], respectively (Figure 6.38).

Figure 6.38 Sample .ZAP file

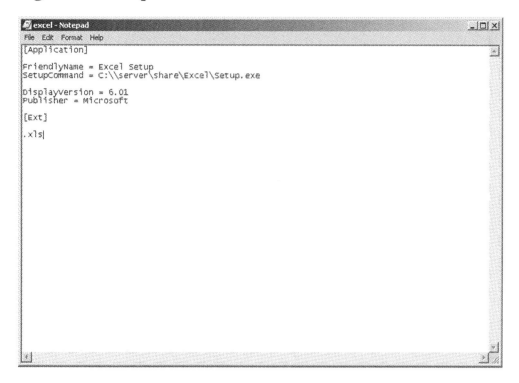

The Application section includes the information necessary to install the application and the information displayed to a user in the Add/Remove Programs control panel. The following are five tags that may be used in the Application section, the first two of which are required:

FriendlyName—The name that appears in the Add/Remove Programs control panel and should be easily identifiable to a user.

SetupCommand—The command that executes when a user chooses to install the program.

DisplayVersion—Displays the version number of the application.

Publisher—Lists the company that produced the program.

URL—Displays the Universal Resource Locator (URL) for a Web page that contains additional information about the program.

The File Extensions section, which is optional, associates file extensions with the application. If used, when a user double-clicks a file with a particular extension, the associated program runs and opens the file.

Customizing Software Installations

When you publish or assign a program, you can optionally implement a software modification file (or .MST file). The .MST file defines changes in the standard installation. For example, you are publishing a money management program for users throughout your worldwide corporation. You want users in Tokyo to have access to information in yen, users in London to work with currency in British pounds sterling and users in the United States to work with dollars. You can create a different OU for each of these geographic regions, create a different GPO for each OU and apply an .MST file to each GPO that defines the currency type to install during installation of the application.

 Note: Modification files are only used during installation of the application and cannot be used to change settings once the application has been installed.

To use a software modification file, follow the steps above for assigning or publishing software. When prompted for the type of deployment, choose Advanced published or assigned (Figure 6.39) and then follow these steps:

1. In the Software Properties window, choose the Modifications property page and then select Add to add a modification file.

Figure 6.39 Deployment Customization

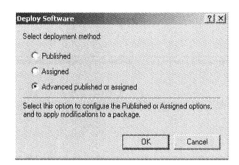

2.   Choose the .MST file you wish to use and then select OK. To add more than one modification file, select Add again and add the other files. When all files have been added and arranged in their proper order, select OK to publish or assign the package.

Tip: When you close the properties page for the software, the package assigns or publishes immediately. Once the package is assigned or published, you cannot add modification files.

Upgrading and Removing Software

Fundamental to a smooth-running network is having all users working with the same version of applications. As updates and patches become available for an application, you want all users to install these changes. However, the work involved with training users on installing the upgrade or on manually installing the software is prohibitive. You can use GPOs to deploy upgrades to software, implement a mandatory upgrade, which runs when a user logs on, or offer an optional upgrade. Software patches and service packs can be automated by redeploying the software.

Implementing a Software Upgrade

To deploy an upgrade, make changes in the Software Installation portion of the Group Policy. To do so, follow these steps:

 Note: Version 1.0 refers to the original installation of the software package, and Version 2.0 refers to the upgrade.

---

1. From the Start Menu, choose Programs, Administrative Tools and then select Active Directory Users and Computers.

2. In the Tree Pane, expand containers as necessary, right-click the Active Directory container associated with the Group Policy you will edit and then choose Properties.

3. In the Container Properties window, choose the Group Policy property page and then double-click the name of the Group Policy you will edit.

4. In the Group Policy snap-in, expand either Computer Configuration or User Configuration, expand Software Settings, and choose Software Installation.

5. In the Details pane, right-click Version 2.0 of the software and choose Properties.

6. In the Software Properties sheet, choose the Upgrades property page (Figure 6.40).

Figure 6.40 Upgrade Assignment

7. Choose Add, select version 1.0 of the package and then select OK.

8. If you want this to be a mandatory upgrade, choose Required Upgrade for existing package (Figure 6.41), otherwise leave this unselected and then select OK.

Figure 6.41 Mandatory Upgrade

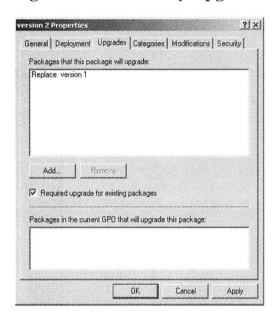

 Note: After performing an optional upgrade, a user can simultaneously run both the new and old versions of the program.

Applying a Service Pack

You can mark a program for redeployment when a service pack or patch for the program becomes available. When you mark a program for redeployment, it is made available again to the users, either as a published application or as an assigned application. When the users run the program, one of three things will occur, depending on how the program was originally deployed (Table 6.2).

Table 6.2 Redeployment Paths

If the application was originally...	The redeployment will...
Published and installed	Update all shortcuts to the program (in the Start menu and on the desktop) and registry settings when the user logs on. The update will occur the first time the user runs th e application.
Assigned to a user account	Update all shortcuts to the program (in the Start menu and on the desktop) and registry settings when the user logs on. The update will occur the first time the user runs the application.
Assigned to a computer account	Update settings the next time the computer is turned on or rebooted.

To install a service pack or patch, follow these steps:

1. Obtain a service pack update that includes an .MSI file. Place the service pack files in the installation folder.

2. From the Start Menu, choose Programs, Administrative Tools and then select Active Directory Users and Computers.

3. In the Tree Pane, expand containers as necessary, right-click the Active Directory container that is associated with the Group Policy you will edit and then select Properties.

4. In the Container properties window, choose the Group Policy property page and then double-click the name of the Group Policy you will edit.

5. In the Group Policy snap-in, expand either Computer Configuration or User Configuration, expand Software Settings and choose Software Installation.

6. In the Details pane, right-click the software package, choose All Tasks and then select Redeploy Application (Figure 6.42).

Figure 6.42 Application Redeployment

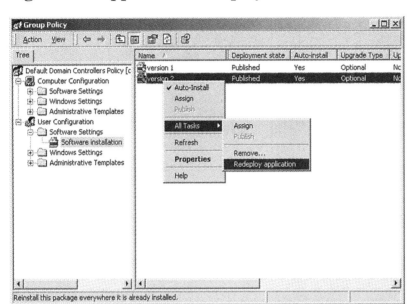

Removing Software

When your company is no longer using a software package, you may wish to remove the software from the client computers. You have the option of mandating removal or making it an option for users. Both removal methods begin the same way:

1. From the Start Menu, choose Programs, Administrative Tools and then select Active Directory Users and Computers.

2. In the Tree Pane, expand containers as necessary, right-click the Active Directory container that is associated with the Group Policy you will edit and then select Properties.

3. In the Container properties window, choose the Group Policy property page and then double-click the name of the Group Policy you will edit.

4. In the Group Policy snap-in, expand either Computer Configuration or User Configuration, expand Software Settings and choose Software Installation.

5. In the Details pane, right-click the software package, choose All Tasks and then select Remove (Figure 6.43).

Figure 6.43 Application Removal

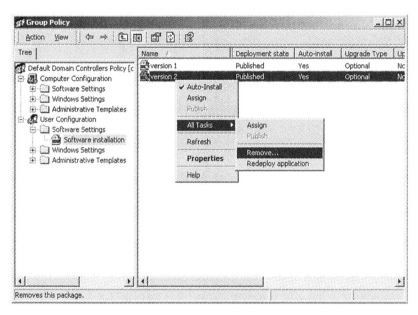

In the Remove Software window, choose Immediately uninstall software from users and computers to make this a mandatory removal, or, to make an optional removal, select Allow users to continue to use the software but prevent new installations and then choose OK (Figure 6.44).

Figure 6.44 Software Removal

Managing Software

In addition to managing the installation of programs, the Windows Installer allows you to manage applications after they have been installed. Windows Installer allows you to do the following:

- Prevent software from being installed through the document associations

- Control and categorize the programs that are listed in the Add/Remove Software control panel

- Force uninstallation when a GPO no longer applies to a user account

Preventing Document Invocation

File extensions are associated with applications. If a user opens a document of an unknown extension, the computer searches the Active Directory for an association. If it finds one and the application has been assigned or published, the application is installed. Often, document invocation is a very useful part of assigning and publishing applications. However, this can result in a user installing an application the user either does not need or should not install. For this reason, this option can be disabled.

Creating Software Categories

Another way in which you can minimize problems caused when users install software is to categorize the software. When you publish an application, you make it available for installation in the Add/Remove control panel. If you publish multiple applications, users may become confused and uncertain about which programs they need to install. To reduce confusion, you can group applications in the Add/Remove control panel. You may wish to group the applications by type (for example, Word Processing, Graphics, Utilities), or by departmental use (Sales Department, Executives, Technicians).

To create software categories, edit any GPO in the domain by following these steps:

1. From the Start Menu, choose Programs, Administrative Tools and then select Active Directory Users and Computers.

2. In the Tree Pane, expand containers as necessary, right-click an Active Directory container that is associated with any Group Policy and then choose Properties.

3. In the Container properties window, choose the Group Policy property page and then double-click the name of any Group Policy.

4. In the Tree pane, expand Computer Configuration (or User Configuration), expand Software Settings, right-click Software Installation and then choose Properties.

5. In the Software Installation Properties window, choose the Categories property page.

6. Choose Add, enter a name for the category and then select OK.

7. Repeat step 6 until all categories have been added and then choose OK.

 Note: Applications are added to the categories during deployment or any time thereafter. Category membership is defined in the Categories property page for the Software package.

Changing Deployment Options

After deploying an application, you may decide to change the way a program is made available to users. To make changes to the deployment of an application, open the Properties window for the application in Software Installation. In the Properties window, choose the Deployment property page (Figure 6.45).

Figure 6.45 Deployment Property Page

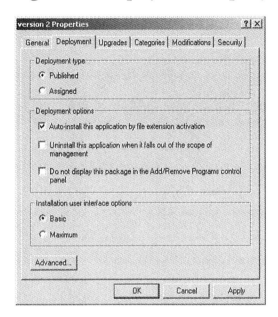

Table 6.3 lists what options you may change and how those changes affect users.

Table 6.3 Deployment Options

Option	Description
Deployment type	Changes the deployment type to either assigned or published. This affects new installations only.
Auto-Install this application by file extension activation	Allows you to enable or disable document invocation. By default, document invocation is enabled.
Uninstall this application when this GPO no longer applies to users or computers	Allows you uninstall and application when a user is removed from an OU. This prevents a user from accessing applications they no longer need to perform their job.

Option	Description
Do not deploy this package in the Add/Remove Programs control panel	Prevents the application from being listed in the Add/Remove Programs control panel. Installation occurs through document invocation or through a shortcut placed on the desktop.
Installation user interface options	Allows you to choose which installation method users see. Some Windows Installer programs offer two different setup interfaces: a basic interface that installs the program without user intervention and a custom interface that requires user input.

Troubleshooting Software Deployment

If you have problems using GPOs to deploy software, there are several likely causes. Refer to Table 6.4 for a list of possible reasons why a user is unable to receive deployed programs.

Table 6.4 Common Problems With Deploying Software

Problem	Possible Solutions
Application does not appear in the Add/Remove Programs control panel	The application was deployed in the wrong OU. The user account or computer account is not a member of the OU to which the GPO is associated. The user is a member of a security group that is preventing the GPO from being applied.
Application appears in the Add/Remove Programs control panel, but shortcuts do not appear in the Start Menu.	The application was published rather than assigned. If you want a shortcut to the installation to appear in the Start Menu, change the deployment type to assigned.

Problem	Possible Solutions
User does not have access to the network share	Verify the network connection by trying to access the share through My Network Places, a command prompt or from the Run window. If the network connection is good, verify that the user account has the proper access permissions for the share.
There are Group Policy conflicts	Verify the GPOs for all containers to which the user account belongs (this includes the Site container, Domain container, and any OUs). If a lower-level OU denies access to the application, this counter acts a higher-level container that assigns the software. Verify the GPOs for the user's computer. Computer policy always overrides user policy.

Vocabulary

Review the following terms in preparation for the certification exam.

Term	Description
ACPI	Windows 2000 uses the Advanced Configuration and Power Interface to handle power management.
AGP	Accelerated Graphics Port
assign	To make a program available for installation using Group Policy. Assigned programs appear on the desktop or the Start Menu.
child objects	An object within an Active Directory container.
conflict	When two or more devices share the same IRQ or I/O address.
console	The main interface of the MMC, the console contains snap-ins.
container	An Active Directory object that contains other objects.
CPU	The Central Processing Unit, which processes all actions, is the brain of the computer.
deploy	To make a program available through the use of Group Policy.
details pane	The right pane of an MMC snap-in, the details pane shows the detailed information or contents of the object selected in the Tree pane.
dip switches	Switches on legacy hardware that allow you to set the IRQ or I/O address.

Term	Description
DMA	Direct Memory Access is a method newer hardware device s use to access memory without requiring intervention from the CPU.
docking station	A base to which a portable computer attaches, the docking station often provides extra drives and network connectivity.
document invocation	The ability to run a program by double -clicking an associated document.
driver	Software used by the operating system to communicate with a piece of hardware.
driver signing	Windows 2000 marks drivers to ensure Windows 2000 compatibility.
folder redirection	Changing the properties of a folder so that its contents appear to be local but are actually stored in a network share.
GPC	The Group Policy container is an Active Directory container that holds information about the replication of the GPO.
GPO	A Group Policy Object is an Active Directory object used to assign Group Policy settings to containers.
GPT	The Group Policy Template is the actual location on the hard drive where Group Policy settings ar e stored.
Group Policy	Group Policy is the Active Directory extension that allows you to control use of Windows 2000 and implement software deployments.
GUID	The Globally Unique Identifier is a 128 -bit number that is assigned to every object in the Active Directory and is always unique to that object.
hardware	The physical components of a computer

Term	Description
hardware profile	A set of hardware devices, as defined in the Device Manager, that defines the hardware setup of the computer.
I/O address	The Input/Output address defines the location of a device in the computer so that other devices and the CPU can communicate with it.
inheritance	When an OU receives the permissions assigned to the OU in which it is contained (its parent).
IPSec	Internet Protocol Security
IrDA	The Infrared Data Association has defined standards for devices that use infrared technology to exchange information.
IrDA-FIR	Fast infrared supports 4 Mbps infrared data transmission.
IrDA-SIR	Serial infrared supports 115,000 bps data transmission.
IrLPT	Infrared technology used to send information from a computer to a printer.
IRQ	The Interrupt Request is used by a device to request attention from the CPU.
IrTran-P	Used to transmit data using infrared technologies from a digital camera or other imaging device to a computer.
ISA `	The Industry Standard Architecture defines a standard method for attaching devices internally in a computer.
jumpers	Small pins and connectors used to set IRQ and I/O settings on legacy cards.
legacy	A non-PnP device.
MMC	The Microsoft Management Console provides the foundation for most administrative tools in Windows 2000.

Term	Description
OU	An Organizational Unit is used in the Active Directory to group similar objects.
parallel port	Also known as the printer port, an external port on most computers used to connect external devices.
PCI	The Peripheral Component Interface is a standard connection for internal devices.
PnP	Plug and Play automatically assigns resource settings to hardware devices.
publish	To make a program available using GPOs. Published applications do not appear on the desktop or Start Menu but can be found in the Add/Remove Programs control panel.
scripts	Small files that run commands and programs, scripts can be assigned to run during logon, logoff, startup, and shutdown.
SCSI	The Small Computer Systems Interface defines a standard for connecting both internal and external devices to a computer.
security group	An Active Directory group that may contain user accounts and other groups and is assigned permissions to resources.
serial port	A port on most computers that allows external devices to be attached.
snap-ins	Modules that run within the MMC, each snap-in handles a different aspect of Windows 2000 management.
software categories	Logical groupings of software types that can be found within the Add/Remove Programs control panel.
TCO	The Total Cost of Ownership defines the expenses involved in building and maintaining a computer network.
Tree pane	The left pane of the MMC, the Tree pane lists the snap-ins included in a console and folders within the snap-ins.

Term	Description
UNC	The Universal Naming Convention defines the location of a resource on a network. It is always in the form \\server_name\share_name.
USB	The Universal Serial Bus is one of the newest methods for attaching external devices to a computer. The USB supports up to 128 devices on one controller.

In Brief

If you want to...	Then do this...
Create a customized MMC	Open a blank MMC module (by entering **MMC** in the Run command from the Start Menu). Add the consoles you want and then save the MMC.
Use a legacy ISA card in Windows 2000	First set the I/O address and IRQ on the card by changing the jumpers or dip switches according the manufacturer's instructions. Then install the card, turn on the computer and run the Add/Remove Hardware control panel.
Use a PnP card in Windows 2000	Install the card and turn on the computer. Windows 2000 will most often automatically detect the card and load the drivers. If not, run the Add/Remove Hardware control panel.
Attach many devices externally to a computer without using a different IRQ for each device	Purchase USB devices and attach them to each other and to the USB port on your computer.
Assign Group Policy settings to all of the computer accounts located in one remote satellite office of your company	Create a GPO with the necessary settings. Assign this GPO to the Site container that is associated with the satellite office site.
Assign Group Policy settings to all users in the domain but exempt three network administrators from these policies	Create a GPO with the necessary settings. Assign the GPO to the Domain container. Create a security group (call it exempt, for example) and place the three user accounts in this security group. Clear all permissions to the GPO for the security group.

Lesson 6 Activities

Complete the following activities to better prepare you for the certification exam.

1. Create a second hardware profile for a computer. Reboot the computer using this new profile, disable the network card and reboot once again using this profile. Can you access the network? Reboot once again, using the original hardware profile. Can you access the network?

2. Create a new OU named TestOU. Copy the administrator account, name it TestAdmin and place this account in the TestOU container. Copy the TestAdmin account and name the copy TestAdmin2.

3. Create a new GPO named TestGPO and associate the GPO with the TestOU container.

4. Make the following changes to the User Configuration portion of the TestGPO: remove the Help menu from the Start Menu, remove the My Network Places icon from the desktop, disable registry editing tools and set the Control Panel to show only the joystick (joy.cpl), date and time properties (timedate.cpl), Add/Remove Programs (appwiz.cpl), and display properties (desk.cpl).

5. Close all open windows, log out and log in as TestAdmin. Check the security settings. Is the My Network Places icon on the desktop? Is Help listed in the Start Menu? Try to edit the registry. Open the control panel and see what is listed. Log out and log in as TestAdmin2. Are the settings the same? Log out and log in using the Administrator account. Are the settings still in effect?

6. Make a folder and share it as Assign. You can use the default share permissions. Obtain a program that uses the new Windows Installer technology (Office 2000 uses it). Copy the installation files and .MSI files to the network share. Edit the TestGPO so that the software package is assigned to user accounts in the TestOU container. Configure the package so that it is not displayed in the Add/Remove Programs control panel.

7. Log out and log in as TestAdmin. Depending on the program package, you should see a shortcut to the program on the desktop or in the Start Menu under programs. Open the shortcut to the program. What happens? Open the Add/Remove Programs control panel and choose Add New Programs. Is the software package listed?

8. Log in as administrator, create a Global security group named Exempt within the TestOU and make TestAdmin2 a member of the group. Remove the restrictions imposed by the GPO on the Exempt group. Log out.

9. Log in as TestAdmin2. Do you have a My Network Places icon on the desktop? Are all of the restrictions removed? Can you install the application? What would you need to do to allow TestAdmin2 the ability to install the application you assigned earlier?

10. Remove all of the restrictions imposed by the TestGPO but maintain the assigned program. Log out and log in as TestAdmin. Did any of the settings persist or were they removed successfully?

Answers to Lesson 6 Activities

1. Right-click My Computer, choose Properties, select the hardware property page and then select Hardware Profiles. Copy the original profile, rename it, move it to the top of the list and then reboot. Make sure you choose the new profile when you reboot. Using the Device Manager, disable the network card. After rebooting, you should not be able to access the network (because the network card is disabled). If you reboot and choose the original profile, you can access the network (because the network card is not disabled in this profile).

2. Open Active Directory Users and Computers. Create an OU, and name it accordingly. In the Tree pane, choose Users. In the Details pane, right-click Administrator (or the original administrator account, if it was renamed) and choose Copy. Enter a first name and a user logon name of TestAdmin. Leave the password blank. Right-click TestAdmin and choose Move. Choose TestOU and select OK. In the Tree pane, choose TestOU and verify that TestAdmin appears in the Details pane. Copy this account and name it TestAdmin2.

3. In the Tree pane, right-click TestOU and choose Properties. Choose the Group Policy property page, select New and enter TestGPO for the name.

4. Choose the TestGPO and then select Edit. Expand User Configuration and then expand Administrative Templates. In the Policy pane, double-click Remove Help menu from Start menu, enable this policy and choose OK. Perform similar steps for the remaining policies (My Network Places is under Desktop, Registry tools are located under System, and the control panel settings are found under Control Panel). For the Control Panel settings, enable Show only specified control panel applets, select Show, choose Add and enter the filename for each of the applets.

5. All of the settings you made should be applied to both accounts. If not, log in as administrator and check your GPO settings. When you log on as administrator, the settings are not applied, since the administrator account is not included in the TestOU container.

6. Edit the TestGPO. Expand User Configuration, expand Software Settings, right-click Software installation, choose New and then select Package. Navigate through My Network Places to access the Assign share you created. Within that share, choose the .MSI file for the software package and select Open. Choose Advanced published or assigned and select OK. In the properties page, select the Deployment property page, choose Assigned and choose Do not display this package.

7. Opening the shortcut to the program should begin the installation program for the application. When installation is finished, the application opens. Each time you access the shortcut thereafter, the program runs. When you open the Add/Remove Programs control panel, you see that the

package is listed in the initial screen, which allows you to remove the package. If you choose Add New Programs, however, the package is not listed as an available application for installation.

8. In the Tree pane of Active Directory Users and Computers, right-click the TestOU, choose New and then select Group. Name the group and choose OK. In the Details pane, double-click the group, select members, choose Add, choose TestAdmin2, select Add and then select OK in each open window to save your configuration changes. In the Tree pane, right-click TestOU and choose Properties. Choose the Group Policy property page, choose TestGPO and then choose Properties. Select the Security property page, select Add, add the Exempt group and choose OK. Choose the Exempt group, clear the check mark in the Allow column next to Read and add a mark in the Deny column next to Apply Group Policy.

9. When you log in as TestAdmin2, none of the Group Policy settings should be applied. You should have full access to those things previously denied, and shortcuts to the assigned program should no longer be present. In order to allow members of the Exempt group access to the assigned program, you would need to create a second GPO, assign the program again in this GPO and make sure the Exempt group is not denied any accesses to this GPO.

10. Since you want to maintain the software assignment, you cannot simply remove the TestGPO or deny the Apply Group Policy permission. Instead, edit the GPO and for every setting you enabled in step 4, choose disabled. When you log in as TestAdmin, you should have the My Network Places icon on the desktop, the Start Menu should contain the Help file, the Control Panel should display all applets, and you should be able to run reedit. Shortcuts to the application should still appear where they did before.

Lesson 6 Quiz

These questions test your knowledge of features, vocabulary, procedures, and syntax.

1. Every device must have a unique_____, but may share a(n) _____.
   A. Port, connector
   B. Connector, port
   C. IRQ, I/O address
   D. I/O address, IRQ

2. Which of the following is the new power management feature of Windows 2000?
   A. Power Manager
   B. Advanced Configuration and Power Interface
   C. Windows 2000 Power and Configuration
   D. Power snap-in for the MMC

3. Which of the following infrared technology transfers information between two computers most quickly?
   A. IrDA-FIR
   B. IrDA-SIR
   C. IrLPT
   D. IrTran-P

4. Which of the following would you use to view the IRQ setting for a network card?
   A. Device Manager
   B. The Network control panel
   C. Active Directory Users and Computers
   D. The IRQ snap-in for the MMC

5. Where are Group Policy settings stored?
   A. In the registry of the local computer
   B. In the user account database
   C. In a subdirectory of the **SYYSVOL** folder
   D. In the GPO folder, under **WINNT**

6. Windows 2000 supports which of the following scripts? (Choose all that apply)
    A. Logon and Logoff
    B. Logon but not Logoff
    C. Startup and Shutdown
    D. Startup but not Shutdown

7. Folder redirection can be applied to which of the following?
    A. Any network share
    B. Any folder on an NTFS or FAT volume
    C. Any folder on an NTFS volume
    D. Only special folders determined by the operating system

8. Which of the following permissions best describe the minimum permission you can assign to a security group so that members may fully manage a GPO?
    A. Full Control
    B. Read and Write
    C. Read
    D. Manage and Change

9. A Group Policy setting applied to a(n)_____ overrides a conflicting Group Policy setting applied to a(n) _____.
    A. Site, Domain
    B. OU, Domain
    C. Domain, OU
    D. Site, OU

10. Using software installation and maintenance, you can automatically install a program on which of the following client computers? (Choose all that apply)
    A. Windows 3.11
    B. Windows 98
    C. Windows NT 4.0
    D. Windows 2000 Professional

Answers to Lesson 6 Quiz

1. Answer D is correct. Every device in a computer must have a unique I/O address and should have a unique IRQ. However, devices may share IRQs but will never share I/O addresses.

   Answers A and B are incorrect. The terms port and connector are not used to describe device resources.

2. Answer B is correct. The Advanced Configuration and Power Interface (ACPI) allows you to control power usage.

   Answers A, C, and D are incorrect. These are fictitious terms.

3. Answer A is correct. All four answers are forms of the infrared technology. IrDA-FIR is the fastest, transmitting data at 4 Mbps.

   Answer B is incorrect. IrDA-SIR transmits data at a maximum of 115 Kbps.

   Answers C and D are incorrect. These infrared technologies are not used for transferring data between computers. IrLPT is used to send information to a printer, and IrTran-P is used to receive information from a digital camera.

4. Answer A is correct. You use the Device Manager to view and change resource settings for all hardware devices in the computer.

   Answer B is incorrect. The Network Control panel does not provide information about the network card and its settings.

   Answer C is incorrect. The Active Directory does not contain resource-level information about devices in the computer.

   Answer D is incorrect. There is no IRQ snap-in for the MMC.

5. Answer C is correct. Group policy settings are stored in Group Policy Templates (GPTs), which are located in the folder `WINNT\SYSVOL\SYSVOL\DOMAIN_NAME\POLI-CIES\{GUID_NAME}`.

   Answer A is incorrect. The registry of the local computer does not store any Active Directory information, including Group Policy settings.

   Answers B and D are incorrect. These do not exist.

6. Answers A and C are correct. Unlike Windows NT 4.0, which only supports Logon scripts, Windows 2000 supports Logon, Logoff, Startup, and Shutdown scripts.

    Answers B and D are incorrect.

7. Answer D is correct. Only certain folders can be redirected to a network share. These folders are: Application Data, Desktop, My Documents, My Pictures, and Start menu.

    Answers A, B, and C are incorrect.

8. Answer B is correct. For a security group to be able to fully manage a GPO, the group only needs Read and Write permissions to the GPO.

    Answer A is incorrect. A group with Full Control can manage a GPO, but this is not the minimum permission needed.

    Answer C is incorrect. A group must also have the write permission to make changes.

    Answer D is incorrect. Manage is not a valid security permission.

9. Answer B is correct. Group Policy settings are applied from most-distant to closest or from the Site container to the Domain container to any OUs. The last Group Policy setting applied overrides any conflicting settings from earlier-applied settings.

    Answers A, C, and D are incorrect. In each of these answers, the earlier applied setting supercedes a more recently applied setting.

10. Answer D is correct. Automatic software installation depends upon Group Policy, which is a part of the Active Directory. Only Windows 2000 computers support the Active Directory.

    Answers A, B, and C are incorrect.

Lesson 7

File Resource and Disk Management

Perhaps the single most common role of a server on a network is as a file server. Users throughout the network need access to common files and placing these files on servers allows you to control access permissions, monitor accesses to the files and maintain a backup strategy. Security of the files (determining who may access what files, how much access a user will have and when the files will be available) is fundamental to administering a file server. Microsoft Windows 2000 has enhanced security features, including file-level encryption and special access permissions. It is also of great importance to make the shared files and folders easy to find on the network, whether the network consists of only a few file servers or a few hundred file servers. Windows 2000 makes use of the Active Directory to publish shared resources, making them easy to find on a network of any size.

In addition to enhanced file management, Windows 2000 contains new technologies for disk management. The major difference in disk management between Windows NT 4.0 and Windows 2000 is the introduction of dynamic and basic disk volumes. Dynamic volumes allow changes to be made to the disk configuration without rebooting the server and support an unlimited number of partitions. Dynamic volumes can be extended to include discontinuous spaces on other disks. Also, the disk configuration information is stored on the disk itself, rather than in the registry so that updates happen immediately. Disk management in Windows 2000 is done using the new Disk Management snap-in for the MMC, which builds upon the Disk Administrator tool of Windows NT 4.0.

After completing this lesson, you should have a better understanding of the following topics:

- File Resource Management

- Disk Management

File Resource Management

Windows 2000 offers several new technologies for managing file resources (files and folders) on a network. In addition to the ability to assign both share permissions and Windows NT File System (NTFS) permissions, which are available in Windows NT 4.0, you can also implement file-level encryption and disk quotas, which limit the amount of space a user can draw on to store files. The advent of the Active Directory has changed how you make file resources available on the network. With Active Directory, you can publish resources in the Active Directory database, and users can access them using the Distributed File System (DFS).

Sharing and Publishing File Resources

Before a folder (or the files within a folder) can be accessed over a network, the folder must be shared. Once shared, the folder can be published in the Active Directory, which makes the folder centrally located and easily accessible to users. There are two methods for sharing a folder. The first method is identical to sharing a folder in Windows NT 4.0. The second method makes use of the new Computer Management snap-in for the Microsoft Management Console (MMC). By now, you should be familiar with Windows Explorer and the MMC.

Sharing a Folder Using Windows Explorer

To share a folder using Windows Explorer, first open Windows Explorer:

1. From the Start Menu, choose Programs, Accessories and then select Windows Explorer.

Tip: Two other methods for opening Windows Explorer are as follows: right-click My Computer and choose Explore or on a Windows-compatible keyboard, use the key combination **WINDOWS KEY-E**.

2. From the Folders (left) pane of Windows Explorer, click on the plus sign (+) next to My Computer to expand it. Expand the hard disk that contains the folder and then expand any other folders necessary to find the folder.

3. Right-click the folder and choose Sharing (Figure 7.1).

Figure 7.1 Folder Sharing

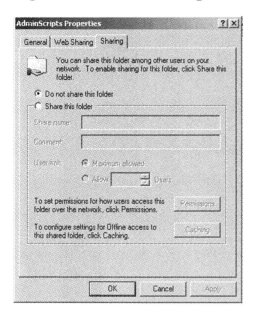

4. In the Sharing property page for the folder, choose Share this folder. If you do not want the shared name (the name that network users see) to be the same as the folder name, type in a new share name and then select Permissions.

 Note: The default share permission in Windows 2000 is the same as in Windows NT 4.0—the Everyone group has Full Control. It is a good practice to remove this permission and assign permissions that are more secure.

5. Before adding other accounts, it is generally wise to remove the Everyone group. To do so, choose the Everyone group and then select Remove.

6. To set the share permission for the folder, choose Add.

7. In the list of User and Group accounts, choose the user or group you wish to add and then select Add. To add more than one account, add the other accounts in the same way. When finished, select OK.

8. From the Share Permissions page, choose one of the user or group accounts you have added and then change the permissions assigned to that group by adding or removing check marks in the Allow column next to each permission (Figure 7.2).

Figure 7.2 Share Permissions

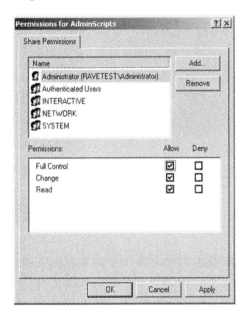

9. You may also wish to deny specific permissions to a group. Be careful using the Deny column—denied permissions override all Allowed permissions. More often than not, simply removing an allowed permission provides the needed security without complicating administration.

10. When you have adjusted permissions for each user or group account, Choose OK in each open window to save your configuration changes. In Windows Explorer, the icon for the folder should have a hand under it, signifying it is shared.

Sharing a Folder Using the Computer Management Snap-In

You can also share a folder using the new Computer Management snap-in for the MMC. Begin by opening the snap-in as follows:

1. Right-click My Computer and choose Manage.

2. From the Tree (left) pane, expand System Tools (if necessary), expand Shared Folders and then choose Shares. The Details (right) pane displays a list of shared folders on the computer (Figure 7.3).

Figure 7.3 Computer Management Snap-In Shared Folders

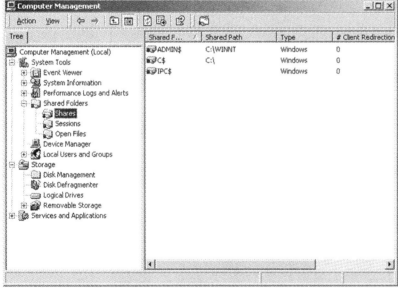

3. From the Tree pane, right-click the Shares folder and choose New File Share. Alternately, you can right-click in the Details pane and choose New File Share, or select the Action Menu and select New File Share.
    The Create Shared Folder Wizard displays.

4. Enter the path to the folder you wish to share or choose Browse and use the Windows Explorer-like interface to choose the folder.

Tip: If the folder has not yet been created, you can choose Browse, explore to the location where you want the new folder, select New Folder and then name the folder.

5. Enter a Share name for the folder. Optionally, you may enter a description as well. If you have the File Services for Macintosh installed, you may opt to make this folder available to Macintosh users (Figure 7.4). Choose Next to continue.

Figure 7.4 Shared Folder Descriptors

6. The wizard offers three pre-defined permission settings from which you may choose or you may select Customize share and folder permissions. If you choose this fourth option, select Custom and follow steps 5 through 9. Table 7.1 lists the three other permission options and the permissions that are set when you choose each option. Make your selection and then select Finish.

7. Answer Yes to create another shared folder or No to finish.

Table 7.1 Pre-Defined Share Permissions

Permission Name	Security Group and Permissions
All users have full control	Everyone—Full Control
Administrators have full control; other users have read-only access	Administrators—Full Control Everyone—Read
Administrators have full control; other us ers have no access	Administrators—Full Control

Publishing a Folder in Active Directory

To make a shared folder easier to find in an Active Directory-based network, you can publish the folder in the Active Directory. To publish a folder in the Active Directory, follow these steps:

1. From the Start Menu, choose Programs, Administrative Tools and then select Active Directory Users and Computers.

2. From the Tree pane, right-click the domain in which the shared folder will reside, choose New and then select Shared Folder (Figure 7.5).

Figure 7.5 Publishing a Shared Folder

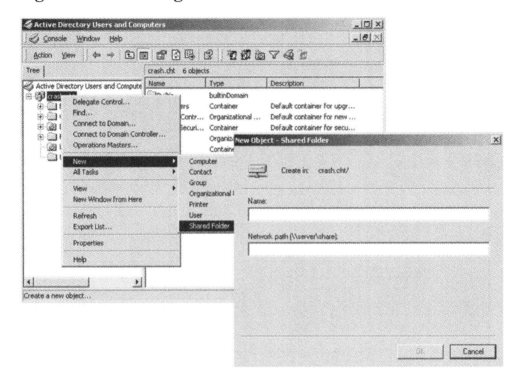

3.   Enter a name for the folder as it will appear in the Active Directory, enter the Universal Naming Convention (UNC) path for the shared folder and then choose OK.

4.   From the Tree pane, choose the domain in which you published the folder and verify that the folder is displayed in the Details pane. The published folder will have the icon of a shared volume (Figure 7.6).

 Note: Every shared resource has a UNC path. The UNC is always in the form **SERVER_NAME****SHARE_NAME**, where **SERVER_NAME** is the name of the computer that has the share and **SHARE_NAME** is the name of the share.

Figure 7.6 Published Folders

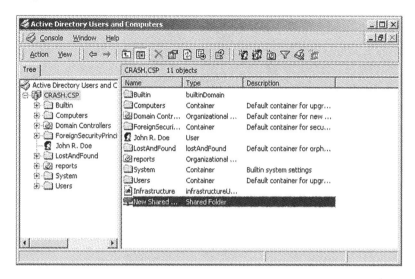

Using the Distributed File System (DFS)

The Distributed File System (DFS) allows you to create a logical directory tree that is composed of several different physical directory trees. The directory tree is the hierarchical structure of volumes, folders, and files that is seen when you use Windows Explorer. Typically, the volumes, folders, and files all reside on the same computer (they are in the same physical place).

Using DFS, you can create a directory structure that contains objects from throughout the network. Creating such a structure greatly simplifies network browsing for users. You can create a DFS for users that contains the network shares they need to access displayed in a logical structure. For example, you can place all of the customer database files in one DFS folder, even if they are stored on several different servers. When users wish to access a customer file, they only need to go to the one DFS folder to find all of the files. In other words, users no longer need to know on which server a resource is located to access that resource.

Note: DFS is available in Windows NT 4.0, but the tools used to create a DFS are cumbersome and confusing. Creating a DFS in Windows 2000 is much easier.

When you create a DFS, you first must decide whether you want to create a stand-alone DFS, in which the entire DFS topology is stored on one computer and which provides no fault tolerance or a fault-tolerant DFS, in which the DFS structure is stored in the Active Directory. A DFS stored in the Active Directory supports integration with the Domain Name System (DNS), multiple levels, and file replication. The first step in creating any distributed file system is to create the root.

Creating a Stand-Alone DFS Root

To create a stand-alone DFS root, begin by opening the Distributed File System console, a snap-in for the MMC:

1. From the Start Menu, choose Programs, Administrative Tools and then select Distributed File System.

2. From the Tree pane, right-click Distributed File System and choose New DFS Root (Figure 7.7).

Figure 7.7 New DFS Root Wizard

3. Enter the name of the server on which the root will be created and then choose Next. The server can be any computer running Windows 2000 Server.

4. If you have already created a shared folder to use as the root, choose that share from the list. To create a new share, enter the local path and folder name and then enter the Share name you wish to use (Figure 7.8).

Figure 7.8 DFS Root Folder Selection

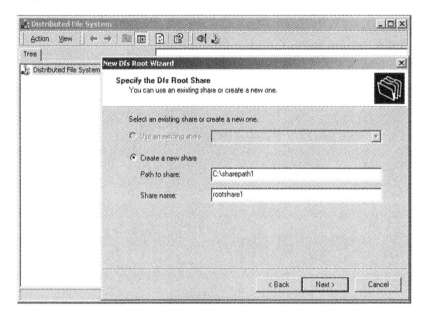

5.   Enter a name for the DFS root. You may also optionally enter a description for this root. When finished, choose Next.

6.   Review the settings you have made and then choose Finish.

 Note: If you enter a path and folder name for a folder that does not exist, you are prompted whether you wish to create and share a new folder.

Creating a Fault-Tolerant DFS Root

Create a fault-tolerant DFS root the same way, by opening the Distributed File System console as follows:

1. From the Start Menu, choose Programs, Administrative Tools and then select Distributed File System.

2. From the Tree pane, right-click Distributed File System and choose New DFS Root.

3. Choose Next to begin the wizard.

4. Choose Create a domain DFS root and then select Next.

5. Choose the domain in which the root will reside and then select Next.

6. Enter the name of a domain controller in the domain that will host the root DFS and then choose Next.

 Tip: A fault-tolerant DFS root is stored in the Active Directory. Therefore, the root must be stored on a domain controller. Once Active Directory replication occurs, the root is accessible over the network, even if the domain controller that hosts the root is unavailable.

7. Review the settings and then choose Finish.

Creating a DFS Link

Once you have created a DFS root, you add child nodes, or links, to the root. Each link points to a network share. If the DFS root is like a volume in a local file system, a link is a folder on that volume. To create a link, begin by opening the DFS console:

1. From the Start Menu, choose Programs, Administrative Tools and then select Distributed File System.

2. From the Tree pane, right-click the DFS Root to which you are adding a link and choose New DFS Link.

3. Enter a name for the link (as it will appear in the DFS tree), enter the UNC path for the share to which the link points and optionally enter a comment for this link. You can also change the cache setting. When you have entered the information, select OK.

Note: The cache setting is the length of time, in seconds, that a client keeps a record of the UNC to which the link points. After the time expires, the client computer queries the DFS server again for the location of the link.

Using NTFS Permissions with File Resources

Controlling access to files is paramount to managing a successful network. As in Windows NT 4.0, you can control network access to Windows 2000 folders using share permissions as well as control local access to folders and files using NTFS permissions. In general, the standard NTFS permissions meet most administrative needs. However, 13 special access permissions are also available to fine-tune settings. Of these, the two most commonly used (and discussed in this lesson) are Change Permissions and Take Ownership.

As in Windows NT 4.0, the effective permission to a Windows 2000 share is the most restrictive of either the Share permission or the NTFS permission. If, for example, a user has Change and Read share permissions to a folder and has been assigned only the Read NTFS permission, the user will have no more than the Read permission on the folder, whether it is accessed over the network or locally. If a user has more than one share permission or NTFS permission to a share, the effective permission is the most restrictive of the combination of the share permissions versus the combination of the NTFS permissions (Figure 7.9).

Figure 7.9 Effective Permissions

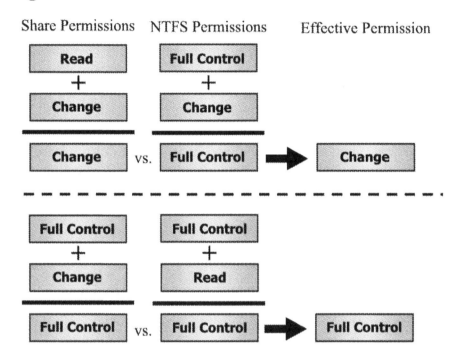

Permissions are inherited from a parent folder by default. When you assign permissions to a folder, these permissions apply to the subfolders and files within the parent. As new folders and files are created within the parent, they also inherit the permissions of the parent. Permission inheritance can be disabled, as explained in the next section.

Assigning NTFS Permissions

To assign NTFS permissions to a folder, begin by opening the Windows Explorer as follows:

1. Right-click My Computer and choose Explore.

2. From the Folders (left) pane, expand volumes and folders as necessary to find the folder on which you will assign permissions.

Note: A folder must reside on an NTFS volume before you can assign NTFS permissions.

3.   Right-click the folder and choose Properties.

4.   From the folder properties window, choose the Security property page (Figure 7.10).

Figure 7.10 Security Property Page

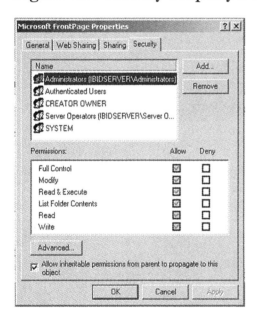

5. Choose Add to add a user or group account. Select the account, select Add and then select OK.

6. From the Name list, choose the account for which you want to assign permissions. In the Permissions box, add or clear check marks in the Allow column next to the appropriate permissions. You may also wish to deny specific permissions. When you have made the necessary changes, select OK.

 Note: You can prevent inheritance of the parent's NTFS settings by clearing the check box next to Allow inheritable permissions from parent to propagate to this object.

Assigning Special NTFS Permissions

Assigning special NTFS permissions begins in the same way:

1. Right-click My Computer and choose Explore.

2. From the Folders (left) pane, expand volumes and folders as necessary to find the folder on which you will assign permissions.

3. Right-click the folder and choose Properties.

4. From the Folder Properties window, choose the Security property page.

5. Choose Advanced.

6. From the Access Control Settings window, choose the Permissions property page, select the user or group account you wish to edit and then choose View/Edit (Figure 7.11).

Figure 7.11 Special NTFS Permissions

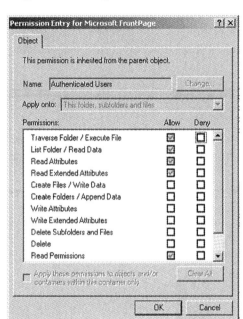

7. From the Permission Entry window, you can apply or deny any one of the thirteen special permissions. When you have made the changes, Choose OK in each open window to save your configuration changes.

Managing Disk Quotas on NTFS Volumes

One of the problems network administrators face is an overuse of a network share for the storage of personal files. If, for example, you redirect the My Documents folder for all users to network shares on the server, the drive space on the server fills up as users save more and more files. You do not wish to discourage use of network volumes for storing files because storage on a network volume simplifies administrative tasks such as auditing and backing up files. Windows 2000 addresses this problem by allowing you to implement disk quotas.

Much like a credit card, volume usage is charged against a user account. The charges are based on file and folder ownership. When a user places a file or folder on a monitored volume or takes ownership of an existing file or folder, Windows 2000 charges the account for the disk space used. The quotas are based on a per-user, per-volume basis.

Tip: Disk Quotas are a feature of the new version of NTFS included with Windows 2000. They are not available on NTFS volumes on a Windows NT 4.0-based server.

Disk quotas have the following characteristics:

*   Disk quotas are based on file and folder ownership

*   Disk quotas are unaffected by compression. Even if an NTFS volume is compressed, users are charged for the uncompressed size of the file or folder

*   Applications report the quota space assigned to the user as the free space on a volume

*   Disk quotas are based on each NTFS volume and are independent from other disk quotas on other volumes

*   Warnings can be implemented to inform a user that he or she is close to using up his or her allotted space

*   Quotas can be enforced, denying access when a user exceeds the limit

Tip: The Administrators security group is exempt from disk quotas.

To enable and define disk quotas, begin by opening the Properties page for an NTFS-formatted volume as follows:

1. Right-click My Computer and choose Explore.

2. From the Folders pane, right-click an NTFS volume and choose Properties.

3. From the Properties window, choose the Quota property page (Figure 7.12).

Figure 7.12 Disk Quota Property Page

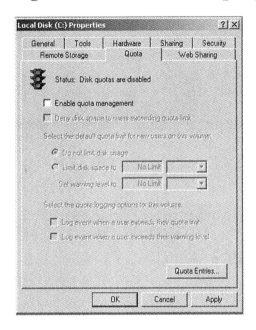

4. Choose Enable quota management. You have the option to adjust the following settings (Table 7.2):

Table 7.2 Disk Quota Options

Option	Description
Deny disk space to users exceeding quota limit	Sends an error message to a user attempting to write to the volume after exceeding the limit.
Do not limit disk usage	Monitors, but does not limit, the volume usage.
Limit disk space to	Sets the maximum size of volume space each user is allowed to use.
Set warning level to	Defines the amount of volume space that can be used before issuing a warning message.
Log event when a user exceeds his/her quota limit	Enters a log entry when a quota is met.
Log event when a user exceeds his/her warning level	Enters a log entry when a user receives a warning.

5.   Once you have defined these settings to fit your needs, choose OK and then select OK again to clear the warning message.

Note: You can view the disk quota log by selecting Quota Entries on the Quota property page or in the System log of the Event Viewer.

Encrypting Files with Encrypting File System (EFS)

EFS is a Windows 2000 file system that allows users to encrypt files and folders on NTFS volumes. When a user encrypts a file, Windows 2000 uses a strong public key-based cryptographic method. Each file has a file encryption key. The file encryption key itself is encrypted using the user's public key (which is obtained from the user's X.509 v3 certificate). The file encryption key is also encrypted using the public key of an authorized recovery agent (a user account with permission to decrypt files). Every encrypted file or folder may have only one creator but may have several recovery agents. Access to an encrypted file is based on a public key and private key pair. This pair of keys is created by Windows 2000 for each user the first time EFS is used.

Some other features of EFS include the following:

Strong file protection—Only the user who encrypted the file (and designated recovery agents) can decrypt and read the file. An administrator cannot read a user's encrypted file, even if the administrator takes ownership of the file.

Transparent EFS—When you use EFS, files are encrypted as you create or place them in an encrypted folder and are decrypted whenever you access them. When the file is closed after use, it is automatically re-encrypted.

Disaster recovery—A User cannot encrypt a file or folder unless at least one public recovery key is available on the system.

 Tip: Windows 2000 creates a default recovery agent so that EFS may be used immediately. By default, the administrator account is designated as the recovery agent.

Secure temporary files—Often an application creates temporary files that are not deleted when the application is closed. You can encrypt the folder in which these temporary files are stored so that unwanted parties cannot gain access.

Paging—EFS keys reside in the system kernel and are stored in the non-paged pool. This ensures that they are never copied to the paging file, where they could be possibly retrieved and used.

Mobility—If an encrypted file is moved from an encrypted folder to an unencrypted folder, the file remains encrypted.

Blocked encryption—Files are encrypted in blocks, and each block has a different file encryption key. The keys are stored in the Data Decryption Field (DDF) and Data Recovery Field (DRF) in the file header.

Enabling and Disabling EFS for a Folder

To enable encryption for a folder, first create a folder on an NTFS volume. Then open Windows Explorer as follows:

1. Right-click My Computer and choose Explore.

2. From the Folders pane, expand My Computer and expand any necessary volumes and folders to find the folder you will encrypt.

3. From either pane, right-click the folder and choose Properties.

4. From the Folder Properties window, choose the General property page and then select Advanced.

5. Choose Encrypt contents to secure data and then select OK in each open window to save your configuration changes.

6. To disable encryption on a folder, deselect Encrypt contents to secure data.

Using CIPHER.EXE

You can also encrypt and decrypt folders and files from the command prompt using the **CIPHER.EXE** command. The format of the **CIPHER.EXE** command is as follows:

```
CIPHER [/E] [/D] [/S:FOLDER_NAME] [/I] [/F] [/Q] [TARGET_NAME]
```

Table 7.3 lists the options available with the **CIPHER.EXE** command and what each option does.

Table 7.3 Cipher.exe Command Options

Option	Description
/E	Encrypt the folder and mark it so that additions to the folder are also encrypted
/D	Decrypt the folder and mark the folder so that future additions to the folder are not encrypted
/S	Perform the operation on this folder and all subfolders
/A	Perform the operation only on the file(s) specified, not their host folders
/I	Ignore any errors and continue the operation
/F	Force encryption, even if a file or folder is already encrypted
/Q	Run in quiet mode (displays only essential information)
TARGET_NAME	Specifies the folder, file, or group of files on which to perform the operation

Tip: You can run the **CIPHER.EXE** command without any options to display the current encryption state of the folder and its subfolders.

Defragmenting Hard Drives

One of the most common tools Windows NT 4.0 administrators need to purchase to maintain a well-running server is a disk defragmenter. As files are written to and deleted from a volume, the free space on the volume becomes discontinuous. This is known as a fragmented disk. As subsequent files are added to the volume, they are broken into smaller pieces, and each piece fills a discontinuous space on the drive.

The file system (FAT, FAT32, or NTFS) keeps track of the location of the file parts on the volume and reassembles the file when it is accessed. This disassembly and reassembly process slows the computer. As the drive becomes more fragmented, there is a noticeable decrease in file system response times. A disk defragmenter searches for all parts of a file, reassembles the file and places it in one continuous part of the disk. Windows NT 4.0 does not include a disk defragmenter. Windows 2000 includes Disk Defragmenter, an MMC snap-in that is part of the Computer Management console.

 Note: Windows 2000 Disk Defragmenter is a newer version of the third-party Windows NT 4.0 utility Diskeeper from Executive Software. It works with FAT, FAT32, and NTFS volumes.

Using Disk Defragmenter

To run Disk Defragmenter, begin by opening the Computer Management console as follows:

1. Right-click My Computer and choose Manage.

2. From the Tree (left) pane, expand Storage and then choose Disk Defragmenter. The Details (right) pane displays the Disk Defragmenter (Figure 7.13).

Figure 7.13 Disk Defragmenter

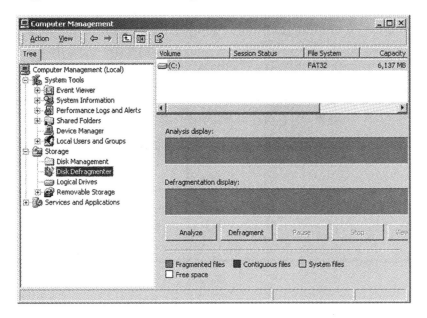

3. From the Details pane, right-click a volume and choose Analyze. When analysis is complete, a summary displays, and you may select to view a detailed report, defragment the drive or close the summary. Choose View Report (Figure 7.14).

Figure 7.14 Defragmenter Analysis Report

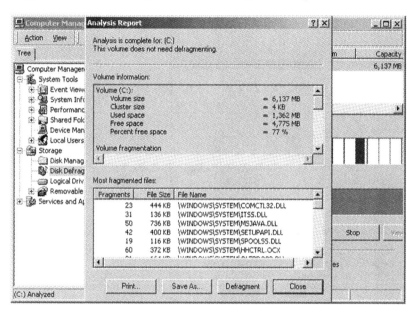

4. The report displays detailed information about the volume and lists all of the files that are fragmented. You may choose to save or print the report. Select Close.

5. From the Details pane, right-click the volume you analyzed and choose Defragment. The defragmentation process begins, and the lower graph shows the progress (Figure 7.15).

Figure 7.15 Defragmentation Progress Display

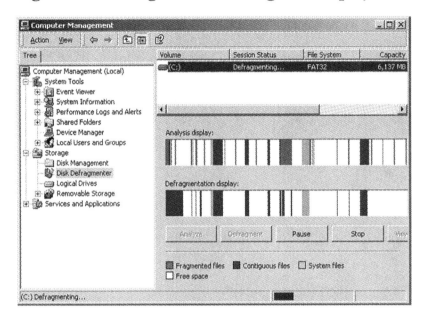

6. When the process is finished, you may choose to view a post-defragmentation analysis report, or you may choose Close.

Disk Management

In addition to enhanced file management capabilities, Windows 2000 offers new disk management features that you should be familiar with. Before discussing disk management in Windows 2000 and how it differs from Windows NT 4.0, a review of some disk terminology is in order.

A hard disk must be partitioned before it can be used. A partition is a logical division of a physical drive; the term volume is synonymous with partition. A drive may contain one partition, or it may contain several partitions.

There are two fundamental partition types: primary and extended. A primary partition is one from which the computer can boot. It contains the files necessary to load an operating system. A primary partition is assigned one—and only one—drive letter. An extended partition cannot be used to store information. An extended partition is divided into logical drives, and each logical drive (which is assigned its own drive letter) contains information. Just as a hard disk cannot be used until you create partitions, an extended partition cannot be used until you create one or more logical drives.

Many of the disk management features and tools are used for fault tolerance. Fault tolerance is the ability of a computer (the hardware or the operating system) to handle a device failure without losing data.

Understanding Windows 2000 Disk Storage Types

Windows 2000 supports two disk storage types: basic and dynamic. Basic disks are those familiar to users of Windows NT 4.0. A basic disk may contain up to four partitions. You may have up to four primary partitions or three primary partitions and one extended partition. The extended partition contains logical drives. Dynamic disks are new to Windows 2000 and offer extended capabilities over basic disks. They support spanned volumes and are not limited in the number of partitions that can be created.

In Windows NT 4.0, basic disks may contain a variety of volume types. In Windows 2000, you can only create primary and extended partitions on a basic disk. However, Windows 2000 dynamic disks support the following five different volume types:

Simple volume—Uses space from only one physical disk (like a primary or extended partition).

Spanned volume—Uses space from two or more physical disks as one logical partition. A spanned volume is like a volume set in Windows NT 4.0.

 Note: Spanned volumes can use a maximum of 32 physical disks.

Mirrored volume—Uses two physical disks to make two identical copies of one partition. A mirrored volume provides fault tolerance in case one of the two hard disks fails. It is like a mirror set in Windows NT 4.0.

Striped Volume—Uses free space on two or more (up to 32) physical disks to make a logical partition. It is similar to a stripe set in Windows NT 4.0

Note: A striped volume differs from a spanned set in the way data is written to each disk. In a spanned set, data is written to the second disk only after the free space on the first disk is used. In a striped volume, data is written consecutively to each disk in the set.

RAID-5 volume—A Redundant Array Of Independent Disks level 5 (RAID-5) volume is the most fault-tolerant volume type and is similar to the Windows NT 4.0 stripe set with parity. A RAID-5 volume uses the equivalent free space of one of the disks in a stripe set to write parity (error-correcting) information. If one of the disks in the RAID-5 array fails, the data can be recreated using the parity information.

 Note: When you upgrade a Windows NT 4.0 server with a mirror set, volume set, stripe set, or stripe set with parity, the volume is maintained, but all disks are initialized as basic disks. In Windows 2000, a basic disk has limited support for these volumes.

Using the Disk Management Snap-In

Windows 2000 disk management is done through a snap-in for the MMC named Disk Management. The Disk Management snap-in is part of the Computer Management console, but, like any other snap-in, it can be run in its own console. When the snap-in is placed in its own console, you can use the snap-in to manage disks on other computers on the network (provided you have administrative rights to access those computers). You can use the snap-in only to manage one computer, but you can add multiple Disk Management snap-ins to one console, each pointing to a different computer on the network.

To access the Disk Management snap-in from within the Computer Management console, follow these steps:

1. Right-click My Computer and choose Manage.

2. If necessary, expand Storage in the Tree pane and then choose Disk Management.

The Details pane is divided into two parts. The upper portion lists all the volumes on the computer with statistics about each volume, including their size, type (basic or dynamic), file system type, and status. The lower portion provides a graphical view of the physical disks in the computer and the logical partitions on these drives (Figure 7.16). This view is much like the Disk Administrator tool in Windows NT 4.0.

Figure 7.16 Disk Management Snap-in

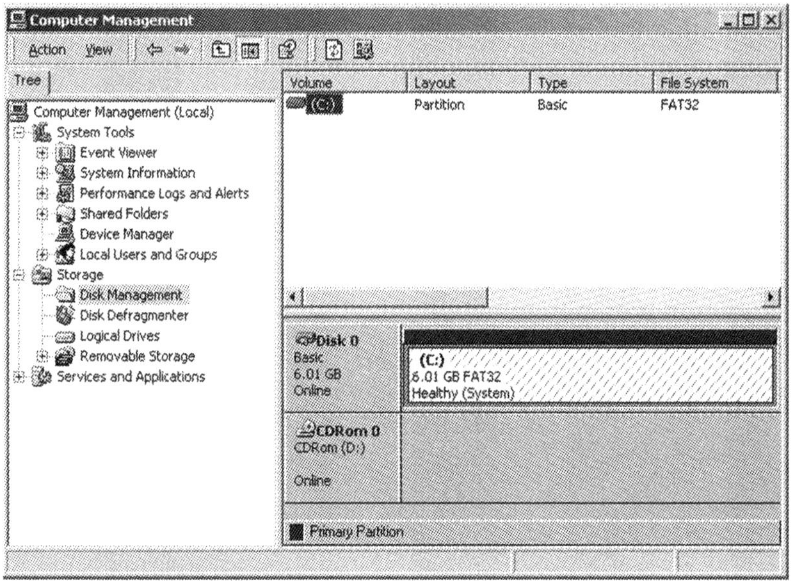

From within the Disk Manager, you can view detailed information about both physical disks and logical partitions. To view detailed information about a physical disk, right-click the icon for the physical disk in the lower portion of the Details pane and then choose Properties (Figure 7.17).

Figure 7.17 Physical Disk Properties Access

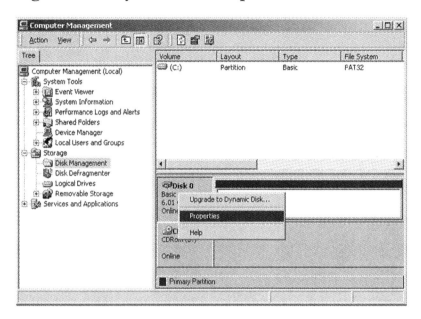

Information displayed for the physical disk includes the disk number, type, status, capacity, unallocated space, device type, manufacturer, and adapter name. The volumes contained on this physical disk also display (Figure 7.18).

Figure 7.18 Physical Disk Properties

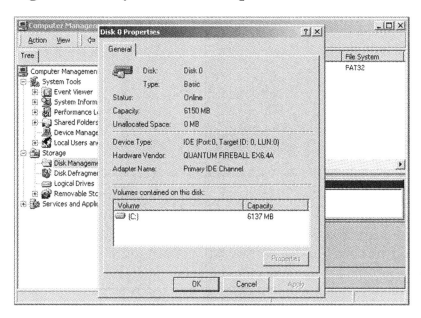

You can also view detailed information about volumes and partitions. In the upper portion of the Details pane, right-click any volume and choose Properties. From the properties page for the volume, you can view information about the volume and perform various tasks. The tasks, which are described in detail below, are accessed through the five property pages associated with the volume properties window. These property pages are as follows:

General—Displays information about the volume size and use, file system and allows you to make settings for volume compression and indexing.

Tools—Provides access to the Error-checking, Backup, and Disk Defragmenter tools.

Hardware—Displays detailed information about the physical nature of the disks in the computer and provides access to the Hardware Troubleshooter.

Sharing—Allows you to view and adjust network sharing settings.

Security—Allows you to view and change NTFS permissions (only available on volumes formatted with the NTFS file system).

Quota—Allows you to view and manage disk quota settings.

Creating Dynamic Volumes

To implement fault tolerance on your server, you should create dynamic volumes. You create dynamic volumes on dynamic disks. You create a dynamic disk when you first add a disk to the server, or you can upgrade a basic disk to a dynamic disk.

 Warning: Windows NT 4.0 does not support dynamic volumes. If you convert a basic disk to a dynamic disk, you will not be able to access the drive or boot older versions of Windows from the dynamic disk.

Converting Storage Types

You can convert a basic disk to a dynamic disk. When you do so, all partitions on the disk are converted to dynamic disk volumes, according to Table 7.4. You can convert a dynamic disk back to a basic disk, but all of the volumes must be deleted first and so all data is lost.

Table 7.4 Basic Disk Partition Conversion

Basic Disk Partition Type	Disk Volume Conversion
System and boot partitions	Simple volumes
Primary partition	Simple volume
Extended partition and logical drives	Extended partition is removed, and its logical drives become simple volumes
Volume set	Spanned volume
Stripe set	Striped volume
Mirror set	Mirrored volume
Stripe set with parity	RAID-5 volume

To convert a basic disk to a dynamic disk, open the Disk Manager as follows:

1. Right-click My Computer and choose Manage.

2. From the Tree pane, expand Storage and then choose Disk Management.

3. From the lower portion of the Details pane, right-click the disk you wish to upgrade and then choose Upgrade to Dynamic Disk (Figure 7.19).

Figure 7.19 Basic Disk Upgrade

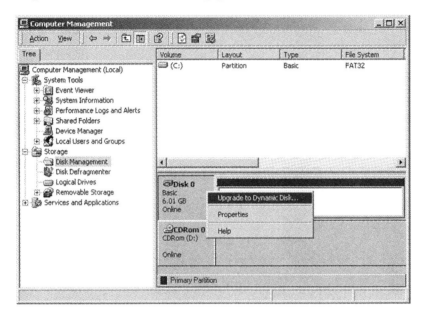

4. Choose the disk(s) you wish to upgrade by placing a check mark in the box next to each and then select OK.

5. Review the settings and then choose Upgrade.

6. If this disk contains the System or boot partitions, you receive several warning messages, and the computer needs to be rebooted. Confirm each of these messages by choosing Yes or OK, as appropriate.

You can also convert a dynamic disk back to a basic disk. Before doing so, make sure you have a complete backup of all data. To revert a dynamic disk to a basic disk, follow these steps:

1. Back up all data contained on the disk.

2. Delete all volumes on the disk.

3. In the lower portion of the Details pane in Disk Manager, right-click the dynamic disk and choose Revert to basic disk.

4. Restore the necessary data from backup.

Warning: Reverting a dynamic disk to a basic disk results in total data loss on that disk.

Creating and Extending Simple Volumes

In many ways, a simple volume in Windows 2000 is like a partition in Windows NT 4.0. However, in Windows 2000, the number of simple volumes on a disk is unlimited, and you can extend (add space to) a simple volume any time after creating it.

Note: A simple volume can be formatted using the FAT, FAT32, or NTFS file system. However, only simple volumes formatted with the NTFS file system can be extended.

To create a simple volume, begin by opening the Disk Manager as follows:

1. Right-click My Computer and choose Manage.

2. From the Tree pane, expand Storage and then choose Disk Management.

3. From the lower portion of the Details pane, right-click any unformatted space on a drive and choose Create Volume.

4. Choose Next to begin the Create Volume Wizard.

5. Choose Simple volume and then select Next.

6. Verify that the proper disk is listed under selected dynamic disks, adjust the size of the volume as necessary and then choose Next (Figure 7.20).

Figure 7.20 Simple Volume Creation

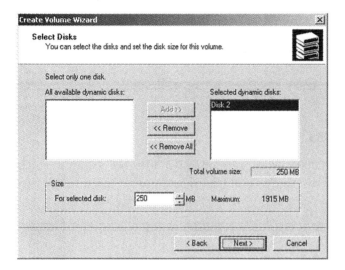

7. Choose Assign a drive letter, select a drive letter for this volume, and then select Next.

8. Unless you wish to format the volume at a later time, choose Format this volume as follows, choose a file system, leave the allocation unit size as Default, and enter a label for the volume. You may also elect to perform a quick format and enable compression (Figure 7.21). After entering the information, select Next.

Figure 7.21 Simple Volume Formatting

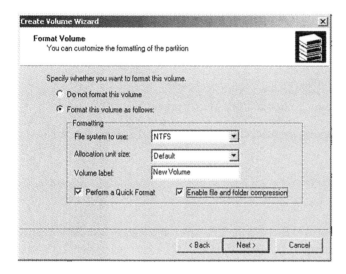

9. Review the settings and then choose Finish.

To extend an existing simple volume, follow these steps:

1. From the lower portion of the Details pane in Disk Management, right-click the simple volume you wish to extend and then choose Extend Volume.

2. Choose Next to begin the Extend Volume Wizard.

3. Choose the disk that contains the free space you will use, enter the amount of free space you wish to use and then select Next.

4. Review the settings and choose Finish.

Creating and Extending Spanned Volumes

Spanned volumes are created in the same fashion as simple volumes. In order to create a spanned volume, you must have at least two dynamic disks in the computer. To create a spanned volume, follow these steps:

1. Right-click My Computer and choose Manage.

2. From the Tree pane, expand Storage and then choose Disk Management.

3. From the lower portion of the Details pane, right-click any unformatted space on a drive and choose Create Volume.

4. Choose Next to begin the Create Volume wizard.

5. Choose Spanned volume and then select Next.

6. Choose the disks on which you wish to create the spanned volume and select Add. At least two disks must be listed in the Selected dynamic disks box (Figure 7.22). Select each disk individually and adjust the amount of space on the disk you wish to use. After making these changes, choose Next.

Figure 7.22 Spanned Volume Disks

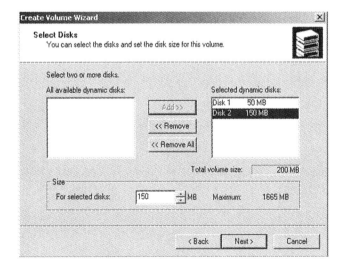

7. Choose Assign a drive letter, select a drive letter for this volume and then select Next.

8. Unless you wish to format the volume at a later time, choose Format this volume as follows, choose a file system, leave the allocation unit size as Default and enter a label for the volume. You may also elect to perform a quick format and enable compression. After entering the information, select Next.

9. Review the settings and then choose Finish.

To extend a spanned volume, follow the steps above for extending a simple volume. Like an extended simple volume, an extended spanned volume acts as one drive, and no portion of it can be deleted without deleting all parts of it simultaneously.

 Note: A spanned volume can only be extended if it is formatted with the NTFS file system.

Creating Striped Volumes

Striped volumes, like spanned volumes, use space on two or more physical disks. Unlike spanned volumes, however, a striped volume writes to all of the disks simultaneously, increasing read and write performance. Data is written to all disks in 64-kilobyte blocks. To create a striped volume, follow these steps:

1. Right-click My Computer and choose Manage.

2. From the Tree pane, expand Storage and then choose Disk Management.

3. From the lower portion of the Details pane, right-click any unformatted space on a drive and choose Create Volume.

4. Choose Next to begin the Create Volume Wizard.

5. Choose Striped volume and then select Next.

6. Choose the disks on which the striped volume will be created. As in creating a spanned volume, you must select at least two disks. For each disk, select the amount of drive space you wish to use for the striped volume and then select Next.

7. Choose Assign a drive letter, select a drive letter for this volume and then select Next.

8. Unless you wish to format the volume at a later time, choose Format this volume as follows, choose a file system, leave the allocation unit size as Default and enter a label for the volume. You may also elect to perform a quick format and enable compression. After entering the information, choose Next.

9. Review the settings and then choose Finish.

Performing Common Disk Management Tasks

In addition to creating dynamic volumes, you can perform several other disk management tasks using the Disk Management snap-in. You cannot create volumes on basic disks, but can—and must—create partitions. In addition, partitions and volumes must be assigned a drive letter. If there is a lack of drive letters, you can mount a drive to a local folder. We will now discuss the processes of partitioning a basic disk, assigning a drive letter and mounting a drive.

Creating Partitions on Basic Disks

By default, all new disks added to Windows 2000 are initialized as basic disks. A basic disk must be partitioned before it can be used. A basic disk may contain up to four partitions. To create a partition, follow these steps:

1. Right-click My Computer and choose Manage.

2. From the Tree pane, expand Storage and then choose Disk Management.

3. From the lower portion of the Details pane, right-click any unformatted space on a basic disk and choose Create Partition.

4. Choose Next to begin the Create Partition Wizard.

5. Choose the type of partition you wish to create (primary, extended, or a logical drive in the extended partition) and then select Next.

6. Enter the size of the partition and then choose Next.

7. Choose Assign a drive letter, select a drive letter for this volume and then select Next.

8. Unless you wish to format the partition at a later time, choose Format this partition with the following settings, choose a file system, leave the allocation unit size as Default and enter a label for

the volume. You may also elect to perform a quick format and enable compression. After entering the information, select Next.

9. Review the settings and then choose Finish.

Changing Drive Letters

In Windows 98, hard disks and removable drives (CD-ROMs, for example) are automatically assigned drive letters. These letters cannot be changed (except for some CD-ROMs). Simply adding another hard disk or another partition can result in some applications failing to work properly. In Windows 98, a CD-ROM or other removable device is always assigned a drive letter after all of the hard disks have been assigned letters. If you have one hard disk and one CD-ROM, the CD-ROM is drive D. If you later add a second hard drive, the CD-ROM becomes the drive E, and applications that use the CD-ROM can no longer find it.

In Windows 2000, as in Windows NT 4.0, you can statically assign drive letters to drives so that they do not change with the addition of other drives. You can assign any drive letter, from C to Z to a partition, volume, or removable storage drive.

 Note: Drive letters A and B are reserved for floppy disk drives. If you have only one floppy disk drive, you can use drive letter B to map a network drive.

Drive letters are assigned in the Disk Management console. Open the console as follows:

1. Right-click My Computer and choose Manage.

2. From the Tree pane, expand Storage and then choose Disk Management.

3. From the Details pane, right-click any partition or volume and choose Change Drive Letter and Path.

4. Choose Edit, choose a drive letter and then select OK.

5. Read the warning message and choose Yes.

The drive letter is changed immediately without the need to reboot or make changes.

Assigning a Drive Path

You may wish to have more volumes or partitions than there are drive letters available. When you wish to surpass this 24-volume limit, you can mount the drive to an empty folder. When you mount a drive, you assign a folder path to a drive. In My Computer or Windows Explorer, the folder to which the drive is mounted appears as another hard disk. When users store files in this folder, the files are actually stored on the volume to which the folder is mounted.

 Note: A mounted drive can be formatted in the FAT, FAT32, or NTFS file system; the folder the drive is mounted to must be empty and must reside on an NTFS volume.

To mount a local drive to a folder, you assign the folder a drive path rather than a drive letter. This process is done through the Disk Management console:

1. Right-click My Computer and choose Manage.

2. From the Tree pane, expand Storage and then choose Disk Management.

3. From the Details pane, right-click the partition or volume you wish to mount and choose Change Drive Letter and Path.

4. If a drive letter is currently listed, choose the drive letter and then select Remove. If necessary, repeat step 3 to reopen the Drive Letter and Path window.

5. Choose Add and then select Mount in this NTFS folder (Figure 7.23).

Figure 7.23 Add New Drive Path

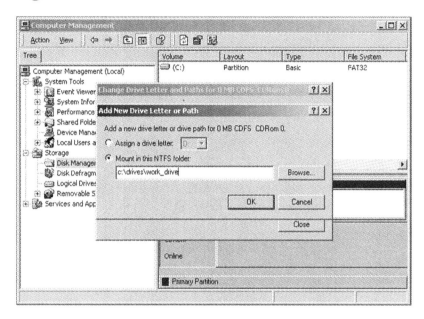

6. Enter the local path to the folder (for example, c:\Documents). If you are uncertain of the path, choose Browse and use the Windows Explorer-like interface to choose the folder. Select OK.

7. The volume appears as any other volume in the Disk Management console, except that it does not have a drive letter associated with it (Figure 7.24).

Figure 7.24 Mounted Drive

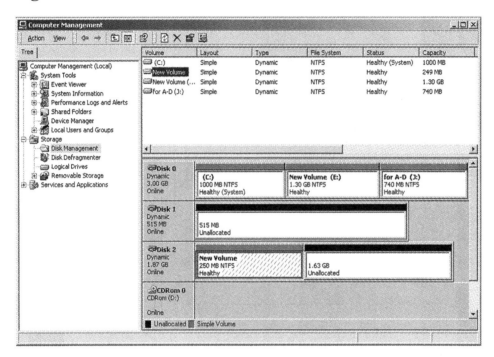

Tip: You can view all of the drive paths used on a system in the Disk Management console. Choose View and select All Drive Paths.

Managing Volume Sets on Basic Disks

When you upgrade Windows NT 4.0 to Windows 2000, the drives automatically convert to basic disk types. If several drives in Windows NT 4.0 are configured as a stripe set with parity and the operating system is upgraded to Windows 2000, the stripe set with parity is maintained but runs on basic disks. Although you cannot create volumes on basic disks in Windows 2000, basic disks do have minimal support for mirror sets, volume sets, stripe sets, and stripe sets with parity to ease the upgrade process. As an administrator, you need to be able to maintain these Windows NT 4.0 volumes within Windows 2000.

Maintaining Mirror Sets

Mirror sets (the Windows NT 4.0 equivalent of a mirrored volume) are maintained when Windows NT 4.0 is upgraded to Windows 2000. They are not converted to mirrored volumes. If one of the disks in a mirror set fails, the status of the mirror set is reported in the Disk Management console as Failed Redundancy, and the status of the disk remains Online (Figure 7.25).

Figure 7.25 Broken Mirror Set

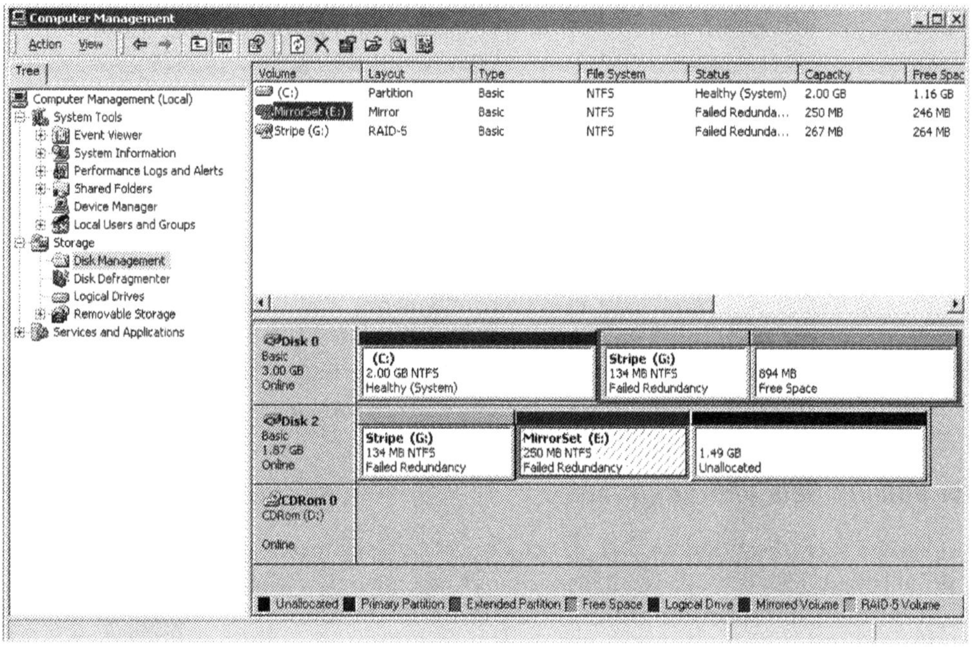

The mirror set can be repaired if you have another basic disk in the computer with sufficient free space. To repair a failed mirror set, use the Disk Management console as follows:

1. Right-click My Computer and choose Manage.

2. From the Tree pane, expand Storage and then choose Disk Management.

3. From the Details pane, right-click the mirror set you want to repair and choose Repair Volume.

4. Follow the steps in the wizard to repair the mirror set.

5. If the Disk Management console does not report the mirror set as Healthy after regeneration, right-click the mirror set and choose Resynchronize Mirror.

 Note: You cannot use a dynamic disk to replace a failed disk in a mirror set.

Mirror sets can also be resynchronized. If one of the two disks is unavailable, and data is written to the other disk, you may need to force synchronization when both disks are available. To do so, right-click the mirror set and choose Resynchronize Mirror.

To stop using the mirror set, you can either break the mirror set or delete it. Breaking a mirror set leaves the data intact on both drives, but the drives become independent of one another and no longer provide fault tolerance. When you delete a mirror set, the data is lost on both disks. To break a mirror set, right-click the mirror set and choose Break Mirror. To delete the mirror set, delete either one of the volumes that make up the set. Right-click either volume and choose Delete Volume.

Working with Volume Sets and Stripe Sets

Volume sets and stripe sets (the Windows NT 4.0 equivalents of spanned volumes and striped volumes) do not provide fault tolerance. As such, they cannot be repaired in Windows 2000 if they fail. For either type, if the set fails, it must be deleted. Once deleted, you may opt to change the disks to dynamic disks, create a spanned or striped volume and then restore the data from tape backup. To delete a volume or stripe set, open the Disk Management console. Right-click any partition involved in the set and choose Delete Volume.

Repairing Stripe Sets with Parity

Stripe sets with parity created in Windows NT 4.0 are maintained when Windows NT 4.0 is upgraded to Windows 2000. Because stripe sets with parity provide fault tolerance, you can attempt to repair such a set using the Disk Management console in Windows 2000. Like a failed mirror set, the Disk Management console reports the status of a failed stripe set with parity as Failed Redundancy, and disk status remains Online. To repair the set, you must have an additional basic disk with the necessary free space installed in the computer.

To repair a failed stripe set with parity, proceed as follows:

1. Right-click My Computer and choose Manage.

2. From the Tree pane, expand Storage and then choose Disk Management.

3. From the Details pane, right-click the stripe set with parity you want to repair and choose Repair Volume.

4. Follow the steps in the wizard to repair the stripe set with parity.

5. When finished, the Disk Management console should report the status of the stripe set with parity as Healthy. If it does not, right-click the stripe set with parity and choose Regenerate Parity.

If you decide you no longer want to use a stripe set with parity, you may remove the set by deleting the volume. You may then choose to create a RAID-5 volume and restore the data from tape backup. To delete a stripe set with parity, right-click the set and choose Delete Volume.

 Warning: Deleting a stripe set with parity deletes all data in the set.

Vocabulary

Review the following terms in preparation for the certification exam.

Term	Description
basic disk	One of two disk types supported by Windows 2000, basic disks support primary and extended partition s and logical drives within the extended partition.
blocks	A file is broken into smaller portions called blocks before being written to a striped volume.
CIPHER.EXE	The command-line utility for encrypting or decrypting a folder or file.
DDF	Data Decryption Field
DFS	The Distributed File System allows you to create a file structure composed of folders and files from a number of different sources.
directory tree	The hierarchical structure of volumes, folders, and files.
disk quotas	Disk quotas allow you to restrict disk usage for all users.
DNS	The Domain Name System provides the overall naming structure of TCP/IP-based networks and Windows 2000 domains.
DRF	Data Recovery Field
dynamic disk	One of two disk types supported by Windows 2000, dynamic disks support five volume types.
EFS	Encrypting File System
encryption	Encrypted data is scrambled so that it cannot be read without the proper security key.

Term	Description
extended	One of two partition types on a basic disk. The extended partition contains logical drive s.
FAT	The File Allocation Table is a file system supported by all Microsoft operating systems, from DOS through Windows 2000.
FAT32	The 32-bit version of the File Allocation Table file system, FAT32 is supported by Windows 98 and Windows 2000 .
fault tolerance	The ability of a computer or operating system to keep data accessible, even if one of the hard disks fails.
fragmented disk	A disk on which data is written in discontinuous blocks.
logical drive	A portion of an extended partition that is assigned its own drive letter and acts as a separate partition .
mirror set	An Windows NT 4.0 fault-tolerant system, in which one hard disk is used to contain an exact copy of the files on another disk.
mirrored volume	The Windows 2000 implementation of a mirror set, a mirrored volume can only exist on dynamic disks.
MMC	The Microsoft Management Console provides a common interface for administrative tools that are in the form of consoles and snap-ins.
mount	To connect a drive volume to a local folder rather than assigning it a drive lett er.
NTFS	The New Technology File System is a file system supported by Windows NT 4.0 and Windows 2000.
NTFS permissions	The right to access files and folders on an NTFS -formatted volume, NTFS permissions apply whether the folder is accessed locally or remotely.

Term	Description
partition	A logical division of a basic disk. There are two partition types: primary and extended.
primary partition	One of two partition types on basic disks, primary partition s may contain the boot files needed to load an operating system.
private key	Half of the key pair used to encrypt and decrypt files and folders, the private key can only be used by the user to whom it is assigned.
public key	Half of the key pair used to encrypt and decrypt files and folders, the public key is attached to the encrypted file or folder.
publish	Publishing a folder in the Active Directory makes the folder easier for users to find.
RAID-5 volume	A disk volume that supports the Redundant Array Of Independent Disks level 5 fault -tolerance system.
recovery agent	A user account that has permission to decry pt a file or folder, even if the agent is not the creator of the encrypted file or folder.
replication	Replication occurs when domain controllers copy the Active Directory database amongst each other.
share permissions	Access rights assigned to a folder that affect what righ ts users have to the folder and its contents when accessed over the network (remotely).
simple volume	On dynamic disks, a simple volume is one which provides no fault tolerance and uses disk space from only one physical disk.
snap-in	An administrative tool in Windows 2000 designed to run within the MMC.

Term	Description
spanned volume	On dynamic volumes, a spanned volume provides no fault tolerance and uses disk space from two or more physical disks.
stripe set	The Windows NT 4.0 equivalent of a striped volume in Windows 2000.
stripe set with parity	The Windows NT 4.0 equivalent of a RAID-5 volume in Windows 2000.
striped volume	In Windows 2000, a striped volume uses two or more physical disks and writes data consecutively to each disk in 64-kilobyte blocks.
topology	The shape and structure of the DFS folder and file hierarchy.
UNC	Universal Naming Convention
volume	A logical division of a drive, a volume on a dynamic disk is similar to a partition on a basic disk.
volume set	The Windows NT 4.0 equivalent of a spanned volume in Windows 2000.

In Brief

If you want to...	Then do this...
Make a folder available over the network	Share the folder using either Windows Explorer or the Computer Management console.
Create a DFS root	Use the Distributed File System console.
Secure a folder over the network to prevent unwanted access	Assign share permissions on the folder.
Secure a file or folder from unwanted access locally or remotely	Assign NTFS permissions on the folder.
Make a file or folder unreadable even if a user has access to it	Use the Encrypting File Service (EFS) or **CIPHER.EXE** to encrypt the file or folder.
Increase disk read and write performance	Defragment the drive using the Disk Defragmenter snap-in.
Combine the free space on several drives into one volume	Create a spanned volume or striped volume.
Provide fault tolerance for data files	Create a mirrored volume or RAID-5 volume and store the data files on it.
Change a dynamic disk to a basic disk without loosing the data contained within	Back up all of the data to a tape backup or other backup system, revert the disk and then restore the data.

Lesson 7 Activities

Complete the following activities to better prepare you for the certification exam.

1. Log in as an administrator. Create a new folder on an NTFS partition named ShareTest. Share the folder, remove the default share permissions and assign the administrator account Full Control permission. Log out and log in as any user other than the administrator. Using My Network Places, attempt to access ShareTest through the network. Now, using Windows Explorer or My Computer, attempt to access ShareTest locally. What happens, and why? Log out.

2. Log in as an administrator. Assign NTFS permissions to ShareTest so that the administrator account has Full Control, the Users group has the default permissions (Read & Execute, List Folder Contents, and Read) and the user account you used in step 1 has been denied the same three permissions (Read & Execute, List Folder Contents, and Read). Log out.

3. Log in as the user with the denied permissions. Can you access the ShareTest folder from the network? Can you access the folder locally? Log out and log in as another user. Can you access the folder locally? Can you delete the contents of the folder? Can you create a test file in the folder? Why or why not? Log out.

4. Log in as administrator. On an NTFS formatted volume, enable disk quotas so that users can use a maximum of 2 MB of drive space. Deny access to users who exceed this limit. Log out.

5. Log in using a non-administrator account. Using Windows Explorer, expand the volume that contains the Windows 2000 system files, expand Program Files and copy the Outlook Express folder. Choose the volume with disk quotas enabled and paste the Outlook Express folder in this volume. What happens? Log out and log in as administrator. Attempt to copy the Outlook Express folder to the volume with quotas enabled. What happens?

6. Analyze and defragment one of the volumes in the computer. Before defragmentation, what is the total fragmentation? How many files are fragmented? After defragmenting the drive, what is the total defragmentation? How many files are still fragmented? Why are there some fragmented files remaining?

7. On a test system with two physical hard disks installed, convert both disks to dynamic disks.

8. Create a spanned volume that uses a portion of both disks. After creating the spanned volume, extend it so that it uses the remainder of one of the two disks.

9. Delete the spanned volume and revert one of the two disks to a basic disk. Do this on the disk that DOES NOT contain the Windows 2000 system files. Create a primary partition on this drive, formatted with the FAT32 file system.

10. Create an empty folder on an NTFS volume named Mounted. Mount the primary partition you created in Step 9 to this folder. How does the folder appear in Windows Explorer? When you store a file in this folder, where are the files actually being stored?

Answers to Lesson 7 Activities

1. Share permissions are only used when the folder is accessed over the network. Since you are logged in as a non-administrator, and only administrators have been granted access to the folder, you cannot access it remotely. When you access the folder through Windows Explorer or My Computer, you are accessing it locally, and the share permissions do not apply.

2. To assign NTFS permissions, right-click the ShareTest folder and choose Properties. Choose the Security property page and add the user accounts as listed.

3. The denied user cannot access the folder locally or remotely. NTFS permissions are used in either scenario. When a folder is accessed remotely, the most restrictive permissions (between the share permissions and the NTFS permissions) become the effective permissions. In this case, the user has been denied to right to read the contents of the folder and receives an Access is Denied message. The other user can read the contents of the folder and can read files within the folder but cannot add files to the folder. The Users group has been granted the Read permission, but not the Write permission.

4. Right-click an NTFS volume in Windows Explorer and choose Properties. Select the Quota property page and enable disk quotas. Change the size setting to 2 MB and select the option to deny disk space to users who exceed the quota limit.

5. In Windows Explorer, you can copy a folder by right-clicking the folder and choosing Copy. When you choose the volume with enabled quotas, right-click on the volume to paste the folder. The Outlook Express folder was chosen because it exists on all installations of Windows 2000 and is typically larger than 2 MB. You can choose any folder over 2 MB. When you attempt to copy the folder, the folder is created, but the contents are not. You receive a message that there is insufficient space on the volume. When you attempt to copy the folder as an administrator, the copy succeeds. Administrators are exempt from disk quotas.

6. Access the Disk Defragmenter from the Computer Management console. Choose a volume and select Analyze. View the report. The statistics regarding total fragmentation and the number of fragmented files can be found in this report and will vary depending on your system. Select Defragment. When defragmentation is finished, view the report again to see what changes have occurred. Some files cannot be defragmented if they are in use by the system.

7. Using the Disk Management console, right-click a disk and choose Upgrade to Dynamic Disk. Repeat for the other disk.

8. Right-click one of the two dynamic disks and choose Create Volume. Create a spanned volume, selecting both disks. The size you select for the volume must be less than the entire space available. After creating the volume, right-click the volume and choose Extend Volume. Select one of the two drives and enter the maximum value for the used space. Note that the spanned volume appears as three parts in the lower portion of the Details pane in the Disk Management console.

9. Right-click on any portion of the spanned volume and choose Delete Volume. Right-click one disk and select Revert to Basic Disk. If this option is not available, you must first delete all other partitions on the disk. You cannot delete the partition containing the Windows 2000 system files. When finished, right-click the unallocated space on the basic disk and choose Create Partition to create the primary partition.

10. Using Windows Explorer, create a new folder on any NTFS volume and name it Mounted. In the Disk Management console, right-click the primary partition and choose Change Drive Letter and Path. Choose Add, select Mount in this NTFS folder, enter the path and name of the folder you just created (for example, D:\Mounted) and then select OK. Reopen the Change Drive Letter and Path window, select the drive letter and select Remove. Note that the volume no longer has a drive letter associated with it. Reopen Windows Explorer and find the folder you created. Note that the icon has changed to represent a hard disk drive.

Lesson 7 Quiz

These questions test your knowledge of features, vocabulary, procedures, and syntax.

1. A fault-tolerant DFS structure is stored where?

   A. On the server on which it is created

   B. On a stripe set with parity

   C. On a mirror set

   D. In the Active Directory

2. Which of the following can use the drive letter B? (Choose all that apply)

   A. A floppy disk drive

   B. A hard disk

   C. A CD-ROM

   D. A mapped network drive

3. Who can open an encrypted file? (Choose all that apply)

   A. Members of the Server Manager group

   B. Anyone with Take Ownership permission

   C. The user who created it

   D. Members of the EfsAdmins group

4. In a striped volume, data is written to each disk in blocks of what size?

   A. 16 kilobytes

   B. 32 kilobytes

   C. 64 kilobytes

   D. Data is not written in blocks on a striped volume.

5. To which of the following can you assign share permissions? (Choose all that apply)

   A. Files on FAT volumes

   B. Folders on FAT volumes

   C. Files on NTFS volumes

   D. Folders on NTFS volumes

6. To which of the following can you assign NTFS permissions? (Choose all that apply)

    A. Files on FAT volumes

    B. Folders on FAT volumes

    C. Files on NTFS volumes

    D. Folders on NTFS volumes

7. After upgrading Windows NT 4.0 to Windows 2000, which of the following Windows NT 4.0 sets can be repaired using the Disk Management console? (Choose all that apply)

    A. Mirror set

    B. Stripe set

    C. Volume set

    D. Stripe set with parity

8. Which of the following volume types can be extended?

    A. Simple volume

    B. Mirrored volume

    C. Striped volume

    D. RAID-5 volume

9. Which of the following volume types can be created on a basic disk?

    A. Simple volume

    B. Spanned volume

    C. Mirror set

    D. You cannot create volumes on basic disks

10. Which of the following rules about NTFS and share permissions is true?

    A. NTFS permissions always supercede share permissions

    B. Share permissions always supercede NTFS permissions

    C. NTFS permissions combine with share permissions to create an effective permission

    D. Share permissions only apply to users remotely accessing a folder

Answers to Lesson 7 Quiz

1. Answer D is correct. A fault-tolerant DFS structure is created on a domain controller, is stored in the Active Directory and is replicated to all Active Directory domain controllers.

    Answer A is incorrect. A stand-alone DFS tree is stored on the local server.

    Answers B and C are incorrect. These two terms relate to Windows NT 4.0 fault-tolerant disk systems. Although the DFS structure could be created on a basic disk with one of these Windows NT 4.0 systems, these are not the best answers.

2. Answers A and D are correct. If there are two floppy drives in a system, the second drive always assumes the letter B. If not, the letter can be used only to map a network drive. It cannot be used for any other local drives.

    Answers B and C are incorrect. The drive letter B cannot be used for any local drives other than a second floppy.

3. Answer C is correct. Only the user who created the file and the recovery agent can open an encrypted file.

    Answer A is incorrect.

    Answer B is incorrect. Even if you take ownership of an encrypted file, you cannot decrypt it without the private key.

    Answer D is incorrect. There is no EfsAdmins group.

4. Answer C is correct. Data is written in 64-kilobyte blocks to each disk in a stripe set.

    Answers A, B, and D are incorrect.

5. Answers B and D are correct. Share permissions do not depend upon the file system, but can only be applied to folders.

    Answers A and C are incorrect. Share permissions cannot be applied to files.

6. Answers C and D are correct. NTFS permissions can be assigned to both files and folders but only those files and folders stored on NTFS-formatted volumes.

    Answers A and B are incorrect. NTFS permissions cannot be used on FAT-formatted volumes.

7. Answers A and D are correct. Only those file systems that provide fault tolerance can be repaired in the event of a failed drive. In this case, the only two sets that provide fault tolerance are mirror sets and stripe sets with parity.

    Answers B and C are incorrect. Stripe sets and volume sets can only be deleted in Windows 2000.

8. Answer A is correct. Only simple volumes and spanned volumes can be extended.

    Answers B, C, and D are incorrect.

9. Answer D is correct. You cannot create any volume type on a basic disk. You can only create primary and extended partitions and logical drives on basic disks.

    Answers A, B, and C are incorrect.

10. Answer D is correct. Share permissions are only applied to users accessing a folder over the network.

    Answers A and B are incorrect. Neither NTFS nor share permissions override the settings of the other.

    Answer C is incorrect. The effective permission is the most restrictive of the NTFS and share permissions, not a combination of the permissions.

Terminal Services

The first computer networks were composed of one or more central servers (called mainframes) and numerous terminals. Users work at the terminals, which are little more than a screen and a network card. Terminals have little or no processing power, permanent storage, or memory and usually cannot operate independently of the network. When a user runs a program, the program uses the processing power of the mainframe. The more users on the network, the higher the demands are on the mainframe.

Most of today's networks consist of clients and servers. A server provides resources on the network, and a client accesses these resources. More specifically, a client computer provides most of the processing power needed by the user. Applications are stored locally on the client computer or on a server, and the application uses the client computer's processor to run. Windows 2000 and Windows NT 4.0 are network operating systems that are designed for the client-server network.

There is now a trend back towards a terminal-server type of network. As the hardware requirements to run Windows 2000 and newer applications increase, companies are finding that many of their older computers cannot run the newer operating systems and applications. Their choices are limited: upgrade the computers to handle the demands of the new operating system or limit what operating system their employees use. Neither choice is a good one. To alleviate this problem, Microsoft has incorporated Terminal Services into Windows 2000, allowing a Windows 2000 server to act as a mainframe and non-Windows 2000 operating systems to act as terminals.

After completing this lesson, you should have a better understanding of the following topics:

*   Terminal Services Overview

*   Terminal Services Installation Planning

*   Terminal Services Installation and Configuration

*   Terminal Services Sessions

*   Terminal Services Applications

*   Client Settings

*   Remote Administration

*   Remote Control

Terminal Services Overview

Terminal Services for Windows allows users of non-Windows 2000 computers to run Windows 2000 services, utilities, and applications. Terminal Services allows a computer unable to run Windows 2000 to participate on a Windows 2000-based network and to run newer applications that would not ordinarily work with the older (or non-Windows) operating system.

Much like the mainframe computer in older mainframe-and-terminal networks, the Windows 2000 Terminal Services server provides the processing power for each client. The server can run multiple copies of Windows 2000, and each copy is sent over the network to a user of Terminal Services.

Tip: Terminal Services can also be used to manage servers remotely. With Terminal Services, an administrator using a non-Windows 2000 computer can run Windows 2000 Server administrative tools.

Understanding how Terminal Services Works

Terminal Services consists of the following three parts:

Terminal Services server—The Terminal Services server handles all processing needs for the Terminal Services session (including keystrokes, mouse movements, video display, and application execution). All users who are logged on to the Terminal Services server receive a unique environment, as if running Windows 2000 on their local machines.

Remote Desktop Protocol (RDP)—RDP is an application layer protocol that uses the TCP/IP protocol suite to transfer information between the Terminal Services server and client.

Note: RDP is based on the International Telecommunication Union (ITU) T.120 Standard.

Terminal Services client—The desktop of the Terminal Services server appears in a window on the client computer. Terminal Services includes support for client computers running Windows for Workgroups 3.11, Windows 95, Windows 98, Windows NT 4.0, Windows CE, and Windows 2000.

Tip: Windows 2000 Terminal Services supports clients running most Windows operating systems. To use Terminal Services with non-Windows operating systems, you can use the third party solution, Citrix MetaFrame. MetaFrame supports clients running DOS, Unix (and Linux), MacOS, and OS/2 Warp.

Terminal Services Installation Planning

Before installing Terminal Services, you must have an understanding of the requirements for both the server and client computers. You should plan your hardware requirements for the Terminal Services server based on the expected number of users that will connect to the server at any given time and their level of use.

Meeting Computer Requirements

One of the main reasons to use Terminal Services is to run Windows 2000 and newer applications on computers that do not have the necessary hardware to run these programs. The lower hardware requirements for clients means higher hardware requirements for the Terminal Services server, which must be able to run multiple copies of Windows 2000 simultaneously.

Client Requirements

In lieu of using a third-party solution, the Terminal Services client must be running one of the Windows operating systems. The hardware requirements depend, in part, on which operating system is running on the client computer. Table 8.1 lists the operating systems that work as Terminal Services clients as well as their associated requirements for Random Access Memory (RAM), Intel processor speed, and video output.

Note: In addition to supporting Intel-based computers, a Terminal Services client is also available for computers based on the Alpha processor.

Table 8.1 Terminal Services Client Hardware Requirements

Operating System	RAM	Processor	Video
Windows for Workgroups 3.11	16 MB	386	VGA
Windows 95	16 MB	386	VGA
Windows 98	16 MB	486	VGA
Windows NT 4.0	16 MB	486	VGA
Windows 2000	32 MB	Pentium	VGA
Windows CE (Handheld PC 3.0)	Vendor-specific	Vendor-specific	Vendor-specific

There are three versions of the Terminal Services client: a 16-bit version for Windows for Workgroups clients, a 32-bit version for clients running Windows 95, Windows 98, Windows NT 4.0, and Windows 2000 and a 32-bit version for computers based on the Alpha processor.

Server Requirements

The hardware requirements for the server depend on the number of concurrent Terminal Services connections to the server and the type of use expected from these connections.

The type of user connecting to the server can make a significant difference in the needs of the server. A basic user—one who generally runs one application at a time—uses far fewer resources than an advanced user who multitasks between several applications. Consider the needs of your users when planning hardware requirements for the Terminal Services server.

Because each user who connects to a Terminal Services demands processing time from the server, you must determine the estimated number of concurrent connections. In addition, each user process requires some of the server's RAM. Table 8.2 lists examples of three server configurations and the approximate number of users supported.

 Note: The hardware examples in Table 8.2 are for a server running nothing but Terminal Services. If your server also provides other services on the network (for example, as a file server, print server, or DNS server), you will need to increase the hardware requirements appropriately.

Table 8.2 Minimum Server Hardware Requirements

Server Configuration	Basic Users Supported	Typical Users Supported	Advanced Users Supported
Single Pentium Pro 200 MHz CPU with 128 MB RAM	25	15	8
Dual Pentium Pro 200 MHz CPU with 256 MB RAM	50	30	15
Quad Pentium Pro 200 MHz CPU with 512 MB RAM	100	60	30

If you are selecting a new computer to use as the Terminal Services server, you should also consider the number and type of hard disks and network cards to install. Hard disk speed—oftentimes the bottleneck in any server—has a strong impact on the performance of a Terminal Services server, since several clients may be simultaneously accessing the same volumes. You should opt for the fastest hard disks and controllers available (typically, fast and fast-wide SCSI disks).

Tip: As a general rule, each Terminal Services client requires an additional 4 to 8 MB of RAM on the server.

In addition, since all of the information must be carried over the network from the server to the clients, you should use the fastest network card that is compatible with your network type. If possible, install multiple network cards to distribute the network traffic.

Licensing Terminal Services

Three licenses are required to use Terminal Services. The Windows 2000 Server running Terminal Services must have a server license. This is the license included when you purchase Windows 2000 Server. Like all other Windows 2000 servers, you must also purchase a Client Access License (CAL) for each computer accessing the server. You may choose Per Seat or Per Server licensing mode for the server.

Tip: In general, you will want to choose Per Seat mode for use with Terminal Services, since it is rarely the only server on the network.

You must also obtain one Terminal Services CAL per connecting client. Windows 2000 Professional ships with one Terminal Services CAL. You need to purchase licenses for all other client operating systems.

Selecting Applications

The final planning stage before installing Terminal Services involves the type of applications the server will provide to clients. In general, if an application is compatible with Windows 2000, it will run over Terminal Services. Windows-based 32-bit applications run significantly more efficiently than 16-bit applications. DOS-based programs may work, but Microsoft does not support running any DOS-based programs with Terminal Services.

 Warning: Running 16-bit Windows applications on a Terminal server greatly reduces the processing ability and available RAM on a server. The number of users who can connect may drop by as much as 40%, and the need for RAM may increase by as much as 50%.

In addition to a lack of support from Microsoft, DOS-based applications may have other problems. Many were written as single-user applications and are not designed to be run by more than one user at a time. In addition, many DOS and older 16-bit Windows applications are custom-designed and may not run on a Terminal server.

Applications that require non-standard hardware (for example, bar code scanners, smart card readers, or graphics tablets) can only be used by a Terminal Services client if the required device is recognized as a keyboard-type device.

Terminal Services Installation and Configuration

After determining the hardware requirements for the Terminal server and preparing the server for installation, you install Terminal Services on both the server and client.

Installing Terminal Services

You begin installation on the server through the Add/Remove Programs Control Panel. For clients, install the software by floppy disk or over the network after the server has been installed.

Terminal Services Server Installation

To begin the Terminal Services installation on the server, follow these steps:

1. From the Start Menu, choose Settings and then select Control Panel.

2. Double-click Add/Remove Programs.

3. Choose Add/Remove Windows Components.

4. From within the Windows Components window, choose the boxes next to Terminal Services and Terminal Services Licensing and then select Next (Figure 8.1).

Figure 8.1 Terminal Services Selection

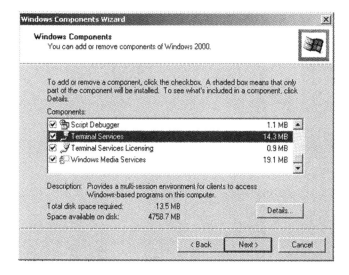

 Note: Terminal Services Licensing configures the server to issue Terminal Services licenses to clients. Terminal Services will only run for 90 days if this option is not installed.

5. Unless you are installing Terminal Services for administrative reasons only, choose Application server mode and then select Next.

6. From the Terminal Services Setup window, choose the permissions that Terminal Services will use and then choose Next.

    The more secure option is to allow only Windows 2000-compatible applications to run Permissions compatible with Windows 2000 Users. Older applications require access to parts of the registry, which is a less secure configuration. If you need to support older applications, choose Permissions compatible with Terminal Services 4.0 Users.

7. If you have previously installed applications on the server, they may be listed in the Terminal Services Setup window (Figure 8.2). The programs listed may not function properly after installation of Terminal Services and may need to be reinstalled. After reviewing the list, choose Next.

Figure 8.2 Application List

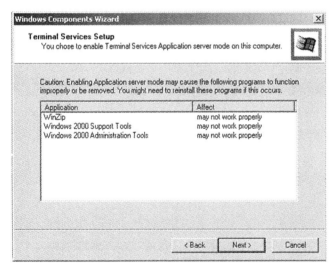

8. Choose whether the Terminal Services License server will supply licenses for the entire enterprise or just the domain (or workgroup) in which the server resides. Also, enter the path for the license server database and then choose Next.

    Terminal Services is now installed.

9.   Choose Finish to complete installation and then select Yes to restart the computer.

Installation of Terminal Services adds the following four snap-ins to the Administrative Tools menu:

Terminal Services Client Creator—Creates floppy disks for installing Terminal Services client software on client computers.

Terminal Services Configuration—Manages the RDP protocol and server settings.

Terminal Services Licensing—Manages Terminal Services CALs.

Terminal Services Manager—Monitors and manages active Terminal Services sessions.

Terminal Services Client Installation

Once the Terminal Services server is installed, you can install the Terminal Services client software on client computers by using floppy disks or by installing the software over the network.

To create client installation floppy disks on the Terminal Services server, follow these steps:

1.   From the Start Menu, choose Programs, Administrative Tools and then select Terminal Services Client Creator.

2.   From the Create Installation Disk(s) window, choose the client software you want to use, the destination floppy drive, whether you want to format the floppy disks before copying the software and then select OK (Figure 8.3).

Figure 8.3 Client Selections

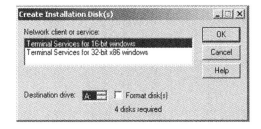

3.   When prompted, insert a floppy disk and choose OK.

4. When the file copy is finished, choose Cancel to close the window, or select OK to create more disk sets.

 Note: You will need either two or four blank floppy disks to create the client installation set, depending on the type of client.

Once the disk set has been created, you can use the floppies to install the client software. On a client computer, follow these steps:

1. Insert the first disk of the set into the floppy drive.

2. From the Start Menu, choose Run.

3. In the Open box, type **A:\SETUP** and then choose OK.

4. Choose Continue. The Terminal Services Client installation begins.

5. Enter a name and organization and then choose OK.

6. Read and accept the license agreement and then choose I Agree.

7. Choose the Setup icon to install Terminal Services client components.

8. Choose whether you want to make the Terminal Services client services available to all users of the computer (select Yes) or just the user that is currently logged on (select No).

9. When prompted, switch disks and choose OK.

10. Choose OK to close the installation window, select Next and then select Finish.

To load the Terminal Services client software over the network, you must first make the installation files available over the network. The following folder contains the installation files for all three types of clients, and it (or each of the client folders) must be shared: \WINNT\SYSTEM32\CLIENTS\TSCLIENT\NET

Tip: Users only need the Read share permission to the installation folder. It is a good practice to remove the Everyone group, add the necessary user or group accounts and assign nothing more than the Read share permission.

Once the folder has been shared, you can install the Terminal Services client software. From a client computer, access the share and run **SETUP.EXE** in the folder that contains the appropriate client files. The setup procedure exactly follows the steps for a floppy installation (without the need to change floppies, of course).

Configuring Terminal Services

You should verify several settings (and change them if necessary) before the Terminal Services server is made available over the network. You can modify the settings in the properties window for each user account. In addition, you can modify the settings for user accounts stored in the Active Directory or for user accounts stored locally on the terminal server. The steps to access the properties page are defined below. However, once the page is opened, the setting choices are identical to the previous options.

Accessing User Properties in Active Directory

To access the property page for a user account in the Active Directory, follow these steps:

1. From the Start Menu, choose Programs, Administrative Tools and then select Active Directory Users and Computers.

2. In the Tree (left) pane, expand the domain and then expand Users (or whichever OU contains the user account you want to modify).

3. In the Details (right) pane, right-click the user account and choose Properties (Figure 8.4).

Figure 8.4 User Account Selection

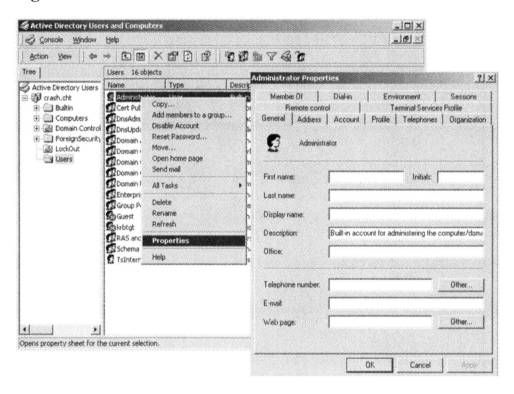

4.   From the User Properties window, choose the Terminal Services Profile property page (Figure 8.5).

Figure 8.5 Terminal Services Profile

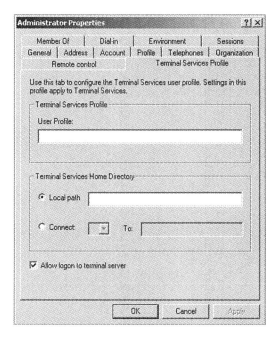

Accessing Local User Properties

If you want to modify settings on a local user account (one that is not stored in the Active Directory), follow these steps:

1. From the desktop, right-click My Computer and then choose Manage.

2. In the Tree pane, expand System Tools, expand Local Users and Groups and then choose Users.

3. From the Details pane, right-click the user account you want to modify and then choose Properties (Figure 8.6).

4. From the User Properties window, choose the Terminal Services Profile property page.

Figure 8.6 Local User Account Selection

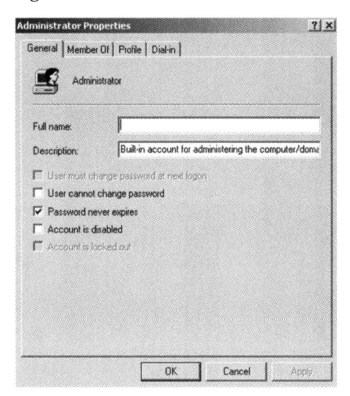

Modifying Terminal Services Settings

After accessing the user property page by one of the two methods provided, you may make changes to the Terminal Services settings. By default, each user who has an account on the Terminal server has permission to log on to the server using Terminal Services. You may disable this setting by deselecting Allow logon to terminal server. You can also define a user profile and home directory for the user account when logging on to the server through Terminal Services (Figure 8.7).

Figure 8.7 Disallowing Use of Terminal Services

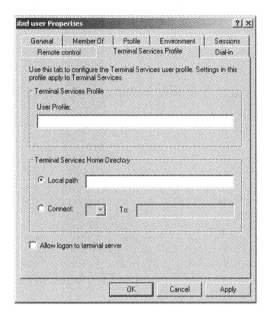

 Note: The settings for a user profile and home directory only take effect when a user accesses the server through Terminal Services. Local logons do not use these settings.

Terminal Services Sessions

After both server and client Terminal Services software has been loaded, and you have configured the security settings for user accounts, the user can establish a Terminal Services connection.

Establishing a Terminal Services Session

To establish a Terminal Services session with a server, do the following from the client computer:

1. From the Start Menu, choose Programs, Terminal Services Client and then select Terminal Services Client.

2. The Terminal Services Client window displays (Figure 8.8). You have several options regarding the connection, as shown in Table 8.3.

Figure 8.8 Terminal Services Client

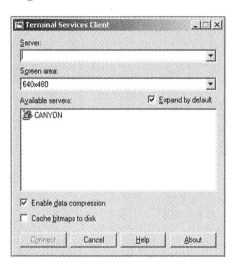

Table 8.3 Terminal Services Connection Options

Option	Description
Server	Enter the name or IP address of the Terminal Services server.
Screen Area	Choose the size of the window that will contain the Terminal Services session. This window size cannot be greater than the client computer's current screen resolution , but it is not dependent on the server's screen resolution.
Available Servers	Choose a server from the expanded list rather than entering an IP address or server name in the first option.
Enable data compression	Data sent from the server is compressed. This requires more processing time from both the server and the client, but it decreases transmission times. Enable this for Terminal Services sessions over slow networks and modem connections.
Cache bitmaps to disk	This option allows graphic portions of the display to be cached locally so they can be refreshed from the client rather than over the network.

3. After making your selections, choose Connect.

4. A window of the specified resolution opens, and the Windows 2000 logon screen displays (Figure 8.9).

Figure 8.9 Terminal Services Logon

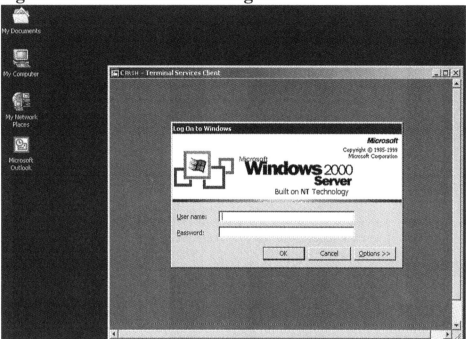

5. Log on using a valid user account and password.

    The desktop of the Terminal Services server displays, including the task bar, Start Menu, and desktop icons (Figure 8.10).

Figure 8.10 Terminal Services Desktop

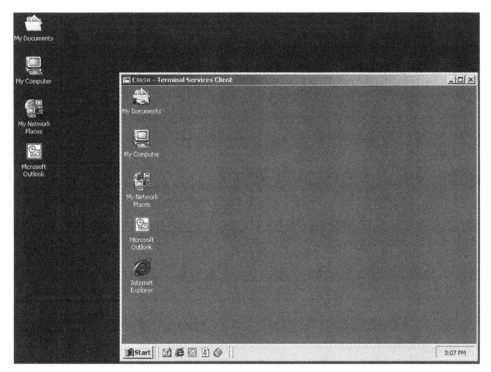

When finished using a Terminal Services connection, you can either close the window or log out. Closing the window maintains a connection to the Terminal Services server in the background and allows programs to continue to run. Logging out disconnects the Terminal Services session and frees server resources.

Terminal Server Applications

Installation of applications on a Terminal server differs from the normal application installation procedure. When you install an application on a server or workstation, certain settings and files are stored within user profiles. In order for applications to work properly over Terminal Services, these files need to be stored in a common location.

Tip: If you attempt to install an application on a Terminal server by running **SETUP.EXE** or AutoPlay you will receive an Installation Failure message, instructing you to use the Add/Remove Programs Control Panel.

Installing Applications on the Terminal Server

You can install applications on a Terminal server in two ways: you can use the Add/Remove Programs Control Panel, or you can run the **CHANGE USER** command. Both methods put the Terminal Services server in install mode, which allows applications to be installed properly for use with Terminal Services.

Change User Command

You can activate the Terminal Services install mode by using the **CHANGE USER** command from a command prompt. From the Start Menu, choose Programs, Accessories and then select Command Prompt. From the command prompt, type the following command:

CHANGE USER /INSTALL

While in install mode, .INI file mapping is disabled, and the system records how Setup installs the files. Install the application and, when finished, type the following command at a command prompt:

CHANGE USER /EXECUTE

The server is now running in execute mode (the default), which allows users to run applications.

Add/Remove Programs

An easier method for installing applications involves the use of the Add/Remove Programs Control Panel. When you run Add/Remove Programs, the **CHANGE USER** commands are issued automatically.

1. From the Start Menu, choose Settings and then select Control Panel.

2. From the Control Panel, open Add/Remove Programs.

3. Choose Add New Programs.

4. Insert the CD-ROM or floppy disk that contains the **SETUP.EXE** file, and then choose CD or Floppy (Figure 8.11).

Figure 8.11 Installation from CD-ROM or Floppy

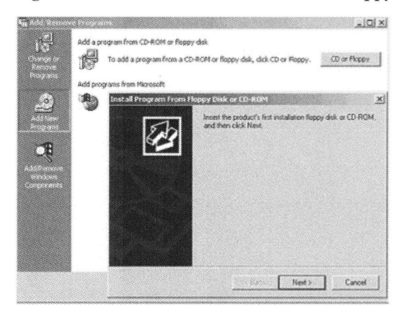

5. Choose Next and Add/Remove Programs will search for the **SETUP.EXE** file.

6. If the file and path in the Open box are correct, choose Next to begin the installation.

7. When installation is complete, choose Next, select Finish, and then close the Add/Remove Programs Control Panel.

Using Compatibility Scripts

Many applications are not designed to work in the multi-user environment needed by Terminal Services. Terminal Services includes application compatibility scripts for many common applications. These scripts modify the registry settings for the application, making it available to multiple users, and protecting files by marking them as read only.

After you install an application, you need to run its associated script. Scripts are located in the \WINNT\APPLICATION COMPATIBILITY SCRIPTS\INSTALL folder and include support for the following programs (Table 8.4):

Table 8.4 Compatibility Scripts

Application	Associated Script File
Corel Perfect Office 7.0 (32-bit)	COFFICE7.CMD
Corel Perfect Office 8.0 (32-bit)	COFFICE8.CMD
Microsoft Exchange Client 5.5	WINMSG.CMD
Lotus SmartSuite 97 (32-bit)	SSUITE97.CMD
Lotus SmartSuite 9.0	SSUITE9.CMD
Microsoft Office 4.3	OFFICE43.CMD
Microsoft Office 95	OFFICE95.CMD
Microsoft Office 97 SR1	OFFICE97.CMD
Microsoft Project 95	MSPROJ95.CMD
Microsoft Project 98	MSPROJ98.CMD
Netscape Communicator 4.0	NETCOM40.CMD
Netscape Navigator 3.0	NETNAV30.CMD

Application	Associated Script File
Microsoft Word 97	MSWORD97.CMD
Microsoft Excel 97	MSEXCL97.CMD
Microsoft Outlook 98	OUTLK98.CMD
Peachtree 2000	PCHTREE6.CMD
Microsoft SNA Server 3.0	MSSNA30.CMD
Microsoft SNA Client 4.0	SNA40CLI.CMD
Microsoft SNA Server 4.0	SNA40SRV.CMD
Microsoft Visual Studio 6.0	MSVS6.CMD
Executive Software DiskKeeper 2.0	DISKPR20.CMD
Qualcomm Eudora 4.0	EUDORA4.CMD
Sybase PowerBuilder 6.0	PWRBLDR.CMD
Visio 5.0	VISIO5.CMD

Notably absent from the list of scripts (Table 8.4) is one for Microsoft Office 2000. To install Office 2000, you must first install the Terminal Services components from the Office 2000 Resource Kit. More information is available at the Office 2000 Resource Kit Web page, at the following address: HTTP://www.microsoft.com/office/ork/2000

Configuring and Running Scripts

To prepare and use a script, follow these steps:

1. Install the application, using the Add/Remove Programs Control Panel or the **CHANGE USER** command.

2. After installation, run the associated script file. To run the script file, right-click My Computer and select Explore.

3. From the left pane of Windows Explorer, expand the drive that contains the system folder, expand WINNT, expand Application Compatibility Scripts and then choose Install (Figure 8.12).

Figure 8.12 Compatibility Scripts

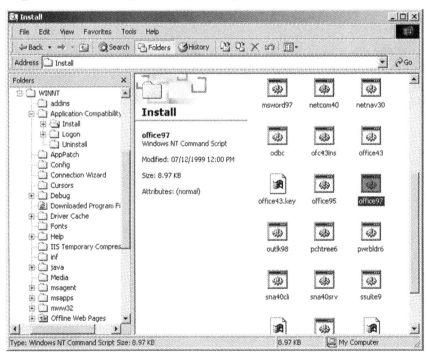

4.   In the right pane, double-click the appropriate script file.

5.   Some script files may require user input before completion. Follow the directions presented by the script, if any.

6.   When complete, the application is ready to be used by Terminal Services clients.

 Note: You must log off and log on again before using the current account for a Terminal Services session.

Client Settings

You can fine-tune the performance of Terminal Services by making changes to the RDP protocol configuration. As the protocol used to transfer data to and from a Terminal Services server, RDP affects all user connections to the terminal server. In particular, you can set time limits on connections.

Configuring Client Settings

To set time limits for users, follow these steps:

1.   From the Start Menu, choose Programs, Administrative Tools and then select Terminal Services Configuration.

2.   In the Tree pane, choose Connections.

3.   In the Details pane, right-click RDP-TCP and then choose Properties (Figure 8.13).

Figure 8.13 RDP-TCP Properties

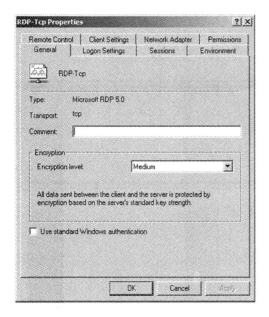

4.   From the RDP-TCP Properties Window, choose the Sessions property page (Figure 8.14).

Figure 8.14 Sessions Property Page

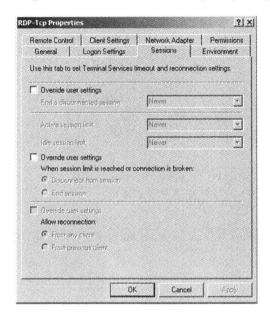

5. You can change several user connection settings in the Sessions property page (Table 8.5). To make connections, first choose Override user settings next to the settings you want to change. Then make your selections and select OK.

Table 8.5 RDP Sessions Selections

Option	Description
End a disconnected session	Specifies how long to retain a session if a session is disconnected without the user logging off.
Active session limit	Specifies how long a user can stay connected to the Terminal server.
Idle session limit	Specifies how long an inactive session can remain connected. Any activity from the user resets the idle time clock.
When session limit is reached or connection is broken	Specifies whether to disconnect the user from the session (which leaves the session open on the server) or to end the session altogether.
Allow reconnection	Specifies from what computer a user can reconnect to a disconnected session.

Remote Administration

The use of Terminal Services is not limited to allowing users of older machines to access Windows 2000 utilities and applications. Terminal Services is also used to provide remote administration of Windows 2000 servers.

If a Terminal server is providing access to multiple users, security settings must be changed to allow access to utilities and applications. However, if Terminal Services is being used for remote administration, the security settings must be more restrictive to prevent unwanted access to the server and to encrypt data transmissions.

Configuring Terminal Services for Remote Administration

Settings to optimize and secure Terminal Services settings for remote administration are made in both the RDP-TCP Properties page and the Terminal Services Server Settings.

RDP Optimization

To make changes to settings in the RDP-TCP page, follow these steps:

1. From the Start Menu, choose Programs, Administrative Tools and then select Terminal Services Configuration.

2. In the Tree pane, choose Connections.

3. In the Details pane, right-click RDP-TCP and then choose Properties.

4. Using Table 8.6 as a reference, choose the appropriate property page and adjust settings as needed.

Table 8.6 RDP-TCP Options

Property Page	Option	Description	Reason
General	Encryption level	Set to High to ensure that sensitive administrative information is not intercepted.	Increase security
Client Settings	Disable the following:	Disable Windows printer mapping, LPT and COM port mapping, and Clipboard mapping. When these are enabled, users can copy sensitive information to the clipboard or send the information to a printer.	Increase security
Network Adapter	Maximum connections	Limit the number of connections.	Increase security
Permissions		By default, the Users group has access to the Terminal Server. Remove this group, and only add user or group accounts for administrators.	Increase security

Property Page	Option	Description	Reason
Sessions	End disconnected session	Specify a time duration for all sessions, freeing up server memory and resources.	Increase performance
Sessions	Idle session limit	Set this value to 5 minutes to prevent unneeded resource use and to ensure security if a session is accidentally left open.	Increase performance and security
Environment	Disable wallpaper	A significant amount of Terminal Services traffic is generated by loading a user's wallpaper. Wallpaper settings are not needed when using Terminal Services for remote administration.	Increase performance

5. Choose OK to save the settings.

Optimizing Server Settings

In addition to making changes to the RDP protocol, you can also adjust server settings to increase performance when using Terminal Services for remote administration. To make changes to the server settings, follow these steps:

1. From the Start Menu, choose Programs, Administrative Tools and then select Terminal Services Configuration.

2. In the Tree pane, choose Server Settings (Figure 8.15).

Figure 8.15 Terminal Services Server Settings

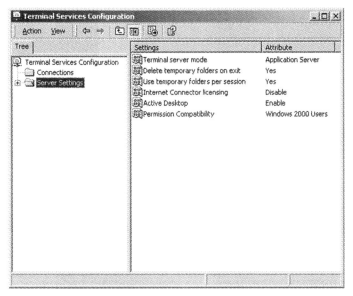

3. In the Details pane, double-click Active Desktop. Choose Disable Active Desktop and then select OK.

    Disabling the Active Desktop reduces the use of server and network resources. Active Desktop is generally not needed to perform remote administrative tasks.

4. Note the setting for the Terminal server mode. If Terminal Services is installed as an Application server, you should change the mode to Remote administration mode.

5. Double-click Terminal server mode.

6. A message displays informing you that mode changes must be made through the Add/Remove Programs Control Panel (Figure 8.16). Choose the link to Add/Remove Programs and the Add/Remove Windows Components Wizard is automatically launches.

Figure 8.16 Mode Change Notification

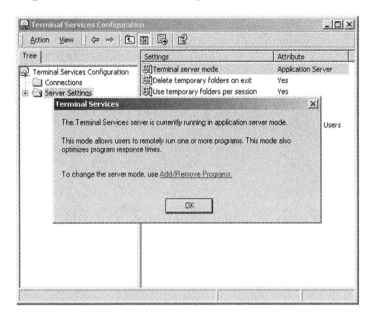

7. From the Add/Remove Windows Components window, select Terminal Services (but do not des-
    elect the check mark) and then select Next (Figure 8.17).

Figure 8.17 Terminal Services Reinstallation

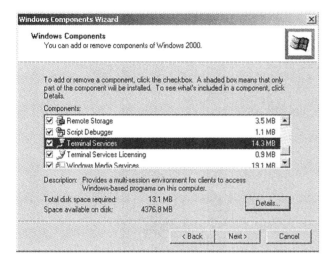

8. Choose Remote administration mode and then select Next.

9. Continue through the remainder of the installation wizard. When complete, reboot the server. After restarting, the server will be running in Remote administration mode.

Remote Control

A final aspect of Terminal Services is the ability for you to monitor and actively control a user's Terminal Services session. Using remote control, you can watch a user's actions to see where difficulties are arising, then take over control of the session to input keyboard and mouse actions so that the user can see the correct way to accomplish tasks.

Configuring Remote Control

Configuration of remote control settings is done in Terminal Services Configuration. To configure settings, follow these steps:

1. From the Start Menu, choose Programs, Administrative Tools and then select Terminal Services Configuration.

2. In the Tree pane, choose Connections.

3. In the Details pane, double-click RDP-TCP.

4. From the RDP-TCP Properties window, choose the Remote Control property page (Figure 8.18).

Figure 8.18 Remote Control Property Page

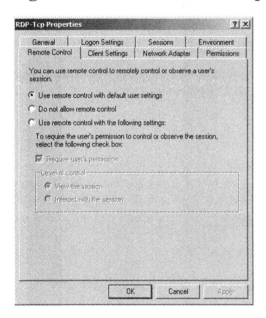

5. Choose Use remote control with the following settings.

6. If you want to require a user's permission for you to remotely control and view his Terminal Services session, ensure that Require user's permission is selected and then select the level of

control. You can deselect Require user's permission to monitor Terminal Services sessions without the user's permission.

7. Choose OK to save your settings and then close Terminal Services Configuration.

 Note: Configuration through RDP-TCP Properties enables remote control for all sessions. If you want to enable remote control for only specific user accounts, configure the user properties in Active Directory or Local Users and Groups.

Using Remote Control

To use remote control to view and control a Terminal Services client, you must run the Terminal Services Manager from within a Terminal Services client window. On a computer with Terminal Services client software loaded, follow these steps:

1. From the Start Menu, choose Programs, Terminal Services Client and then select Terminal Services Client.

2. Choose a Terminal Services server, a screen area (which must be equal to or greater than the user's session) and then select Connect.

 Note: If the screen size you select is smaller than that of the user, your screen size automatically adjusts when you choose to the user's session.

3. Log on to the Terminal Services with a user account with administrative access.

Warning: If you are running the Terminal Services client software on a Windows 2000 computer, it is easy to get the two screens confused. Terminal Services Manager must be run from within the Terminal Services client window, not from the Windows 2000 desktop.

4. From the Terminal Services client window Start Menu, choose Programs, Administrative Tools and then select Terminal Services Manager.

5. In the Tree pane, choose the Terminal server to which the user is connected (Figure 8.19).

Figure 8.19 Terminal Server Selection

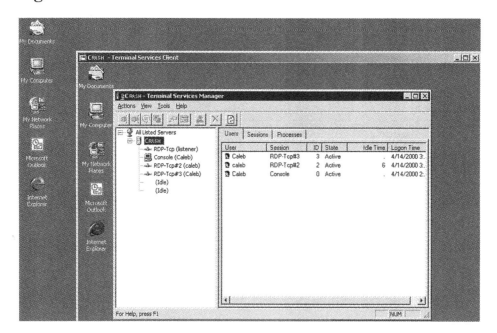

6. In the Users pane, right-click the user session you want to control and choose Remote Control (Figure 8.20).

Figure 8.20 User Session Selection

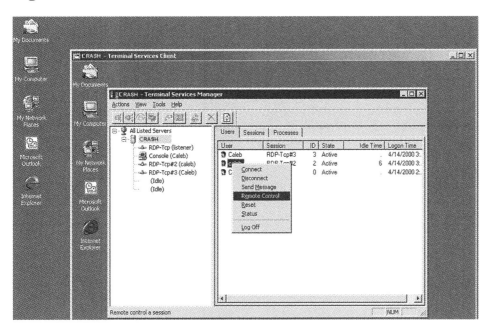

7. Choose an exit hot key combination and then select OK.

The exit hot key combination is the key combination used to end a remote control session. The combination should not be something you are likely to type while helping the user. The default is **CONTROL-*** (using the * on the numeric keypad).

8. The user's Terminal Services session appears. Your mouse and keyboard actions are now sent directly to that session, not your own.

If you configured remote control to require a user's permission, a significant pause occurs while the user responds to your request.

Tip: Keeping track of sessions can be difficult. When using remote control, you are controlling a Terminal Services session within a Terminal Services session within your local logon session.

9. When you are finished monitoring or controlling the remote session, use the exit hot key combination to end the remote session.

10. Close Terminal Services Manager and then log off from your Terminal Services session.

Vocabulary

Review the following terms in preparation for the certification exam.

Term	Description
bottleneck	The slowest part of a system, the bottleneck in a computer is often the hard drive.
CAL	A Client Access License permits a client computer to access resources on a Windows 2000 server.
CHANGE USER	The Change User command is used to put a Terminal Services server in install mode (for installing applications) or execute mode (for running applications).
client	Any computer on a network that accesses resources on a server.
execute mode	The default mode for a Terminal server, execute mode allows users to run applications.
install mode	Install mode is used on a Terminal server to install applications.
ITU	The International Telecommunication Union is an intergovernmental organization through which telecommunications standards are developed.
mainframes	Mainframes are computers designed to handle all of the computations needed for client computers.
RAM	Random Access Memory is used to stores active programs and the operating system.
RDP	Remote Desktop Protocol is the protocol used to transfer Terminal Services session information. It requires the use of the TCP/IP protocol suite.

Term	Description
remote control	Remote control is a feature of Terminal Services that allows you to monitor and control another user's Terminal Services session.
SCSI	Small Computer System Interface
server	Any computer that shares resources over the network.
snap-in	An administrative tool designed to work within the Microsoft Management Console (MMC).
terminal	A device used to access a mainframe on older networks. A terminal generally cannot operate independently of the network.
Terminal server	A Windows 2000 server running Terminal Services .
Terminal Services	Terminal Services are network services provided with Windows 2000 Server that allow users to display and use the Windows 2000 desktop environment on com puters that cannot run Windows 2000. Terminal Services are also used for remote administration of Windows 2000 servers.

In Brief

If you want to...	Then do this...
Allow users to run Windows 2000 on outdated computers currently running Windows 3.11	Install a Terminal Services server and then load Terminal Services client software on the older computers.
Allow Macintosh users to run a Windows 2000 window	Install a Terminal Services server and then install Citrix MetaFrame, or another third-party solution, on the Macintoshes.
Administer a server from your computer running Windows NT 4.0 Workstation	Install Terminal Services on the server in Remote administration mode. Load the Terminal Services client software on your workstation.
Increase Terminal Services connection speed	Replace slow hard drives and network cards on the server with faster ones. Configure Terminal Services to end disconnected and idle sessions, disable the use of wallpaper and disable Active Desktop.
Permit only three specific users to connect to a Terminal server	Place the three user accounts in a group. Grant access to the Terminal server only to that one group.
Guide a Terminal Services user through a complicated process without leaving your desk	Use remote control to take over the user's Terminal Services session. The user can watch as you move your mouse and make selections.
Ensure that an application will run properly under Terminal Services	Install the application and then run the associated script file.

Lesson 8 Activities

Complete the following activities to better prepare you for the certification exam.

1. Install Terminal Services on a test server. Make sure it is installed in Application server mode. Also, if you have not done so already, create two user accounts that have administrative access to the server (name them Admin1 and Admin2, perhaps).

2. Create a floppy disk set for Terminal Services client installation. Select the client software for a computer using the Windows 2000 operating system.

3. Share the client installation folder with the minimum share permissions to grant Admin1 and Admin2 access. Load the Terminal Services client software on the client computer using this network share.

4. Using the floppy set, load the client software on the Terminal Services server. The server will now be both a Terminal Services server and client.

5. Using the **CHANGE USER** command, install Office 97 or another application that has an associated script file on the Terminal server and use the script file to prepare the program for Terminal Services use.

6. Enable remote control on the server, requiring user permission. Allow the remote administrator to monitor and control the user's session.

7. From the client computer, initiate a Terminal Services session, and log on to the server using the Admin1 account.

8. On the server, initiate a client session, logging on with the Admin2 account.

9. From the Server, remotely control the Admin1 client session. From the Admin1 session, you will need to grant permission to Admin2 when prompted. From the server, change the user's background color to a bright color.

10. As Admin2, end the remote session, log out from the session on the server and then log out Admin1 from the session on the client. On the server, initiate another Terminal Services client session, logging in this time as Admin1. Did the desktop settings remain?

Answers to Lesson 8 Activities

1. On the server, use the Add/Remove Programs Control Panel to install Terminal Services. If the server is domain controller, create the two user accounts in the Active Directory. If it is a stand-alone server, create the two user accounts locally. To create local accounts, right-click My Computer and choose Manage. Expand System Tools, expand Local Users and Groups and then select Users.

2. From the Start Menu (on the server), choose Programs, Administrative Tools and then select Terminal Services Client Creator. Choose Terminal Services for 32-bit x86 windows.

3. The client installation folder is \WINNT\SYSTEM32\CLIENTS\TSCLIENT\NET. Share this folder and set the share permissions such that only the two Admin accounts are listed, and each has only the Read permission.

4. If you insert the first floppy disk in the server and try to run **SETUP.EXE**, you will be notified that you cannot install applications on the Terminal Services server without using Add/Remove Programs. Use the Add/Remove Programs Control Panel to run **SETUP.EXE** on the first disk of the set and then follow the screen instructions.

5. Before loading the program, run **CHANGE USER /INSTALL** from a command prompt. Load the program, run the script file and then run **CHANGE USER /EXECUTE**. It does not matter which program you load. The purpose of this activity is to give you experience with the script files and **CHANGE USER** command.

6. Enable remote control using the Terminal Services Configuration snap-in. Access the RDP-TCP Properties window and then choose the Remote Control property page. When you enable remote control, the default setting requires permission from the user but only allows you to monitor. Change this to allow control of the session.

7. On the client computer, run Terminal Services Client, choose the server and then choose Connect. When the logon screen appears, log on using the Admin1 account.

8. On the server, run Terminal Services Client, choose the same server and then select Connect. When the logon screen appears, log on using the Admin2 account. You will now have a copy of the server's desktop running in a window on the server's desktop.

9. From within the Terminal Services session on the server, open Terminal Services Manager. Right-click the Admin1 session and choose Remote Control. Select a hot key combination and then select OK. On the client computer, confirm the notification. On the server, you may begin altering the client computer's desktop settings. Right-click the desktop and choose Properties. Make changes that will be noticeable.

10. On the server, use the exit hot keys to end the remote session and from the Start Menu (in the Terminal Services session window), choose Shut Down and then select Log Off Admin2. On the client computer, log Admin1 off in the same way. On the server, establish another Terminal Services session and login as Admin1. The desktop settings you made remotely have been preserved.

Lesson 8 Quiz

These questions test your knowledge of features, vocabulary, procedures, and syntax.

1. What is the minimum amount of RAM needed to run the Terminal Services client on any Windows desktop platform?

    A. 8 MB

    B. 16 MB

    C. 32 MB

    D. 64 MB

2. Which type of application runs most efficiently over a Terminal Services connection?

    A. DOS-based

    B. 16-bit Windows-based

    C. 32-bit Windows-based

    D. Macintosh-based

3. Which of the following licenses are required to use Terminal Services? (Choose all that apply)

    A. CAL licenses for each client accessing the server

    B. Terminal Services CAL licenses for each client accessing the server

    C. Remote control license

    D. Server license for the Windows 2000 server running Terminal Services

4. Which of the following client operating systems includes a Terminal Services CAL? (Choose all that apply)

    A. Windows 3.11

    B. Windows 98

    C. Windows NT 4.0 Workstation

    D. Windows 2000 Professional

5. How must you install applications on a Terminal Services server?

    A. By using the AutoPlay feature

    B. By using the Add/Remove Hardware Control Panel

    C. By running `SETUP.EXE`

D. By using the `CHANGE USER /INSTALL` command

6. How do you install Terminal Services client software?

    A. By creating installation disks using the `CREATE DISK /INSTALL` command

    B. By creating installation disks using Terminal Services Client Creator

    C. By creating installation disks using Terminal Services Floppy Creator

    D. By connecting to the \WINNT\Terminal Services\Clients folder and running `SETUP.EXE`

7. Where do you configure remote control settings?

    A. Terminal Services Configuration, RDP-TCP properties

    B. Terminal Services Configuration, remote properties

    C. Terminal Services Client Creator

    D. Active Directory Sites and Services

8. Which protocol(s) is (are) used with Terminal Services?

    A. TCP and IP only

    B. RDP and TCP/IP

    C. RDP only

    D. IP and RDP

9. When installing Terminal Services client software over the network, what is the minimum share permission users need?

    A. Read

    B. Read and Write

    C. Change

    D. Full Control

10. By default, what is the time limit on idle Terminal Services sessions?

    A. 5 minutes

    B. 30 minutes

    C. 3 hours

    D. No time limit

Answers to Lesson 8 Quiz

1. Answer B is correct. For any Windows desktop operating system, you must have at least 16 MB RAM installed. For Windows 2000, the minimum is 32 MB.

    Answers A, C, and D are incorrect.

2. Answer C is correct. 32-bit Windows applications are the most efficient applications.

    Answer A is incorrect. Many DOS programs may not work at all over a Terminal Services connection, let alone be the most efficient.

    Answer B is incorrect. 16-bit Windows applications may decrease the number of users who can connect by 40% and reduce the amount of available RAM by 50%.

    Answer D is incorrect. Macintosh-based programs do not run under Windows 2000.

3. Answers A, B, and D are correct. You must have a server license, a CAL license for each client, and a Terminal Services CAL for each client.

    Answer C is incorrect. You do not need to purchase a license to use remote control.

4. Answer D is correct. Only Windows 2000 Professional ships with one Terminal Services CAL.

    Answers A, B, and C are incorrect. None of these operating systems come with Terminal Services CALs. To use them, you must purchase CALs.

5. Answer D is correct. The **CHANGE USER /INSTALL** command puts the server in install mode, allowing applications to be installed.

    Answers A and C are incorrect. **SETUP.EXE** and AutoPlay will not work until the server is running in install mode.

    Answer B is incorrect. You can use the Add/Remove Programs Control Panel but not the Add/Remove Hardware Control Panel.

6. Answer B is correct. To install Terminal Services client software, you create installation floppies using Terminal Services Client Creator.

    Answers A and C are incorrect. Neither is a valid command or utility.

Answer D is incorrect. You can install Terminal Services client software by accessing a network share, but the location is not \WINNT\Terminal Services\Clients.

7. Answer A is correct. Remote control settings are configured by opening Terminal Services Configuration, accessing the RDP-TCP Properties window and then selecting the Remote Control property page.

    Answers B, C, and D are incorrect.

8. Answer B is correct. Terminal Services uses the RDP protocol, which requires the presence of the TCP/IP protocol suite.

    Answers A, C, and D are incorrect. Each of these answers lists protocols that are used, but the answers are incomplete.

9. Answer A is correct. Users need nothing more than Read permission on the share to access and run the Terminal Services client installation.

    Answers B, C, and D are incorrect. Each of these options gives the user more access than is needed and may be a security problem.

10. Answer D is correct. By default, no time limits are imposed on Terminal Services clients.

    Answers A, B, and C are incorrect.

Network Security and Remote Access

The two fundamental aspects of network security are user authentication and data encryption. Authentication ensures that before any data is transmitted between two computers, each user can verify the identity of the other user. Data encryption ensures that if the data is intercepted during transmission, it cannot be read by the intercepting user.

Remote access is the service that allows users to connect to a Local Area Network (LAN) from remote points. Inherent to remote network access are problems with slow network connections and data security. New enhancements to remote access help compress data and provide on-demand lines, reducing problems created by slow Wide Area Network (WAN) links. For data security, remote access takes advantage of several new security features in Windows 2000, including new protocols and data encryption methods.

After completing this lesson, you should have a better understanding of the following topics:

- Distributed Security Services
- Smart Cards
- Internet Protocol Security (IPSec)
- Remote Access

Distributed Security Services

As companies increase their presence on the Internet and use the Internet as the backbone for intra-company networking and remote access, the need to incorporate security technologies into corporate networks also increases. Windows 2000 distributed security services meets this challenge by adding new features to the existing Windows NT 4.0 security architecture that simplify administration, improve performance and incorporate Internet security protocols.

Distributed security services is an umbrella term that includes the following features:

1. Integration with Active Directory

2. Support for the Kerberos Version 5 authentication protocol

3. Network authentication and data integrity using public-key technologies, Secure Socket Layer (SSL), and CryptoAPI

Integrating Security with Active Directory

Windows 2000 implements multiple methods for achieving authentication and encryption on the network. These methods are integrated with Active Directory, providing a high level of security within the fundamental network structure. Active Directory provides the underlying structure of Windows 2000 networks and provides user logon authentication.

Active Directory Overview

Windows 2000 uses the Active Directory as the repository for user account information. The Active Directory is a hierarchical structure of objects. A domain may contain thousands of objects, including computer accounts, user accounts, and user groups. You organize these objects by placing them in Organizational Units (OUs). An OU is a container object, an Active Directory object that contains other objects.

The Active Directory structure allows for expandability and supports a much larger number of user and group accounts than the domain structure of Windows NT 4.0. In Windows NT 4.0, user accounts are stored in a secure portion of the domain controller's registry. The registry has a maximum size that limits the number of accounts within a domain. Active Directory, although limited, supports many more objects (more than 1 million objects per domain).

Active Directory Security

The detailed structure of Active Directory allows you to assign fine-grained access rights to objects. Every object in the Active Directory has an Access Control List (ACL), a list of user and group accounts that have been granted or denied access to that object. When assigning permissions, you can assign them to the entire object or to only certain properties of the object. For example, you can grant a user permission to change user passwords but not be able to change any other user information.

The Active Directory structure also lends itself to delegation of administrative tasks. By assigning specific permissions to OUs, you can delegate control over those OUs without sacrificing security on other OUs within the directory. In Windows NT 4.0, a user with access permissions to change user accounts has permission to change all user accounts. In Windows 2000, an administrator can control all user accounts within an OU, but may not be able access the security information stored elsewhere in the Active Directory.

Using Encryption Keys for Security

Network security requires user authentication and data encryption. Both users and computers can be authenticated, the former for logging on to the network and accessing resources and the latter for transmitting data. The data that is transmitted can be encrypted, which renders it unreadable by any computer other than the intended receiver.

 Note: When discussing network security, it is often useful to imagine two people sharing sensitive information face-to-face. Each person needs to identify the other party (network authentication). To avoid eavesdropping, both parties may communicate in a secret code (data encryption).

When information transmits across a network, it is important for the receiving computer to know with certainty the identity of the sending computer. It is also important that the data is encrypted. In a secure network, an unauthorized user should not be able to access the network. Likewise, an authorized user should not be able to receive information intended for another user. Windows 2000 uses digital certificates (and associated encryption keys) to identify users on the network.

Digital Certificates

A digital certificate is a form of identification on a network. When data needs to be sent securely across a network, the sender and the receiver use digital certificates. On networks, it is impossible to identify (in person) the user with whom you are exchanging information. Digital certificates provide the means of verifying identities without requiring physical proximity.

A digital certificate is issued by a trusted third party called a Certificate Authority (CA). There is an ever-increasing number of CAs on the Internet, and most of them use the industry-standard X.509 Version 3 certificate. A company or user must apply for a digital certificate. The CA performs numerous checks of the company to verify the identity, and the amount of effort a CA puts forth in verification must be publicly available. The result is that when you receive a digital certificate from another party, you can be relatively certain that the identity of that party has been verified. You can also check the level of verification that was performed before trusting the certificate.

 Tip: Windows 2000 fully supports the X.509 Version 3 standard and uses it for many security protocols, including Authenticode, CryptoAPI, and SSL/TLS.

A digital certificate contains a key pair that consists of two cryptographic (or encryption) keys: a public key and a private key. A key is a mathematical function that scrambles the data sent. The data encrypts using one key and can only be decrypted (reorganized) using the other key. The keys are mathematically related to one another but are complex enough that it is impossible to determine one key from the other.

The public key, as the name implies, is available to anyone on the network. However, the client that generates the key pair keeps the private key confidential. No other user on the network can obtain this private key.

Note: The complexity of the mathematical functions in keys makes it nearly impossible to recreate a key. If you obtain a public key, you cannot use the information within to make a copy of the associated private key.

Encrypting Data

Using the public key of a key pair, you can send an encrypted message to the holder of the private key. For example, user A wants to send encrypted data to user B (Figure 9.1). The sender encrypts the data using the encryption algorithm stored in the B's public key. Upon receipt of the data, B decrypts the data using the private key of the key pair. Since the data was encrypted with B's public key, it can only be decrypted using B's private key, held by no one else but User B.

Figure 9.1 Data Encryption

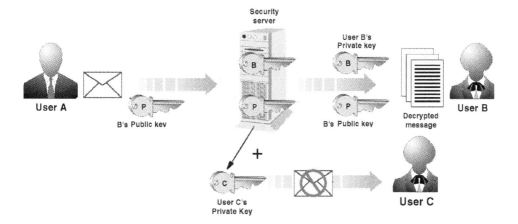

Signing a Message

Encryption keys can also sign a message as proof of authentication. For example, suppose user A wants to send information to user B and wants B to know with certainty that the message came from A. (Figure 9.2).

Figure 9.2 Message Signing

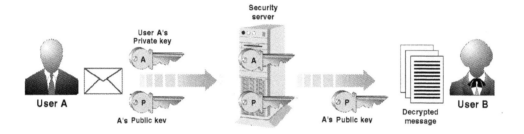

User A encrypts the data with A's own private key and then sends the data to B. Upon receipt, B uses A's public key to decrypt the data. Since the data was encrypted using A's private key (which no one else has), B can be certain of A as the sender.

Tip: Even if the data is encrypted, it is not secure. Anyone can eavesdrop by using A's public key to decrypt the message. However, the message cannot be altered, since the private key is needed to resend the data.

Encryption with Signing

You may have to send securely encrypted data that is also signed. To do so, you combine the methods for both encryption and signing (Figure 9.3).

Figure 9.3 Encryption and Authentication

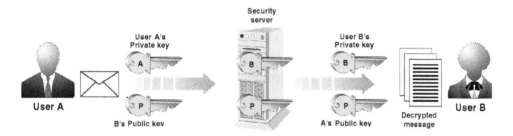

In this case, user A encrypts the data using A's private key, then encrypts the data again using B's public key. Upon receipt of the message, B decrypts the data using B's private key (which only B has ensuring security) and then decrypts the data using A's public key (which ensures A is the original sender of the information).

Using Kerberos for Security

Within a Windows 2000 network, there are two methods for authenticating users. The Windows NT LAN Manager protocol (NTLM) is the default for network authentication in Windows NT 4.0. It is used in Windows 2000 to support non-Windows 2000 clients. The second authentication method supported by Windows 2000 is Kerberos Version 5, which is the default in Windows 2000.

Note: Kerberos protocol is defined in Request For Comments (RFC) 1510. RFC documents are available on the Internet at the following Web address: http://www.rfc-editor.org

Kerberos is more efficient, more secure and more widely used than NTLM. The benefits of Kerberos include the following:

Mutual authentication—With NTLM, servers can confirm a client's identity, but clients cannot verify servers. Using NTLM, servers on a network are assumed to be authentic. With Kerberos, no assumptions are made. Clients can verify servers, and servers can verify one another.

Efficient authentication—With Kerberos authentication, a client receives credentials when logging on to the network. The client can then use these credentials to access other servers. With NTLM, the client needs to be re-authenticated by a domain controller for every server it accesses.

Interoperability—Kerberos is a network standard, unlike NTLM, which is a Microsoft-specific protocol. Using Kerberos enables interoperability with other networks that use Kerberos.

Simplified trusts—Trusts between Windows 2000 domains are all two-way, transitive trusts. Kerberos makes this possible. With NTLM, all trusts must be one-way, non-transitive trusts.

Delegated authentication—Kerberos allows network services to impersonate a client on the client's behalf. The service can access resources needed on other servers by acting as the client.

 Note: NTLM uses delegated authentication but only for resources on the local computer. Kerberos can use delegated authentication locally and over the network.

Kerberos uses encryption keys, but does not use a key pair. Instead, Kerberos uses secret key cryptography (or shared secret keys). With shared secret keys, two clients both know the secret key (hence shared secret). This dual knowledge of a secret encryption helps each client verify the other. If only two people know a secret password, and you are one of the people, anyone who tells you the secret password must be the trusted person.

Kerberos Authentication

Suppose a client wishes to access secure information on a server. The client wants to be sure that the server is the correct machine, and the server needs to verify the client's identity as well. The client sends a message to the server that contains information encrypted with the secret key (Figure 9.4).

Figure 9.4 Kerberos Verification

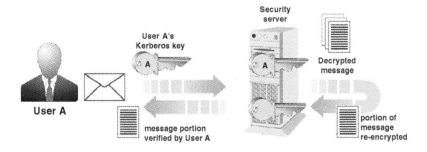

The server decrypts the message using the secret key, extracts a small portion of the original message and encrypts it again with the secret key. The client, upon receiving the new message, decrypts it and verifies that a portion of the original message is contained within.

Since the server could decrypt the message using the secret key, it knows that the client used the secret key and must be authentic. Since the client received a portion of the original message in return, it knows that the server successfully decrypted the message using the secret key and therefore must be authentic as well.

Key Distribution Center (KDC)

If every client needs a secret key for each server, and every server needs a secret key for each client, the number of keys generated would be astronomical. To solve this potential problem, Kerberos uses a trusted intermediary to handle key distribution. This intermediary is called the Key Distribution Center (KDC).

A secure server on the network is designated as the KDC. When a user logs on to the network, the user's password is put through a one-way hashing function, generating a cryptographic key. This key is called the long-term key. This key is always used to identify the user. The KDC uses a user's long-term key to generate a session key that is only used once—for a single session between a client and server—and then discarded.

When a client wants to talk to a server, it asks the KDC for a session key. The KDC produces two copies of the session key, one for the client and one for the server. Both keys are then passed on to the client (Figure 9.5). The KDC does not send a copy of the session key to the server. It sends the server's copy to the client, and it becomes the client's responsibility to send the other key to the server.

Figure 9.5 Session Key Distribution

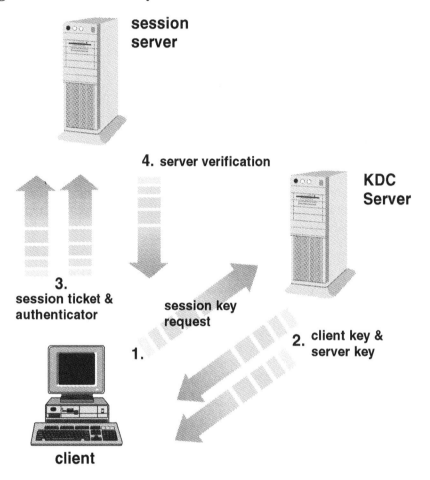

 Note: Due of the nature of networks, a message sent from the KDC may arrive at the client long after it arrives at the server, causing inefficient use of server time. The KDC does not send a session key to the server to prevent these server wait times.

The package sent to the client includes the session key, encrypted with the client's long-term key and the same session key for the server, encrypted with the server's long-term key. The portion encrypted for the server is called the session ticket.

When the client initiates contact with the server, it sends the session ticket (which is encrypted with the server's long-term key) and an authenticator, which is encrypted with the new session ticket. Upon receiving this information, the server first decrypts the session ticket to obtain the short-term session key, and then uses the session key to decrypt the authenticator.

Using session keys, the server can be certain of the identity of the requesting client. The KDC sends the session key encrypted with the client's long-term key. Only the intended client can decrypt it and use the session key to send a copy of the session ticket to the server.

If the client needs to verify the identity of the server, the server can encrypt a portion of the client's authenticator using the session key and send it back to the client. Again, only the designated server could decrypt the client's message, obtain the session key and use that key to send a message back to the client.

Understanding Secure Sockets Layer (SSL) and Transport Layer Security (TLS)

When companies conduct business over the Internet, they need to make available a secure channel through which customers can provide credit card numbers, bank account numbers, and other sensitive information. The Secure Sockets Layer (SSL) 3.0 protocol is a network protocol created by Netscape that uses public key technology to establish a secure connection between a Web client and Web server.

 Note: A standard Web connection uses Hypertext Transfer Protocol (HTTP). A secure connection uses HTTPS, the S representing secure.

An SSL session begins when a Web browser accesses a Web page requiring SSL. The steps that occur during an SSL connection are as follows:

1. The Web browser establishes a connection to a secure Web page (Figure 9.6).

Figure 9.6 SSL Process

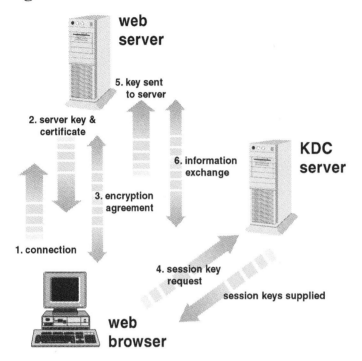

2. The Web server sends the browser a copy of its public key and its certificate (which confirms the server's identity).

3. The Web server and browser agree on a level of encryption (usually either 40-bit or 128-bit encryption).

4. The Web browser obtains a session key from a KDC, encrypts it using the server's public key and sends the encrypted key to the Web server.

5. The server decrypts the session key using its own private key

6. The server and browser exchange information using the session key.

Microsoft has proposed Transport Layer Security (TLS) to the Internet Engineering Task Force (IETF) as a new standard for SSL. It is entirely based on SSL 3.0 but is not fully compatible with SSL. Microsoft often refers to the protocols as SSL/TLS, indicating their similar purpose and use.

Note: More information on the proposed TLS protocol can be found in RFC 2246.

Understanding CryptoAPI (CAPI)

CryptoAPI (CAPI) is an Application Programming Interface (API) that allows applications to encrypt and digitally sign data. The applications do not actually perform the encryption and signing functions but pass these jobs on to Cryptographic Service Providers (CSPs). A CSP, which can be software- or hardware-based, is responsible for generating the public and private keys for the session.

 Tip: CryptoAPI is supported by Microsoft Windows 95, Windows 98, Windows NT 4.0, and Windows 2000.

Using Authenticode

Authenticode uses digital signatures to verify the origin and integrity of software downloaded from the Internet. When Internet Explorer downloads digitally-signed code, Authenticode verifies the digital signature and often prompts the user if the sender can be trusted to run the code on the local computer.

Smart Cards

When security keys are generated, they are often stored in the local computer's Random Access Memory (RAM). RAM memory is erased frequently, so storing security keys in the RAM is safer than storing them on a hard disk, but they are still susceptible to unauthorized access. Smart cards, which are credit card-sized devices, can be used to store private and shared keys more securely. Smart cards provide a better storage solution for private information (like security keys) because they provide the following:

- Removable storage, so that secure data travels with the user rather than staying in the computer

- Tamper-resistant storage

- Isolate security information from the rest of the computer

A smart card has an embedded microprocessor and embedded memory and attaches to the computer through a smart card reader. The internal memory stores the private information, and the internal processor can be used to process security requests from within the card, limiting the number of external processes that can access the information.

Smart cards are used in Windows 2000 to do the following:

- Logon to a network using security certificates

- Authenticate an SSL connection over the Internet

- Send and receive secure e-mail using Microsoft Outlook and Microsoft Outlook Express

Understanding Smart Card Compatibility

The Personal Computer Smart Card (PC/SC) Workgroup, an industry group of PC and smart card manufacturing companies and operating system designers, develops specifications for smart cards. The PC/SC Workgroup membership includes Microsoft, Intel, Sun Microsystems, Hewlett Packard, Toshiba, Siemens, Schlumberger, Bull, and GemPlus.

 Note: The latest specifications on smart cards can be found at the PC/SC Workgroup's Web page on the Internet at the following address: http://pcscworkgroup.com.

Microsoft's primary role in the development of smart cards has been full operating system support for the cards and readers. Windows 95 and Windows 98 support smart card use for Internet security. Windows NT 4.0 and Windows 2000 also support using smart cards for logons, including remote access connections.

Microsoft is also developing device-independent APIs that allow applications to use smart cards. The program platform, called Smart Card for Windows, uses two common programming languages— Microsoft Visual C++ and Microsoft Visual Basic. Using these programming languages ensures that many programmers can implement smart card usage without learning a new language.

Internet Protocol Security (IPSec)

IPSec, an Internet Protocol (IP)-based network security protocol, works at the network layer of the Open Systems Interconnection (OSI) model to provide application-independent authentication, data integrity, and encryption. IPSec works with TCP/IP-based networks to provide security against internal and external attacks. It is also used to provide encryption on remote access connections using a Virtual Private Network (VPN). IPSec encapsulates data carried on the network in an Encapsulated Security Payload (ESP), ensuring data security and authenticity.

 Note: The OSI model provides a standard structure on which networks are developed. The Internet Protocol (IP) part of the TCP/IP protocol suite works at the Network Layer of this model. This allows application-independence.

IPSec was designed by the Internet Engineering Task Force (IETF), and is included as part of the Windows 2000 operating system as Windows IP Security. The advantages of using IPSec include the following:

Standardization—IPSec is based on the OSI model, a networking standard that ensures multi-platform compatibility.

Transparency—IPSec works at the Network Layer of the OSI model, making it hidden from applications. You do not need to rewrite applications to make use of IPSec.

Authenticity—IPSec provides strong authentication services to prevent falsely-claimed identities.

Confidentiality—IPSec ensures that data is not intercepted and interpreted en route to its intended destination.

Encryption—IPSec provides data encryption.

Centralization—Management tools for IPSec are centralized to simplify administration.

Dynamism—IPSec uses dynamic rekeying to change the security keys mid-session, further reducing the chances of an attack.

Configuring IPSec

IPSec is configured using the IP Security Policy Management snap-in for the MMC. You can add the snap-in to a pre-existing console (the security console you created for the security configuration tools), or you can open an empty console and add the snap-in as follows:

1. From the Start Menu, choose Run.

2. Type **MMC** in the Open box and then choose OK.

3. The MMC opens with an empty console.

4. From the menu bar, choose Console and then select Add/Remove Snap-in.

5. Choose Add.

6. The Add Standalone Snap-in window is displayed.

7. Choose IP Security Policy Management and then select Add.

   The Select Computer window is displayed (Figure 9.7).

Figure 9.7 Computer Selection

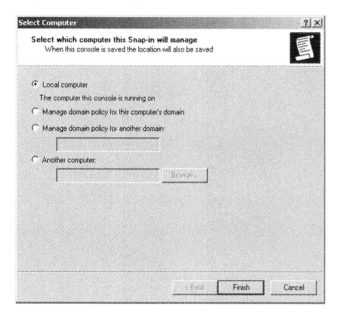

8.   Choose the management option (Table 9.1) and then select Finish.

Table 9.1 Management Options

Option	Description
Local computer	Manages the computer on which the console is running.
Manage domain policy for this computer's domain	Allows you to manage the domain IPSec policy, rather than just the local computer policy.
Manage domain policy for another domain	Allows you to type the name of a remote domain you wish to manage.
Another computer	Allows you to manage the local security settings for a computer other than the one on which the console is running.

9.   Choose Close to return to the Add/Remove Snap-in page.
     The list of snap-ins now includes the snap-in you added (Figure 9.8).

Figure 9.8 Added Snap-in

10. Choose OK to return to the console. If you wish, you can save the changes to the console.

Once you have added the snap-in to a console, you can use the management tools to configure IPSec settings. You can configure the following settings:

•   Requiring a server to accept only data sent using Kerberos

•   Requiring the use of a third-party CA to authenticate all IP data

•   Filtering IP addresses

•   Adjusting Key Exchange values

Remote Access

Remote access is the server-based service that allows users to connect to a LAN from remote computers. Users connect to the network by using a modem to dial in to a dial-up server (a server with a collection of modems) or by tunneling through the Internet with a VPN. A VPN uses tunneling protocols to create a secure passageway through the otherwise very public Internet lines.

Remote access must be both efficient and secure. An employee dialing into your corporate network from a laptop does not have the luxury of a 10- or 100-MB connection, so data transmissions should be compressed to reduce transmission delays. If the employee accesses your network over the Internet using a VPN, the data carried to and from the employee's computer travels through public lines and must be secure to prevent eavesdropping. Remote access for Windows 2000 uses several new protocols and a new tunneling protocol to ensure data is secure and compressed.

Understanding New Remote Access Protocols

Windows NT 4.0 supports many security protocols, including the Password Authentication Protocol (PAP), Challenge Handshake Authentication Protocol (CHAP), and the Shiva Password Authentication Protocol (SPAP). In addition, Windows NT 4.0 uses the Point-to-Point Tunneling Protocol (PPTP) to provide an encrypted tunnel through public lines, creating a Virtual Private Network (VPN).

Windows 2000 supports the security protocols used by Windows NT 4.0 and also includes support for several new security protocols, including the Extensible Authentication Protocol (EAP), Remote Authentication Dial-in User Service (RADIUS), and IPSec. Layer Two Tunneling Protocol (L2TP) replaces PPTP as the default tunneling protocol, and Windows 2000 introduces the use of the Bandwidth Allocation Protocol (BAP) used to control remote access connections.

Extensible Authentication Protocol (EAP)

EAP, which is used during the user logon process, does not provide network or data security directly, but rather provides a framework for remote access security. EAP allows the remote access client and server to negotiate an authentication method. EAP is extensible, providing APIs so that developers can create new authentication methods to work with EAP. Out of the box, EAP supports the following two authentication protocols:

MD5-CHAP—The Message Digest 5 Challenge Handshake Authentication Protocol encrypts user-names and passwords using the MD5 algorithm.

TLS and smart cards—When you are using smart cards for network security, EAP uses TLS with the smart card for data encryption.

 Note: EAP is defined and described in RFC 2284.

Remote Authentication Dial-in User Service (RADIUS)

RADIUS provides remote authentication of user logons. There are two components to a RADIUS network: a RADIUS client and a RADIUS server. Both computers are servers. The RADIUS client is typically a dial-up server, which then becomes a client to the RADIUS server (Figure 9.9). The separation of dial-up server and authenticator allows a company to locate dial-up servers globally but maintain a centralized user account database on the RADIUS server.

Figure 9.9 RADIUS

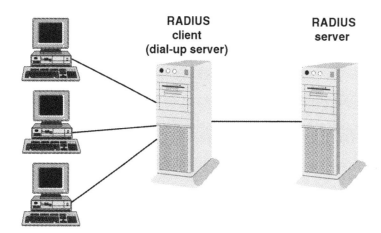

The RADIUS client is often a dial-up server for an Internet Service Provider (ISP). When a user connects to the RADIUS client, the client sends the logon information to the RADIUS server, and the server authenticates the logon process.

The Windows 2000 RADIUS server is called the Internet Authentication Service (IAS) server. The IAS server provides authentication for RADIUS client requests using several possible methods, including such as PAP, CHAP, EAP, Dialed Number Identification Service (DNIS), and Automatic Number Identification (ANI) service. DNIS authenticates a user, based on the number called by the user, and ANI uses the number from which the user called (ANI is also known as Caller ID).

 Note: More information on RADIUS can be found in RFC 2138 and RFC 2139.

Layer Two Tunneling Protocol (L2TP)

L2TP creates an encrypted tunnel through a public network. Although its purpose is very similar to PPTP, there are many differences between the two (Table 9.2). Both PPTP and L2TP use the Point-to-Point Protocol (PPP) to initiate a session, but after the session is established, the two protocols function differently.

Table 9.2 PPTP and L2TP Comparison

Feature	PPTP	L2TP
Network protocol support	Requires an IP-based network.	Can use IP, Frame Relay, X.25, or Asynchronous Transfer Mode (ATM).
Header compression	Not supported. Header size is 6 bytes long.	Uses header compression to reduce the header size from 6 bytes to 4 bytes.
Tunnel authentication	Not supported, but if PPTP is used with IPSec, IPSec provides tunnel authentication.	Supported.
Data encryption	Uses PPP encryption.	Uses IPSec for encryption.

 Note: For more information on L2TP, see RFC 2661.

Bandwidth Allocation Protocol (BAP)

Windows NT 4.0 and Windows 2000 remote access servers support multilink technologies. Multilink combines two or more physical lines into one logical connection, increasing the bandwidth (speed) achieved by that connection. For example, you can combine two 56-Kbps modems into one multilink connection, creating an access rate of 128-Kbps.

With Windows NT 4.0, multilinks are static. Once created, they cannot be changed during a session. Windows 2000, using BAP and the Bandwidth Allocation Control Protocol (BACP), allows multilink connections to dynamically change as demands dictate. If a line is needed to connect a new remote access client, and all lines are currently used in multilink connections, BAP can remove a line from a multilink session and make it available for the new client. Likewise, if a line becomes available, and a particular session needs more bandwidth, BAP can add the available line to the session (Figure 9.10).

Figure 9.10 On-Demand Line Allocation

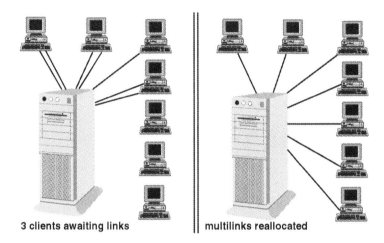

3 clients awaiting links | multilinks reallocated

Configuring Remote Access Clients

Configuration of remote access involves setup on both the server and the client. Outbound connections—those from the client to the server—are set up using the Network Connection Wizard. Using the wizard you can create dial-up connections, connections to a VPN, and direct cable connections.

Creating a Dial-up Connection

Before you can create a dial-up remote access connection, you must have installed and configured a modem. To create an outbound dial-up connection on a Windows 2000 computer, follow these steps:

1. From the Start Menu, choose Settings and then select Network and Dial-up Connections.

2. Double-click Make New Connection.

3. Choose Next to begin the Network Connection Wizard.

4. Choose the type of dial-up connection you wish to create and then select Next (Figure 9.11).

   Dial-up to private network creates a connection to a remote access server, which is what you are doing. Dial-up to the Internet creates a connection to an ISP.

Figure 9.11 Dial-up Connection Choices

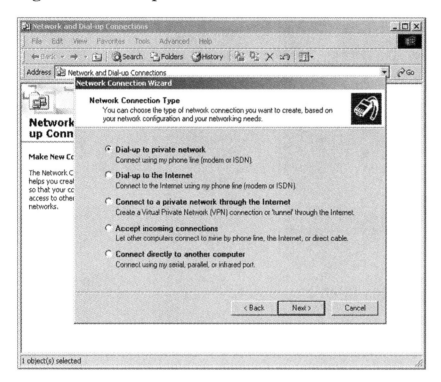

5. If you chose to connect to a private network, enter the phone number and then select Next. If you want the computer to determine which dialing rules to use, based on the user's location, select Use dialing rules, enter an Area code and select a country (Figure 9.12).

Figure 9.12 Dialing Options

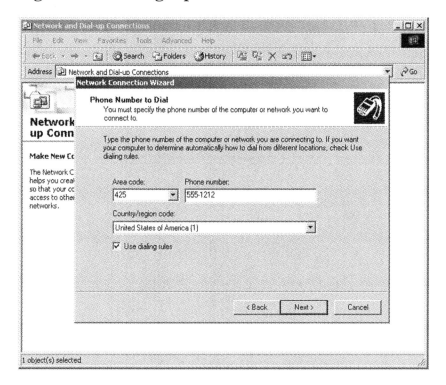

6. Choose whether the dial-up connection will be used by all users of the computer or only the currently active account and then select Next.

7. If you wish to make the connection available to all users, you may choose to use this dial-up computer to provide access to other computers on the network. To do so, select Enable Internet Connection Sharing for this connection and then select Next.

8. Enter a name for the dial-up connection and then choose Finish.

Tip: Internet Connection Sharing enables a Windows 2000 computer to act as a small-scale proxy server, providing dial-on-demand access to the Internet for other computers on the LAN. The use of Internet Connection Sharing is designed for small networks using the TCP/IP protocol and DHCP and is not intended to replace the use of proxy servers on larger networks.

Connecting to a VPN

The Network Connection Wizard is also used to create a connection to a VPN. To set up a VPN connection, follow these steps:

1. From the Start Menu, choose Settings and then select Network and Dial-up Connections.

2. Double-click Make New Connection, and then choose Next to begin the wizard.

3. Choose Connect to a private network through the Internet and then select Next.

4. If you want to establish a dial-up connection before connecting to the VPN, you can opt to do so by selecting Automatically dial this initial connection, and then choosing a previously created dial-up connection. Otherwise, choose Do not dial the initial connection and then select Next.

5. Type the IP address or Fully Qualified Domain Name (FQDN) for the remote access server, and then choose Next.

6. Choose whether this connection will be for all users or just the current user, and then select Next.

7. Enable Internet Connection Sharing, if necessary, and then choose Next.

8. Type a name for the VPN connection, and then choose Finish.

9. If you wish to connect immediately, type a username and password, and then choose Connect. Otherwise, select Cancel (Figure 9.13).

Figure 9.13 VPN Connection

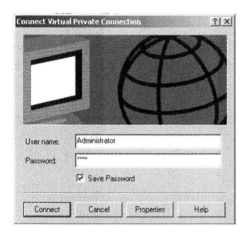

Direct Cable Connection

A direct cable connection can be made between computers. In general, direct cable connections are used for the temporary transfer of information if the network is inoperable or for learning the remote access setup process without the use of modems. To configure a direct cable connection, follow these steps:

1. From the Start Menu, choose Settings and then select Network and Dial-up Connections.

2. Double-click Make New Connection and then choose Next to begin the wizard.

3. Choose Connect directly to another computer and then choose Next.

4. Choose whether this will be the host or guest computer and then select Next. The guest initiates the connection and accesses resources on the host.

Note: If a computer belongs to a domain, you cannot use the Network Connection Wizard to make the computer a host for a direct-cable connection. You must use Routing and Remote Access to do so.

5. Choose the serial, parallel, or infrared port that connects to the other computer and then select Next.

6. Choose whether this connection is for all users or just the current user and then select Next.

7. Type a name for the connection and then choose Finish.

Configuring Remote Access Servers

On the server side of a remote access connection, configuration is done through either the Network Connection Wizard or the Routing and Remote Access (RRAS) snap-in. If the server is a member of a domain, you must use RRAS. If the server is a member of a workgroup, you can use the Network Connection Wizard. Since you have seen how to use the wizard, and since most servers are members of domains, the following steps involve using RRAS.

Configuring Dial-up Connections

To configure a dial-up server, follow these steps:

1. From the Start Menu, choose Programs, Administrative Tools, and then select RRAS.

2. In the Tree (left) pane, right-click the server and choose Configure and Enable Routing and Remote Access (Figure 9.14).

Figure 9.14 RRAS Configuration

3. Choose Next to begin the wizard.

4. Choose Remote access server and then select Next.

5. Verify that all of the protocols you wish to use over the remote access connection are listed, choose Yes, all of the required protocols are on the list and then select Next (Figure 9.15).

Figure 9.15 Protocol List

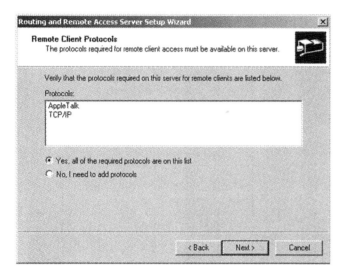

 Note: If you choose No, I need to add more protocols, the wizard ends prematurely. You must add the needed protocols and then re-run the wizard.

6. Configure the server to issue IP addresses to connecting clients and then choose Next. You may choose to have adresses assigned automatically by a DHCP server or the remote access server (select Automatically), or you may assign a specific range of addresses to use (select From a specified range of addresses) (Figure 9.16).

Figure 9.16 IP Address Assignment

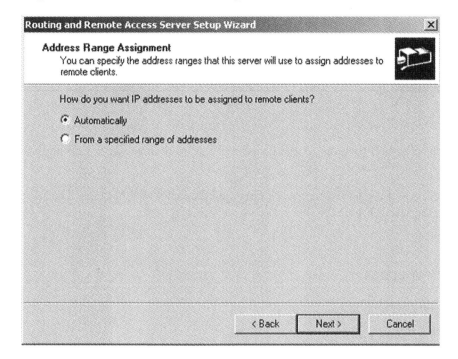

7. Choose whether you want this remote access server to use a RADIUS server (in other words, to be a RADIUS client) and then select Next.

8. Choose Finish to end the wizard and save your settings. RRAS is started automatically.

Configuring Inbound VPN Ports

When you first enable RRAS, ten VPN ports are created, five using L2TP and five using PPTP. All of the ports are disabled by default. You can configure these ports and must enable them before they can be used to receive inbound VPN connections.

Note: You are not limited to only ten VPN connections.

To configure VPN ports, follow these steps:

1. From the Start Menu, choose Programs, Administrative Tools, and then select Routing and Remote Access.

2. In the Tree (left) pane, expand the server, right-click Ports and then choose Properties. The Ports Properties Window is displayed (Figure 9.17).

Figure 9.17 Ports Properties

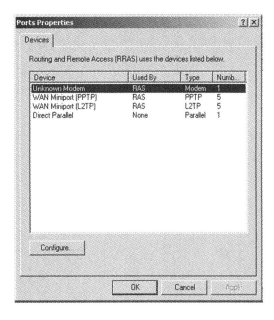

3. Choose the device you wish to configure and then select Configure (Figure 9.18). For a VPN, you should select either WAN Miniport (PPTP) or WAN Miniport (L2TP).

Figure 9.18 Device Configuration

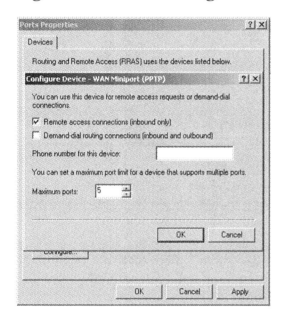

4. From within the Configure Device window, choose whether the device will accept inbound connections, perform demand-dialing, as well as the number of virtual ports that can be used. Make your selections and then select OK.

5. Choose OK again to save your changes.

Tip: Modems and direct-cable ports can also be configured from the Ports Properties window.

Understanding Remote Access Policies

Remote access policies work in conjunction with Active Directory settings to determine which users can connect to a remote access server, and how and when they can make these connections. To successfully create a remote access policy, you need to configure the following three parameters:

User dial-in permissions—Settings are made in Active Directory or on the local machine and closely resemble the RAS settings in Windows NT 4.0.

Remote access policy conditions—Conditions include information about the user and connection that must be matched before access is granted.

Remote access profiles—Profiles dictate the type of connection, including the number of lines to be used and the type of encryption.

 Note: For a server in a domain, user permissions are set in Active Directory Users and Computers. For a server in a workgroup, user settings are changed in Local Users and Groups.

Remote Access Policy Evaluation

Windows 2000 evaluates a remote access policy in the order of conditions, permissions, and profile for the user. If the policy conditions are met, the user and remote access permissions are verified. If the user has permission to connect, the profiles are matched. A user must match at least one remote access profile before access is allowed.

Creating a Remote Access Policy

To effectively implement remote access, you need to create a remote access policy. To do so, you implement dial-in settings for user accounts in Active Directory, then create a policy in Routing and Remote Access, and then edit the policy conditions and profile. The following steps assume the remote access server is a member of a domain.

To configure user dial-in permissions in the Active Directory, follow these steps:

1. From the Start Menu, choose Programs, Administrative Tools and then select Active Directory Users and Computers.

2. From the Tree pane, expand the server and then choose Users (Figure 9.19).

Figure 9.19 Active Directory Users Container

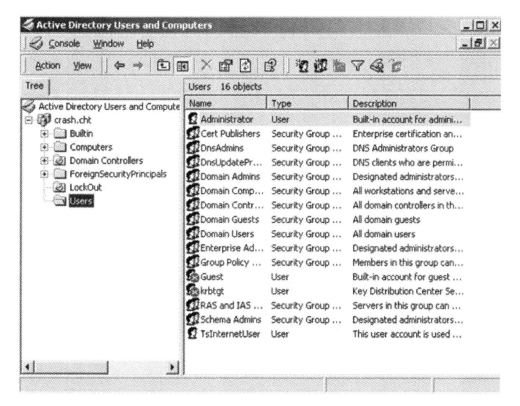

3. In the Details pane, choose the user or group account you wish to edit and then select Properties.

4. From the User Properties window, choose the Dial-in property page (Figure 9.20).

Figure 9.20 Dial-in Property Page

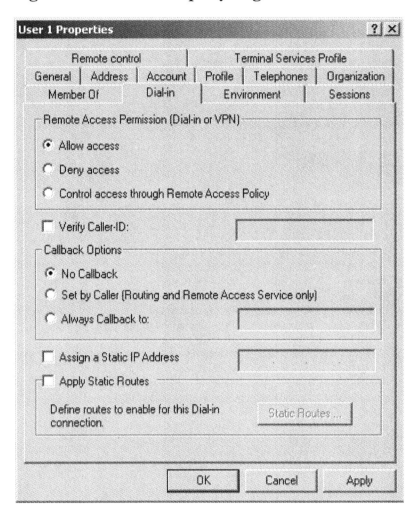

5.   Choose Allow Access, and then make other changes as desired, based on the information in Table 9.3. When finished, select OK to save the changes.

Tip: You can also choose Control access through Remote Access Policy. This setting allows permissions to be determined solely by the remote access policy.

Table 9.3 Dial-in Settings

Option	Description
Verify Caller ID	If the proper caller ID equipment is installed at both ends of the connection, Windows 2000 will match the caller's phone number with the one you enter here and deny access if they do not match. This option is not available in a mixed-mode domain.
Callback Options	You can have the remote access server call the user back before establishing a connection. The Set by Caller option does not increase security, but saves the caller long-distance phone charges. The Always callback to option increases security by requiring the user to be at a pre-determined phone number.
Assign a Static IP Address	Specify an IP address that will always be assigned to this user when establishing a remote access connection. This option is not available in a mixed-mode domain.
Apply Static Routes	This is used with dial-on-demand settings to update routing tables. This option is not available in a mixed-mode domain.

After making changes to the user permissions, close Active Directory Users and Computers. You can then configure the remote access policy conditions. To create policy conditions, follow these steps:

1. From the Start Menu, choose Programs, Administrative Tools and then select Routing and Remote Access.

2. In the Tree pane, expand the server, right-click Remote Access Policies and then choose New Remote Access Policy (Figure 9.21).

Figure 9.21 New Remote Access Policy Creation

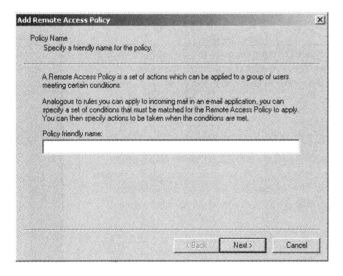

3. Type a name for the new policy and then choose Next.

4. From the Conditions window, choose Add to add new conditions.

5. Choose the condition you wish to add and then select Add. For example, select Day-and-Time-Restrictions and then select Add.

6. Depending on the condition selected, you will be presented with a window to define the conditions. If you chose Day-and-Time-Restrictions, you now specify the hours during which a connection is permitted or denied (Figure 9.22).

Figure 9.22 Time-of-Day Constraints

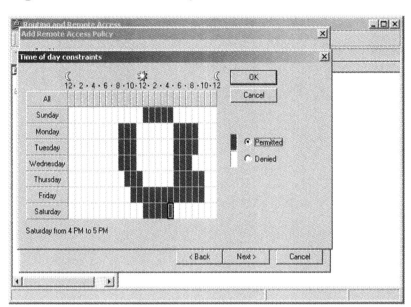

7. After adding and setting all of the conditions you wish to use, choose Next.

8. Choose whether the conditions are to be used to grant access or to be used as filters, denying access if they are met and then select Next.

9. Choose Finish to close the wizard.

The final stage in configuring a remote access policy is to define the profile. To edit the profile for a remote access policy, follow these steps:

1. In the Tree pane of the Routing and Remote Access snap-in, expand the server and choose remote access Policies.

2. In the Details pane, right-click the policy you wish to edit and choose Properties (Figure 9.23).

Figure 9.23 Profile Editing

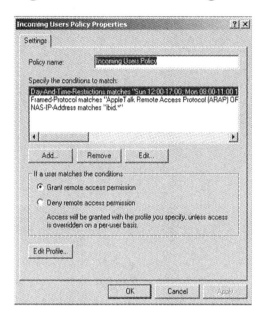

3.   From the Policy Properties window, choose Edit Profile.

4.   In the Edit Dial-in Profile window, make changes to the profile according to the following table (Table 9.4) and then choose OK.

Table 9.4 Edit Dial-In Profile Options

Property Page	Option	Description
Dial-in Constraints	Disconnect if idle for	Sets a time limit for inactive sessions.
	Restrict maximum session to	Sets a maximum time limit for the session.
	Restrict access to the following days and times	Prevents connections during hours and days you set.

Property Page	Option	Description
	Restrict dial-in to this number only	Only allows connections made through a specified phone number.
	Restrict dial in media	Only allows connections made using the selected media types.
IP	IP Address Assignment Policy	Determines how IP addresses are issued.
	IP Packet Filters	Allows filtering of both inbound and outbound IP packets.
Multilink	Multilink Settings	Can be used to restrict a user to only one line or to enable Multilink.
	BAP Settings	Allows you to reduce a Multilink connection to fewer lines when network traffic drops below a specified threshold.
Authentication	Choose the authentication methods, which are allowed for this connection	You may choose which authentication methods can be used, and whether to allow PPP clients to use the connection without negotiating an authentication method.
Encryption	Choose the level(s) of encryption that should be allowed by this profile	Choose what levels of encryption will be allowed. If encryption is required, deselect No Encryption. If strong encryption is needed, also deselect Basic.
Advanced		Adjust advanced settings, including specific modem and line connection settings.

Vocabulary

Review the following terms in preparation for the certification exam.

Term	Description
ACL	Every object in the Active Directory has an associated Access Control List, which defines who can access the object and how.
Active Directory	Active Directory is a directory database that provides the underlying structure of Windows 2000 networks.
ANI	Automatic Number Identification service, also known as Caller ID, identifies a user, based o n the phone number from which the user called. (ANI is also known as Caller ID).
API	An Application Programming Interface provides standard programming components that developers can use to build applications.
ATM	Asynchronous Transfer Mode
Authenticode	An authentication tool that verifies the source of programs and code that are downloaded from the Internet .
BACP	The Bandwidth Allocation Control Protocol dynamically changes the number of lines used in a Multilink, based on network demands.
BAP	The Bandwidth Allocation Protocol works with BACP to determine what a Multilink line needs.
CA	A Certificate Authority is a trusted third-part computer that verifies the identity of servers and clients using digital certificates.
CAPI	CryptoAPI is an Application Programming Interface that provides security-related building blocks for developers to use in building applications.

Term	Description
CHAP	The Challenge Handshake Authentication Protocol provides a security key to encrypt the username and password before the client sends this informati on to the dial-in server.
container object	An object in Active Directory that contains other objects.
CryptoAPI	CryptoAPI (CAPI) is an Application P rogramming Interface (API) that allows applications to encrypt and digitally sign data. See CAPI.
CSP	A Cryptographic Service Provider s is responsible for generating the public and private key s for a session.
data encryption	Using a mathematical function (encryption key) to scramble data, rendering it unreadable by anyone without the key.
dial-in settings	User account settings that determine when and how a user can access a Remote Access server.
digital certificate	A digital certificate is issued by a CA to verify the identity of both parties in a secure transmission.
distributed security services	A general term for several security features of Windows 2000, including support for Kerberos , SSL, and CryptoAPI.
DNIS	Dialed Number Identification Service authenticates a user, based on the phone number called by the user.
dynamic rekeying	The ability of a protocol to change the security keys being used during a session.
EAP	The Extensible Authentication P rotocol allows a client and server to negotiate an authentication method before the user logs on to the network.
encryption key	A method of scrambling data according to a mathematical function. The data can only be unscrambled using a related key.

Term	Description
ESP	Using IPSec, data is carried on the network in an Encapsulated Security Payload , ensuring data security and authenticity.
FQDN	The Fully Qualified Domain N ame consists of a computer's hostname and full domain name (for example, www.lightpointlearning.net).
HTTP	The HyperText Transfer Protocol is a protocol that formats and transmits.
HTTPS	The Secure Hypertext Transfer Protocol transmits Web page s securely over the Internet .
IAS	The Internet Authentication Service acts as a RADIUS server.
IETF	Internet Engineering Task Force
Internet Connection Sharing	A service included in Windows 2000 tha t acts as a proxy server for small networks using the TCP/IP protocol.
IP	The Internet Protocol is one part of the TCP/IP protocol suite, and is used to identify individual computers on a network.
IPSec	IP Security is a group of tools that provide secure data transmissions on networks using the TCP/IP protocol.
ISP	An Internet Service Provider is a company that provides Internet access to users.
KDC	The Key Distribution Center issues short-term session keys to users, based on their long-term keys.
Kerberos	An authentication protocol that uses session tickets and shared secret keys to provide user authentication and data encryption.

Term	Description
key pair	A key pair is a matched set of a private key and a public key.
L2TP	Layer 2 Tunnel Protocol is a tunneling protocol that can be used with various transmission protocols and provides compression and tunnel authentication.
LAN	A Local Area Network consists typically of fewer than 100 computers all within the same area.
long-term key	When a user logs on to a network, the account is assigned a long-term security key, which may be used to obtain sessions keys from a KDC.
MD5-CHAP	Message Digest 5 Challenge Handshake Protocol is used to encrypt usernames and passwords, and is supported by EAP.
MMC	The Microsoft Management Console provides a common structure in which administrative tools (snap-ins) can run.
Multilink	A Multilink combines several physical lines into one logical connection, thereby increasing bandwidth for that connection.
NTLM	The Windows NT 4.0 LAN Manager protocol is used on non-Windows 2000 networks to authenticate users during logon. It is supported by Windows 2000 for compatibility with non-Windows 2000 operating systems.
OSI	The Open System Interconnection model defines a seven-layer structure upon which network protocols are designed and built.
OU	An Organization Unit is an Active Directory object used to organize and group other objects to simplify administration.
PAP	Compares a username and password (which are not encrypted before sending) to an encrypted database to verify logon.

Term	Description
PC/SC	Personal Computer/Sound Card
policy conditions	Remote Access conditions that must be met before a Remote Access connection is established.
PPP	The Point-to-Point protocol provides dial-up connections to TCP/IP-based networks.
PPTP	The Point-to-Point Tunneling Protocol is a tunneling protocol that works with IP-based networks and uses PPP for data encryption.
private key	One half of a key pair, the private key is known only to the holder of the key, and cannot be obtained or copied by anyone else.
profiles	Remote Access profiles specify certain criteria that define the Remote Access connection.
proxy server	A server that provides access to the Internet for other computers. The proxy server has the only direct connection to the Internet, and other computers go through the proxy to send and receive information.
public key	One half of a key pair, the public key is available to everyone on the network.
RADIUS	Remote Authentication Dial-in User Service allows dial-in servers to use a remote server for user authentication .
RADIUS client	The RADIUS dial-in server that requests user authentication information.
RADIUS server	The RADIUS server that provides user authentication information to the RADIUS client.
RAM	Random Access Memory is used as temporary storage of information on a computer.

Term	Description
RFC	A Request For Comments is a public document that describes a new Internet technology, so that others may implement it.
RRAS	Routing and Remote Access Service is used on Windows 2000 domain member servers to configure Routing and Remote Access features.
secret key cryptography	Uses a shared secret key that only two people (or computers) know.
session key	Issued by a KDC, the session key is used to encrypt data for only one session, and then is discarded.
session ticket	The session ticket contains the session key encrypted with the server's long-term key, and is sent to the server by the client, not the KDC.
shared secret keys	Another name for secret key cryptography.
sign	A sending computer will sign, or mark, a data transmission so that the receiving user can verify the source.
smart cards	A credit card-sized attachment for computers that contains its own processor and RAM, and can be used to store sensitive information, including security keys.
snap-in	The form administrative tools take in Windows 2000 to work within the MMC.
SPAP	The Shiva Password Authentication Protocol is a proprietary implementation of PAP.
SSL	Secure Sockets Layer is a network protocol used to transmit sensitive data over the internet.
TLS	The Transport Layer Security protocol has been introduced by Microsoft as an enhancement to—and possible replacement of—SSL.

Term	Description
tunneling	The process of creating a secure channel through public lines, through which encrypted data may travel safely.
VPN	Virtual Private Networks uses tunneling protocols to send data over public lines as if they were private.
WAN	Wide Area Network
Windows IP Security	The Windows 2000 implementation of IPSec .
X.509 Version 3	An industry standard digital certificate format, X.509 is the most widely used type of certificate.

In Brief

If you want to...	Then do this...
Prevent intercepted data from being read	Implement data encryption.
Verify the user with whom you are sharing information	Use a key pair and a Certificate Authority.
Receive sensitive information from customers on your company Web page	Implement SSL.
Implement a VPN	Use Network Connection Wizard on the client computer and RRAS on the server to configure the VPN connection and policy settings.
Implement a VPN over an ATM-based network	Use the L2TP protocol rather than PPTP.
Configure a remote access server to only accept connections from members of one group	Using RRAS, add the attribute Windows-Groups to the policy conditions.
Remove user authorization ability from dial-up servers and place it on one central server	Implement RADIUS.
Prevent a user from accessing the network remotely	Do nothing. By default, the dial-in permission is not granted.

Lesson 9 Activities

Complete the following activities to better prepare you for the certification exam.

1. Write out the steps involved in encrypting data using a key pair.

2. Write out the steps involved in digitally signing data (by both the client and the server) using a key pair.

3. List the process of encrypting and signing data between a client and server using a key pair.

4. Set up a Windows 2000 computer as a remote access client. Create a direct cable connection, making this computer the guest.

5. Set up a Windows 2000 server as a remote access server and configure it as the host for a direct cable connection. At this point, do not configure any conditions or profiles. Make sure you grant dial-up access to the user account you use on the client computer and to the Administrator's group.

6. Using a null-modem cable (available at most computer stores), connect the two computers and establish a remote access session.

7. Disconnect the direct cable connection. On the server, implement the following policy conditions: users can remotely access the network from 9 a.m. to 5 p.m. weekdays, and only members of the Administrators group are allowed remote access. Set the server's date and time to 1 p.m. on any weekday.

8. Attempt to make another connection to the server, using a user account that is not in the Administrators group but has been granted the dial-in permission. Can you connect?

9. Change the time on the server to 11 p.m. on any day of the week. Again, attempt to connect from the client, this time using an account in the Administrator's group. Can you connect?

10. Finally, set the time on the server to within the permissible hours for connection and attempt to connect using an account in the Administrator's account.

Answers to Lesson 9 Activities

1. The sender uses the receiver's public key to encrypt the data. Upon receipt, the receiver uses the private key to decrypt the data.

2. The sender encrypts the data using the sender's private key. The receiver decrypts the data using the sender's public key, removes a portion of the data and encrypts this new packet with the receiver's private key. The original sender decrypts the new packet using the receiver's public key.

3. The server encrypts the data using the server's private key and then encrypts again using the receiver's public key. The receiver decrypts the data, first with the receiver's private key and then with the sender's public key.

4. Use the Network Connection Wizard to set up the direct cable connection.

5. If the server is a member of a domain, use RRAS to enable remote access and then enable the serial or parallel port you will use. In Active Directory Users and Computers, modify dial-in permissions for the Administrators group and for the individual user account.

    If the server is not in a domain, configure the direct-cable connection using the Network Connection Wizard and adjust the user and group settings in Local Users and Groups.

6. Null-modem cables are generally designed to connect one serial port to another. Verify that you are attaching the cable to the proper port on each computer and that those ports are the ones you selected when configuring the direct cable connection. Do not proceed past this step until you have successfully connected.

7. Using RRAS, implement a new remote access policy. Access the Properties window for the policy and add the two conditions. In the list of conditions, choose Day-and-Time-Restrictions, adjust the time settings and then select Windows-Groups. Select Add and select the Administrators group.

    To set the server's time, double-click the time in the lower-right corner of the task bar.

8. You cannot connect because you are not in the Administrator's group, and membership in this group is one of the required conditions.

9. You cannot connect because you are not connecting during the permissible time.

10. You can connect, because the two conditions have been successfully met.

Lesson 9 Quiz

These questions test your knowledge of features, vocabulary, procedures, and syntax.

1. What is the most widely used digital certificate type?
    A. X.509
    B. X.905
    C. SSL
    D. TLS

2. What is the name of the group of application programming tools that provides security utilities for developers?
    A. API
    B. CAPI
    C. APIC
    D. CryptoPIA

3. A smart card has which of the following features? (Choose all that apply)
    A. Built-in hard drive
    B. Built-in memory
    C. Its own processor
    D. Plugs in to a CD-ROM drive

4. What is the technology used to verify programming code downloaded from the Internet called?
    A. CryptoAPI
    B. Active Directory
    C. Authenticode
    D. AuthiCode

5. The _____ defines who has access to an Active Directory object.
    A. HCL
    B. ACL
    C. AFC
    D. NFL

6. What protocol does a Windows 2000 VPN use to establish a secure tunnel?

   A. L2TP

   B. PPP

   C. P2TP

   D. TPTP

7. Which of the following statements is true?

   A. PPTP can use IP or Frame-relay-based networks.

   B. L2TP has built-in data encryption.

   C. PPTP supports tunnel authentication.

   D. L2TP uses header compression.

8. What tool is used to configure a remote access server in a workgroup?

   A. RRAS

   B. Network Connection Wizard

   C. RAS Wizard

   D. A remote access server cannot be a member of a workgroup. It must belong to a domain.

9. What is the order of a remote access policy evaluation?

   A. Permissions, conditions, profiles

   B. Profiles, conditions, permissions

   C. Conditions, permissions, profiles

   D. Conditions, profiles, permissions

10. Which of the following connections can be created using the Network Connection Wizard? (Choose all that apply)

    A. Direct cable guest

    B. Direct cable host

    C. VPN

    D. Dial-up access to the Internet

Answers to Lesson 9 Quiz

1. Answer A is correct. X.509 is the most commonly-found digital certificate type, and is supported by Windows 2000.

    Answer B is incorrect. X.905 is not a digital certificate type.

    Answers C and D are incorrect. SSL and TLS are not digital certificates. They are network security protocols.

2. Answer B is correct. CAPI, or CryptoAPI, provides developers with an Application Programming Interface (API) of security tools.

    Answers A, C, and D are incorrect. These are all fictitious terms.

3. Answers B and C are correct. A smart card has an integrated processor and RAM so that it can process and store security information.

    Answer A is incorrect. Smart cards are not large enough to contain hard disks.

    Answer D is incorrect. Smart cards require a special smart card reader to interface with the computer.

4. Answer C is correct. Authenticode is used to verify the source of programs downloaded from the Internet.

    Answer A is incorrect. CryptoAPI is a programming interface.

    Answer B is incorrect. Active Directory provides the underlying structure of Windows 2000 networks and is not concerned with Internet downloads.

    Answer D is incorrect. It is a fictitious term.

5. Answer B is correct. The Access Control List (ACL) determines access privileges to Active Directory objects.

    Answer A is incorrect. The Hardware Compatibility List (HCL) lists hardware that work with Windows 2000.

    Answer C and D are incorrect.

6. Answer A is correct. Virtual Private Networks use either Point-to-Point Tunneling Protocol (PPTP) or Layer 2 Tunneling Protocol (L2TP) to create a secure tunnel.

    Answers B, C, and D are incorrect. These are fictitious terms.

7. Answer D is correct. L2TP supports header compression and tunnel authentication.

    Answer A is incorrect. PPTP only works with IP-based networks.

    Answer B is incorrect. L2TP relies upon IPSec for data encryption.

    Answer C is incorrect. PPTP does not support tunnel authentication but can use IPSec for tunnel authentication.

8. Answer B is correct. On a workgroup, you use the Network Connection Wizard to configure remote access.

    Answer A is incorrect. RRAS is used to configure a remote access server on a domain.

    Answer C is incorrect. This is not a real Windows 2000 tool.

    Answer D is incorrect. remote access servers can exist in either a domain or workgroup.

9. Answer C is correct. When a remote access policy is evaluated, the conditions necessary to establish the connection are first checked. If they are met then the user's permissions are verified. Finally, the Active Directory profile is evaluated.

    Answers A, B, and D are incorrect.

10. Answers A, B, C, and D are all correct. All of these connection types are created using the Network Connection Wizard. Answer B is incorrect only on servers that are domain members, but this was not specified.

Disaster Protection and Recovery

Computers are not infallible. Network administrators know well that they cannot rely upon a computer or a network of computers to run indefinitely without problems. Computer hardware is sensitive to the slightest environmental changes. These changes include static electricity or a power surge and can cause immediate failure. Hard disk drives, on which data that includes the operating system and user data is stored, are the most likely components to fail, since they have the only moving parts in a computer. In some ways, hard drives are also the most important components in a server because they hold user data for the entire network.

Microsoft Windows 2000 includes several features to help with disaster protection and recovery. Many of these are geared toward recovering from a failed hard drive. You can do little to prevent hardware from failing, but you can do a great deal to prepare for such failures. Being prepared for computer failures allows you to recover quickly, minimize lost productivity and minimize lost data.

After completing this lesson, you should have a better understanding of the following topics:

- Windows 2000 Disaster Protection Features

- Fault-Tolerant Volumes

- Advanced Startup Options

- Recovery Console

- Data Backup and Restoration

Windows 2000 Disaster Protection Features

Computer disasters usually come in two varieties—a hardware failure or an operating system failure. You solve most hardware failures by determining which component failed and then replacing that component. If the component is a hard drive, recovery includes not only replacing the hard drive, but also restoring the data stored on that drive.

If the computer failure is a problem with the operating system (Microsoft Windows NT 4.0 or Windows 2000), troubleshooting can become more complex. Typically, operating system failures result from an incompatibility with a hardware device or application, and failures occur soon after the installation. A good disaster recovery program includes documenting all changes made to your computer. If an operating system failure occurs, you can refer to your documentation to see what changes, if any, have recently occurred.

Windows 2000 uses many of the same disaster recovery methods as Windows NT 4.0. As in Windows NT 4.0, you can create fault-tolerant volumes in Windows 2000. A fault-tolerant volume uses two or more hard disks to store data and is designed so that if one of the hard disks fails, the data stored on the volume remains intact. Also like Windows NT 4.0, Windows 2000 comes with a tape backup utility. This tool has been greatly improved and is now based on the Seagate BackupExec software. Both fault-tolerant volumes and the Backup utility help with hardware failures, and the Backup utility aids in recovering from severe operating system failures.

Understanding New Disaster Protection Features

New to Windows 2000 are startup options that help you diagnose operating system and hardware problems. Using the startup options, you can run Windows 2000 in Safe Mode, a special diagnostic mode that only loads the minimal drivers needed to run the system. A driver is a small program that allows the operating system (Windows 2000) and applications to communicate with a particular device in the computer. Every device in a computer has a driver. Many, including drivers for the keyboard, mouse, and disk controllers are included with the Windows 2000 operating system.

Other startup options include the Last Known Good option, debugging mode, and the Directory Services Restore Mode. Directory Services Restore Mode allows you to recover a corrupted Microsoft Active Directory database on a domain controller.

Also new in Windows 2000 is the Recovery Console, a special command-line interface that allows you to replace corrupted files, enable and disable services, and repair a corrupted boot sector.

Fault-Tolerant Volumes

Fault-tolerant volumes protect against data loss in the event of a hard disk failure. They do not prevent disk failures but are designed to keep data accessible when a disk fails.

 Note: You cannot create fault-tolerant volumes on a computer running Microsoft Windows 2000 Professional. The fault tolerance features are only available on servers.

Microsoft Windows 2000 Server supports two types of fault-tolerant volumes:

Mirrored volumes—Mirrored volumes create an exact copy of the data stored on one disk to another disk. If either disk fails, the mirrored volume still contains all of the data, and the data remains accessible to users. Mirrored volumes are similar to mirror sets in Windows NT 4.0.

RAID-5 volumes—RAID-5 volumes, known as stripe sets with parity in Windows NT 4.0, use a minimum of three hard disks. One disk in the set stores parity (error-checking) information. If one of the disks in the volume fails, the parity information is used to recreate the data as the data is accessed.

 Note: Parity information is not stored on just one disk, but is staggered across all disks in the RAID-5 volume. The parity information uses the space equivalent of one hard disk.

Using Fault-Tolerant Volumes

To implement fault-tolerant volumes, the following criteria must be met:

1. You must use Windows 2000 Server, Advanced Server, or Datacenter Server

2. You can only create volumes only on dynamic disks (not basic disks)

3. For a mirrored volume, you must have at least two physical disks installed

4. For a RAID-5 volume, you must have at least three physical disks installed

After creating fault-tolerant volumes, you use them as any other volume. The disparate physical disks share one drive letter, and data is read from—and written to—the volume like any other partition. The fault-tolerant features of the volume are transparent to the user.

 Note: The system and boot partitions cannot be part of a RAID-5 volume, but they can be mirrored to provide fault tolerance of the operating system.

Creating a Mirrored Volume

To create a mirrored volume, follow these steps:

1. From the desktop, right-click My Computer and select Manage.

2. From the Tree (left) pane of the Computer Management console, expand System Tools, expand Storage and then select Disk Management (Figure 10.1).

    The Disk Management snap-in is displayed in the Details (right) pane.

Figure 10.1 Computer Management Console

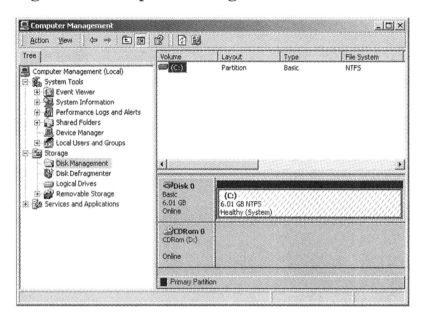

3. In the lower half of the Details (right) pane, right-click an area of unallocated space and then select Create Volume (Figure 10.2).

 Tip: If you right-click on an area of unallocated space and do not have Create Volume as an option, you are using a basic disk. You must use dynamic disks for fault-tolerant volumes.

Figure 10.2 Create Volume

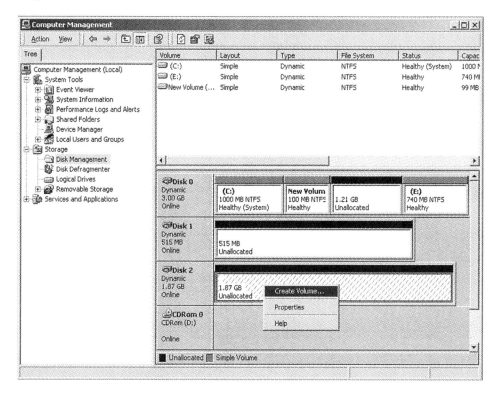

4. Click Next to begin the Create Volume Wizard.

5. Select Mirrored volume and then click Next.

6. From the list of available disks, select the second disk you want to use for the mirrored volume and then click Add (Figure 10.3).

    Two dynamic disks are shown in the "Selected dynamic disks" list.

Figure 10.3 Available Disks

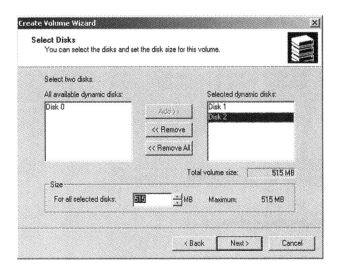

7.   In the "For all selected disks" box, enter the amount of disk space to use on each disk and then click Next (Figure 10.4).

 Note: The maximum volume size is the amount of free space on the smaller of the two disks.

Figure 10.4 Mirrored Volume Size

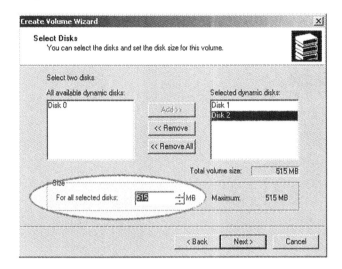

8. From the drop-down menu, select a drive letter for the volume (or accept the default) and then click Next (Figure 10.5).

Figure 10.5 Drive Letter Assignment

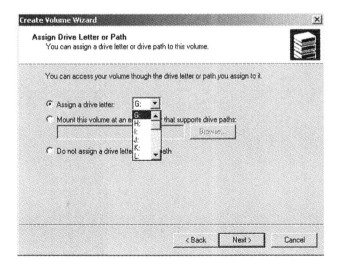

9. Choose a file system and type a label name for the volume and then click Next (Figure 10.6).

Figure 10.6 Volume Format

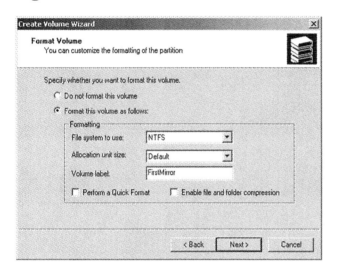

10. Click Finish to close the wizard and begin the volume format.

The mirrored volume appears in the lower half of the Details pane as two separate partitions sharing the same drive letter. Each reports a healthy state (Figure 10.7).

Figure 10.7 New Mirrored Volume

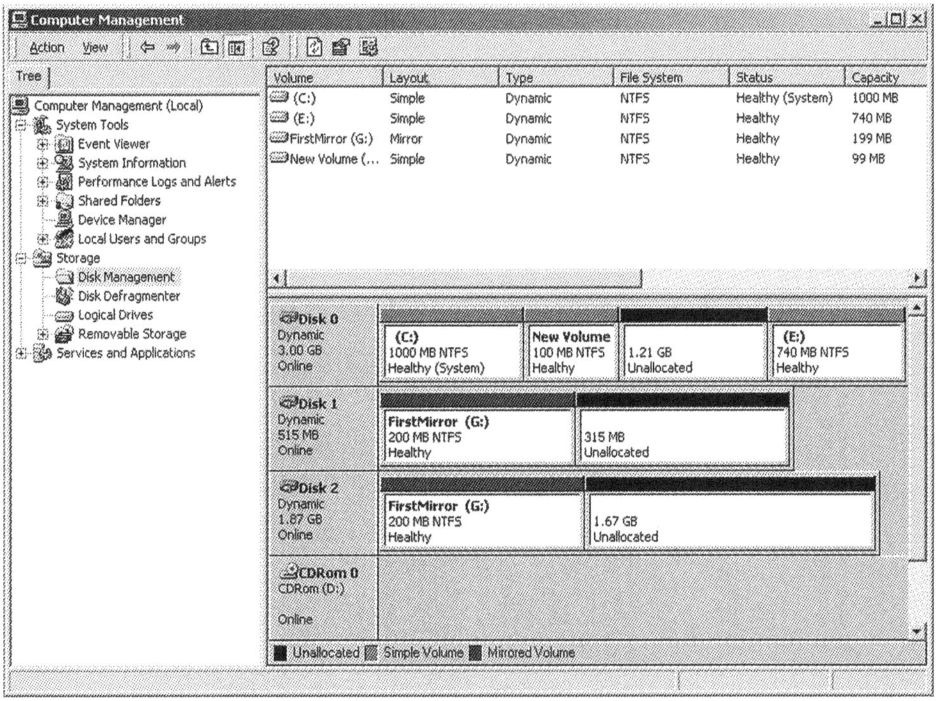

Creating a Mirror of an Existing Volume

You can also create a mirror of an existing volume that provides fault-tolerance to a volume already containing data. To do so, follow these steps:

1. Right-click the existing volume and choose Add Mirror (Figure 10.8).

Figure 10.8 Add Mirror

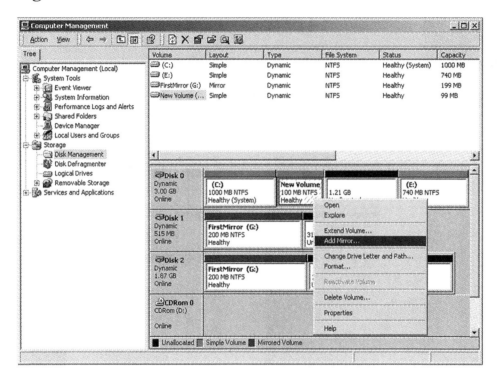

2.   Select the disk you wish to use for the mirror and then click Add Mirror (Figure 10.9).

 Note: In the Add Mirror window, Windows 2000 lists only dynamic disks with sufficient free space to mirror the selected volume.

Figure 10.9 Disk Selection

The new volume appears in the lower half of the Details pane and the mirror generates.

Creating a RAID-5 Volume

The process of creating a RAID-5 volume is nearly identical to that for creating a mirrored volume. To create a RAID-5 volume, follow these steps:

1. From the desktop, right-click My Computer and select Manage.

2. From the Tree (left) pane of the Computer Management console, expand System Tools, expand Storage and then select Disk Management.

3. In the lower half of the Details (right) pane, right-click an area of unallocated space and then select Create Volume.

4. Click Next to begin the Create Volume Wizard.

5. Select RAID-5 Volume and then click Next.

6. From the list of available disks, select the disks to be used for the RAID-5 volume and then click Add (Figure 10.10).

    You must use at least three disks for a RAID-5 volume.

Figure 10.10 Disk Selection

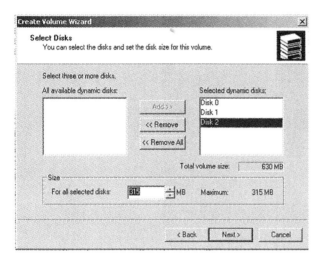

7. In the "For all selected disks" box, enter the amount of disk space to use on each disk and then click Next.

8. From the drop-down menu, select a drive letter for the volume (or accept the default) and then click Next.

9. Choose a file system and type a label name for the volume and then click Next.

10. Click Finish to close the wizard and begin the volume format.

Recovering a Failed Mirror Volume

When one member of a fault-tolerant volume fails, data is preserved. However, the volume is no longer fault-tolerant, and a second disk failure will result in data loss. A failed mirrored volume is reported in the Disk Management snap-in as "Offline," "Missing," or "Online (Errors)."

Tip: If Disk Management reports the status as Offline or Missing, confirm that the hard disk is still attached to the computer and has power. If the disk was just disconnected, you can regenerate the mirrored volume after reattaching the disk and rebooting.

When one disk in a mirrored volume fails, you need to replace the disk and then follow these steps:

1. From the desktop, right-click My Computer and select Manage.

2. From the Tree (left) pane of the Computer Management console, expand System Tools, expand Storage and then select Disk Management.

3. In the lower half of the Details (right) pane, right-click the disk that still contains the data in the mirrored volume and then select Remove Mirror.

4. From the Remove Mirror window, select the failed disk and then click Remove Mirror (Figure 10.11).

Figure 10.11 Remove Mirror Selection

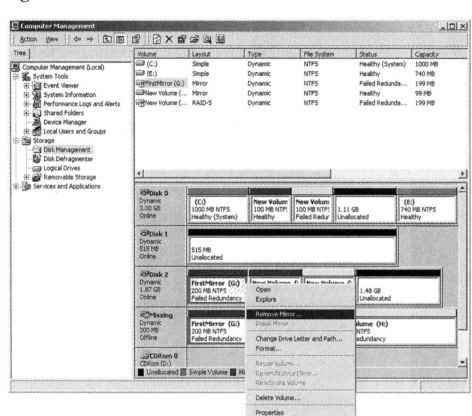

5. Click Yes to confirm the deletion of the failed mirror.

6. Right-click the healthy volume that contains the formerly mirrored data and then select Add Mirror.

7. Select the new disk and then click Add Mirror.

The mirrored volume is regenerated on the new disk.

Recovering a Failed RAID-5 Volume

When one disk of a RAID-5 volume fails, the data on that disk is recreated by Windows 2000 using the parity information. However, the RAID-5 volume is no longer fault-tolerant, and you need to replace the failed disk as soon as possible. To recover a failed RAID-5 volume, replace the failed hard disk drive and then follow these steps:

1. From the desktop, right-click My Computer and select Manage.

2. From the Tree (left) pane of the Computer Management console, expand System Tools, expand Storage and then select Disk Management.

3. In the lower half of the Details (right) pane, right-click the RAID-5 partition on any of the disks and choose Repair Volume (Figure 10.12).

Figure 10.12 Repair Volume

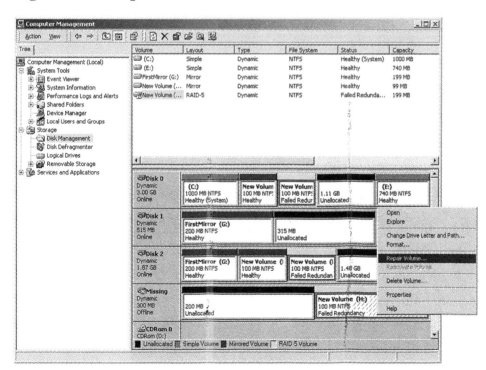

4.   Select the new disk as a replacement for the failed drive and then click OK. The RAID-5 volume is regenerated.

Advanced Startup Options

When starting a Windows 2000 server, you have several startup options. Under normal circumstances, Windows 2000 boots normally. However, if the boot process fails, you can use the advanced startup options to diagnose boot problems. When the boot process first begins, the following message is displayed:

Starting Windows...

For troubleshooting and advanced startup options for Windows 2000, press F8.

Press **F8** to pause the boot process and display the list of advanced startup options. The Windows 2000 Advanced Options Menu (Figure 10.13) displays.

Figure 10.13 Advanced Options Menu

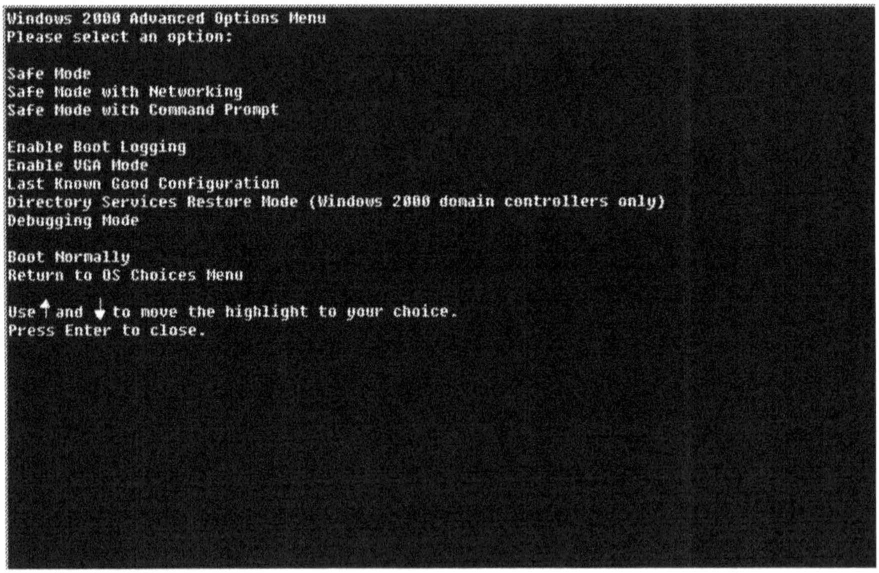

Comparing Advanced Startup Options

When you access the Windows 2000 Advanced Options Menu, you are presented with nine startup choices. Each of the choices boots Windows 2000 differently, as described in Table 10.1.

Table 10.1 Advanced Startup Options

Option	Description
Safe Mode	In Safe Mode, the server boots with only the minimal drivers needed to start the computer. Mouse, keyboard, hard drive, and basic Video Graphics Array (VGA) video drivers are loaded, as are the system services. A log file is also created of the boot process.
Safe Mode with Networking	This mode is the same as Safe Mode, except network access is also enabled. To access the network, the drivers for the Network Interface Card (NIC) and the network protocols are loaded.
Safe Mode with Command Prompt	Like Safe Mode, Safe Mode with Command Prompt loads only the minimal drivers. Rather than booting to the Graphical User Interface (GUI), this option boots directly to a command prompt.
Enable Boot Logging	Enable Boot Logging boots the server normally, loading (or trying to load) all of the drivers, and creates a log file (**\WINNT\NTBTLOG.TXT**). The log file contains a listing of all drivers and services the system attempts to load during the boot process and whether the driver or service loaded properly.
Enable VGA Mode	Enable VGA Mode loads all of the drivers of a normal boot, except it loads only the basic VGA drivers rather than the normal video card. Many boot errors occur after loading an incorrect video driver. You can reboot in VGA Mode and remove the incorrect drivers.

Option	Description
Last Known Good Configuration	As in Windows NT 4.0, Windows 2000 supports the Last Known Good Configuration. The state of the computer is recorded when you successfully log on. If you cannot reboot successfully, you can restore the server to this last known good condition.
Directory Services Restore Mode (Windows 2000 domain controllers only)	On Windows 2000 domain controllers, you can use this option to perform maintenance of the Active Directory and restoration of the SYSVOL folder.
Debugging Mode	Debugging Mode sends debugging information to another computer through a cable attached to the serial port of the server.
Boot Normally	Performs a normal boot of the server.

Using Safe Mode

Of the boot options listed in Table 10.1, Safe Mode is the one you will most likely use. Select Safe Mode (or Safe Mode with Networking), the server boots and displays the drivers as they are loaded. The Windows 2000 logon screen displays, and you log on normally. After logging on, a Safe Mode message displays (Figure 10.14).

Figure 10.14 Safe Mode Warning

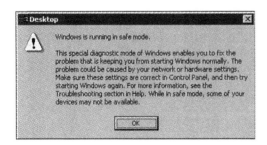

Once in Windows 2000 Safe Mode, you can make appropriate changes to the server configuration. If you know what driver or application was recently loaded, use Device Manager to remove or disable the driver or use Add/Remove Programs to remove the application. If you are uncertain of the cause of the boot errors, check the Event Viewer logs, or the boot log file (**\WINNT\NTBTLOG.TXT**). After making changes, reboot the server and allow Windows 2000 to boot normally. If the boot process fails again, reboot in Safe Mode and look again for the problem.

Using Last Known Good

Last Known Good Configuration restores the server to its state when you last successfully logged on. To restore a server to its last known good state, follow these steps:

1. As the server boots, press **F8** to access the Advanced Startup Options Menu.

2. Using the arrow keys, select Last Known Good Configuration and then press **ENTER**.

3. From the Hardware Profile/Configuration Recovery Menu screen, press **L** and then press **ENTER**.

Tip: Unfortunately, the Last Known Good selection screen has not become less cryptic with the release of Windows 2000. If you remember to press **L** and then **ENTER**, you will load the Last Known Good configuration.

Recovery Console

The Recovery Console is a command-line interface that allows you to start and stop services, control service startup options, format drives and copy files from floppies and CD-ROMs to your hard disks. Although the Recovery Console does not use the GUI, you are required to log on to the computer using the Administrator user account and password.

Note: Although the Recovery Console looks like the Windows 2000 Command Prompt or an MS-DOS screen, it functions very differently.

Loading the Recovery Console

There are two ways to access the Recovery Console. If your server is not booting, even in Safe Mode, you can run the Recovery Console from the Windows 2000 CD-ROM (if your computer supports booting from the CD-ROM) or the Windows 2000 Setup floppies.

Alternately, you can configure the Windows 2000 startup menu (which lists the operating system choices at the beginning of the boot process) to include the Recovery Console. This must be done from within Windows 2000 and can only be done before you experience boot problems. To install the Recovery Console as a startup option, follow these steps:

1. Insert the Windows 2000 Server CD-ROM and then close any windows that open automatically.

2. From the Start Menu, choose Programs, choose Accessories and then select Command Prompt.

3. From the Command Prompt, type the following command where D is the drive letter for your CD-ROM drive:

    ```
    D:\I386\WINNT32.EXE /CMDCONS
    ```

4. From the Windows 2000 Setup window, click Yes to install the Recovery Console (Figure 10.15).

    The Setup process loads the necessary files without further user intervention.

Figure 10.15 Recovery Console Installation

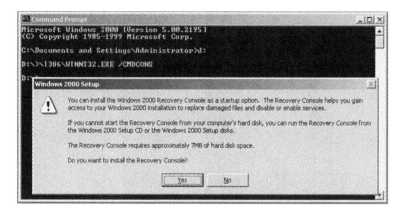

5.   When Setup completes, Click OK to close the window and then close the Command Prompt.

The Recovery Console has been added to the list of startup options and will be available the next time the server is restarted.

Using the Recovery Console

To use the Recovery Console, you can either boot from the Windows 2000 Setup floppies or CD-ROM or from the startup menu.

Accessing Recovery Console from the CD-ROM

To access the Recovery Console from the CD-ROM, boot the computer from the CD-ROM and then follow these steps:

 Note: These steps also apply to accessing the Recovery Console from the Windows 2000 Setup boot disks.

1.   From the first user-input screen, press **ENTER** to continue.

2.   From the Welcome to Setup screen, press **R** to repair a Windows 2000 installation.

3.   From the Windows 2000 Repair Options screen, press **C** to use the Recovery Console.

4.   Select the installation of Windows 2000 you wish to use (by typing the corresponding number from the displayed list) and then press **ENTER** (Figure 10.16).

Figure 10.16 Installation Selection

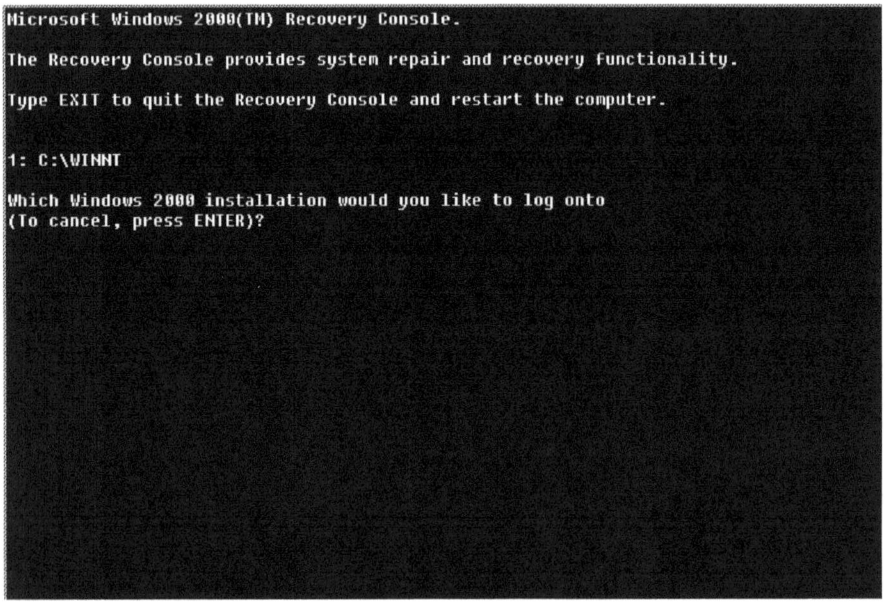

```
Microsoft Windows 2000(TM) Recovery Console.

The Recovery Console provides system repair and recovery functionality.

Type EXIT to quit the Recovery Console and restart the computer.


1: C:\WINNT

Which Windows 2000 installation would you like to log onto
(To cancel, press ENTER)?
```

5.   Type the password for the Administrator account, and then press **ENTER**.
     A **C:\WINNT** prompt is displayed, and you are now in the Recovery Console.

Accessing Recovery Console from the Startup Menu

To access the Recovery Console from the startup menu, follow these steps:

1. Boot the server.

2. From the startup menu, choose Windows 2000 Recovery Console from the list of operating systems and then press **ENTER** (Figure 10.17).

Figure 10.17 Startup Menu

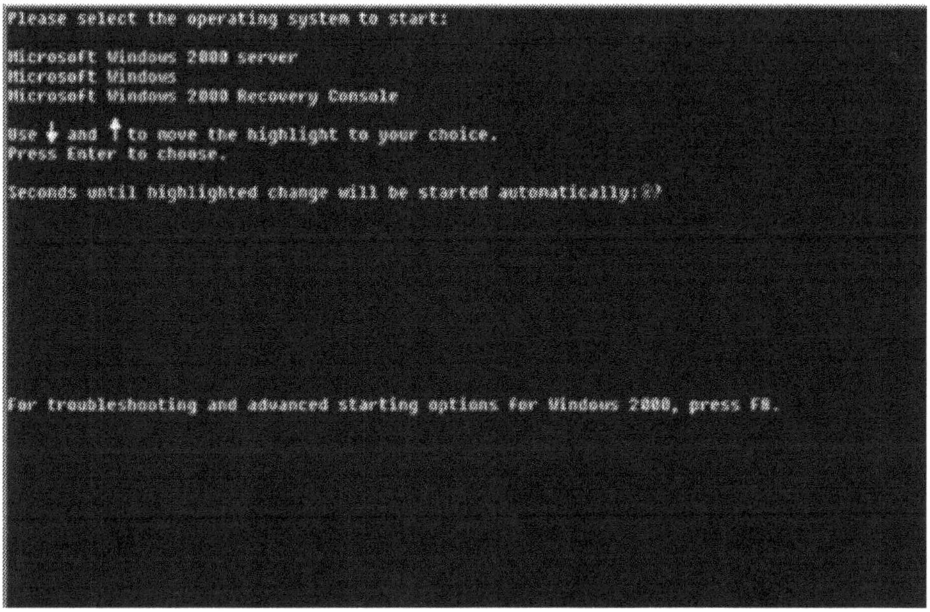

3. Select the installation of Windows 2000 you wish to use (by typing the corresponding number from the displayed list) and then press **ENTER**.

4. Type the password for the Administrator account and then press **ENTER**.

Recovery Console Commands

The Recovery Console resembles the Windows 2000 Command Prompt but has a more limited set of usable commands. To obtain a list of commands, type **HELP** at the command prompt and then press **ENTER**. Table 10.2 lists the available commands and their function. More detailed information about individual commands can be obtained by typing **HELP [COMMAND]**, where **[COMMAND]** is the command about which you want details.

Table 10.2 Recovery Console Commands

Command	Description
ATTRIB	Changes the attributes (hidden, read-only, system, and compressed) for a file or folder.
BATCH	Executes commands in a text file as a batch file.
CHDIR (CD)	Changes the working directory or displays the name of the current directory.
CHKDSK	Performs a check on the disk and displays a status report.
CLS	Clears the screen.
COPY	Copies a file to another location.
DELETE (DEL)	Deletes one or more files.
DIR	Provides a list of the files and folders in a directory.
DISABLE	Disables a system service or device driver.
DISKPART	A text-based disk partition management utility that allows you to view, delete, and create partitions.

Command	Description
ENABLE	Enables a system service or device driver.
EXIT	Exits Recovery Console and restarts the computer.
EXPAND	Extracts a file from within a compressed archive (like a .CAB file).
FIXBOOT	Rewrites the partition boot sector onto the system (bootable) partition.
FIXMBR	Repairs the Master Boot Record (MBR).
FORMAT	Formats a disk.
HELP	Displays a list of these commands.
LISTSVC	Lists the available drivers and services on the computer.
LOGON	Logs on to a Windows 2000 installation.
MAP	Displays all drive letter mappings.
MKDIR	Creates a new subdirectory within the current working directory.
MORE	Used with type to display a long text file in screen-sized portions.
RENAME (REN)	Renames a file.
RMDIR (RD)	Removes (deletes) an empty directory.
SET	Displays and sets the environmental variables.

Command	Description
SYSTEMROOT	Sets the current working directory as the system root (the directory that contains the Windows 2000 files).
TYPE	Displays the contents of a text file.

Data Backup and Restoration

The single-most important tool for data protection and recovery in the event of failure is a data backup and restoration program. Although fault-tolerant volumes provide some measure of data recovery, if more than one disk fails (say there is a fire in your server room), your data is lost.

Backing up data on some form of removable storage (magnetic tape, CD-ROM, floppies) allows you to have the data off-site in a safe location in the event of catastrophe. Performing frequent and regularly-scheduled backups ensures that you have a recent copy of the data, and that there will be little loss of productivity.

Windows NT 4.0 includes a minimal but sufficient tape backup utility. This utility allows you to back up and restore data to tape drives only, and requires external commands to schedule backups. Windows 2000 includes a greatly-enhanced Backup utility that permits data backups to several types of removable storage and backup scheduling from within the application.

Using the Backup Utility

To open the Backup utility from the Start Menu, choose Programs, choose Accessories, choose System Tools and then select Backup. The Backup utility opens with the Welcome property page (Figure 10.18).

Figure 10.18 Backup Utility Welcome Page

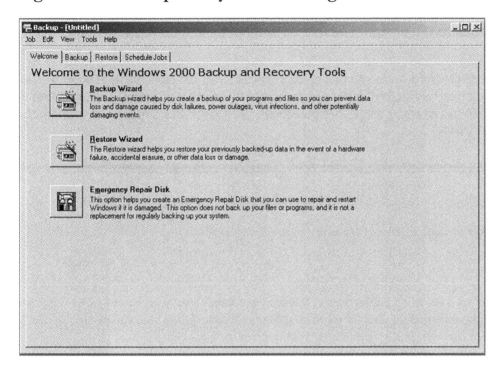

From the Welcome property page, you can run the Backup and Restore wizards and build an Emergency Repair Disk.

Creating an Emergency Repair Disk (ERD)

An Emergency Repair Disk (ERD) is used to repair a corrupt installation of Windows 2000. The ERD does not back up any data and is not intended as a method of backup. However, if Windows 2000 becomes corrupt, you can often re-run the Windows 2000 Setup and use the ERD to restore the system to a working state. To create an ERD, follow these steps:

1.   From the Welcome property page of the Backup utility, select Emergency Repair Disk. Alternately,

2.   From the menu bar, choose Tools and then select Create an Emergency Repair Disk.

3. Insert a blank, formatted floppy disk into drive A and then click OK. You may also select to copy the registry to the repair directory.

Tip: The ERD wizard saves information to a special repair directory, \WINNT\REPAIR. The repair directory stores information necessary to restore the System State, so information in this directory should not be altered. Changes to this directory may render the ERD useless.

4. When the file copy and floppy creation are complete, click OK to close the wizard.

5. Store the ERD in a safe location away from the server.

System State

The System State is a collection of information and system components necessary to run a Windows 2000 computer. This information can be backed up using the Backup Utility, and you need to be familiar with what is contained in the System State before performing a backup.

The information included in the System State depends on the Windows 2000 operating system (Server or Professional) and the role of the computer on the network. Table 10.3 lists three operating system configurations and the information included in a backup of the System State.

Table 10.3 System State Contents

Operating System	Included Components
Windows 2000 Professional	Registry Component Services Class Registration database System startup files
Windows 2000 Server as a member server	Registry Component Services Class Registration database System startup files Certificate Services database
Windows 2000 Server as a Domain Controller	Registry Component Services Class Registration database System startup files Certificate Services database Active Directory SYSVOL folder

When you back up data and the System State using the Backup utility, you have two choices. You may use the Backup Wizard, or you can create a backup job by manually selecting the data to be backed up.

 Note: The Component Services Class Registration database is known as the COM+ database in Windows NT 4.0.

Backup Wizard

The Backup Wizard is the easiest method for backing up data to removable storage. To perform a backup using the Backup Wizard, follow these steps:

1. From the Start Menu, choose Programs, choose Accessories, choose System Tools and then select Backup.

2. From the Welcome property page of the Backup utility, select Backup Wizard.

3. Click Next to begin the wizard.

4. From the What to Back Up screen, select whether you want to back up all of the data on the computer, only selected files (including files over the network) or only the System State and then click Next (Figure 10.19).

Figure 10.19 What to Back Up

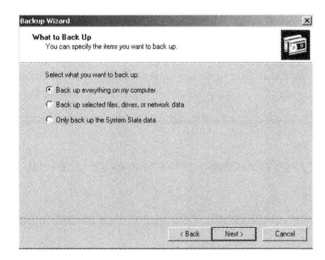

If you choose to back up everything or only the System State, the Where to Store the Backup screen is displayed. If you chose to back up only selected files, the Items to Back Up screen is displayed.

5. From the "Items to Back Up" screen, expand folders and directories as necessary and then place check marks in the boxes next to the items you wish to back up (Figure 10.20). After selecting the files and folders to back up, click Next.

Figure 10.20 Backup Selection

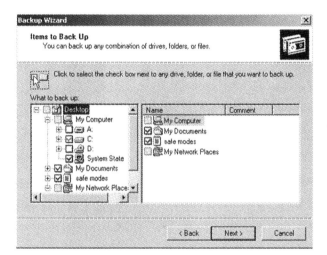

6. In the Where to Store the Backup screen, choose a backup media type and the name of the backup media (or file name if you are saving the backup to a file) and then click Next (Figure 10.21).

Figure 10.21 Backup Destination

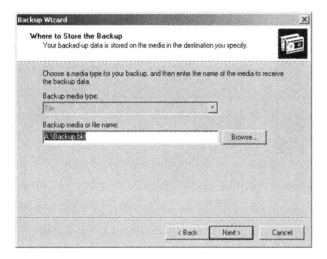

7. From the Completing the Backup Wizard screen, click Advanced.

8. Select the type of backup you wish to perform based on the information in Table 10.4 and then click Next.

Table 10.4 Backup Types

Option	Description
Normal	Backs up all of the selected files and marks each one as having been backed up.
Copy	Backs up all of the selected files but does not mark them as having been backed up.
Incremental	Backs up only the selected files that have not been backed up previously or have changed since the last backup. Files are marked as having been backed up.

Option	Description
Differential	Backs up only the selected files that have not been backed up previously or have changed since the last backup. Files are not marked as having been backed up.
Daily	Backs up only the selected files that have changed the same day the backup is run. Files are not marked as backed up.

9. Choose whether you want the Backup utility to verify the data after backup and whether to use hardware compression (if the tape drive supports this feature) and then click Next.

Tip: The verify process compares all files in the backup to those on the computer. This procedure generally doubles the time needed to complete a backup.

10. Select whether the new data will be added to another backup set on the medium ("Append this backup to the media") or whether it will overwrite the media ("Replace the data on the media with this backup") and then click Next.

    If you choose to replace the data, you also have the option of restricting access to the media for the owner of the data and the Administrator account only.

11. Type a label for the backup session and, if you are using new media (or replacing old data), enter a media label and then click Next (Figure 10.22).

Figure 10.22 Backup Label

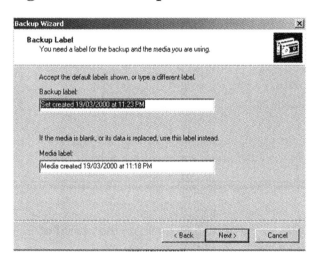

12. From the When to Back Up screen, select whether you want to back up the data now or later (Figure 10.23). If you want to begin the backup now, choose Now, click Next and then proceed to step 16.

Figure 10.23 When to Back Up

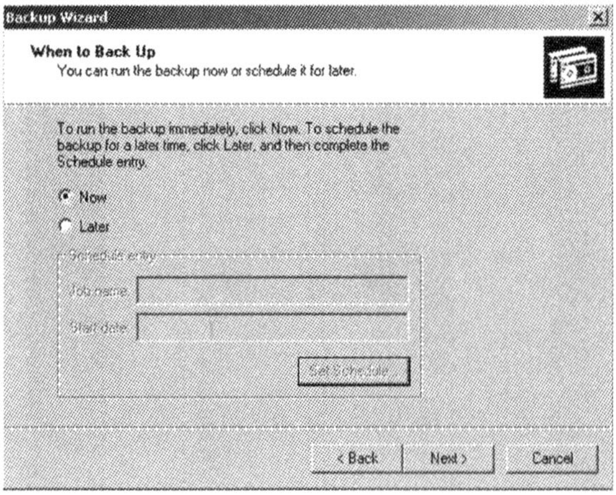

13. If you chose Later, the Set Account window displays. Enter a user name and password for an account that has permission to perform a backup and then click OK (Figure 10.24).

Figure 10.24 User Account Information

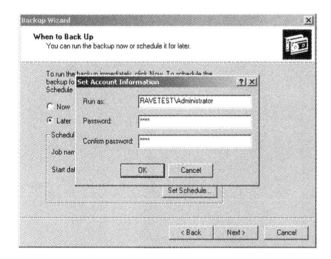

14. Enter a name for the backup job and then click Set Schedule to set the time and date for the backup.

15. From the Schedule Job window, adjust the time and date for the backup and then click OK (Figure 10.25).

Figure 10.25 Backup Schedule

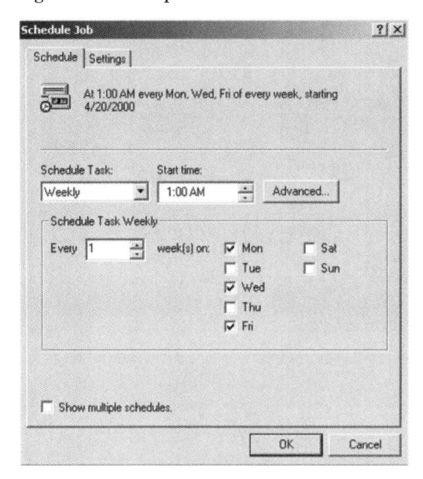

16. Verify the backup settings and then click Finish to begin the backup.

Tip: Familiarize yourself with the Settings property page in the Schedule Job window. These settings allow you to fine-tune a backup schedule.

Creating a Backup Job

To create a backup job without using the Backup Wizard, follow these steps:

1. From the Start Menu, choose Programs, choose Accessories, choose System Tools and then select Backup.

2. From the Backup utility, select the Backup property page (Figure 10.26).

Figure 10.26 Backup Property Page

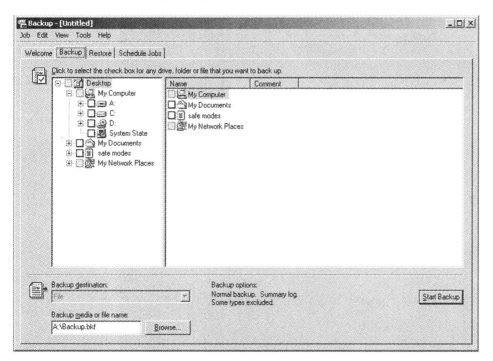

3. Select the files and folders (including the System State) you wish to back up. Choose a backup destination and then click Start Backup.

4. From the Backup Job Information screen, type a description for the backup job and select whether this job will append or replace other backup jobs. If you wish to adjust the advanced

settings and schedule, as described in the previous steps, select either Advanced or Schedule (Figure 10.27). After you have set the features, click Start Backup.

Figure 10.27 Backup Job Information

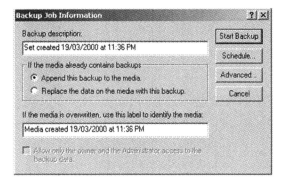

When a system failure occurs or when a file or folder is accidentally deleted, you can use the Backup utility to restore the lost data. As when backing up data, you can restore data manually or by using the Restore Wizard.

Restore Wizard

To restore data using the Restore Wizard, follow these steps:

1. From the Start Menu, choose Programs, choose Accessories, choose System Tools and then select Backup.

2. From the Welcome property page, select Restore Wizard.

3. Click Next to begin the wizard.

4. From the What to Restore page, select the location of the backup set and then select the files and folders in the set you wish to restore (Figure 10.28).

Figure 10.28 Restore Options

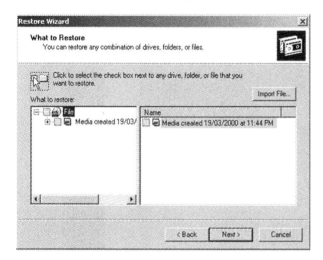

5. From the Completing the Restore Wizard page, select Advanced.

6. Determine where the files will be restored and then click Next. Your three choices are:

    Original location—Places the files and folders in the original folder from which they were backed up and maintains the original directory structure.

    Alternate location—Maintains the original directory structure of the data but places the data in whichever folder you select.

    Single folder—Restores all of the files and folders to one folder without preserving the directory structure.

7. From the How to Restore window, select how the files should be restored. Determine whether the restored files should not replace any files in the directory, replace files of the same name, only if they are older than the backup copy or to always replace the files on the destination with the backup copy (Figure 10.29). After making a selection, click Next.

Figure 10.29 How to Restore

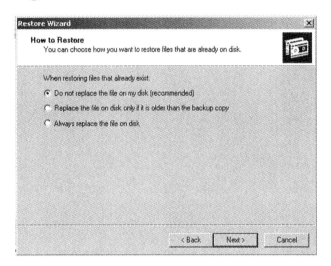

8. From the Advanced Restore Options window, select whether you want to restore security settings on the files and then click Next.

9. Review the settings and then click Finish.

Manual Restoration

If you wish to restore files and folders without using the Restore Wizard, follow these steps:

1. From the Start menu, choose Programs, choose Accessories, choose System Tools and then select Backup.

2. From the Backup Utility, select the Restore property page.

3. Select the media that contains the backup set, select the backup set and then select the files and folders you wish to restore (Figure 10.30). Also select the destination for the restored files and then click Start Restore.

Figure 10.30 Restore Property Page

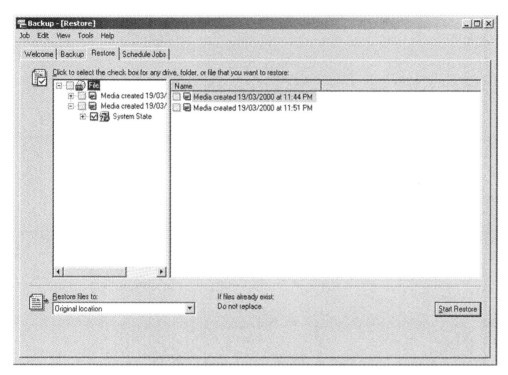

4. From the Confirm Restore window, click OK.

Restoring the Active Directory

When the Active Directory on a domain controller becomes corrupt, you restore it using the Backup utility, if your backup includes the System State information. After restoring the Active Directory, Windows 2000 re-indexes the Active Directory and compares its copy to that of its replication partners and updates the Active Directory as necessary.

Directory Service Restore Mode

If the Active Directory is damaged to the point that you cannot reboot and log on to the domain controller, you must boot the computer in Directory Service Restore Mode. To do so, follow these steps:

1. Reboot the computer. When prompted, press **F8** to access the Advanced Startup Options Menu.

2. Using the arrow keys, select Directory Service Restore Mode and then press **ENTER**.

3. If you have more than one Windows 2000 installation, select the one on which you are performing the recovery and then press **ENTER**.

   The computer boots in Safe Mode.

4. Log on using an administrator account and password.

5. From the Start Menu, choose Programs, choose Accessories, choose System Tools and then select Backup.

6. Select the Restore property page and insert the backup medium on which the System State is stored.

7. Expand the backup medium and then check the box next to System State (Figure 10.31).

Figure 10.31 System State Selection

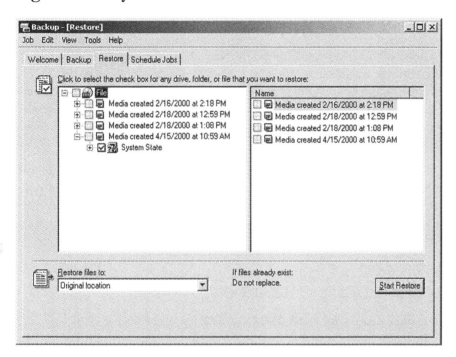

8. Verify that the files will be restored to their original location and then click Start Restore.

 Note: Restoring the System State to the original location always overwrites the current System State.

---

9. Click OK to confirm the overwrite warning and then click OK to restore the System State.

10. When the restore is complete, click Close and then click Yes to reboot the server.

Authoritative Restore

The very nature of a distributed environment, like that created by Windows 2000 using Active Directory, presents problems when restoring deleted objects. A domain controller compares its copy of the Active Directory to that of other domain controllers. New changes to the database are replicated (copied) to all other domain controllers. When you restore a deleted object to the Active Directory, those files retain their older time-and-date stamp. In other words, they are not seen as new changes. When replication occurs, the changes are viewed as old and are replaced by a "newer" version of the Active Directory database. Shortly after you restore deleted Active Directory objects, Active Directory deletes them again.

To prevent the restored files from being deleted during the next replication, you perform an authoritative restore. An authoritative restore overrides the time stamp on the files, permitting them to be replicated. To perform an authoritative restore, follow the steps for restoring the Active Directory, except for the last step. Rather than clicking Yes to reboot the server, click No and then follow these steps:

1. From the Start Menu, choose Run.

2. In the Open box, type **NTDSUTIL.EXE** and then click OK.

    A command prompt window opens with an **NTDSUTIL.EXE:** prompt (Figure 10.32).

Figure 10.32 NTDSUTIL.EXE

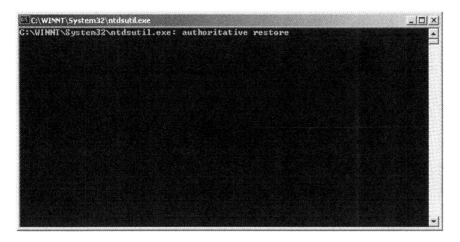

3. Type **AUTHORITATIVE RESTORE** and then press **ENTER**.

 Note: This command is only available when the server is running in Directory Service Restore Mode.

---

4. Type **RESTORE SUBTREE [DISTINGUISHED_NAME_OF_OBJECT]**, where [distinguished_name_of_object] is replaced with the distinguished name of the object you just restored.

 Note: The distinguished name for an Active Directory object is always in the form: **OU=[OU name],DC=[domain name],DC=[higher-level domain name]**. For example, the distinguished name for an OU named "sales" in the ibidpub.com domain is **OU=sales,DC=ibidpub,DC=com**.

---

5. Click Yes to confirm the authoritative restore.

6. When the authoritative restore is finished, type **QUIT**, and then type **QUIT** again to close the console.

7. Restart the server for the changes to take effect.

Vocabulary

Review the following terms in preparation for the certification exam.

Term	Description
Active Directory	Active Directory is a directory database that provides the underlying structure of Windows 2000 networks.
authoritative restore	A method of restoring Active Directory objects so they are not deleted during replication.
boot partition	The partition that contains the system (Windows 2000) files.
boot sector	The first portion of the system partition, the boot sector contains information needed to boot the operating system.
copy backup	Backs up selected files without marking them as backed up.
daily backup	Only backs up files changed the same day the backup is run.
Device Manager	A tool in Windows 2000 that displays hardware devices in the computer and allows you to enable and disable the devices and change drivers.
differential backup	Backs up files that have not been backed up previously or have changed since the last back up and does not mark the files.
Directory Services Restore Mode	A special version of Safe Mode that allows you to restore and repair the Active Directory.
distinguished name	The full name of an Active Directory object, in the form OU=[name],DC=[name],DC=[name].
driver	Software used by the operating system to communicate with a piece of hardware.

Term	Description
ERD	The Emergency Repair Disk is a floppy disk used to rebuild a corrupted installation of Windows 2000.
fault-tolerant volume	A collection of two or more partitions that provide data redundancy in case one member of the volume fails.
GUI	Graphical User Interface is the common desktop interface of Windows 2000.
incremental backup	Backs up files that have not been backed up previously or have changed since the last back up and marks the files.
Last Known Good	A Windows 2000 boot option that restores the System State to the state when a user last successfully logged on locally.
MBR	Master Boot Record
mirrored volumes	A fault-tolerant volume that uses one disk to exactly mirror the contents of the other disk.
NIC	The Network Interface Card provides the physical connection between the computer and the network.
normal backup	A normal backup backs up all selected files and folders and marks them as backed up.
parity	A mathematical function from which missing data can be recreated, parity is used in RAID-5 volumes to provide fault tolerance.
RAID-5 volumes	Fault-tolerant volumes that use at least three hard disks to store data.
Recovery Console	A boot or setup option in Windows 2000, the Recovery Console allows you to perform administrative tasks on a computer that is not properly booting Windows 2000.
replication	The process Windows 2000 uses to copy the Active Directory database among domain controllers.

Term	Description
Safe Mode	A Windows 2000 boot option that loads only the minimal drivers needed to use Windows 2000.
startup menu	The menu displayed when you press **F8** during the boot process.
system partition	The partition that contains the boot file s needed to load the operating system.
System State	A collection of information, including the Registry and system startup files, that can be backed up and restored using the Backup utility.
VGA	Video Graphics Array is the standard video driver type compatible with all video cards used in Windows 2000 and is used in Safe Mode and VGA Mode.
VGA Mode	A Windows 2000 boot option that loads all normal drivers except the video card drivers and loads instead standard VGA drivers.

In Brief

If you want to...	Then do this...
Keep data files accessible in the event of hard drive failure	Store the files on a fault-tolerant volume.
Prevent data loss in the event of two concurrent hard drive failures	Implement a backup strategy ahead of time. Restore the data after replacing the failed drives.
Keep data files accessible in the event of two concurrent hard drive failures	No Windows 2000 fault-tolerant method maintains file integrity if more than one drive fails.
Fix a Windows 2000 installation that fails to boot after loading new video card drivers	Boot the computer in VGA Mode, uninstall the incorrect video drivers, install the proper drivers and reboot the server.
Back up the registry files to a single file	Use the Backup utility. Select System State as the only object to back up and select File for a destination.
See what driver is causing a boot up failure	Read the boot log file, NTBTLOG.TXT.
Use the Recovery Console.	Load the Recovery Console as a startup option (using the **CMDCONS** command) or boot the computer from the Windows 2000 CD-ROM and choose Recovery Console at the appropriate time.

Lesson 10 Activities

Complete the following activities to better prepare you for the certification exam.

1. On a server with three hard disks, create a mirrored volume, using partitions on the first disk (Disk 0) and the third disk (Disk 2). On the same server, create a RAID-5 volume using all three disks.

2. Copy the **\WINNT** directory, or any other directory, to both the mirrored set and the RAID-5 volume.

3. Install the Recovery Console as a boot up option.

4. Restart the server and boot to the Recovery Console. Using the **DISKPART** command, delete all partitions on the third disk.

5. Restart the server normally and ensure files on both the mirrored volume and the RAID-5 volume are still accessible.

6. Run the Disk Management snap-in. Restore the mirrored volume and the RAID-5 volume on the "new" disk (the disk has not changed, but Windows 2000 recognizes it as a new one).

7. Restart the computer using the Recovery Console and disable the mouse service ("MOUCLASS"), and then reboot the server in normal mode. Verify that the mouse is not responding. Log on.

8. Restart the computer using the Recovery Console. Enable the mouse service and then reboot the server normally.

9. From the Device Manager, disable the mouse driver. Reboot the computer normally, but DO NOT LOG ON. When the logon screen is displayed, verify that the mouse pointer is not present and then shut the computer off. Restart the computer and use the Last Known Good Configuration. Verify that the mouse pointer is present. Log on.

10. Using the Backup utility, back up the System State to a file on drive C. Restore the System State. If possible, do this step on a test computer configured as a domain controller.

Answers to Lesson 10 Activities

1. From the desktop, right-click My Computer and select Manage. Select Disk Management in the Tree pane. Select unallocated space on the first disk and choose Create Volume. Follow the steps to create the mirrored volume. Repeat the steps for the RAID-5 volume.

2. From the desktop, right-click My Computer and choose Explore. In the left pane, select a folder, right-click the folder and choose Copy. Right-click one of the fault-tolerant volumes and select Paste. Repeat for the other fault-tolerant volume.

3. Insert the Windows 2000 CD-ROM. From a command prompt, run the following command: **D:\I386\WINNT32.EXE /CMDCONS**

4. From the Recovery Console, type **DISKPART**. Use the arrow keys to select a partition on the third disk and then press **D** to delete the partition. Press **ENTER** and then press **L** to confirm the deletion. Repeat this step for the other partition on the third disk. Press ESC to exit **DISKPART**.

5. Using Windows Explorer, open each of the volumes and verify that the files and folders are still viewable.

6. From the desktop, right-click My Computer and select Manage. Select Disk Management in the Tree pane. Before restoring the volumes, you must set the disk as a dynamic disk. The appropriate wizard appears automatically. Right-click the mirrored volume, remove the mirror and then create a new one. Right-click the RAID-5 volume, choose Repair Volume and choose the new disk.

7. From the startup menu, choose Recovery Console. Log on and from the Recovery Console prompt, type **DISABLE MOUCLASS**. Type **EXIT** to reboot the computer.

8. From the startup menu, choose Recovery Console. Log on and from the Recovery Console prompt, type **ENABLE MOUCLASS SERVICE_SYSTEM_START**. Type **EXIT** to reboot the computer.

9. From the desktop, right-click My Computer and choose Properties. Select the Hardware property page and then select Device Manager. Expand "Mice and other pointing devices," right-click the name of the mouse and select Disable. Answer Yes to the prompt and then Yes to reboot the server. After rebooting, it is important to not log on or else the disabled mouse configuration will be stored as the last known good. Turn the server off and then on again. Press **F8** to access the Advanced Options menu and select Last Known Good Configuration. Press **L**, and then press **ENTER**.

10. Use the Backup utility and either use the Backup Wizard or create a backup job. If you do this on a domain controller, you will find that after backing up the System State you cannot restore the System State without rebooting in Directory Services Restore Mode.

Lesson 10 Quiz

These questions test your knowledge of features, vocabulary, procedures, and syntax.

1. Which tool do you use in Windows 2000 Professional to create a mirrored volume?

    A. Computer Management

    B. Disk Management

    C. Disk Administrator

    D. You cannot create a mirrored volume in Windows 2000 Professional

2. A RAID-5 volume requires a minimum of how many disks?

    A. 2

    B. 3

    C. 4

    D. 5

3. From the Recovery Console, which command allows you to view partition information?

    A. **DISKPART**

    B. **VIEWPART**

    C. **PARTVIEW**

    D. **FDISK**

4. What is the name of the boot log file?

    A. **BOOTLOG.TXT**

    B. **NTBOOT.TXT**

    C. **NTBTLOG.TXT**

    D. **NTLOG.TXT**

5. Which restore method restores all backed up files to the same folder without preserving the original directory structure?

    A. Alternate location

    B. Single folder

    C. Original location

    D. Chaos

6. What tool or command is used to create an Emergency Repair Disk?

    A. **MAKEERD.EXE**

    B. **ERD.CMD**

    C. **ERD.EXE**

    D. Backup utility

7. If you want to provide fault tolerance for the boot partition, which type of volume can you use? (Choose all that apply)

    A. Mirrored volume

    B. RAID-5 volume

    C. Extended volume

    D. Stripe set

8. In Windows 2000 Professional, what is included in a backup of the System State? (Choose all that apply)

    A. Registry

    B. Component Services Class Registration database

    C. System startup files

    D. Active Directory

9. Which of the following drivers is NOT loaded when using Safe Mode?

    A. VGA video drivers

    B. NIC drivers

    C. Hard disk controllers

    D. Mouse drivers

10. A RAID-5 volume is the equivalent of which Windows NT 4.0 set?

    A. Mirror set

    B. Stripe set

    C. Stripe set with parity

    D. Volume set

Answers to Lesson 10 Quiz

1. Answer D is correct. You cannot create fault-tolerant volumes on Windows 2000 Professional.

   Answers A and B are incorrect. Disk Management, a snap-in in the Computer Management console, is the tool used to create fault-tolerant volumes on computers running Windows 2000 Server.

   Answer D is incorrect. Disk Administrator is a Windows NT 4.0 tool.

2. Answer B is correct. A RAID-5 volume requires a minimum of three hard disks.

   Answer A is incorrect. A mirrored volume can use two disks but not a RAID-5 volume.

   Answers C and D are incorrect.

3. Answer A is correct. From a Recovery Console, you view, delete and create partitions using the **DISKPART** command.

   Answers B and C are incorrect. These are not valid commands.

   Answer D is incorrect. **FDISK** is a DOS utility for viewing partitions.

4. Answer C is correct. The boot log file is called **NTBTLOG.TXT** and is stored in the **\WINNT** directory.

   Answers A, B, and D are incorrect.

5. Answer B is correct. The Single folder restore option places all of the files into one folder and removes any existing folder hierarchy.

   Answers A is incorrect. The alternate location option will maintain the folder structure while copying the files and folders to a new location.

   Answer C is incorrect. Original location restores the files to their original location and preserves the folder structure.

   Answer D is incorrect.

6. Answer D is correct. The Backup Utility is used to create an Emergency Repair Disk (ERD).

   Answers A, B, and C are incorrect. These are fictitious commands.

7. Answer A is correct. The boot partition, which contains the system files, can be part of a mirrored volume.

   Answer B is incorrect. The boot and system partitions cannot be members of a RAID-5 volume.

   Answer C is incorrect. Although you can create an extended partition with the boot partition, this does not provide any fault tolerance.

   Answer D is incorrect. A stripe set is a Windows NT 4.0 partition and does not provide fault tolerance.

8. Answers A, B, and C are correct. The System State on a Windows 2000 Professional includes three items: the Registry, the Component Services Class Registration database, and the system startup files.

   Answer D is incorrect. The Active Directory is part of the System State only on Windows 2000 domain controllers.

9. Answer B is correct. In Safe Mode, the Network Interface Card (NIC) drivers are not loaded. They are loaded if you choose Safe Mode with Networking.

   Answers A, C, and D are incorrect. Each of these drivers is loaded in Safe Mode, as all are needed for minimal operation of Windows 2000.

10. Answer C is correct. RAID-5 volumes work in the same way as stripe sets with parity in Windows NT 4.0.

   Answer A is incorrect. A mirror set in Windows NT 4.0 is equivalent to a mirrored volume in Windows 2000.

   Answers B and D are incorrect. Neither of these partition schemes provides fault tolerance.

GLOSSARY

Term	Description
ACL	Every object in the Active Directory has an associated Access Control List, which defines who can access the object and how.
ACPI	Windows 2000 uses the Advanced Configuration and Power Interface to handle power management. Advanced Configuration and Power Interface is a configuration standard for laptop computers.
Active Directory	Active Directory is a directory database that provides the underlying structure of Windows 2000 networks.
Active Directory-integrated zone	A DNS zone that is stored in the Active Directory database and is copied during Active Directory replication .
active partition	The partition from which an operating system boots.
AGP	Accelerated Graphics Port
ANI	Automatic Number Identification service, also known as Caller ID, identifies a user, based on the phone number from which the user called. (ANI is also known as Caller ID).
API	An Application Programming Interface provides standard programming components that developers can use to build applications.
APIPA	Automatic Private IP Addressing is the ability of a client computer to assign its own IP address in the absence of a DHCP server.
APM	Advanced Power Management is a union of the BIOS and operating system to manage power.
assign	To make a program available for installation using Group Policy . Assigned programs appear on the desktop or the Start Menu.

Term	Description
ATM	Asynchronous Transfer Mode
Authenticode	An authentication tool that verifies the source of programs and code that are downloaded from the Internet.
authoritative restore	A method of restoring Active Directory objects so they are not deleted during replication.
AXFR	Full zone transfer occurs is when the primary DNS server transfers the database file in its entirety to secondary servers.
BACP	The Bandwidth Allocation Control Protocol dynamically changes the number of lines used in a Multilink, based on network demands.
bandwidth	The rate at which data can be carried across a network connection.
BAP	The Bandwidth Allocation Protocol works with BACP to determine what a Multilink line needs.
basic disk	One of two disk types supported by Windows 2000, basic disks support primary and extended partitions and logical drives within the extended partition.
BDC	The Backup Domain Controller is the computer in a Windows NT 4.0 network that receives and stores a read-only copy of the directory database.
BIND	Berkeley Internet Name Domain
BIOS	The Basic Input-Output System on a computer is the read-only programming used by the computer to access its hardware.
bit	A binary digit, a bit is represented by a 0 or 1.
blocks	A file is broken into smaller portions called blocks before being written to a striped volume.
boot partition	The partition that contains the system (Windows 2000) files.

Term	Description
boot sector	The first portion of the system partition, the boot sector contains information needed to boot the operating system.
bottleneck	The slowest part of a system, the bottleneck in a computer is often the hard drive.
broadcast	Method of sending information to all computers on a TCP/IP network.
CA	A Certificate Authority is a trusted third-part computer that verifies the identity of servers and clients using digital certificates .
CAL	A Client Access License permits a client computer to access resources on a Windows 2000 server.
CAPI	CryptoAPI is an Application Programming Interface that provides security-related building blocks for developers to use in building applications.
CHANGE USER	The Change User command is used to put a Terminal Services server in install mode (for installing applications) or execute mode (for running applications).
CHAP	The Challenge Handshake Authentication Protocol provides a security key to encrypt the username and password before the client sends this information to the dial-in server.
child domain	A domain under the root domain that uses part of the root domain's name as its own.
child objects	An object within an Active Directory container.
CIPHER.EXE	The command-line utility for encrypting or decrypting a folder or file.
CIW	Client Installation Wizard.
client	Any computer on a network that accesses resources on a server.

Term	Description
clustering	Grouping two or more servers together for combined processing.
CN	The Common Name is one component of the distinguished name in the Active Directory naming convention.
complete trust domain model	A Windows NT 4.0 domain model in which all domains are master domains and resources domains, and all domains trust one another.
conflict	When two or more devices share the same IRQ or I/O address.
connection object	An Active Directory object that points a domain controller to its replication partners.
console	The main interface of the MMC, the console contains snap-ins.
container	An Active Directory object that contains other objects.
container object	An object in Active Directory that contains other objects.
continuous namespace	The hierarchical structure of a domain tree where each layer of the tree shares a common DNS domain name.
copy backup	Backs up selected files without marking them as backed up.
CPU	The Central Processing Unit, which processes all actions, is the brain of the computer.
CryptoAPI	CryptoAPI (CAPI) is an Application Programming Interface (API) that allows applications to encrypt and digitally sign data. See CAPI.
CSP	A Cryptographic Service Provider is responsible for generating the public and private keys for a session.
daily backup	Only backs up files changed the same day the backup is run.
data encryption	Using a mathematical function (encryption key) to scramble data, rendering it unreadable by anyone without the key.

Term	Description
DC	The Domain Component is one part of the distinguished name in the Active Directory naming convention.
DCPROMO.EXE	The domain controller promotion utility is used to promote member servers to domain controllers and demote controllers to member servers.
DDF	Data Decryption Field
deploy	To make a program available through the use of Group Policy .
details pane	The right pane of an MMC snap-in, the details pane shows the detailed information or contents of the object selected in the Tree pane.
Device Manager	A tool in Windows 2000 that displays hardware devices in the computer and allows you to enable and disable the devices and change drivers.
DFS	The Distributed File System allows you to create a file structure composed of folders and files from a number of different sources.
DHCP	Dynamic Host Configuration Protocol is a service for automatically assigning IP addresses and settings.
dial-in settings	User account settings that determine when and how a user can access a Remote Access server.
differential backup	Backs up files that have not been backed up previously o r have changed since the last back up and does not mark the files.
digital certificate	A digital certificate is issued by a CA to verify the identity of both parties in a secure transmission.
dip switches	Switches on legacy hardware that allow you to set the IRQ or I/O address.
directory	A listing of the objects in a network and their associated properties.

Term	Description
directory database	Contains user and group accounts and permissions to resources in the network.
directory service	A service that provides network information to users and applications.
Directory Services Client	Allows a Windows 95 or Windows 98 computer to participate on an Active Directory domain without upgrading the operating system to Windows 2000.
Directory Services Restore Mode	A special version of Safe Mode that allows you to restore and repair the Active Directory.
directory tree	The hierarchical structure of volumes, folders, and files.
disk quotas	Disk quotas allow you to restrict disk usage for all users.
distinguished name	An Active Directory name that lists an object's relative distinguished name and the containers in which the object is found, in the form OU=[name],DC=[name],DC=[name].
distributed security services	A general term for several security features of Windows 2000, including support for Kerberos, SSL, and CryptoAPI.
DMA	Direct Memory Access is a method newer hardware devices use to access memory without requiring intervention from the CPU .
DNIS	Dialed Number Identification Service authenticates a user, based on the phone number called by the user.
DNS	Domain Name Service resolves IP addresses to hostnames , and hostnames to IP addresses. The Domain Name System provides the overall naming structure of TCP/IP-based networks and Windows 2000 domains. The Domain Name System translates computer names to network addresses and is a fundamental part of Active Directory and the Internet.

Term	Description
docking station	A base to which a portable computer attaches, the docking station often provides extra drives and network connectivity.
document invocation	The ability to run a program by double-clicking an associated document.
domain	A logical grouping of computers that share a common directory database.
domain name server	A server running the DNS service.
domain namespace	The hierarchical structure of domain names from the root domain down through first-level and second-level domains and subdomains.
domain naming master	An operations master that controls the addition and removal of domains in the forest.
DRF	Data Recovery Field
driver	Software used by the operating system to communicate with a piece of hardware.
driver signing	Windows 2000 marks drivers to ensure Windows 2000 compatibility.
dual-boot, multiple-boot	Setting up a computer to boot from more than one operating system.
dynamic disk	One of two disk types supported by Windows 2000, dynamic disks support five volume types.
dynamic DNS	The ability of DNS to automatically update itself using the Active Directory database.
dynamic rekeying	The ability of a protocol to change the security keys being used during a session.
dynamic update	A new feature of both DNS and DHCP that allows DHCP to update the DNS database as changes occur on the network.

Term	Description
Dynamic Update Protocol	A protocol that allows clients and the DHCP server to update the DNS database as changes occur on the network.
EAP	The Extensible Authentication Protocol allows a client and server to negotiate an authentication method before the user logs on to the network.
EFS	Encrypting File System
encryption	Encrypted data is scrambled so that it cannot be read without the proper security key.
encryption key	A method of scrambling data according to a mathematical function. The data can only be unscrambled using a related key.
ERD	The Emergency Repair Disk is a floppy disk used to rebuild a corrupted installation of Windows 2000.
ESP	Using IPSec, data is carried on the network in an Encapsulated Security Payload, ensuring data security and authenticity.
execute mode	The default mode for a Terminal server that allows users to run applications.
extended	One of two partition types on a basic disk. The extended partition contains logical drive s.
extended partition	A partition that can contain logical drive s.
FAT	The File Allocation Table is a 16-bit file system supported by DOS, Windows, Windows 95 and 98, Windows NT 4.0 , and Windows 2000.
FAT32	The 32-bit version of the File Allocation Ta ble file system, FAT32 is supported by Windows 98 and Windows 2000 .
fault tolerance	The ability of a computer or operating system to keep data accessible, even if one of the hard disks fails.

Term	Description
fault-tolerant volume	A collection of two or more partitions that provide data redundancy in case one member of the volume fails.
file-level encryption	Requiring permission to open or read files.
folder redirection	Changing the properties of a folder so that its contents appear to be local but are actually stored in a network share.
forest	Two or more domains that do not share a common namespace.
forward lookup query	The process a DNS server uses when trying to resolve a host name or IP address beyond its zone of authority.
forward lookup zone	The portion of the DNS database file used for resolving host names to IP addresses.
FQDN	The Fully Qualified Domain Name consists of a computer's hostname and full domain name (for example, www.lightpointlearning.net).
fragmented disk	A disk on which data is written in discontinuous blocks.
global catalog server	An Active Directory domain controller that contains information on objects in the entire forest, not just one domain.
GPC	The Group Policy container is an Active Directory container that holds information about the replication of the GPO.
GPO	A Group Policy Object is an Active Directory object used to assign Group Policy settings to containers.
GPT	The Group Policy Template is the actual location on the hard drive where Group Policy settings are stored.
Group Policy	Group Policy is the Active Directory extension that allows you to control use of Windows 2000 and implement software deployments.
GUI	Graphical User Interface is the common desktop interface of Windows 2000.

Term	Description
GUID	The Globally Unique Identifier is a 128-bit number that is assigned to every object in the Active Directory and is always unique to that object.
HAL	Hardware Abstraction Layer.
hardware	The physical components of a computer
hardware profile	A set of hardware devices, as defined in the Device Manager, that defines the hardware setup of the computer.
HCL	The Hardware Compatibility List is published by Microsoft and lists computer hardware that has been verified to work with Windows 2000.
hibernate	A method of shutting down Windows 2000 that restores the system state upon waking.
host	Any object (computer, printer, etc.) on a TCP/IP network.
host name	The name of a host on a TCP/IP network; DNS resolves host names to IP addresses.
hot swapping	Interchanging hardware components while the computer is running.
HTTP	The Hypertext Transfer Protocol is a protocol that formats and transmits data and Web pages.
HTTPS	The Secure Hypertext Transfer Protocol transmits Web pages securely over the Internet.
I/O address	The Input/Output address defines the location of a device in the computer so that other devices and the CPU can communicate with it.
IAS	The Internet Authentication Service acts as a RADIUS server.
IETF	Internet Engineering Task Force

Term	Description
IIS	Internet Information Service.
incremental backup	Backs up files that have not been backed up previously or have changed since the last back up and marks the files.
infrastructure master	An operations master that controls changes in group membership within a domain.
inheritance	When an OU receives the permissions assigned to the OU in which it is contained (its parent).
install mode	Install mode is used on a Terminal server to install applications.
Internet Connection Sharing	A service included in Windows 2000 that acts as a proxy server for small networks using the TCP/IP protocol.
interval	The setting that determines how often domain controllers look for changes in the Active Directory.
IP	The Internet Protocol is one part of the TCP/IP protocol suite, and is used to identify individual computers on a network.
IP address	The 32-bit number used to identify hosts on a TCP/IP network in the form of aaa.bbb.ccc.ddd.
IPP	Internet Printing Protocol allows printing across the Internet.
IPSec	IP Security is a group of tools that provide secure data transmission s on networks using the TCP/IP protocol.
IPv4	IP version 4 is the current version of the IP protocol that supports 32-bit addressing.
IPv6	IP version 6 is the proposed new version of the IP protocol that will support 128-bit addressing.
IrDA	The Infrared Data Association has defined standards for devices that use infrared technology to exchange information.

Term	Description
IrDA-FIR	Fast infrared supports 4 Mbps infrared data transmission.
IrDA-SIR	Serial infrared supports 115,000 bps data transmission.
IrLPT	Infrared technology used to send information from a computer to a printer.
IRQ	Interrupt Request is used by any device inside the computer to request information from the processor.
IrTran-P	Used to transmit data using infrared technologies from a digital camera or other imaging device to a computer.
ISA	The Industry Standard Architecture defines a standard method for attaching devices internally in a computer.
ISP	An Internet Service Provider is a company that provides Internet access to users.
iterative request	A complete or partial request for information. DNS servers send lookup queries as iterative requests.
ITU	The International Telecommunication Union is an intergovernmental organization through which telecommunications standards are developed.
IXFR	Incremental zone transfer is when the primary DNS server sends only the changes to secondary servers.
jumpers	Small pins and connectors used to set IRQ and I/O settings on legacy cards.
KCC	The Knowledge Consistency Checker is a service that automatically creates connection objects and ensures replication occurs properly.
KDC	The Key Distribution Center issues short-term session keys to users, based on their long-term keys.

Term	Description
Kerberos	An authentication protocol that uses session tickets and shared secret keys to provide user authentication and data encryption.
key pair	A key pair is a matched set of a private key and a public key.
L2TP	Layer 2 Tunnel Protocol is a tunneling protocol that can be used with various transmission protocols and provides compression and tunnel authentication.
LAN	A Local Area Network consists typically of fewer than 100 computers all within the same area.
Last Known Good	A Windows 2000 boot option that restores the System State to the state when a user last successfully logged on locally.
LDAP	Lightweight Directory Access Protocol
LDIF	LDAP Data Interchange Format
legacy	Hardware that does not support PnP.
local installation	Installing software on the computer at which you are working.
logical drive	A portion of an extended partition that is assigned its own drive letter and acts as a separate partition.
long-term key	When a user logs on to a network, the account is assigned a long-term security key, which may be used to obtain sessions keys from a KDC.
lookup zone	The scope of information a DNS server has within its database file.
mainframes	Mainframes are computers designed to handle all of the computations needed for client computers.
manual tombstoning	Marking a record for deletion in WINS.

Term	Description
master DNS server	The DNS server that contains a master copy of the database file. It can be a primary or secondary DNS server.
master domain	In Windows NT 4.0, a master domain is one that contains user and groups accounts and is trusted by other domains.
MBR	Master Boot Record
MD5-CHAP	Message Digest 5 Challenge Handshake Protocol is used to encrypt usernames and passwords, and is supported by EAP.
member server	A server that does not provide any directory services to the network.
migration	The process of changing a computer or network from an older operating system to a newer one.
mirror set	A Windows NT 4.0 fault-tolerant system, in which one hard disk is used to contain an exact copy of the files on another disk.
mirrored volume	The Windows 2000 implementation of a mirror set, a mirrored volume can only exist on dynamic disks.
mirrored volumes	A fault-tolerant volume that uses one disk to exactly mirror the contents of the other disk.
mixed mode	In Windows 2000, a domain mode that supports both Active Directory domain controllers and Windows NT 4.0 domain controllers.
MMC	The Microsoft Management Console provides a common interface for administrative tools that are in the form of consoles and snap-ins.
mount	To connect a drive volume to a local folder rather than assigning it a drive letter.
multicast	A method of simultaneously sending information to several computers over a TCP/IP network.

Term	Description
multicast scope	A range of IP addresses defined in the DHCP service reserved for multicasts.
Multilink	A Multilink combines several physical lines into one logical connection, thereby increasing bandwidth for that connection.
multi-master replication	All replication partners are peers—they all contain read-write copies of the directory database.
multiple master domain model	A Windows NT 4.0 domain model in which more than one domain contains user and group accounts.
name resolution	The process of converting a network address to a name or a name to an address.
namespace	The logical region in which a name can be resolved to an address. The hierarchical structure of the DNS naming system, in which a child domain's name contains the parent domain's name.
native mode domain	All domain controllers must run Windows 2000.
native-mode	When all Windows 2000 domain controllers only support Active Directory, and no longer function as domain controllers for a Windows NT 4.0 network.
NBT	NetBIOS over TCP/IP allows the use of NetBIOS names on a TCP/IP-based network.
NetBEUI	A protocol designed by Microsoft, originally designed for small single-segment networks.
NetBIOS	Network Basic Input-Output System is a protocol that uses names to identify computers on a network. It was originally designed as part of NetBEUI.
NetBIOS name	A name assigned to a computer on a NetBIOS-based network to identify it. Also called a WINS name.

Term	Description
network share	A folder that has been shared so that it is accessible over the network.
NIC	The Network Interface Card provides the physical connection between the computer and the network.
non-transitive trust	A trust relationship that exists between two domains and cannot be inherited by other domains.
normal backup	A normal backup backs up all selected files and folders and marks them as backed up.
NSLOOKUP.EXE	A command-line program used for testing DNS.
NTFS	The New Technology File System is a file system supported by Windows NT 4.0 and Windows 2000.
NTFS permissions	The right to access files and folders on an NTFS -formatted volume, NTFS permissions apply whether the folder is accessed locally or remotely.
NTLM	The Windows NT 4.0 LAN Manager protocol is used on non - Windows 2000 networks to authenticate users during logon. It is supported by Windows 2000 for compatibility with non -Windows 2000 operating systems.
offline folders	Network shares that are available even when not connected to the network.
one-way trust	A trust relationship where one domain trusts another without the second domain trusting the first.
operation master	A domain controller that performs a special role in the domain or forest that can only be performed by one do main controller.
option classes	Settings within DHCP that allow you to assign IP addresses based on user-definable parameters.

Term	Description
OSI	The Open System Interconnection model defines a seven-layer structure upon which network protocols are designed and built.
OU	Organizational Units are used to group objects within the Active Directory for management and administrative purposes.
PAE	Physical Address Extensions allows programs to access RAM beyond 4 GB.
PAP	Compares a username and password (which are not encrypted before sending) to an encrypted database to verify logon.
parallel port	Also known as the printer port, an external port on most computers used to connect external devices.
parent	A domain that contains a child domain, the parent is closer to the root than are its child domains.
parity	A mathematical function from which missing data can be recreated, parity is used in RAID-5 volumes to provide fault tolerance.
partition	A logical division of a basic disk. There are two partition types: primary and extended.
PC/SC	Personal Computer/Sound Card
PCI	The Peripheral Component Interface is a standard connection for internal devices.
PDC	In Windows NT 4.0, the Primary Domain Controller is the only domain controller with a read-and-write copy of the directory information.
PDC emulator	An operations master that acts as a Windows NT 4.0 PDC for non-Windows 2000 computers in a domain.
peers	Two or more computers that have equal importance or act in the same role.

Term	Description
Per Seat	A licensing mode that assigns a CAL to a specific client machine.
Per Server .	A licensing mode that assigns a series of CALs to a server.
persistent connections	A setting in Windows 2000 WINS that allows WINS servers to replicate data without establishing a connection every time.
PnP	Plug and Play automatically assigns resource settings to hardware devices.
policy conditions	Remote Access conditions that must be met before a Remote Access connection is established.
PPP	The Point-to-Point protocol provides dial-up connections to TCP/IP-based networks.
PPTP	The Point-to-Point Tunneling Protocol is a tunneling protocol that works with IP-based networks and uses PPP for data encryption.
primary DNS server	The DNS server that has the master database file. Changes to the DNS file occur on the primary DNS server.
primary partition	The partition from which an operating system can boot (if it is also active). One of two partition types on basic disks, primary partitions may contain the boot files needed to load an operating system.
private key	Half of the key pair used to encrypt and decrypt files and folders; the private key can only be used by the user to whom it is assigned.
profiles	Remote Access profiles specify certain criteria that define the Remote Access connection.
protocol	The set of rules computers use to communicate over a network.
protocol suite	A collection of protocols designed to work in unison. TCP/IP is an example of a protocol suite.

Term	Description
proxy server	A server that provides access to the Internet for other computers. The proxy server has the only direct connection to the Internet, and other computers go through the proxy to send and receive information.
public key	Half of the key pair used to encrypt and decrypt files and folders, the public key is attached to the encrypted file or folder.
publish	Publishing a folder in the Active Directory makes the folder easier for users to find. To make a program available using GPOs. Published applications do not appear on the desktop or Start Menu but can be found in the Add/Remove Programs control panel.
PXE	Pre-Boot Execution Environment; allows a computer to boot from the NIC.
RADIUS	Remote Authentication Dial-in User Service allows dial-in servers to use a remote server for user authentication.
RADIUS client	The RADIUS dial-in server that requests user authentication information.
RADIUS server	The RADIUS server that provides user authentication information to the RADIUS client.
RAID	Redundant Array of Independent Disks.
RAID-5 volume	A disk volume that supports the Redundant Array Of Independent Disks level 5 fault-tolerance system, that use at least three hard disks to store data.
RAM	Random Access Memory is used to store active programs and the operating system.
RAS server	Remote Access Server

Term	Description
RDP	Remote Desktop Protocol is the protocol used to transfer Terminal Services session information. It requires the use of the TCP/IP protocol suite.
recovery agent	A user account that has permission to decrypt a file or folder, even if the agent is not the creator of the encrypted file or folder.
Recovery Console	A boot or setup option in Windows 2000, the Recovery Console allows you to perform administrative tasks on a computer that is not properly booting Windows 2000.
recursive request	A request for complete information. A client sends a recursive request to a DNS server for the IP address of another computer.
relative distinguished name	The portion of the distinguished name that applies specifically to the object and not to its containers.
remote control	Remote control is a feature of Terminal Services that allows you to monitor and control another user's Terminal Services session .
replication	The process of copying database information from one server to another, which is used by DNS, Active Directory, and WINS.
replication partners	Two computers that are configured to transmit the directory database with each other.
resource domain	A domain that does not contain user and groups accounts and trusts a master domain.
reverse lookup zone	The portion of a DNS database file that resolves IP addresses to host names.
RFC	A Request For Comments is a formal, public proposal defining a new technology or an update to an existing technology.
RID	The Relative Identifier is a number assigned to objects in a domain . Every RID is unique within the domain.

Term	Description
RID master	An operations master responsible for allocating RIDs to domain controllers so that the domain controllers can assign the RIDs to objects.
RIS	Remote Installation Service is used to install Windows 2000 remotely.
rollback strategy	A strategy that allows you to return a network to its previous state if problems arise during upgrades.
ROM	Read Only Memory; can only be read, not altered.
root domain	The first domain created in Active Directory.
RPC	Remote Procedure Call
RRAS	Routing and Remote Access Service is used on Windows 2000 domain member servers to configure Routing and Remote Access features.
Safe Mode	A Windows 2000 boot option that loads only the minimal drivers needed to use Windows 2000.
schedule	The time period during which replication can occur between sites.
schema	The entire scope of an Active Directory forest. The schema defines all objects within an Active Directory.
schema master	An operations master that controls all changes to the schema.
scope	In DHCP, a range of IP addresses that the DHCP server can issue to requesting clients.
scripts	Small files that run commands and programs, scripts can be assigned to run during logon, logoff, startup, and shutdown.
SCSI	The Small Computer Systems Interface defines a standard for connecting both internal and external devices to a computer.

Term	Description
secondary DNS server	A DNS server that receives a copy of the master DNS database file through replication. Changes to the DNS file cannot be made on a secondary server.
second-level domain	In the namespace, one level below first-level domains. Typically a company name, university name, or other unique and identifiable name.
secret key cryptography	Uses a shared secret key that only two people (or computers) know.
security group	An Active Directory group that may contain user accounts and other groups and is assigned permissions to resources.
segment	One section of a TCP/IP network separated from other segments by a router.
serial port	A port on most computers that allows external devices to be attached.
server	Any computer that shares resources over the network.
session key	Issued by a KDC, the session key is used to encrypt data for only one session, and then is discarded.
session ticket	The session ticket contains the session key encrypted with the server's long-term key, and is sent to the server by the client, not the KDC.
share permissions	Access rights assigned to a folder that affect what rights users have to the folder and its contents when accessed over the network (remotely).
shared secret keys	Another name for secret key cryptography.
SID	Security Identifier.
sign	A sending computer will sign, or mark, a data transmission so that the receiving user can verify the source.

Term	Description
simple volume	On dynamic disks, a simple volume is one which provides no fault tolerance and uses disk space from only one physical disk.
single domain model	In Windows NT 4.0, a domain model that consists of only one domain.
single master domain model	In Windows NT 4.0, a domain model that consists of one master domain and numerous resource domains.
site	A physical grouping of computers where all computers are members of the same TCP/IP subnet connected by a high-speed link.
site link	Defines the connection between sites and dictates when and how replication will occur.
site link bridge	A collection of two or more site links.
site links	A logical connection between sites that you create to govern replication between the sites.
smart cards	A credit card-sized attachment for computers that contains its own processor and RAM, and can be used to store sensitive information, including security keys.
SMTP	Simple Mail Transfer Protocol
snap-in	An administrative tool designed to work within the Microsoft Management Console (MMC), each snap-in handles a different aspect of Windows 2000 management.
SNTP	Simple Network Time Protocol
software categories	Logical groupings of software types that can be found within the Add/Remove Programs control panel.
spanned volume	On dynamic volumes, a spanned volume provides no fault tolerance and uses disk space from two or more physical disks.

Term	Description
SPAP	The Shiva Password Authentication Protocol is a proprietary implementation of PAP.
SRV	The Service Resource record in DNS allows computers to search for servers in the DNS database based on the server's role in the network.
SRV records	Service Resource records
SSL	Secure Sockets Layer is a network protocol used to transmit sensitive data over the internet.
startup menu	The menu displayed when you press **F8** during the boot process.
static IP address	An IP address that does not change and is manually entered when configuring TCP/IP on a host.
stripe set	The Windows NT 4.0 equivalent of a striped volume in Windows 2000.
stripe set with parity	The Windows NT 4.0 equivalent of a RAID-5 volume in Windows 2000.
striped volume	In Windows 2000, a striped volume uses two or more physical disks and writes data consecutively to each disk in 64 -kilobyte blocks.
subdomain	In the domain namespace, one or more levels below the second -level domain, usually used for organizational purposes within a corporation or other large network.
superscope	A DHCP scope that contains several smaller scopes.
switch	A module for the Microsoft Management Console (MMC).
synchronize	To force replication between a BDC and PDC so that the BDC has the latest updates to the directory database.
system partition	The partition that contains the boot files needed to load the operating system.

Term	Description
system root	The folder or directory into which Windows 2000 is installed; usually `C:\WINNT`.
System State	A collection of information, including the Registry and system startup files, that can be backed up and restored using the Backup utility.
TCO	The Total Cost of Ownership defines the expenses involved in building and maintaining a computer network.
TCP/IP	Transmission Control Protocol / Internet Protocol is the network protocol used by DNS, Active Directory, and the Internet.
terminal	A device used to access a mainframe on older networks. A terminal generally cannot operate independently of the network.
Terminal server	A Windows 2000 server running Terminal Services.
Terminal Services	Terminal Services are network services provided with Windows 2000 Server that allow users to display and use the Windows 2000 desktop environment on computers that cannot run Windows 2000. Terminal Services are also used for remote administration of Windows 2000 servers.
TLS	The Transport Layer Security protocol has been introduced by Microsoft as an enhancement to—and possible replacement of—SSL.
top-level domain	In the domain namespace, the first level below the root level; typically a two- or three-letter domain name (for example, com, edu, gov, ca).
topology	The shape and structure of the DFS folder and file hierarchy.
transitive trust	A trust relationship where the trusts between two domains are inherited by their subdomains.
tree	Two or more domains that share a common DNS namespace.

Term	Description
Tree pane	The left pane of the MMC, the Tree pane lists the snap-ins included in a console and folders within the snap-ins.
trust	A logical connection between two Windows NT 4.0 domains that allows the sharing of user and group information.
TTL	Time To Live
tunneling	The process of creating a secure channel through public lines, through which encrypted data may travel safely.
two-way trust	A trust relationship where both domains trust each other.
UNC	The Universal Naming Convention defines the location of a resource on a network. It is always in the form \\server_name\share_name.
Unicode	Computer characters used to support languages other than English.
upgrade pack	A software update supplied by the software manufacturer that makes the application compatible with Windows 2000.
UPS	An Uninterruptible Power Supply is a battery that provides temporary power to your computer if the main power is lost.
URL	Universal Resource Locator is the address used to connect to hosts and resources over the Internet using a Web browser.
USB	The Universal Serial Bus is one of the newest methods for attaching external devices to a computer. The USB supports up to 128 devices on one controller.
user principal name	A user's login name and domain name (joe@domain.com).
VGA	Video Graphics Array is the standard video driver type compatible with all video cards used in Windows 2000 and is used in Safe Mode and VGA Mode.
VGA Mode	A Windows 2000 boot option that loads all normal drivers except the video card drivers and loads instead standard VGA drivers.

Term	Description
volume	A logical division of a drive, a volume on a dynamic disk is similar to a partition on a basic disk.
volume set	The Windows NT 4.0 equivalent of a spanned volume in Windows 2000.
VPN	Virtual Private Networks use tunneling protocols to send data over public lines as if they were private.
WAN	A Wide Area Network is one or more LANs connected over a distance of miles.
Windows IP Security	The Windows 2000 implementation of IPSec.
WINS	Windows Internet Naming Service is a service that keeps track of NetBIOS names on a network.
X.509 Version 3	An industry standard digital certificate format, X.509 is the most widely used type of certificate.
zone transfers	The process of sending the DNS database file from the master DNS server to secondary servers.
zone, zone of authority	The group of computers for which a DNS server has domain name information.

Index

75-83, 86-90, 92-93, 100-106, 108, 111-
112, 114-119, 121, 125, 137-143, 146-149,
156-157, 160-162, 164, 171, 176, 182-185,
217-218, 223, 234, 239, 241, 244-247, 249-
252, 254, 258, 264, 266, 269, 271-273, 318,
359, 366-367, 369, 372, 376-377, 382, 388,
392, 417, 419, 421, 423-431, 433, 436-438,
440-442, 447, 450, 452-453, 455, 457-458,
464-467, 469, 478-482, 488-491, 493, 496,
498-502, 504-505, 508-509, 520-521, 523,
525-526, 528-529, 542, 544-547, 549, 552,
554, 569-571, 576-577, 581

printer, 6, 22, 55, 194, 219, 280-281, 283, 288, 357
  driver, 288-289, 293-295, 527, 545, 576

private key, 380, 419, 474-477, 482, 521

programming interfaces, 108

protocol, 3, 6, 22-23, 51, 53-56, 66-67, 77, 79, 83,
  88, 90, 92, 103-105, 112, 125, 129-130, 133,
  161-162, 223, 234, 283, 318, 423, 431, 447,
  452, 468, 470, 471-472, 477-478, 481, 483,
  485, 489-492, 496, 500, 523, 525
  HTTP, 12, 38, 58, 61, 234, 445, 477, 481, 484
  HTTPS, 481
  network, 2-7, 9-12, 15-18, 22-24, 28-29, 32,
    34-36, 48-56, 58-59, 61, 65-69, 72, 74, 77,
    79-81, 86, 88-89, 92-93, 104, 107-108, 110-
    116, 120, 124, 126, 135, 140-141, 143, 146-
    147, 156-157, 161-164, 166, 168, 170-172,
    174-176, 182-185, 193, 209, 223-231, 233-
    235, 237-251, 253-255, 257, 259, 261, 263-
    265, 267, 269-273, 278, 295, 306-307, 314,
    318-319, 327, 329, 333, 351-358, 359-361,
    365, 367, 371-372, 376, 388, 391, 401, 413,
    415, 417, 419-421, 423, 426-428, 431-433,
    453, 464, 468, 470, 471-475, 477-479, 481,
    483-485, 487, 489-491, 493-499, 501, 503,

505, 507, 509, 511, 513, 515, 517, 519-521,
  523-526, 554, 556, 582
  RDP configuration, 474
  TCP/IP, 21-22, 43, 45, 51, 53, 55-56, 58, 60,
    66-67, 79, 81, 92, 94-98, 100-101, 105-106,
    109, 112, 124, 135, 151, 154, 159, 160, 162,
    408, 423, 461, 468, 470, 485, 496, 514, 516,
    585, 588, 592-593, 596-597, 600, 602, 604-
    607
  X., 27, 81, 90, 101, 287, 380, 455, 474, 505,
    522, 524
proxy, 6, 81, 496
  server, 2-4, 6-8, 10, 12, 14-18, 20, 22, 26, 28-
    30, 32, 34-35, 38, 47-53, 55, 57-66, 69-73,
    75-83, 86-90, 92-93, 100-106, 108, 111-
    112, 114-119, 121, 125, 137-143, 146-149,
    156-157, 160-162, 164, 171, 176, 182-185,
    217-218, 223, 234, 239, 241, 244-247, 249-
    252, 254, 258, 264, 266, 269, 271-273, 318,
    359, 366-367, 369, 372, 376-377, 382, 388,
    392, 417, 419, 421, 423-431, 433, 436-438,
    440-442, 447, 450, 452-453, 455, 457-458,
    464-467, 469, 478-482, 488-491, 493, 496,
    498-502, 504-505, 508-509, 520-521, 523,
    525-526, 528-529, 542, 544-547, 549, 552,
    554, 569-571, 576-577, 581

proxy server, 6, 496

public key, 318, 380, 474-477, 481-482, 521

publish, 143, 327, 329-330, 332-333, 340, 359-
  360, 365

PXE, 32

query, 34, 60-61, 76-79, 104, 140, 161

quotas, 15, 360, 376-377, 413, 415
  disk, 1, 3, 6, 12-15, 19, 23, 25, 30, 32, 34-37,
    48, 50-52, 112, 217, 245, 273, 277-278,
    282, 326, 359-361, 363, 365, 367, 369, 371,

www.ingramcontent.com/pod-product-compliance
Lightning Source LLC
Chambersburg PA
CBHW080129060326
40689CB00018B/3724